# AN OLD
# CREED
# FOR THE
# NEW SOUTH

**Recent Titles in**
**Contributions in Afro-American and African Studies**
*Series Advisors: John W. Blassingame and Henry Louis Gates, Jr.*

Voices from Under: Black Narrative in Latin America and the Caribbean
*William Luis, editor*

Contemporary Public Policy Perspectives and Black Americans: Issues in an Era of Retrenchment Politics
*Mitchell F. Rice and Woodrow Jones, Jr., editors*

Student Culture and Activism in Black South African Universities: The Roots of Resistance
*Mokubung O. Nkomo*

The Cinema of Ousmane Sembene, A Pioneer of African Film
*Françoise Pfaff*

Philanthropy and Jim Crow in American Social Science
*John H. Stanfield*

Israel in the Black American Perspective
*Robert G. Weisbord and Richard Kazarian, Jr.*

African Culture: The Rhythms of Unity
*Molefi Kete Asante and Kariamu Welsh Asante, editors*

Writing "Independent" History: African Historiography, 1960–1980
*Caroline Neale*

More Than Drumming: Essays on African and Afro-Latin American Music and Musicians
*Irene V. Jackson, editor*

More Than Dancing: Essays on Afro-American Music and Musicians
*Irene V. Jackson, editor*

Sterling A. Brown: Building the Black Aesthetic Tradition
*Joanne V. Gabbin*

Amalgamation!: Race, Sex, and Rhetoric in the Nineteenth-Century American Novel
*James Kinney*

Black Theatre in the 1960s and 1970s: A Historical-Critical Analysis of the Movement
*Mance Williams*

# AN OLD CREED FOR THE NEW SOUTH

## Proslavery Ideology and Historiography, 1865–1918

 John David Smith

CONTRIBUTIONS IN AFRO-AMERICAN AND
AFRICAN STUDIES, NUMBER 89

Greenwood Press

WESTPORT, CONNECTICUT • LONDON, ENGLAND

**Library of Congress Cataloging in Publication Data**

Smith, John David, 1949–
An old creed for the New South.

(Contributions in Afro-American and African studies,
ISSN 0069-9624 ; no. 89)
Bibliography: p.
Includes index.
1. Slavery—United States—Historiography.   2. United
States—Intellectual life—1865–1918.   I. Title.
II. Series.
E441.S655 1985       973'.0496'0072       84–27935
ISBN 0-313-23648-8 (lib. bdg.)

Library of Congress Catalog Card Number: 84-27935
ISBN: 0-313-23648-8
ISSN: 0069-9624

First published in 1985

Greenwood Press
A division of Congressional Information Service, Inc.
88 Post Road West, Westport, Connecticut 06881

Printed in the United States of America

10  9  8  7  6  5  4  3  2  1

**Copyright Acknowledgment**

The author and publisher are grateful for permission to quote from the following
source: *American Negro Slavery* by Ulrich B. Phillips. Copyright 1918 by D. Appleton & Co., renewed 1946 by Lucie M. Phillips. A Hawthorn book. Reprinted by permission of E. P. Dutton, a division of New American Library.

# Contents

Contents

# Acknowledgments

I began this book a decade ago. At the University of Kentucky Charles P. Roland first introduced me to the ways of the Southland and then directed this study in its infancy. I remain in his debt for his patience, his insistence on clear exposition, and, through the years, his unflagging support and friendship. Holman Hamilton also inspired me to pursue the historian's craft. He left a legacy of excellence in the classroom, in the fruits of his prodigious pen, and in the manner in which he encouraged young scholars. In Lexington I developed a friendship with Thomas H. Appleton, Jr., and James C. Klotter. Through the years I have subjected them to virtually every word I have written on the historiography of slavery. Nevertheless, Tom and Jim remain my most thoughtful critics and closest friends.

August Meier, Eugene D. Genovese, and Jim Klotter kindly read an earlier version of this volume. They provided searching criticism and suggested possible avenues for revision. While in Fort Wayne, Indiana, I received encouragement daily from Mark E. Neely, Jr. Long before I could digest my own material, Mark grasped the vital nexus between postbellum proslavery ideology and historiography. At a 1978 session of the Southern Historical Association, James L. Roark and Elizabeth Fox-Genovese suggested ways to strengthen my assessment of early black writers on slavery. Upon relocating in Columbia, South Carolina, I met Charles W. Joyner, who urged me to broaden the focus of my research. At Southeast Missouri State University, Franklin D. Nickell

Acknowledgments

smoothed the way for my research jaunts across the Mississippi River to Carbondale, where John Y. Simon always offered encouragement and sound judgments. In 1981–1982 a fellowship from the American Council of Learned Societies enabled me to research and write full-time. In 1982–1983 a James Still Fellowship from the Andrew W. Mellon Foundation and an Albert J. Beveridge travel grant from the American Historical Association facilitated my research on free blacks. A fellowship in 1983 from the American Political Science Association and Project '87 enabled me to study the Black Codes in Don E. Fehrenbacher's Stanford University seminar on slavery and race.

I completed my revisions of *An Old Creed for the New South* after moving to Raleigh in 1982. In the last stretch I received immensely valuable suggestions from Tom Appleton, Stanley L. Engerman, David Gilmartin, Jim Klotter, Randall M. Miller, and Mark Neely. Each read final drafts of the manuscript with remarkable care and keen insight. The labors of these valued friends improved this book immeasurably. I also esteem the contributions of the following colleagues at North Carolina State University, who either critiqued individual chapters or provided timely advice and support: James E. Easley, Jr., Linda O. McMurry, William C. Harris, Walter A. Jackson, Charles Carlton, and Joseph P. Hobbs. At a critical juncture I profited as well from the wise counsel of Joel Williamson of Chapel Hill.

Through the years I have also accumulated debts to numerous librarians and archivists. Among them, special thanks go to Alexander M. Gilchrist, Bonnie Reed, William J. Marshall, Vivian MacQuown, and Robin S. Barnard at the University of Kentucky; Jacqueline Goggin at the Library of Congress; Daniel T. Williams at Tuskegee Institute; Allen H. Stokes at the University of South Carolina; Carson Holloway at the University of North Carolina at Chapel Hill; Ann S. Smith at North Carolina State University; Susan Pallone at the Public Library of Fort Wayne and Allen County; Mary Canada at Duke University; Ruth Harrod at Indiana University-Purdue University, Fort Wayne; Maribeth Needels and James W. Hart at Southeast Missouri State University; Judith A. Schiff at Yale University; Jane Thomas at the Joint University Libraries, Nashville; Charlynn S. Pyne and Esme E. Bhan at Howard University; and Susan E. Davis at the Schomburg Center for Research in Black Culture, New York Public Library. Historian Fred A. Bailey of Abilene Christian University shared with me the fruits of his research in the Tennessee Civil War Veterans Questionnaires.

Finally, I wish to thank several people who supplied behind-the-scenes support over so many years. My parents, Doris and Len Smith, always understood my commitment to this book and backed the project in every way. Ruth B. Nicholson served on my staff at the Historic Columbia Foundation and reminded me again and again that not all scholars find their callings in the classroom. When I finally did gain an opportunity to teach, I benefited from the aid of student assistants Mitchell Stroder at Southeast Missouri State University, and Paul Peterson and Lee Bumgarner at North Carolina State University.

# AN OLD
# CREED
# FOR THE
# NEW SOUTH

# Introduction

The slave went free; stood a brief moment in the sun; then moved back
again toward slavery.

—W. E. B. Du Bois[1]

In 1959 historian Stanley M. Elkins published a masterful historio-
graphical essay on black slavery, one that remains insightful and influential today. Commenting on postemancipation thought about slavery,
Professor Elkins remarked that following Appomattox the peculiar institution held little interest for Americans. "Throughout a good part of
the postwar generation," wrote Elkins, "a moratorium on that subject
was observed everywhere with surprising unanimity."[2] Elkins assumed
that after the close of the Civil War, whites and blacks alike quickly
swept slavery's skeleton aside. In his view Americans simply expunged
from their thinking an institution that for years had dominated the country's politics, split the nation in two, and, finally, sparked America's
bloodiest war. Although critics have identified major weaknesses in
Elkins's work,[3] no one has challenged this comment on the early historiography of slavery. Most historians have themselves ignored the
broad role slavery played as idea and symbol in postbellum American
thought.[4] That is not to say, of course, that scholars have sidestepped
such important questions as the dynamics of emancipation, the interplay
of race and class during Reconstruction, the evolution of sharecropping,
and the rise of segregation. Indeed, these topics continue to attract much
of the best recent scholarship in the field of Southern history. But
following Elkins's lead, students of Southern history, race relations,

and intellectual history imply—by their avoidance of the subject—that Americans after the Civil War virtually wiped slavery from their consciousness.

Black slavery, though abolished by the Thirteenth Amendment, retained a key place in American racial thought from Reconstruction to World War I. Although the Civil War sounded the death knell for slavery, in the years following Appomattox there was no discernible loss of interest in the peculiar institution. Slavery, a subject that virtually turned the world of antebellum Americans upside down, remained a major topic of discussion for a broad spectrum of Americans, including ex-planters, former abolitionists, U.S. Army officers, historians, folklorists, novelists, physicians, and "race thinkers." Black slavery assumed a whole new significance after the war. Although its destruction was now codified firmly in law, years of abuse and institutionalized degradation of blacks left a profound legacy to American life and thought.

The importance of slavery to late nineteenth- and early twentieth-century thinking has been vastly understated by modern scholars. Despite Elkins's assertion, in these years slavery held an unusual attraction for writers, north and south, black and white. Not since the late antebellum years had so much attention been devoted to it. A recent computer-based bibliography identified well over six hundred books and articles on slavery published in the years 1865–1889. More than two thousand slavery items, including theses and dissertations, appeared in the period 1890–1920.[5] Interest in slavery took various forms. In the years 1867–1912, for example, the New York *Times* published articles on such diverse aspects of slavery as the uncertain legal status of a freedwoman, the Northwest Ordinance, and textbook treatments of the peculiar institution.[6] Late in the period under consideration, other newspapers devoted surprisingly detailed coverage to the activities of elderly former bondsmen. Ex-slaves, especially the venerable black mammies and uncles, were honored by black colleges and Confederate veteran groups alike.[7] Editorial after editorial endorsed the establishment of old-age homes and the awarding of pensions to indigent ex-slaves. Obituaries eulogized the passing of former slaves.[8] During the age of Jim Crow, then, the American public seemed to have almost an insatiable curiosity about slavery and the bondsmen.[9]

What caused this unusual concern with the long-defunct, peculiar institution? Many influential writers, including J. L. M. Curry, Theodore Roosevelt, and William E. Dodd, identified black slavery with the broad racial, social, and economic issues of their own day. For them slavery served as a crucial metaphor, a comparative model for what they perceived as new forms of servitude.[10] Some employed the term *slavery* to condemn unequal power relationships, including those involved in the struggle between labor and capital, tariff protectionism, and American imperialism in the Caribbean and the Pacific.[11] Others used *slavery* metaphorically to describe the conflicting relationship between blacks and whites. In 1875, for example, northern writer Charles Nordhoff observed that in spite of the Thirteenth Amendment, southern blacks were still enslaved by the ethos of menial work. That resulted, he noted, not only from the blacks' essential ignorance and poverty, but from overwhelming white racism as well. Thirty years later journalist Walter Hines Page sensed the same dual nature of black enslavement. Blacks, according to Page, languished "in economic bondage and a bondage likewise to the white man's race-feeling."[12]

In its broadest sense, slavery provided a metaphor that explained and justified race relations in the postwar South. This was a period of severe racial tension. Many race-related questions remained unsolved after Appomattox. What was to be the social, economic, and political role of the freedmen? How would blacks react to their new social status? And how would they fare physically without the alleged protection offered by slavery? Americans glanced backward to slavery for answers to these and other questions. They employed slavery as a constant touchstone, a reference point for contemporary issues. In doing so, a broad spectrum of writers contributed a vast literature, polemic as well as historical, on the subject of slavery. In spite of the racism and sectional chauvinism of much of their work, they posed many salient questions, unearthed valuable source materials, and pioneered methods of inquiry employed by subsequent researchers. In short, the early students of slavery anticipated much later scholarship

This book explores the place of black slavery in American thought, especially historiography, in the half-century following emancipation. Whereas other studies have furthered our understanding of race relations from Reconstruction to World War I, this work focuses as minutely as possible on images of slavery during these years.[13] Slavery as idea and symbol played an important role in shaping the ways that blacks and whites reacted to one another in the postemancipation world. Part One examines attitudes toward slavery from the end of the Civil War to the turn of the century. Despite an apparent decline of interest in the subject in the 1870s and 1880s, continuity of ideology—proslavery as well as antislavery—characterized the entire period.[14] After Appomattox the old arguments appeared anew, virtually unchanged in spite of slavery's demise. Abolitionists and other friends of the blacks continued to condemn the horrors and indignities of enslavement. They hammered away at the unwillingness of whites to liberate the blacks in spirit as well as in deed. The neoabolitionists identified roadblocks—flagrant vestiges of slavery—in virtually every avenue of black life. Republican politicians used the neoslavery of the postbellum period for partisan purposes. It armed them with ammunition aplenty with which to battle white southerners and Democrats alike. And even more so than their white friends, ex-slaves and their descendants sensed the legacy of bondage that survived emancipation. Postwar blacks never fully blotted out the nightmares of two hundred years of forced and degrading labor. They likened the racial discrimination and proscription that surrounded them to the old peculiar institution. Slavery constantly reminded blacks of white greed, hegemony, injustice, and inhumanity.

White, especially southerners, focused so intensely on slavery that for many the subject became almost an obsession. They viewed the peculiar institution in a radically different light than blacks did. Many mourned slavery's demise and defended the old order with the zeal of the antebellum proslavery ideologues.They wove threads of slave fealty and loyalty into the fabric of the Lost Cause. Former masters agonized over the loss of control over their ex-bondsmen. "Even after the death of slavery," writes historian George C. Rable, "elements of the pro-slavery argument retained their vitality, and traditional southern racial ideas became, in some cases, even more powerful and entrenched." No matter how "profusely southerners might welcome emancipation, many unconsciously, and a number both consciously and publicly, looked back longingly on the former glories of plantation slavery."[15] A common theme pervades most of these postabolition writings on slavery. While few openly advanced the actual return to chattel slavery, many white writers revived elements of the old proslavery argument. During Reconstruction and on through the Progressive Era, one writer after another extolled the virtues of the old peculiar institution. They once again described slavery as a beneficent school where, unlike under freedom, the blacks lived in harmony with the whites. In return for the fruits of their labor, the bondsmen received adequate food, clothing, and housing. According to this new proslavery argument, slaves reaped humane treatment from their paternalistic masters. Cruel, abusive slave-holders were rare. And the domestic slave trade only occasionally divided slave families. Quite openly, the new breed of white proslavery ideologues viewed slavery as preferable to freedom for blacks.

Slavery, of course, no longer figured as a legitimate force in American law or race relations. But in the hands of these writers it gave whites a familiar yardstick with which to gauge solutions to contemporary racial discord. "Thus," writes historian Guion Griffis Johnson, "when the old social and economic structure fell with the Civil War, the South immediately began the erection of a new structure upon the basis of the old philosophy. By the turn of the twentieth century that adjustment had become fixed in a biracial social and economic order." For some, no doubt, the proslavery argument symbolized a yearning for a simpler, lost civilization. For others it represented a conscious attempt to undo the results of Union victory in the Civil War. Regardless of motive, the new proslavery theorists described the diverse benefits of slavery for blacks and whites alike. Their rhetoric dominated the postwar generations. It bolstered well southern propaganda against federal control in the region. And it propped the racial settlement upon which the New South movement rested.[16]

To be sure, very few whites advocated reenslavement. But the vast majority continued to envision blacks as slavelike inferiors. They remained unequivocally determined to keep blacks entrenched as a subordinate laboring class. They refused to admit that blacks would work without compulsion or, at the very least, white supervision. Whites loathed surrendering the etiquette of slavery. They clutched dearly to every shred of racial control and discipline that smacked of slavery. As blacks asserted their new free status, demanding equal economic and political opportunities, white southerners scrambled to adapt the old proslavery argument to the new order of things. They resurrected virtually all of the old rationales for enslaving blacks. And when the dog-eared arguments in favor of slavery lost any sense of relevancy, whites trotted out new ones. Drawing heavily on the findings of physicians and "race thinkers," whites concluded that, without slavery's guardianship, the freedmen were destined to extinction as a race. According to Rable, "Though many of the more obscure and theoretical aspects" of the proslavery argument "became moot points after 1865, the death of slavery failed to destroy the institution's intellectual foundation."[17]

The polemics of the post–Civil War years established the ideological underpinnings for the first generation of historians of slavery. The early historiography of slavery illustrates most clearly the legacy of proslavery thought in America up to 1918. Historians assumed a prominent role in the espousing of the new proslavery argument. Part Two analyzes the vast corpus of historical writings on slavery that first emerged around the time of America's centennial. Taken as a whole, these diverse articles, books, and theses substantiate the argument that there was serious, broad discussion of slavery into the twentieth century. Indeed, throughout the late nineteenth century and up through the Progressive Era, slavery captured the attention of a surprisingly large number of amateur as well as professional historians.[18] Scholars without portfolio as well as academics in the then-emerging graduate schools established the peculiar institution as one of the most popular subjects of historical inquiry of their day. These historians wrote amidst the postwar slavery debate. Many conducted their research at a time when state legislatures were fastening the repressive Jim Crow system on black southerners. Mostly whites, they imbibed not only the bitter racism of the age but also the proslavery views that triumphed after Appomattox. By the turn of the century, legalized segregation and proscription ruled in the South. Yet de facto segregation and race hatred also existed north of the Mason–Dixon line.

Surrounded by new forms of racial control—debt peonage, serfdom, wage slavery—historians, north and south, examined slavery in order to gain some perspective on the contemporary scene. Their writings not only recounted the old proslavery argument but redefined and adapted it to changes in post-Victorian American life. Historians kept alive the notion (one with great appeal to whites in the age of segregation) that the two races could live together in harmony only when blacks were legally subordinate to whites. Concurrently, these scholars worked under other influences as well, especially the pervasive forces of nationalism and scientism central to late nineteenth-century American thought. The peculiar institution, itself a subject charged with emotion and partisanship, challenged historians who sought to write a truly national history. It also posed problems for scholars who prided themselves on employing "scientific" methods in their quest of "objective" history. Sharing their age's general awe of Darwinian science, they followed the formula—tracing the evolution of institutions over time—popularized by Professor Herbert Baxter Adams at The Johns Hopkins University. The study of slavery fit this mold perfectly.

Or so the practitioners of "scientific" history believed. Despite their determined efforts at detachment and scholarly rigor, the first generation of historians of slavery succumbed to the dictates of the old slavery debate. Ideology ultimately prevailed over historical method. On the subject of black slavery, at least, historians practiced far less than they preached. In their books and articles on slavery they abandoned the "scientific" ideal. Much in the tradition of the abolitionists, the Nationalist historians and a large group of black writers met the proslavery barrage of the postwar years head-on. These writers, far fewer in number than the proslavery forces, comprised two widely divergent groups.

The white neoabolitionists condemned slavery vigorously, yet subscribed to contemporary racism and held little commitment to black advancement. They used history to chart a new nationalism and, almost in spite of themselves, established the institutional features of slavery later scholars would study. The black neoabolitionists, pioneer black historians, teachers, editors, and clergymen, brought to their task a sense of immediacy. Some indeed had felt the sting of the lash. Others blamed slavery for the second-class citizenship they inherited as freed men and women. These black critics contributed much to the early historiography of slavery, and their work prefigured some of the best recent scholarship on the subject. Early black writers exposed the new proslavery doctrine for what it was—thinly veiled racism. In 1905, conservative white historian Walter Lynwood Fleming remarked disapprovingly that whenever blacks discussed slavery, "we hear the clank of chains and the cutting swish of the lash; the slaves, we infer, hate the whites with a consuming hatred, and the cruel masters endeavor to crush out the human feelings of the black."[19] As Fleming correctly observed, many blacks emphasized the brutal, oppressive, exploitative aspects of slavery. They noted the ways in which the conditions of labor for blacks in the postwar South, including sharecropping, peonage, and the convict lease system, drew heavily for their existence upon the heritage of slavery.

But in spite of black historians' impassioned attacks on slavery, the new proslavery argument ultimately carried the day in the age of segregation. The vast majority of white students of slavery writing in these years, from James C. Ballagh to Ulrich B. Phillips, pointed to slavery's overall benefits for the blacks. They interpreted slavery as a benign school in which blacks fared better than as freedmen. They revived, refined, updated, and modified many of the same arguments espoused by antebellum and postbellum proslavery writers. Without question, the students at Johns Hopkins and their disciples unearthed invaluable information pertaining to slavery as an institution on the state and local levels. Their contributions to the development of North American slave studies unfortunately have been long overlooked by specialists in the slavery field. And even Phillips's most vehement critics now admit his salient contributions. Notwithstanding the historian's flagrant racism and condescension, Phillips identified and popularized plantation records as sources, developed the comparative method, and integrated economic questions into the study of slavery. With penetrating insight, he probed the complexities of the master-slave relationship. Phillips's many important writings, especially *American Negro Slavery* (1918), set a standard for twentieth-century scholarship on the peculiar institution. The entire body of works analyzed here renders these years a truly formative period in the historiography of slavery. They underscore the significant degree to which the early investigators pioneered many of the sources, topics, and conclusions of modern researchers.

But in doing so, early historical writings on slavery reinforced the existing structural framework of race relations. Proslavery in cast and content, they buttressed white supremacy and justified the second-class citizenship accorded blacks in these years. At the very time whites were depicting slavery in sentimental, patriarchal terms, blacks were losing hard-fought economic, political, and civil rights. The new proslavery school, though clearly identifiable from Reconstruction through the Gilded Age, surfaced most clearly in the 1890s. Slavery's new apologists filled scholarly monographs and journals, popular magazines and newspapers, with a historical rationale for the contemporary repression of blacks— mob terror, lynching, segregation, disfranchisement. Studying the position of blacks early in the new century, reform journalist Ray Stannard Baker observed: "Many Southerners look back wistfully to the faithful, simple, ignorant, obedient, cheerful, old plantation Negro and deplore his disappearance. They want the New South, but the old Negro."[20]

But black men and women of the New South refused to behave like "old Negroes." They steadfastly rejected the abject role of slave. Undaunted, whites continued in their polemical and historical writings to defend an institution that kept antebellum blacks under wraps. This ongoing proslavery rhetoric, then, supplied the intellectual base for the new chains of ignorance, poverty, and racial discrimination that bound blacks in the New South. Slavery's heritage constantly reminded whites of black inferiority and of the simpler racial dynamic of that golden age when whites were masters and blacks were slaves. The history of slavery conjured up images of racial order and discipline. For most white southerners slavery symbolized a lost ideal. Alternative modes of race control, no matter how severe, never quite held the same meaning in a slaveless world.

## NOTES

1. Du Bois, *Black Reconstruction in America: An Essay Toward a History of the Part Which Black Folk Played in the Attempt to Reconstruct Democracy in America, 1860–1880* (New York, 1935), 30.

2. Elkins, *Slavery: A Problem in American Institutional and Intellectual Life* (Chicago, 1959), 5.

3. See Ann J. Lane, ed., *The Debate over Slavery: Stanley Elkins and His Critics* (Urbana, 1971).

4. Two notable exceptions are Pete Daniel, "The Metamorphosis of Slavery, 1865–1900," *Journal of American History*, 66 (June, 1979): 88–99, and William L. Van Deburg, *Slavery & Race in American Popular Culture* (Madison, 1984).

5. See John David Smith, *Black Slavery in the Americas: An Interdisciplinary Bibliography, 1865–1980*, 2 vols. (Westport, 1982) and computer printouts for periods 1865–1889 and 1890–1920 in possession of the author.

6. See "Remnants of the Slave System—the Law of Apprenticeship," New York *Times*, October 18, 1867; "The Ordinance of 1787," ibid., October 21, 1882; "Virginians Object to Elson's History," ibid., February 28, 1911. For other examples, see "Emancipation in Russia and the United States," New York *Times*, April 8, 1877; "Slaves in the Olden Days," ibid., October 1, 1882; "Days of Slavery in Ohio," ibid., November 12, 1882; "The Underground Road," ibid., March 11, 1899; and "Race War Coming, Dr. Giddings Says," ibid., September 26, 1912.

7. See, for example, "Ex-Slaves Guests of Bishop College," New York *Age*, January 5, 1914; "U.C.V. to Honor Wartime Slave," ibid., January 18, 1914; "Eleven Former Slaves Dined by Owner's Sons," ibid., May 13, 1915; "South Still Honors 'Old-Time' Negro," Philadelphia *Public Ledger*, May 2, 1915; "To Erect Monument for Negro 'Mammies,' " *Afro-American Ledger*, June 15, 1915; " 'Black Mammy' Day Observed," St. Louis *Republic*, October 14, 1915; "Black Mammy," *Christian Science Monitor*, October 21, 1918. These newspaper clippings, as well as those cited in the following two notes, are located in the Slavery and Race Problem Files, Tuskegee Institute.

8. See, for example, "Homes for Ex-Slaves," Indianapolis *Freeman*, February 2, 1915; untitled article in New York *Town Topics*, July 15, 1915; "Home

for Ex-Slaves Helped by Atlantans," Atlanta *Constitution*, April 19, 1918; "Slaves Who Deserve Pensions," Montgomery (AL) *Advertiser*, July 12, 1913; "Will Tallahassee Heed?" Palatka (FL) *Advocate*, October 2, 1915; untitled article in Columbia (SC) *State*, April 27, 1915; "Devoted Ex-Slave Dies at Selma," Montgomery *Advertiser*, November 18, 1913; " 'Auntie' Gibbs, Aged 137, Dies in Memphis," New York *Globe*, October 8, 1915; "Negro Body Servant of Southern Soldier Dies," Montgomery *Advertiser*, August 15, 1915; "Negro Confederate Buried with Honors," Atlanta *Constitution*, October 19, 1915. See also Robert Timmons, "Aged Ex-Slaves Gather at Home of Old Master," in *The Possibilities of the Negro in Symposium* (Atlanta, 1904), 69–73.

   9. See, for example, Memphis *Journal and Guide*, July 4, 1914; "Herald's News Photograph Contest," New York *Herald*, July 10, 1915; "Slavery in California," Riverside (CA) *Enterprise*, September 5, 1916; "Former Slaves in Celebration," Brooklyn *Eagle*, October 23, 1916; " 'Deacon' Smith Has Double Anniversary," Middletown (CT) *Press*, October 17, 1917; "Movement Is Started to Care for Ex-Slaves," Atlanta *Constitution*, December 25, 1917; "Slavery Kept Up in Illinois after Lincoln Freed Negroes," Chicago *Journal*, October 5, 1920; "How the Last of the Slaves Was Captured," New York *Sun*, January 4, 1920; "How Traffic in Slaves Flourished in Marlborough in the Early Days of the Nation," Poughkeepsie (NY) *Courier*, June 20, 1920.

   10. Curry to Booker T. Washington, June 3, 1898, in Louis R. Harlan, ed., *The Booker T. Washington Papers*, 13 vols. to date (Urbana, 1972– ), 4:427; Roosevelt to James Ford Rhodes, November 29, 1904, Theodore Roosevelt Papers, Manuscript Division, Library of Congress; Dodd to Oswald Garrison Villard, July 3, 1906, Oswald Garrison Villard Papers, Houghton Library, Harvard University; Dodd to Edwin Mims, September 15, 1906, Edwin Mims Papers, Joint University Libraries, Nashville; William J. Strong, "Blacklisting: The New Slavery," *Arena*, 21 (March 1889): 273–292; James A. Skilton to Andrew Dickson White, August 14, 1896, Andrew Dickson White Papers, Cornell University; Charles B. Spahr, *America's Working People* (New York, 1900), 90; editorial, "Feudalism or Slavery," *Independent*, 55 (April 2, 1902): 805–806; "Slavery in Alabama," ibid., (June 11, 1903): 1416–1417; Moorfield Storey, *Negro Suffrage Is Not a Failure* (Boston, 1903), 10; Richard Barry, "Slavery in the South To-Day," *Cosmopolitan Magazine*, 42 (March, 1907): 481–491; Raymond, "Slave Laws Halt South's Progress," Chicago *Tribune*, January 5, 1908; David Y. Thomas, "Social Aspects of the Slavery Question," *Dial*, 51 (November 1, 1911): 330; editorial, "What Is Slavery?" *Independent*, 74 (February 20, 1913): 389; Thomas Pearce Bailey, *Race Orthodoxy in the South and Other Aspects of the Negro Question* (New York, 1914), 346; Herbert J. Seligmann, "Slavery in Georgia, A.D. 1921," *Nation*, 112 (April 20, 1921): 591.

11. Anon., "A New Slavery among Us," *National Anti-Slavery Standard*, 29 (April 17, 1869): 1; George Fitzhugh, "The Freedman and His Future: II. A Rejoinder," *Lippincott's Magazine*, 5 (February, 1870): 304; Stephen J. Field and Joseph P. Bradley in *U.S. Supreme Court Reports, Vols. 82–85* (Rochester, 1884), 413, 421; E. J. Donnell, *Slavery and "Protection"! An Historical Review and Appeal to the Workshop and the Farm* (New York, 1882), 3; anon., *Slavery and Polygamy Reestablished under the Jurisdiction of the United States So Far as It Can Be Done by Authority of William McKinley, in Carrying on His Effort to Deprive the People of the Philippine Islands of Their Liberty* (Brookline, MA, 1899); Caroline H. Pemberton to W. E. B. Du Bois, December 12, 1903, W. E. B. Du Bois Papers, University of Massachusetts, Amherst; Storey, *Negro Suffrage Is Not a Failure*, 19.

12. Nordhoff, *The Cotton States in the Spring and Summer of 1875* (New York, 1876), 105; Page, *The Rebuilding of Old Commonwealths: Being Essays towards the Training of the Forgotten Man in the Southern States* (New York, 1905), 125.

13. Though pioneer studies of slave folk culture support the overall argument of this book, I have largely excluded them from the present study. For an analysis of the early literature in this field, see John David Smith, "The Unveiling of Slave Folk Culture, 1865–1920," *Journal of Folklore Research*, 21 (April, 1984): 47–62.

14. The terms *proslavery* and *antislavery* appeared regularly after the Civil War. The *National Anti-Slavery Standard*, for example, published a column, "Pro-Slavery," well after Appomattox. It reprinted "extracts from the Pro-Slavery Press, North and South, as serve best to illustrate the character of Slavery and the spirit of its champions and apologists." See vol. 26, December 30, 1865, p. 1.

15. Rable, "Bourbonism, Reconstruction, and the Persistence of Southern Distinctiveness," *Civil War History*, 29 (June, 1983): 138, 139.

16. Johnson, "The Ideology of White Supremacy, 1876–1910," in Fletcher Melvin Green, ed., *Essays in Southern History* (Chapel Hill, 1949), 135.

17. Rable, "Bourbonism, Reconstruction, and the Persistence of Southern Distinctiveness," 140.

18. My use of the term *historians* is deliberately broad. It encompasses those writers who identified slavery as a topic of historic significance. The authors whose works I analyze, then, are not limited to "trained" historians in the modern sense of that term.

19. Fleming, "The American Negro Academy," *Publications of the Southern History Association*, 9 (January, 1905): 50.

20. Baker, *Following the Color Line: An Account of Negro Citizenship in the American Democracy* (New York, 1908), 44.

# PART ONE

# The Old Arguments Anew: Proslavery and Antislavery Ideology in the Postwar Mind

# 1

# Emancipation and the Origins of the New Proslavery Argument

## I

Slavery as an idea died a slow death in the half-century after Appomattox. Even before the war's end, white southerners contemplated shaping their peculiar institution to the new order of things should the Confederacy fail. Early in 1865 a Virginian explained, "What the form of slavery, or what name will be given to it by Yankee ingenuity, we cannot foresee, but that the thing itself will continue, and that the negroes will have to work harder and fare worse than slaves have ever worked or fared before in the Southern States, is as certain as the rising of tomorrow's sun." Union victory, emancipation, and the Reconstruction amendments outlawed the ownership of chattels personal once and for all. But while slavery as an institution was deemed forever dead, as an ideal it was never laid fully to rest. No sooner had Lee's men stacked their guns than southern whites, reinforced by northern conservatives, began a new offensive on the slavery question. To be sure, few southerners openly advocated reenslavement. Repeatedly whites denied accusations that they sought to reenslave the blacks.[1] But the spirit of slavery remained alive in the South. Proslavery ideology surfaced again immediately after the war. It lingered in every corner of the former Confederacy.

Writing, for example, in May, 1865, a U.S. Army officer stationed in eastern North Carolina expressed concern over the sentiments of

whites in Sampson and Duplin counties. Residents there, wrote Colonel
Elias Wright, ''much regret the loss of slavery . . . deplore the presence
of free negroes and the colored soldiery among them . . . very much fear
'servile insurrection' . . . [and] some of them have a lingering hope that
something may yet turn up to restore to them the old domestic relations
of master and slave.'' And many white southerners, explained General
Benjamin H. Grierson in June, 1865, continued to ''clutch on to slavery
with a lingering hope to save at least a relic of their favorite yet barbarous
institution for the future.'' In August, 1865, the *Nation* charged that
white southerners sought to ''retain the slaveholding spirit without keeping the slaves.'' Two years later, one South Carolinian advised another
to abandon any hopes of reenslavement. Whites, argued Joseph E.
Holmes, must forsake the ''hard words and frowning looks'' toward
blacks that signified their desire to keep them enslaved. He predicted
that such reactionary thought would only lead to race war.[2]

Slavery as symbol and as idea assumed a whole new role in postemancipation southern society. Why did white southerners focus so
keenly on slavery after its abolition? What was there about the peculiar
institution that fostered such resistance to social change? Slavery enabled
white southerners to explain, to defend, to justify their lost civilization
from ongoing abolitionist attacks. It also provided a vital link to the
past at a time when the South was occupied by what residents perceived
as an alien invasion force. Uncomfortable with the new free labor
system, many longed for the control mechanisms inherent in slavery.
In Baton Rouge, Louisiana, for example, two white women in 1866
complained that their servants refused to act like slaves. ''They want
to treat the Negroe as of old,'' remarked James A. Payne, but the blacks
''wont put up with it.'' In North Carolina a white overseer discharged
two freedmen in 1868 because, he explained, the blacks ''have got to
work and act slave fashion or they cant stay with me.'' Representatives
of virtually every segment of the South's white community viewed
slavery in a positive light, extolling its many virtues and bemoaning its
all too sudden passing.[3]

By reviving elements of the old proslavery argument, white southerners vented their innermost frustrations. For Ryland Randolph, race-
baiting editor of Tuscaloosa, Alabama's *Independent Monitor*, blacks
were suited only for servitude—''to wait on the tables and brush off
flies.'' Those blacks who accepted white supremacy were to ''be re-

warded with plenty of work, porridge and kind treatment.'' In 1869
Randolph eulogized slavery as

a God-send for the negro race. Negroes, as bondsmen, were happier, more
sleek and greasy-looking, and better clothed, than they are now. We never hear
the ringing horse-laughs, the picking of banjoes, beating of tamborines, and
knocking of feet against puncheon-floors, that formerly marked their *sans souci*
existence. Instead thereof, they may be heard to grumble, in squads, collected
in fence-corners; and may be seen with ashy faces, grim countenances, and
squalid appearance generally.

Whites like Randolph could barely comprehend the meaning of emancipation. A contributor to the *Southern Cultivator* in 1865 described
the freedman as

a monstrosity . . . a hand without muscles, a glass eyeball, and a shin-plaster
. . . a tender without any locomotive; fuel, coals . . . without any machinery. A
nigger without any master is latent power off the track. Put him off by himself,
you can get him along only by pushing so constant and severe, that it costs
more than it comes to. Tackle him to an engine, in the shape of a white man,
and the long train laden with industrial products goes with a rush.

Or perhaps such blatant racists grasped freedom's message all too well.
For them the prospect of blacks being their social and political equals
was anathema. Yankees could dictate the new order of race relations,
but in the minds of many postemancipation southern whites, the black
man remained a slavelike inferior.[4]
   Convinced that emancipation proved gravely harmful to ex-masters
and ex-slaves alike, many whites during Reconstruction fashioned a
new proslavery argument. It encompassed virtually all of the familiar
antebellum rationales for slavery plus a bevy of defenses fitted to the
peculiar circumstances of the postwar South. With secession and the
specter of civil war no longer at issue, whites found themselves free to
espouse a new, even more romanticized image of slavery. Yet their
writings—unabashedly sympathetic to the peculiar institution—closely
resembled antebellum southern propaganda. After many years of countering charges that slavery was cruel and exploitative, white southerners
now went on the offensive to set the record straight. They blasted Yankee
hypocrisy. Had not New Englanders grown rich from the Atlantic slave

trade, only to abandon the Africans when the traffic in human flesh proved no longer profitable? According to a contributor to the *Southern Cultivator*, the Africans arrived as

untrained savages, deficient in personal vigor, size and stature, with no intellectual cultivation whatever, and no just notions of religious truth. Under our supervision and care, the products of negro labor have almost clothed the world. Contact with and direction from the white man has educated him fully to the half-civilized state—a position he has hitherto reached in no other country.

And early in 1866, a North Carolina journalist identified no fewer than twelve advantages that slavery offered blacks. He described the slavery system as a virtual paradise where the blacks were fed, clothed, sheltered, relieved from cares, nursed, mourned, buried, educated, elevated, disciplined, improved, and, most important, civilized.[5]

Two years later a writer in *Scott's Monthly Magazine* summarized virtually all of the new defenses of slavery. Drawing heavily on history to support his proslavery ideas, Russ James lauded slavery's merits, condemned its premature abolition, and grieved over the condition of the freedmen. Through world history, James insisted, slavery had existed as a means for civilized people to elevate a backward one. Slavery advanced the blacks in ways the abolitionists never could comprehend. In Africa the black was "barbarous, idolatrous, and utterly depraved. *As a Southern slave*, he . . . obtained a knowledge of the true God; was affectionate to his family, and was immeasurably in advance of his ancestors, intellectually and morally. And all this in less than three centuries." Emancipation, however, represented a disastrous step backward for them.

In many parts of the South, they are sinking into the most degrading and revolting superstition. . . . They have become insubordinate and habitual violators of law and order. Our prisons are swarming with them, while many have expiated a short, though bloody, career of crime upon the scaffold. As a race, they are passing rapidly away, nearly one million having perished in the short space of three years.

Idleness, crime, disease, and starvation replaced Christianity, obedience, thrift, and prosperity. "The history of these unfortunate people

everywhere," concluded James, "has been that freedom, suddenly bestowed, has been ruinous and destructive."[6]

Emancipation obviously overturned the lives of southern whites. They
reeled in shock at what they deemed the altered deportment and poor
agricultural performance of their former bondsmen. Abolition rocked
the very basis of southern white society.[7] Writing in 1867 from Rapides
Parish, Louisiana, a planter shared his troubled musings with readers
of *DeBow's Review*. "I live surrounded by my former slaves," he wrote,
"and some times for a little while I look upon the whole change as a
dream." Others described their thoughts on slavery more as nightmares.
Without slaves, some white elites wondered, who would perform household chores? The mere idea of having to do menial work shocked some
of them. In some it conjured up images of themselves being enslaved
by their former bondsmen and the hated Yankees. Both ideas sat poorly
with a people who defended their peculiar institution from charges of
cruelty with the claim that the whites, not the blacks, had been the only
real slaves under the old regime. For these whites, emancipation meant
more than the simple loss of property. It meant the repudiation of
control—of racial order and discipline—dictated by a master class.
Whites feared that the new order of things would usher in catastrophic
changes, not only black political equality but social equality as well.
White southerners shuddered at the thought that they would become
subservient to blacks and, equally horrifying, to northerners.[8]

Across the region, white southerners sensed this reversal of roles.
Mrs. Eva B. Jones of Augusta, Georgia, held nothing but contempt for
"Our Yankee masters" who "think that *their* term of slavery having
expired, that the shackles they have abandoned, more firmly riveted,
will do for us their former owners." Later that year a North Carolinian
echoed these fears: northern misrule and black misbehavior had made
southern whites "fit subjects for slaves."[9] Observing blacks after two
years of freedom, H. Rives Pollard, editor of Richmond's *Southern
Opinion*, impugned "the sullen and impudent crowd of blacks . . . mo-
reour masters than our servants." According to an ex-slaveholder from
Richmond County, North Carolina, nothing was "more deplorable, or
more galling, than for those who have been born free . . . to be *in subjection*, to the stupid and ferocious black." Many shared the sentiments
of unreconstructed rebel and poet Paul H. Hayne. So wedded to the
past was Hayne that in 1885 he still remarked bitterly that blacks refused

to act like slaves. Although two decades had elapsed since emancipation, he condemned the blacks' "servile *insubordination*, & impudence!" Surrounded by "emancipated Ethiopia," wrote Hayne, the whites were enslaved this time around.[10]

Convinced that they were held captive by alien forces in their midst, white southerners expected the worst from their ex-slaves and were seldom disappointed. Incidents throughout the South proved to them that emancipation had ushered in the much-dreaded social revolution. Soon after Appomattox whites watched in disbelief as their once faithful servants either fled to the Yankees or became disobedient hired laborers. At the very time when whites sought to reorder their world, blacks set out to test their newfound freedom. Reports circulated that blacks refused to labor, committed violent crimes, and fraternized openly with whites of the opposite sex.[11] The presence of large numbers of U.S. Colored Troops only added insult to injury. Whites fumed at the alleged abusive language and behavior of the black occupation forces that reportedly incited the freedmen to "liberate" hogs, horses, and provisions belonging to their ex-masters. To make matters worse, late in 1865 rumors circulated widely that if the former slaves failed to receive land from the government, they would rise en masse at Christmas. Such fears spread as whites observed with dismay the destruction of their beloved South. Without slavery, charged editor Pollard, the region would become "a grand roming ground for lazaroni, . . . freed Africans, imported Africans, mulattos, miscegenates of every hue and degree of mongrelism, and greazers."[12]

## II

Immediately after Appomattox the uncertain legal status of blacks, and the general disorder prevailing in the South, postponed the full impact of slavery's demise. Because emancipation was such a bitter pill, masters made every effort to delay or postpone its full impact upon "their" blacks as well as upon themselves. Confusion reigned in the South in the spring of 1865. As they watched their society crumble around them, slaveholders prayed that somehow their peculiar institution—and their way of life—might be spared. In northeast Mississippi, minister/teacher/farmer Samuel A. Agnew noted the uncertainty with which whites approached emancipation. "The negroes," explained Agnew in May, 1865, "evidently think they are free, but they may be too hasty in their conclusions." A week later he recorded that "The general opinion now is that slavery is dead but some still are incredulous because they do not want to believe it. Just like Lee's surrender it is an unpalatable truth. . . . " In Perry County, Alabama, a planter chafed under his inability to control his ex-slaves' comings and goings. "Joy go with them," explained Hugh Davis, Jr., in May, 1865, "but if this military order, unconstitutional as it is, does not protect them always, all who have left or leave had better look out for I have a settlement with them all my own way too."[13]

Such wishful thinking tended to appear most commonly in the more remote areas of the South. In parts of Arkansas, for example, slaveholders withheld the news of freedom from the blacks as long as possible. In July, 1865, Colonel Charles Bentzoni issued an order informing Arkansas slaveholders that blacks had been freed effective January 1, 1863. He warned whites that anyone who held blacks as slaves after that day owed the laborers two and one-half years back pay. In Texas some masters kept their blacks enslaved as late as November, 1865. And in the following month a Freedmen's Bureau agent reported that a Kentucky slaveholder refused to surrender a black child, his former property, to its mother. In February, 1866, Freedmen's Bureau officials in Nashville reported that many blacks remained enslaved in Kentucky. General Clinton B. Fisk explained that according to the Louisville *Democrat*, emancipation only fanned the burning embers of slavery in the Commonwealth. Recently, wrote Fisk in February 1866, "the slavery question has become more unsettled than ever." Many Kentuckians, "believing its doctrines, practice accordingly, and still hold freedmen *as slaves*."[14]

But such confusion did not last for long. On December 13, 1865, twenty-seven states ratified the Thirteenth Amendment, abolishing slavery once and for all. Blacks now stood free and, on paper at least, could own land, perhaps attend school, and relocate as they wished. How did whites respond to being masters without slaves? A few expressed relief that the incubus of slavery was finally removed. They admitted guilt and even explained Confederate defeat as a result of God's displeasure with the peculiar institution. In April, 1865, for example, Dr. William N. Mercer of Adams County, Mississippi, recorded these ideas in his diary:

That slavery is an evil, I have never doubted, and for more than twenty years have been convinced it could not be preserved, in opposition to the spirit of the age, the dictates of humanity and the teaching of experience. In regard to my personal own interests, I would have been perfectly willing to have manumitted my own slaves. But I did not believe that an immediate, and so great, a change would have been to their advantage.


A contributor to *The Land We Love* wrote that slavery had failed to shepherd the slaves' spiritual needs as well as it catered to their physical wants. "Since we failed to come up to the full measure of our obligation, we have been punished for our neglect." Others blamed slavery for teaching blacks lessons that had to be unlearned: crime and immorality. And some admitted that their fears of the unprofitability of free black labor had been unfounded all along.[15]

But the overwhelming mass of white southerners protested emancipation vigorously. They refused to apologize for slavery. The vast majority in fact defended slavery, mourned its passing, and openly praised the peculiar institution as preferable to freedom for blacks. An ex-slaveholder, for example, declared point-blank that owning bondsmen was no crime. "Abraham[,] Isaac & Jacob . . . were slave holders & I am very willing to be classed with them," he declared. Whites agreed that emancipation, not slavery, deserved condemnation. South Carolina's Wade Hampton denounced the Thirteenth Amendment as illegal, dishonest, immoral; it denied whites what he considered their natural right "to direct, to instruct and to protect" the blacks. Many censured emancipation as a blatant crime, what Mrs. Eva B. Jones termed "a most unprecedented robbery." According to the editor of the Charlotte *Church Intelligencer*, setting free the slaves amounted to "the greatest crime against humanity . . . since the French revolution."[16]

Freedom, charged the editor of another Carolina paper, the Wilmington *Daily Dispatch*, was a curse for the blacks, not a blessing. Removed from the protection of their masters, they now had to endure winters without adequate food, clothing, or shelter. Such were "the crimes," complained the editor, "committed in the name of Freedom!" For North Carolina blacks, emancipation guaranteed "freedom to suffer, freedom to shiver in the cold, freedom to starve in the streets, freedom to die miserable, loathsome deaths, uncared for and alone." Others branded emancipation a violation of property rights guaranteed by the Constitution. Some even demanded compensation from the victorious Yankees. For these whites, abolition symbolized a curse, a blight, "a violation of one of the fundamental laws of God's government of men, and the gravest national errour of the Christian era.''[17]

As they came face to face with emancipation, whites expressed uncertainty, shock, and bewilderment at the behavior of their ex-slaves. Observing the free blacks around him in July, 1865, Alabama cotton planter John Horry Dent concluded that "their demoralization is complete . . . indifference and idleness is their course." And he envisioned dire consequences for the freedmen.

Their future will be want, misery and wretchedness. . . . [With] no one to care for them, guide and protect them, they will meet with ill treatment, rowdiness and many wrongs from the whites. Time will show in this great experiment whether as Slaves or Freedmen they were best off. Without being properly controlled, managed, directed and constantly employed, they will fast run into ruins, vagabondism and every species of vice.

Dent deemed the different deportment of blacks as slaves and as freedmen worthy of special note. Confederate defeat meant to him the loss of three-quarters of his $200,000 fortune, including 137 slaves. In Dent's plantation journal for August, 1865, he listed in parallel columns words that measured for him the ways in which the blacks had changed. Labelling his journal entry "The Contrast," the Alabamian described the slave as contented, cheerful, obedient, industrious, and domestic. But as a freedman, these qualities disappeared. Now the black, charged Dent, was discontented, soured, insolent, idle, and wandering. "The Past," Dent wrote, "has shown that the Negro as a slave was a contented and happy being." The future, according to the planter, was uncertain. Recent experience, however, had given him reason to doubt freedom's success.[18]

Three months earlier, in May, Sam and Jack, two of Dent's former slaves, had fled from his plantation to the protection of General Benjamin H. Grierson's U.S. cavalry. The blacks, wrote Dent, "were wild and reckless with the idea of their freedom." By mid-August the two blacks had returned to their ex-master, looking "very ill and used up. They ask pardon," Dent explained, "and promise to do better, saying they had their fill of the Yankees." The change in his former slaves' behavior was more than this planter could bear. "To say that Dent criticized freedmen for not being slaves is only a small exaggeration," concludes historian Ray Mathis. "A life of paternalism could not be discarded overnight like an old-fashioned garment."[19]

Unable or unwilling to grasp the importance of freedom to the blacks, some whites quickly lashed out at their ex-slaves. ''What a miserable set of ungrateful wretches they are!'' wrote a planter with holdings in Mississippi and Arkansas. Others were more contemplative. For example, Dr. John H. Parrish of Greensboro, Alabama, mourned the passing of slavery as well as the broad impact of emancipation on southerners' way of life. ''The loss of our servants,'' wrote Parrish, ''destroys the nature of all other property.'' Mrs. Ella Gertrude Clanton Thomas of Augusta, Georgia, became so distraught by emancipation that she simply was unable to discuss the subject. Because her family's fortune had been invested entirely in bondsmen, Confederate defeat suddenly transformed her ''from a state of affluence to comparative poverty.'' Her life in shambles, Mrs. Thomas was stunned. She dreaded living amidst free blacks—where ''everything is entirely reversed.'' ''I alone know,'' lamented Mrs. Thomas, ''the effect the abolition of slavery has had upon me.'' It shook her faith in God. Writing in October, 1865, she explained that ''if the *Bible* was right then slavery *must be*— Slavery was done away with and my faith in God's Holy Book was terribly shaken. For a time I doubted God. . . . I was bewildered . . . I felt all this and *could not* see God's hand—the Negroes suddenly emancipated from control were wild with their newly gained and little understood freedom.'' In Chapel Hill, North Carolina, Mrs. Cornelia P. Spencer shared this sense of total economic and social upheaval. ''There are many . . . slave-owners in the South,'' she explained, ''who take this spoiling of their goods anyway but joyfully.'' One of them, Mrs. Laura E. Buttolph, chafed under Yankee rule in Liberty County, Georgia. In June, 1865, Union troops were there, she noted, principally ''to keep the county in order—particularly the colored population.'' Times certainly had changed. ''There are to be *no more bondsmen and no more whippings*,'' lamented Mrs. Buttolph. As blacks quickly stopped acting like slaves, their former masters experienced new feelings of hopelessness and betrayal. Conquered, degraded, humiliated, and robbed of their slave property, southern whites had little doubt that their world had indeed been turned upside down.[20]

## III

But whites still retained the color of their skin. Throughout Reconstruction, planters and poor whites alike continued to perceive themselves as masters of any and all blacks. The postwar South, writes political scientist Daniel A. Novak, retained "a metamorphosized slave psychology. It . . . simply adapted its laws to meet the formal strictures of the Civil War amendments, in order to retain as much of its old rules of labor control as possible." Whites continued to run the South, to make the rules, even in the midst of Reconstruction. They complained that their northern conquerors lacked an understanding of the need to dominate blacks because they misunderstood blacks in general and the nature of slavery in particular. According to the Reverend Agnew of Mississippi, the Yankees failed to grasp the degree to which the black character cried out for control. Living among blacks, Yankees would soon comprehend that "the negroe must be governed in some way."[21]

Several recent studies have detailed the various ways in which southern whites reacted to their crisis.[22] Most whites sought to define the new relationships with blacks in terms that would allow them to retain maximum control over blacks. Convinced of the revolutionary proportions of the new order of things, they determined to continue hegemony over the blacks. As a result, the freedmen quickly became ensnarled in a web of economic, legal, and extralegal restraints—labor contracts, the Black Codes, vagrancy legislation, lien laws, convict labor, enticement laws, and debt peonage. Neoslavery remained alive and well in the South.

Their need to control the ex-slaves consumed southern whites during Reconstruction. They predicted that without white control the freedmen would either languish and become public wards or perish. "To one who knows him," wrote an influential North Carolinian in 1866, "the negro is but an overgrown child." Without an arsenal of state laws regulating them, the freedmen would feed themselves inadequately, abuse their children, drink excessively, and squander their earnings. At the very least, wrote North Carolinian T. P. Devereux, penal laws should tie the black people either to the soil or to some mechanical trade. According to South Carolina rice planter Dr. J. R. Sparkman,

The negro left to himself as a race has never advanced beyond demi-civilization. And if under the control of a superior race (call it slavery, bondage, servitude, or villenage,) the facts are made patent, . . . his physical wants are better supplied—his moral condition improved, his domestic happiness promoted, his proclivities to vice and crime controlled, and he is made a contributor to the general comfort and welfare of mankind. . . .

The "helpless" condition of the freedmen in Texas persuaded Caleb
G. Forshey, a former Confederate officer, to conclude "that the highest
condition the black race has ever reached or can reach, is one where
he is provided for by a master race." In the opinion of these unreconstructed southerners, postwar conditions proved that blacks required
strict regulation by whites.[23]

The Black Codes passed by southern legislatures in 1865–1866 indicate the sorts of control mechanisms preferred by whites during Presidential Reconstruction. In Florida, for example, the legislators
responsible for drafting laws applicable to blacks praised "the benign,
but much abused and greatly misunderstood institution of slavery."
Florida's bondsmen were "the happiest and best provided for laboring
population in the world." But the freedmen, "suddenly deprived of the
fostering care and protection of their old masters, . . . are now to be
seen like so many children gambling upon the brink of the yawning
precipice—careless of the future, and intent only on revelling in the
present unrestrained enjoyment of the newly found bauble of 'freedom.' " Defining blacks as an "inferior and dependent class," the
Floridians outlined various legal means—punishments, prohibitions,
qualifications—of setting whites on a higher plane. Blacks, for example,
were prohibited from keeping firearms, and they were to be imprisoned
for crimes for which whites would be merely fined. The essential lesson
for freedmen, concluded the lawmakers, was that "*liberty* is not license,
and that labor is ordained of God, and a necessity of their condition."[24]

Under Texas law, as in all of the former Confederate states, the
freedmen labored under strict contracts. Much as under slavery, the
whites still dictated the terms of the work environment. Unlike under
slavery, the blacks were now free to contract with the parties of their
choice, "but when once chosen, they shall not be allowed to leave their
place of employment, until the fulfillment of their contract, unless by
consent of their employer, or on account of harsh treatment or breach
of contract on the part of the employer." True, laborers possessed a
lien of one-half of the crop to ensure the payment of wages. And
employers were to be fined double the amount due the laborer should
they default on payment or treat their employees inhumanely. Nevertheless, the stamp of slavery remained embedded on Texas's Black
Code. The employee was expected to "obey all proper orders of his
employer" and was liable for fines if proven disobedient. Talking back,
swearing, neglecting duty, leaving the farm without permission, enter-

taining visitors during work hours—such infractions might be tolerated
in the case of white workers, but were strictly forbidden in the case of
ex-slaves.[25]

South Carolinian Edmund Rhett kept slavery in the forefront of his
mind as he served in 1865 as a member of his state's commission to
revise laws pertaining to blacks. He thought long and hard over the
nature of the new control whites should hold over the freedmen. The
results of his work later were incorporated into South Carolina's famous
Black Code. Rhett assumed that blacks would work only by coercion.
He damned emancipation as "unwise, injurious, and dangerous to our
whole system, pecuniary and social." Yet whites had to accept abolition. It was crucial, reasoned Rhett, that whites take steps to keep the
black "as near to his former condition as Law can keep him, that he
should be kept as near to the condition of slavery as possible, and as
far from the condition of the white man as is practicable." In other
words, the new status of the freedman "should to the utmost extent
practicable be limited, controlled, and surrounded with safe guards, as
will make the change as slight as possible." Rhett's goal, he explained
in no uncertain terms, was to preserve "our labor system, and, indeed
. . . our social system."[26]

Uppermost in Rhett's mind was preventing blacks from owning land.
Once the black was denied land, Rhett said, "it will . . . cut off all
competition between the white and black man. The black man must
then forever labor upon the capital of the white man, and the white man
must take care of him, or else he will soon have no labor." To keep
blacks in line, Rhett proposed vagrancy legislation as well as bills to
enforce contracts and to discipline black laborers. White plantation
supervisors, he suggested, should be allowed to mete out the same
corporal punishments employed in the U.S. Army. If blacks could be
denied their forty acres and a mule, he wrote, whites could restore racial
order. In Rhett's mind, this restoration involved granting blacks a status
much like that of English aliens, "upon the footing of a denizen."[27]

South Carolina's Black Code joined Mississippi's as the most no-
torious legal attempts to retain the substance of slavery during Reconstruction. (Both were finally overturned by the Freedmen's Bureau.)
While all of the Codes acknowledged the blacks' free status, at best
they provided what Harold M. Hyman and William M. Wiecek have
described as "severely truncated forms of freedom." They reenacted
the race-control and labor-discipline features of the slave codes, pro-

viding detailed listings of blacks' civil disabilities. According to Hyman and Wiecek:

They defined racial status; forbade blacks from pursuing certain occupations . . . forebade [sic] owning firearms . . . controlled the movement of blacks by systems of passes; required proof of residence; prohibited the congregation of groups of blacks; restricted blacks from residing in certain areas; and specified an etiquette of deference to whites. . . . The Codes forbade racial intermarriage and provided the death penalty for blacks raping white women, while omitting special provisions for whites raping black women. They excluded blacks from jury duty, public office, and voting. Some Codes required racial segregation in public transportation. Most Codes authorized whipping and the pillory as punishment for freedmen's offenses.

The Codes placed the freedmen on a legal par with antebellum free blacks but denied them equality with whites in civil rights. According to Hyman and Wiecek, they established a class of Americans "excluded by law because of race and color from the capacity to protect itself in courts equally with whites through testimony, to be fully responsible for marketplace decisions, or to live without fear of prejudiced application of criminal justice." And the vagrancy and apprentice clauses— placing unemployed adults and children of indigent blacks under the control of white employers—smacked clearly of slavery.[28]

While it would be unfair to assert that the Black Codes represented a mere subterfuge for slavery, the acts clearly were designed to keep blacks as close to bondage as possible. The Codes are especially important because they illustrate the first steps taken by whites to effect racial control after emancipation. "Through these codes," wrote one of their early students, "the mind of the South uttered its first and last untrammeled word upon the status of the freedmen." The mere wording of the various state laws suggests the types of slavelike behavior whites expected from their former bondsmen. For example, the police ordinance for blacks in St. Landry Parish, Louisiana, sought to maintain the public order, "comfort and correct deportment" of the freedmen. Blacks needed passes even to enter the parish and could not be absent from their employers after ten o'clock at night. They were prohibited from renting or owning property in the parish, and any blacks residing there were "required to be in the regular service of some white person, or former owner, who shall be held responsible for the conduct of said negro.'' Mississippi's Code included a catch-all section levying fines and possible imprisonment for any black

committing riots, routs, affrays, trespasses, malicious mischief, cruel treatment to animals, seditious speeches, insulting gestures, language, or acts, or assaults on any person, disturbance of the peace, exercising the function of a minister of the Gospel without a license . . . vending spirituous or intoxicating liquors, or committing any other misdemeanor, the punishment of which is not specifically provided for by law.

Similarly, South Carolina's Code included among the categories of vagrants ''those who are engaged in representing publicly or privately, for fee or reward, without license, any tragedy, interlude, comedy, farce, play, or other similar entertainment, exhibition of the circus, sleight-of-hand, wax-works, or the like.'' The master of an apprentice was authorized ''to inflict moderate chastisement and impose reasonable restraint upon his apprentice, and to recapture him if he depart from his service.''[29]

With such laws emanating from southern state capitals, not surprisingly individuals openly advocated whipping blacks and other vestiges of slavery. According to one editor, ''nothing impresses'' the freedmen ''half so beneficially as a thorough mauling.'' Early in 1866, an Alabama planter put this theory into practice when he discovered a freedman slaughtering one of his pigs. ''I caught him in the very act,'' wrote Albert Davis, ''& gave him a genteel old fashioned thrashing & spared him from going to jail.'' Others spoke vaguely of reenslavement. Talk of putting blacks back in chains—no matter how farfetched—cropped up repeatedly in the postwar years. Surrounded by hostile whites who begrudged them their freedom, and cognizant of the vagrancy and other restrictions of the Black Codes, blacks took such rhetoric seriously. The Virginia correspondent of the New Orleans Daily Picayune observed in October, 1865, that blacks refused to sign labor contracts, ''believing it a sort of slavery.'' So fearful of reenslavement were blacks in Jefferson County, Mississippi, that in September, 1865, they refused to sign labor contracts for the next year. In their minds, merely agreeing to a labor contract meant signing themselves back as their ex-masters' bondsmen. What Charles H. Otken in 1894 referred to as ''the great bugbear reenslavement'' appeared in many forms.[30]

Early in Reconstruction the U.S. Army and Freedmen's Bureau aided whites in using black fears of reenslavement to accomplish various ends. Federal soldiers and agents often assisted former masters in reclaiming and punishing their ex-bondsmen. As William S. McFeely has explained, the Freedmen's Bureau served as a conservative force to impose order, stability, and racial discipline on blacks. Throughout the South agents implored the freedmen to accept their new responsibilities. Some sympathized with the ex-slaveholders who were trying to restore control over the blacks. When, for example, in August, 1865, soldiers whipped blacks who had attacked a white overseer, Georgia freedmen appeared "mystified—thunderstruck that they should receive such treatment . . . at the hands of their friends." Observing U.S. troops stationed at Port Royal Island in February, 1866, Laura M. Towne quipped that "They are often more pro-slavery than the rebels themselves, and only care to make the blacks work." In North Carolina, Captain John C. Barnett, assistant superintendent of the Freedmen's Bureau, warned the blacks that once the army left the state, they would have to fend for themselves: "You must know that your freedom has taken away that interest which your former masters had for you. When in slavery you were their property—they valued you as dollars and cents—and it was their interest to feed, clothe, and nurse you in sickness; but now that interest has gone." Convinced that blacks in western North Carolina misunderstood the meaning of freedom, Barnett in October, 1865, informed them of their rights and responsibilities. While the blacks were free to contract with the employers of their choice, they were expected "to labor and work out your own solution; and, unless you do, you go back to slavery, or a condition far worse." Other Freedmen's Bureau officers, however, took just the opposite tack. They discouraged blacks from signing labor agreements because they judged the conditions too similar to slavery. According to an outraged white employer, the military prejudiced the blacks against him. The credulous blacks had been brainwashed into believing that if they contracted with local planters, "they would be branded and become slaves again!" While government officials assured the freedmen that they would not be reenslaved, blacks heard conflicting messages as well: they would continually have to prove themselves worthy of freedom and beware of whites who still perceived them as slaves.[31]

The threat of reenslavement also played a role in southern politics during Reconstruction. Writing in 1867 from Greensboro, Alabama, Dr. John H. Parrish noted the rapid increase of blacks in Republican political organizations such as the Loyal League. Republicans taught the blacks, alleged Dr. Parrish, that not only were whites their enemies, but that if the Democrats returned to power, they would reenslave the blacks. Southern Democrats reasoned that it was in their best political interest to convince the blacks that they would not be reenslaved. "Yes," wrote a Richmond County, North Carolinian, to former jurist Thomas Ruffin, "let them be told *their freedom* is a fixd fact and will not, ever be attempted to be changed." Otherwise swarms of freedmen would vote for the Republicans. The blacks needed to be reassured that "the continuance of their freedom" did not depend "upon the ascendancy of the Radical party."[32]

Reenslavement, no matter how untenable, loomed in the minds of more than a handful of hopeful, but nevertheless unrealistic, white southerners. Running as a candidate for the Mississippi State Convention in August, 1865, W. L. Brandon adamantly denied charges that he was an emancipationist. He fought for four years to uphold slavery, which, Brandon explained, "I am as fully persuaded to-day as ever, was the true status of the negro. . . . Slavery," he informed the voters of Wilkinson County, "has been taken from us," but only "until we can get control once more of our own State affairs." In the following year a Virginian testified before the Joint Committee on Reconstruction on plans in his state to reenslave the freedmen. Former slaveholders "intend—while they cannot reorganize slavery exactly as it was, and call it slavery, and buy and sell as they did before—by a hocuspocus arrangement to get the service of their former slaves, and tyrannize over them and the poor white people as formerly." Local vagrancy and patrol laws, he predicted, would force the black man to place "himself under the protection of some white man who will take him as a sort of master." Such whites argued unpersuasively that defeat in war did not destroy their constitutional rights to hold slave property. A few dreamed of compensation—as if Confederate defeat had not settled that question permanently. While it is doubtful that these writers seriously expected to undo the Thirteenth Amendment, the terms in which they couched their proslavery ideas and appeals underscore the importance of slavery to the racial thought of the period.[33]

During the transition from slavery to freedom whites indeed were loath to relinquish control over "their" blacks. Reluctant to accept emancipation, North Carolinian William A. Graham in May, 1865, informed his ex-slaves that he would continue to feed and clothe them "as usual." He also agreed to pay them "wages out of the crops, where I thought them earned." All decisions, however, "must be left to me," insisted Graham, "and my authority to remain the same" as under slavery. Donald MacRae, another planter unwilling to surrender the substance of slavery, refused to allow the blacks who worked for him to come and go at will. In September, 1865, he reprimanded Zilla, an ex-slave, for leaving for the day without his permission. "I told her," wrote MacRae, "that though I acknowledge her freedom, I do not acknowledge her right to do as she wishes without my consent, and that if she tried it again she could not come back." These white southerners, then, refused to surrender hegemony over their ex-slaves. Their treatment and expectations of blacks remained unchanged, as if slavery had only been modified, not abolished. In 1869 a contributor to *Scott's Monthly Magazine* summed up this idea nicely. "The form of servitude may be changed," he said, "not the fact."[34]

## NOTES

1. Editorial, Richmond *Daily Dispatch*, January 4, 1865; editorial, "Re-Enslavement," Columbia (SC) *Christian Neighbor*, 1 (October 29, 1868): 122; Marcel, "A Trip in South Carolina," *Nation*, 1 (July 27, 1865): 106; Charles Nordhoff, *The Cotton States in the Spring and Summer of 1875* (New York, 1876), 10, 56; J. C. Delavigne, "The Troubles in the South," *Southern Magazine*, 16 (May, 1875): 518; H. S. Fulkerson, *The Negro; As He Was; As He Is; As He Will Be* (Vicksburg, 1887) 17.

2. Report of Wright, May 29, 1865, Governors' Papers, William W. Holden, North Carolina Division of Archives and History; Report on Operations, April 17–May 29, 1865, June 4, 1865, in *Official Records of the War of the Rebellion*, 128 vols. (Washington, 1880–1901), ser. 1, vol. 49, pt. 1, p. 301; editorial, "Slavery and Slaveocracy," *Nation*, 1 (August 17, 1865): 202; Holmes to Nickels Holmes, November 24, 1867, Nickels Holmes Papers, Duke University.

3. James A. Payne to Mrs. Kate F. Sterrett, June 10, 1866, in John D. Barnhart, ed., "Reconstruction in the Lower Mississippi," *Mississippi Valley Historical Review*, 21 (December, 1934): 393; R. M. Abbott to Thomas Ruffin, March 25, 1868, in J. G. de Roulhac Hamilton, ed., *The Papers of Thomas Ruffin*, 4 vols. (Raleigh, 1920), 4:198.

4. Randolph quoted in Allen W. Trelease, *White Terror: The Ku Klux Klan Conspiracy and Southern Reconstruction* (New York, 1971), xl, xli, 253–254; Paul S. Taylor, *Slave to Freedman* (Berkeley, 1970), 25–26.

5. "Editorial," *Land We Love*, 2 (November, 1866): 70–72; ibid., 1 (Sep-

tember, 1866): 380; anon., "The Massachusetts Slave Trade," *DeBow's Review*, a.w.s., 2 (August, 1866): 296–297; "Memories of the War," ibid., 3 (March, 1867): 225; anon., "The Enterprise and Energy of the South," *Land We Love*, 2 (February, 1867): 273; editorial, "Slavery Revived by the Radicals," Richmond *Southern Opinion*, October 10, 1868; Ella Gertrude Clanton Thomas Diary, October 22, 1868, Duke University; W., "Facts and Predictions," *Southern Cultivator*, 23 (1865): 134; editorial, "A Plea for the Negro," Raleigh *Daily Standard*, January 23, 1866.

6. James, "Historical Sketch of Slavery," *Scott's Monthly Magazine*, 5 (April, 1868): 192, 196, 198, 199.

7. The literature on the transition from slavery to freedom is especially rich. I have benefited most from the following: Joel Williamson, *After Slavery: The Negro in South Carolina during Reconstruction, 1861–1877* (Chapel Hill, 1965), 67–94, 96–97, 243–257, 275–276, 298; W. McKee Evans, *Ballots and Fence Rails: Reconstruction on the Lower Cape Fear* (Chapel Hill, 1966), 66–67, 69–89, 139, 208, 210, 249–250; Taylor, *Slave to Freedman*, 10, 13, 15, 20, 24–27, 29–33, 35–37, 40, 45, 50, 57, 64, 67, 71–72, 82; Peter Kolchin, *First Freedom: The Response of Alabama's Blacks to Emancipation and Reconstruction* (Westport, 1972), xviii–xix, 23, 34, 36, 42, 45, 194; James L. Roark, *Masters without Slaves: Southern Planters in the Civil War and Reconstruction* (New York, 1977), 70, 95, 104–107, 111, 120, 131, 141, 157–159, 198, 207, 235n; Dan T. Carter, "Fateful Legacy: White Southerners and the Dilemma of Emancipation," *Proceedings of the South Carolina Historical Association* (1977): 49–63; Jonathan M. Wiener, *Social Origins of the New South, Alabama, 1860–1885* (Baton Rouge, 1978), 3, 35, 38–39, 42, 47, 51, 53, 54, 57, 61, 69, 70, 71–73; Leon F. Litwack, *Been in the Storm So Long: The Aftermath of Slavery* (New York, 1979), passim; Lawrence N. Powell, *New Masters: Northern Planters during the Civil War and Reconstruction* (New Haven, 1980), 97–122; Ronald L. F. Davis, "Labor Dependency among Freedmen, 1865–1880," in Walter J. Fraser, Jr., and Winfred B. Moore, eds., *From the Old South to the New: Essays on the Transitional South* (Westport, 1981), 155–165, and *Good and Faithful Labor: From Slavery to Sharecropping in the Natchez District, 1860–1890* (Westport, 1982), 3–11, 58, 76, 89–111, 169–178, 181–183, 189–195; J. William Harris, "Plantations and Power: Emancipation on the David Barrow Plantations," in Orville Vernon Burton and Robert C. McMath, eds., *Toward a New South? Studies in Post–Civil War Southern Communities* (Westport, 1982), 246–264; Michael Wayne, *The Reshaping of Plantation Society: The Natchez District, 1860–1880* (Baton Rouge, 1983), 7, 28, 39, 41–44, 50–51, 119–122, 134–135, 148–149, 195, 202–203; Eric Foner, *Nothing but Freedom: Emancipation and Its Legacy* (Baton Rouge, 1983), 54, 60, 66, 68; Litwack, "The Ordeal of Black Freedom," in Fraser and Moore, eds., *The Southern Enigma: Essays on Race, Class and Folk Culture* (Westport,

36                                                    The Old Arguments Anew

1983), 5–23; George C. Rable, *But There Was No Peace: The Role of Violence in the Politics of Reconstruction* (Athens, 1984), 16–32.

8. "Editorial Department," *DeBow's Review*, a.w.s., 3 (March 1867): 332; Ella Gertrude Clanton Thomas Diary, May 29, 1865, p. 70; John W. Norwood to Thomas Ruffin, August 6, 1865, in Hamilton, ed., *The Papers of Thomas Ruffin*, 3:463; Samuel A. Agnew Diary, January 5, 1866, Southern Historical Collection, University of North Carolina at Chapel Hill.

9. Mrs. Eva B. Jones to Mrs. Mary Jones, June 13, 1865, in Robert M. Myers, ed., *The Children of Pride* (New Haven, 1972), 1274. See also Eliza B. Tillinghast to David Ray Tillinghast, June 13, 1865, Tillinghast Family Papers, Duke University; David Schenck Diary, March 16, June 14, 1865, Southern Historical Collection, University of North Carolina at Chapel Hill; M., "Treatment of Laborers," *Southern Cultivator*, 25 (February, 1867): 42; Edward Conigland to Thomas Ruffin, December 4, 1865, in Hamilton, ed., *The Papers of Thomas Ruffin*, 4:46; James Mallory Diary, January 23, 1866, Southern Historical Collection, University of North Carolina at Chapel Hill; James A. Payne to Mrs. Kate F. Sterrett, December 27, 1875, in Barnhart, ed., "Reconstruction in the Lower Mississippi," 395.

10. "Whites or Blacks," *Southern Opinion*, October 19, 1867. See also "Negrodom" in ibid., December 21, 1867; W. F. Leak to Thomas Ruffin, March 13, 1868, in Hamilton, ed., *The Papers of Thomas Ruffin*, 4:194; Hayne to Charles Gayarré, July 7, 1885, Paul Hamilton Hayne Papers, Duke University. Such images persisted through the postemancipation decades. See, for example, Weldon N. Edward to Thomas Ruffin, October 11, 1866, in Hamilton, ed., *The Papers of Thomas Ruffin*, 4:134, and P. M. E., "Concentrative Immigration, the True Policy of the South," *Land We Love*, 6 (February, 1869): 313.

11. John H. Parrish to Henry Watson, June 19, July 30, 1865, Henry Watson, Jr., Papers, Duke University; Earl Schenck Miers, ed., *When the World Ended: The Diary of Emma LeConte* (New York, 1957), 102.

12. Samuel A. Agnew Diary, October 11, November 3, 8, 22, 23, 1865; Ella Gertrude Clanton Thomas Diary, July 23, 1865. See also Dan T. Carter, "The Anatomy of Fear: The Christmas Day Insurrection Scare of 1865," *Journal of Southern History*, 42 (August, 1976): 345–364; E. G. Baker to Messrs. Irby and Ellis and Mosely, October 22, 1865, in Ira Berlin, Joseph P. Reidy, and Leslie S. Rowland, eds., *Freedom: A Documentary History of Emancipation, 1861–1867* (Cambridge, 1982), 748; editorial, "Are Not Capulet and Montague Dead?" *Southern Opinion*, August 12, 1867.

13. Samuel A. Agnew Diary, May 8, 15, 1865; Hugh Davis Farm Book, May 18, 1865, quoted in Weymouth T. Jordan, *Hugh Davis and His Alabama Plantation* (University, AL, 1948), 160.

14. Claude Oubre, *Forty Acres and a Mule: The Freedmen's Bureau and*

*Land Ownership* (Baton Rouge, 1978), 30–31, 192; William S. McFeely, *Yankee Stepfather: General O. O. Howard and the Freedmen* (New Haven, 1968), 68, 160; W. G. Bond to J. H. Cochrane, December 19, 1865, in Berlin et al., eds., *Freedom*, 706; *Report of Clinton B. Fisk to Maj. General O. O. Howard, February 14, 1866*, 39th Congress, 1st session, House Executive Document 70 (Washington, 1866), 236.

15. William N. Mercer Diary, April 10, 1865, William N. Mercer Papers, Louisiana State University; Eliza J. Thompson to Benjamin S. Hedrick, May, 1865, Benjamin S. Hedrick Papers, Duke University; J. L. Tucker, *The Relations of the Church to the Colored Race* (Jackson, MS, 1882), 2–3, 5–8, 12, 14; anon., "Mistaken Sympathy; or, Mistaken Figures," *Land We Love*, 1 (September, 1866): 356; Nordhoff, *The Cotton States*, 22, 23, 56; Arney R. Childs, ed., *The Private Journal of Henry William Ravenel, 1859–1887* (Columbia, 1947), 219, 242–243, 246–247, 268; C. Vann Woodward, ed., *Mary Chesnut's Civil War* (New Haven, 1981), 803; "Letter from Dr. Cloud," *Southern Cultivator*, 25 (December, 1867): 364–365; K., "Slavery Not the Source of All the Evils in the South," ibid., 26 (February, 1868): 61–62; Joseph B. Killebrew Autobiography, vol. 1, pp. 214–215, Southern Historical Collection, University of North Carolina at Chapel Hill.

16. Lon Taylor to S. F. Patterson, February 12, 1866, Lindsay Patterson Papers, Southern Historical Collection, University of North Carolina at Chapel Hill; Hampton to Andrew Johnson, August 25, 1866, in Charles E. Cauthen, ed., *Family Letters of the Three Wade Hamptons, 1782–1901* (Columbia, 1953), 131; Mrs. Eva B. Jones to Mrs. Mary Jones, June 13, 1865, in Myers, ed., *Children of Pride*, 1274; "The Problem of the Negro Race," Charlotte *Church Intelligencer*, 6 (June 21, 1866): 90.

17. "The Celebration of the Anniversary of the Emancipation Proclamation," Wilmington *Daily Dispatch*, January 2, 1867; editorial, "The Freedmen," Raleigh *Daily Sentinel*, January 11, 1866; Paul H. Hayne to Charles Gayarré, April 14, 1885, Hayne Papers; William B. Greene, *The Sovereignty of the People* (Boston, 1868), 29; Lillian A. Kibler, *Benjamin F. Perry: South Carolina Unionist* (Durham, 1946), 412; Elias Dodson to Thomas Ruffin, February 16, 1866, in Hamilton, ed., *The Papers of Thomas Ruffin*, 4:50–51; editorial, "Shall We Have a Negro War?" *Southern Opinion*, September 26, 1868.

18. John H. Dent Plantation Journal, July 6, 1865, vol. 6, pp. 111, 125, Troy State University, Troy, Alabama; Ray Mathis, *John Horry Dent: South Carolina Aristocrat on the Alabama Frontier* (University, AL, 1979), 212–213.

19. "Negro List 1864 and 1865," Dent Plantation Journal, vol. 6, p. 73; ibid., May, 1866, vol. 7, p. 13; ibid., August 16, 1865, pp. 73, 125; Mathis, *John Horry Dent*, 220.

20. Alex McRae to Donald MacRae, March 5, 1866, Hugh MacRae Papers, Duke University. See also Howell Cobb to wife, December, 1866, in Ulrich B. Phillips, ed., *The Correspondence of Robert Toombs, Alexander H. Stephens, and Howell Cobb* (Washington, 1913), 684; Kenneth Raynor to Thomas Ruffin, July 5, 1869, in Hamilton, ed., *The Papers of Thomas Ruffin*, 4:222; Parrish to Henry Watson, Jr., July 30, 1865, Watson Papers; Ella Gertrude Clanton Thomas Diary, June, 1865, October 9, 14, 1865; Spencer, *The Last Ninety Days of the War in North Carolina* (New York, 1866), 186; Cornelia P. Spencer Diary, July 4, 1865, Southern Historical Collection, University of North Carolina at Chapel Hill; Mrs. Laura E. Buttolph to Mrs. Mary Jones, June 30, 1865, in Myers, ed., *Children of Pride*, 1279. See also Ella Gertrude Clanton Thomas Diary, May 29, 1865; Samuel A. Agnew Diary, July 24, 31, November 27, December 7, 1865; John Paris, ''The Moral and Religious Status of the African Race in the Southern States,'' unpublished manuscript [1877?], John Paris Papers, Southern Historical Collection, University of North Carolina at Chapel Hill.

21. Novak, *The Wheel of Servitude: Black Forced Labor after Slavery* (Lexington, 1978), 41; editorial, ''The U.S. Emancipation Movement,'' Charlotte *Church Intelligencer*, 5 (March 16, 1865): 96; Eliza B. Tillinghast to David Ray Tillinghast, June 3, 1865, Tillinghast Family Papers; Josiah Nott, *The Negro Race: Its Ethnology and History* (Mobile, 1866), 5; Agnew Diary, July 20, 1865.

22. Pete Daniel, *The Shadow of Slavery: Peonage in the South, 1901–1969* (New York, 1972), xi, 11, 13, 23, 29, 58, 96, 127, 138; Robert Higgs, *Competition and Coercion: Blacks in the American Economy, 1865–1914* (Cambridge, 1977), 37–61; Jay R. Mandle, *The Roots of Black Poverty: The Southern Plantation Economy after the Civil War* (Durham, 1978), 3–51; Daniel, ''The Metamorphosis of Slavery, 1865–1900,'' *Journal of American History*, 66 (June, 1979): 88–99; Litwack, *Been in the Storm So Long*, 387–449; Roger L. Ransom and Richard Sutch, *One Kind of Freedom: The Economic Consequences of Emancipation* (Cambridge, 1977), 22–39, 185–186; Donald Spivey, *Schooling for the New Slavery: Black Industrial Education, 1868–1915* (Westport, 1978), 6, 11; Novak, *The Wheel of Servitude*, 16, 28, 29, 41, 84, 90.

23. Devereux to Jonathan Worth, October 20, 1866, Legislative Papers, 1866–1867, North Carolina Division of Archives and History; Sparkman, ''Results of Emancipation,'' *Land We Love*, 4 (November, 1867): 21; Forshey testimony, March 28, 1866, in *Report of the Joint Committee on Reconstruction*, 39th Congress, 1st session, House of Representatives Report 30 (Washington, 1866), part 4, p. 131. See also G. A. N., ''Laborers Wanted,'' *Southern Cultivator*, 25 (March, 1867): 69.

24. See Theodore Brantner Wilson, *The Black Codes of the South* (University, AL, 1965), 43–44, 48, 53, 69, 72, 114, 116–117, 138–140, 142–144,

146–147, 152; Donald G. Nieman, *To Set the Law in Motion: The Freedmen's Bureau and the Legal Rights of Blacks, 1865–1868* (Millwood, NY, 1979), 72–77, 98; C. H. DuPont and A. J. Peeler, "Report of the General Assembly of the State of Florida," in *Senate Journal of the State of Florida* (Tallahassee, 1865), 56, 57, 54, 59, 60.

25. *General Laws of the Regular Session of the Eleventh Legislature of the State of Texas* (Austin, 1866), 77–79.

26. Rhett to Armistead Burt, October 14, 1865, Armistead Burt Papers, Duke University.

27. Ibid.

28. Hyman and Wiecek, *Equal Justice under Law: Constitutional Development, 1835–1875* (New York, 1982), 319, 320.

29. John Mecklin, "The Black Codes," *South Atlantic Quarterly*, 16 (July, 1917): 258. Representative Black Codes appear in *Letter of the Secretary of War, . . . Reports of the Assistant Commissioners of Freedmen, and a Synopsis of Laws respecting Persons of Color in the Late Slave States*, 39th Congress, 2nd session, Senate Executive Document 6, 2 vols. (Washington, 1867), 1:170–230 (cited hereafter as *Letter of the Secretary of War*); *Laws of Mississippi, 1865*, quoted in Walter Lynwood Fleming, ed., *Documentary History of Reconstruction*, 2 vols. (Cleveland, 1906–1907), 1:290; *Acts of the General Assembly of the State of South Carolina, Passed at the Sessions of 1864–1865* (Columbia, 1866), 303, 293–294.

30. William A. Graham, Jr., to William A. Graham, September 15, 1865, in Max R. Williams, ed., *The Papers of William Alexander Graham, Volume VI, 1864–1865* (Raleigh, 1976), 359; editorial, "Aroused at Last by the Insults of the Negro," *Southern Opinion*, August 15, 1868; Jordan, *Hugh Davis and His Alabama Plantation*, 163; "Matters in Virginia," New Orleans *Daily Picayune*, October 22, 1865; George D. Humphrey, "The Failure of the Mississippi Freedmen's Bureau in Black Labor Relations, 1865–1867," *Journal of Mississippi History*, 45 (February, 1983): 34; Nieman, *To Set the Law in Motion*, 38; Report of General Davis Tillson, November 1, 1866, in *Letter of the Secretary of War*, 1:50; Otken, *The Ills of the South or Related Causes Hostile to the General Prosperity of the Southern People* (New York, 1894), 7.

31. McFeely, *Yankee Stepfather*, passim; editorial, "Future Relations of Slaves and Slaveowners," New York *Times*, May 8, 1865; "Gen. Howard on Free Labor," *Freedmen's Journal*, 2 (January, 1866): 1; "Free Labor," *Southern Cultivator*, 24 (April, 1866): 87; John Robert Kirkland, "Federal Troops in the South Atlantic States during Reconstruction: 1865–1877" (Ph.D. Diss., University of North Carolina at Chapel Hill, 1968), 331–346; Nieman, *To Set the Law in Motion*, 55–65, 222; John Jones to Mrs. Mary Jones, August 21, 1865, in Myers, ed., *Children of Pride*, 1292; Laura M. Towne to Rosabel Towne, February 23, 1866, Penn School Papers, Southern Historical Collection,

University of North Carolina at Chapel Hill; "Circular to the Freedmen of North Carolina," October 1, 1865, in Williams, ed., *The Papers of William Alexander Graham*, 376, 377–378; Charles L. Price, "John C. Barnett, Freedmen's Bureau Agent in North Carolina," *East Carolina University Publications in History*, 5 (1981): 51–74; Henry Watson, Jr., to Julia, December 16, 1865, Watson Papers.

32. Parrish to unidentified correspondent, May 28, 1867, Watson Papers; W. F. Leak to Thomas Ruffin, March 17, 1868, in Hamilton, ed., *The Papers of Thomas Ruffin*, 4:194.

33. Brandon to the voters of Wilkinson County, August 6, 1865, in "Report of Carl Schurz on the States of South Carolina, Georgia, Alabama, Mississippi, and Louisiana," in *Message of the President of the United States*, 39th Congress, 1st session, Senate Executive Document 2, (Washington, 1865), 101; testimony of Jaquelin M. Wood, February 9, 1866, *Report of the Joint Committee on Reconstruction*, 39th Congress, 1st session, House of Representatives Report 30 (Washington, 1866), part 2, p. 86; Marcel in *Nation*, 1 (July, 1865): 106.

34. Graham to David L. Swain, May 11, 1865, in Williams, ed., *The Papers of William Alexander Graham*, 311; MacRae to Julia MacRae, September 4, 1865, MacRae Papers; E. B. Teague, "Relations of the Races," *Scott's Monthly Magazine*, 7 (April, 1869): 255.

# 2

## Reconstruction and the Fashioning of the New Proslavery Argument

The old proslavery argument found a new home in the reconstructed South. While few postbellum writers publicly endorsed reenslavement, during Reconstruction many nevertheless revived the essential ingredients of the old proslavery argument. Harkening back to antebellum days, proslavery theorists relied on one old standby after another to defend southern slavery. Slavery's new apologists, for example, repeatedly denied charges that masters wantonly sold their blacks. Slave sales, they argued, resulted either from some serious fault in the bondsman or from the master's benign wish to reunite a slave family. Another weapon in the proslavery arsenal was the loyalty of the slaves themselves during the Civil War. If they had been mistreated, reasoned Cornelia P. Spencer of North Carolina, the slaves certainly would have rebelled or, at the very least, fled at the first opportunity. But they remained loyal servants almost until the end. And if slavery so debased the blacks, asked the editor of the Raleigh *Standard*, how "in nine months time, [did] those formerly down-trodden, ruined barbarians, by some *hocus pocus*" become the social and political equals of the whites? The Reverend A. Toomer Porter, rector of Charleston's Church of the Holy Communion, put the question another way: If slavery was so thoroughly cruel and destructive, he asked in 1882, how, then, did the North judge the blacks worthy of citizenship so soon after their alleged brutalization?[1]

At the core of the new defenses of slavery lay the humane, uplifting treatment allegedly accorded the bondsmen. In 1867 Louisiana's Shreveport *Southwestern* defended slavery as "but the transition state through which all peoples pass from barbarism to a progressive civilization." Two decades later, in *The Negro: As He Was; As He Is; As He Will Be*, proslavery ideologue H. S. Fulkerson lauded slavery as an "unquestioned good, physically and morally." Apologists for slavery pointed to the institution's broad educational benefits for the ignorant Africans. Every slave owner, they said, became in an important sense a teacher, a missionary, a ward. Slavery, averred a contributor to the *Southern Review*, served as a vital "preparatory school." Enrolled in the peculiar institution, the black race "attained the highest point of civilization, intelligence, and moral elevation ever reached by it in all its known history." A contributor to the *Land We Love* praised the dynamic quality in slavery that left the bondsmen uniformly "happy, thriving, contented." In exchange for their masters' patriarchal care and protection, the slaves "cheerfully rendered a faithful service, obedience and affection." They "spent their days in healthful easy employment, their powers never overtasked, their nights under good shelters in healthful sleep, with plentiful supplys of food, with no thought of the past, no care for the morrow." According to this author, slavery was a system of "mild and beneficent restraint, which . . . admitted full and free enjoyment, permitted no excesses full of remorse and bitter consequences."[2]

Another of slavery's defenders challenged Senator Charles Sumner's accusation that masters abused the blacks, both physically and psychologically. Citing census data, he insisted that rates of suicide, insanity, blindness, and physical deformity among slaves paled when compared with the rate of these problems in the North. "The fact is the negro was the best-fed, the best clothed, the best cared-for and least-worked laborer on the globe." This line of thought, invoking a comparative perspective, remained popular with white southerners well into the twentieth century. Writing to her brother living in New York in June, 1865, a North Carolinian praised slavery as "the most humane system of labor in the world." In her opinion the bondsmen actually worked fewer hours, on the average, than did European immigrants in the North. The editor of *DeBow's Review* shared this opinion. In 1867 he remained convinced that the slaves fared better than had other peasant classes worldwide. Slavery merged the best interests of labor and capital, making it attractive to blacks and whites alike. Writers identified certain benefits in slavery—care for the elderly, guaranteed work year-round—that were absent from the free labor system. Fulkerson underscored that in most cases the slaves received better treatment than did free laborers in the Gilded Age. Slaves never starved, he said, and they worried little about "lock-outs" by hostile capitalists.[3]

Much as during the antebellum period, after Appomattox white southerners again employed the Bible to buttress their argument that blacks fared better as slaves than as freedmen. As historian Charles R. Wilson has argued, southern preachers continued after Appomattox to praise slavery for teaching blacks lifelong lessons in morality, hard work, and religion. They pointed to the old ex-slaves as examples of "good" blacks and looked with fright at the devilish young blacks reared without slavery's restraints. Ministers employed the scriptures to support the point that emancipation was a backward step for blacks and whites alike. In his widely circulated pamphlet, *The Negro: What Is His Ethnological Status?* "Ariel" (Nashville publisher and clergyman Buckner H. Payne) maintained that God disapproved of any attempt to equalize the races. "Ariel" based his theory on the supposition "That the negro being created before Adam, consequently . . . is a beast in God's nomenclature." The author argued that calamities in the Bible were God's punishments for miscegenation between white descendants of Adam and Eve and blacks. Without souls and without immortality, reasoned "Ariel," blacks could not worship God. And because blacks were beasts, not men, God frowned on attempts to make them equal. To "elevate a *beast* to the level of a son of God," charged "Ariel," was tantamount to insulting the Creator. As a result, "The states or people that favor this equality and amalgamation of the white and black races, God will *exterminate*." Up to this time slaveholders had been chosen by God to prevent just this calamity. But with slavery's destruction, only two alternatives remained for the black man, concluded "Ariel": "You *must send him back to Africa or re-enslave him*."[4]

Some racial thinkers doubted that the freedmen possessed even the first option set forth by "Ariel." Writing in 1868, for instance, "A Minister" (D. G. Phillips of Louisville, Georgia) argued that because God had created blacks before the rest of mankind, and because the serpent who deceived Eve had been a Negro, blacks were doomed "to perpetual menial crouching slavery." Forever incapable of being the equals of whites, blacks would remain enslaved. Drawing upon the Bible, "facts," and "history," "A Minister" asserted that all attempts at emancipation were futile. "Reader," he exhorted, "whether you be a pro or anti-slavery man," you must grasp the naked truth: blacks must wallow in abject slavery or suffer extermination. While the black legally was no longer a chattel, the abolitionists had won but a temporary victory. According to the theologian, "to take him [the black] out of his condition of slave and force him into an unsought condition of manhood is to fight against God, and the consequences must be direful in the end."[5]

Reflecting on the origins of his argument, "A Minister" explained in 1868 that "My theory was not hatched by me. The 'ovum' was the property of Dr. [Samuel A.] Cartwright—the moulding alone mine. The theory is true—it will prevail."[6] By mentioning Cartwright, "A Minister" linked his biblical defense of slavery to the ideas of one of the Old South's foremost scientific apologists for the peculiar institution. For years Cartwright, a Louisiana physician, had identified indigenous black diseases and immutable ethnological characteristics among the slaves. Blacks succumbed to "drapetomia" (running away) and "rascality" when mismanaged, said Dr. Cartwright. He referred to the Bible and to his years of medical practice among blacks to support his rationale for keeping blacks enslaved. Drawing heavily on the racist anthropology and pseudoscience of their day, Cartwright and the like-minded Dr. Josiah C. Nott declared that blacks were so radically inferior to whites that their destiny included only two alternatives: perpetual servitude to whites or extermination. The blend of biblical and scientific arguments for black inferiority lay at the core of many postbellum defenses of slavery. Few northern or southern whites in 1865, or for that matter, in 1918, questioned the inherent racial differences between the Negro and the Caucasian. In their minds, developments in anthropometrics and biology confirmed, not challenged, racial stereotypes in America that dated back to the seventeenth century. Whites viewed blacks as a weak, backward people, untouched by what they vaguely termed Anglo-Saxon traditions of work and self-government. Most white Americans remained convinced that the black man possessed unique racial qualities that suited him to slavery. They prophesied that emancipation would destroy him and mire the nation in racial conflict. Enslavement had been the black's brightest hour.[7]

## II

The impact of such fears was not lost on conservative northern Democrats, who unleashed bitter proslavery diatribes during Reconstruction.

The Copperheads joined the humanitarian, religious, and pseudoscientific defenders of slavery to further their own political ends. They played upon racial ambivalence among white northerners, predicting that emancipation would breed "mongrelization" or race war. In July, 1865, for example, the racist Chicago *Times* railed against emancipation. "The whole country," complained the editor, "priests; newspapers; politicians, white, black, yellow; Fourth of July; Hail Columbia, and everything else—are 'going it' exclusively on account of the negro." As a result, all white Americans were becoming enslaved: "Our negro masters crack their whips over our legislators and our priests, and thus control our laws and our religion They have established a tyranny over us worse than that of the Pisistratids. . . . The more we do for our sable masters, the more exacting are they in their demands." According to the editor, whites needed to rise up against "abolitionists, niggers and miscengenationists." Writing in 1868, the editor of New York's ultra-conservative *Old Guard* openly commended slavery. The black, he wrote, "can only exist in one or the other condition—in his African savagery or under the care and guidance of his white master, and even an Abolition lunatic would call the latter preferable." Slavery, explained another Copperhead, was the blacks' "normal condition, for [as slaves] they multiplied quite as fast as the white people." The bondsmen, "guided and cared for by their masters, were probably the healthiest and happiest four millions of human creatures that ever lived upon the earth."[8]

The Copperheads depended heavily on religion and science to uphold their defenses of the peculiar institution. God's design, explained Dr. J. R. Hayes of the District of Columbia, was for the blacks to remain forever subordinate to the whites. Divine will positioned the blacks at the lowest rung on the human family ladder. "The negro's imperfect anatomical construction," wrote Hayes, "fixes him . . . next in gradative series in mammals created just below him." Hayes not only found blacks deficient in "psychical or mental development," but he criticized their inferior odor, hair, "unctuous skin, . . . prognathous skull, receding forehead, protruding jaw, thick lips, flat nose, expanded nostrils, crooked legs and flat feet." If God had intended the blacks to be free, he asked, "would millions of them have permitted another race to hold them in slavery . . . and when freed, freed only as an incident of war?"[9]

Far from viewing slavery as a sin, northern racists praised it as one of "the fundamental laws of organic life." By enslaving blacks, whites not only obeyed "natural law and industrial necessity . . . irrevocable

as a law of gravitation." Blacks, northern conservatives wrote again
and again, were as different from and inferior to whites as the different
subgroups of animals within a species. According to one author, the
laws of nature proved that "Wherever the negro occupies the relation
of servitude to the white man, all is happiness and prosperity. Where
he does not, all is social chaos and blight." Another remarked that the
black man possessed unique racial qualities that kept him depraved and
suited to slavery.

The negro race has no history, no learning, no literature, no laws. For six
thousand years he has been a *savage*. . . . He has never invented anything, or
advanced a single step in civilization when left to himself. He is sunk in the
grossest superstitions, and is guilty of the most revolting practices. The only
ones that have ever shown any advancement are those who have been brought
to this country and placed under the control of Christian masters.

In the midst of the passage of the Black Codes, a Copperhead looked
back with affection to the old slave codes. He described them not only
as essential for regulating the barbarous blacks, but "far more humane
than that of the law revealed by Moses." Writing in 1866, the editor
of Wisconsin's LaCrosse *Democrat* maintained that thanks to emancipation, the black man "is worse off to-day under the drippings of this
New England mercy than under the care of his former master." And
conservative northerners, like their fellow racists in Dixie, also predicted
that emancipation in the South would breed just as catastrophic results
as it had in Haiti and Jamaica. Emancipation, they agreed, was a cruel,
unconstitutional trick by "the Mongrel Party." It let loose "the natural
instincts of the negro," wrote a northerner in 1869, "and he has already
commenced his march backward towards his own native barbarism."[10]
    Copperheads concluded that slavery, not freedom, was the natural
condition for the black man. In their opinion, abolition was not only
impracticable but impossible.[11] This theme merged the biblical theory
of writers such as "Ariel" with the ethnological thrust of the North's
most outspoken proslavery ideologue, Dr. John H. Van Evrie of New
York. According to historian George Fredrickson, Van Evrie was in no
sense a scientist, but rather a blatant antiblack propagandist, "perhaps
the first professional racist in American history."[12] The very term *slavery* had meaning only for whites of Euro-American heritage, not Africans, said Dr. Van Evrie. Reversing the entire notion of slavery and

freedom, Van Evrie and other Negrophobes purported that blacks experienced freedom only while enslaved. The first of six *Anti-Abolition Tracts* published by Van Evrie, Horton and Company in 1866 argued that *"When they* [blacks] *live the life that they are designed for, they are free; when they do not, they are slaves."* Black slavery was described simply as the set of laws established by God for what He deemed an inferior, servile race. Consequently, the "so-called slavery" or "imaginary slavery" of the South was not slavery at all. In reference to the black man, "slavery" was "a stupid misnomer." Slavery was the implementation of God's will that Caucasians "shall govern them [blacks] by *specific* rules and regulations, suited to their nature."[13]

To such writers, reenslavement, or some other form of racial control, seemed the only solution to the race question. Blacks would perish, explained another Copperhead in 1869, "unless some lucky turn of the tide of fortune places them back again under the direction and control of their old masters, and only true friends." Adopting the proslavery idea so prevalent in the South, a northern observer in 1877 judged the conditions—housing, clothing, food, health—under slavery as preferable to those enjoyed by the freedman. According to George R. Stetson, as a slave "the Negro was a better member of society than he is today . . . or perhaps, ever will be." Northern conservatives reported that emancipation had worsened race relations and ushered in social chaos. They predicted that abolition would result in either total racial amalgamation or race war.[14]

## III

The Mason-Dixon line provided no dividing line for such sentiment. In the South, ideas of the blacks' natural qualifications for slavery appeared regularly during Reconstruction. The black man was uniquely equipped for perpetual bondage by nature, wrote South Carolina's G. Manigault in 1868. "Of all races," he explained, the black "alone accepts servitude as a decree of nature." His "natural docility . . . a certain sluggishness of body and mind, a sense of inferiority" made him a perfect slave—"the most easily governed and most incapable of ruling of all people." Another writer argued that "Nature" demanded that blacks and whites live together only in the relation of slaves and masters. But with that relation no longer a reality, a new alternative—"some form of subordination of the inferior race"—had to be fashioned.

Blacks, explained Georgian J. R. Ralls in 1877, would only prosper in some slavelike status.

A servile disposition . . . seems to be an inherent and firmly fixed trait in the negro character. He cannot . . . enjoy anything like rational liberty. When not in a state of slavery, under the task-master, who subdues his will and controls his physical man, he is led by the stronger impulses of his nature in pursuit of something that will exercise dominion over him. It matters but little with him what may be the form or character of the servitude he renders, so long as he has something that will accept the homage that instinct . . . prompts him to bestow.

The new system of racial control would have to coerce the freedmen to work, all the while providing them the protection and maintenance of slavery.[15]

White southerners not only believed that blacks made natural slaves, but amassed evidence of black behavior and physical deterioration that convinced them the ex-bondsmen could not survive as freedmen. During Reconstruction and up to World War I, whites continually observed changes in blacks that persuaded them that emancipation unsuited the freedmen. Repeatedly they defended the peculiar institution by citing the alleged retrogression of emancipated blacks toward savagery. They delighted in citing the history of Liberia and emancipation in the Caribbean as examples of the deterioration of blacks freed from white control. Left to themselves, the blacks reportedly refused to work, succumbed to gross immorality and, in the case of Haiti, massacred first the whites and then the mulattoes.[16] Writing in 1866, for example, Dr. Josiah C. Nott, still espousing scientific apologies for slavery, informed General O. O. Howard of the Freedmen's Bureau that the nightmarish history of emancipation in Haiti and Jamaica portended an equally dismal future for the South's freedmen. As a subordinate the black reached his full potential. But as a freeman, absent from white guidance, he lapsed into barbarism. "History," Nott argued, "proves . . . that a superior and inferior race cannot live together practically on any other terms than that of master and slave, and that the inferior race . . . must be expelled or exterminated." The Alabama physician and ex-slaveholder added that whenever the black "is removed from the controlling influence of the superior race, and is left to his own interests, he soon sinks into savagism."[17]

Whites interpreted the deficiencies of free blacks as a function of their overall deterioration. Georgia physician W. T. Grant praised slavery because it alone guarded the black "against a relapse into his original condition of black ignorance and unmitigated barbarism." The black was "truly bettered in being enslaved," argued Grant, because contact with whites tempered his "native ferocity and grossness." But alas, without the guardianship of slavery, blacks reportedly were on the road to destruction as a race; in the opinion of editor H. Rives Pollard, they would move "backward into the barbarism of the Bushman, and the fiendishness that belongs to tribes that hide in the African jungles." According to these writers, emancipation signaled not only the end of progress for blacks, but their physical demise as well.[18]

Even before Appomattox, reports began to circulate throughout the South of widespread suffering, disease, and death among the freed blacks, especially those congregating in the cities. Emancipation, whites concluded, must mean the eventual elimination of the race. Early in 1865, for example, Mary Jones, wife of the Reverend Charles Colcock Jones of Georgia, predicted that freeing the slaves would result in "their extermination. All history . . . proves them incapable of self-government; they perish when brought in conflict with the intellectual superiority of the Caucasian race." Later in the year, during the blacks' first summer of freedom, rumors spread that they were indeed dying en masse.[19] Throughout these years whites compiled medical information that, to them, proved that blacks fared better as bondsmen than as freedmen. Since the blacks' emancipation, their infant mortality rate reportedly had skyrocketed, and the adults supposedly were dying off as well. Many authors concluded that freedom was anything but a boon for the black man. It represented, in fact, the black's one-way ticket to racial extinction. Without the guardianship offered by slavery, blacks soon would follow the path of the American Indian. For years after emancipation, laymen and physicians alike agreed that blacks suffered diseases as freedmen that were unknown to their race as slaves. Insanity, venereal disease, feticide, drunkenness, and other maladies threatened, they said, the very future of the freedman.[20]

Such statements confirmed Dr. Nott's 1866 pessimistic prognosis that, removed from the medical care of their former masters, most blacks would succumb to illness and die. For years he had linked the physical well-being of blacks to slavery. Incorporating Lamarckian and Darwinian theories of racial evolution, Nott remained convinced that free blacks first would stagnate, then retrograde, and finally die off. Blacks would remain "what God made them," Nott lectured General Howard, "and your [Freedmen's] Bureau can no more unmake, or thwart the laws of nature than it can pluck the sun from the heavens." Endorsing Nott's predictions, the editor of Charlotte's *Church Intelligencer* branded the emancipation edict the "death-warrant of the negro race." The numerous ailments thought endemic to free blacks convinced a contributor to the Richmond *Examiner* "that the negro is not equal to the burdens of freedom." That blacks could not withstand the physical demands of emancipation, he said, "shows that the negroes are not of that 'perdurable stuff' of which freedmen should be made." Removed from the care of the whites, blacks were expiring quickly. "As children need parents," gibed the correspondent, "so do negroes need masters."[21] The freedman's supposed declining birth rate, coupled with his alleged increasing death rate, led another writer to conclude "that the negro thrives in servitude and dies out in freedom." As a freedman he would "dwindle and die out," falling hopelessly by the wayside in the struggle for existence.[22]

Whites claimed to have found abundant evidence that blacks retrogressed without slavery's stewardship. They noted repeatedly the freedmen's degraded physical state and their frightful day-to-day living conditions and behavior. Denied white support, blacks reportedly suffered from inadequate food, clothing, shelter, and medical care. Late in 1865, for example, Alabama planter Henry Watson, Jr., recounted the tragedy of ex-slave Anthony, his sick wife, and seven children. The freed family was tottering on the brink of starvation. Because Anthony was now a freedman, explained Watson, he was "bound to clothe, feed, support, lodge, warm and pay medical bills for his wife and children. His wages are not worth to me the support of his family now that I shall not be remunerated hereafter by the labor of his children. . . . He talks very seriously about his condition, says he is worse than ever before . . . that all the black people are worse off than when slaves." "What was the negro before the war?" asked ex-Governor Zebulon B. Vance of North Carolina in 1869. "A simple, happy, and affectionate bondsman. What is he now? Fast merging into a ragged, starving, dangerous vagabond."[23]

Southern whites blamed emancipation for unleashing negative qualities in blacks that reportedly had been controlled by enslavement. No longer held in check by the slaveholder's precept and example, free blacks reveled in sin, neglected their households, and mistreated their children. Black families, complained the editor of the *Southern Cultivator*, were disintegrating without the guardianship previously offered by the slave masters. Commenting on the state of affairs in Alabama late in 1866, William F. Samford remarked that " 'Civilization' is 'marching two steps backwards' like the truant boy went to school, 'to one forward' in our 'Africa' down here. The negroes here spend their time in going to 'funerals,' religious howlings, promiscuous sexual intercourse, thieving and 'conjuring.' " From Thomasville, Georgia, a clergyman complained, "My observation convinces me that freedom has had a decidedly injurious influence upon the moral character of the blacks." On the one hand, the freedmen "are ever envious of the superiority of the whites and clamorous for equality while using every means to appropriate their property." For their part, the whites "are inspired with contempt for the blacks and constantly irritated and provoked by their bad conduct."[24] Whites agreed that black religion became more emotional, more savage without the restraints and direction imposed by slavery and the master class. The freedmen consumed liquor at a rate unknown during slavery. And not only were blacks more licentious and sensual than before, but now they were even prone to rape white women. So said the white South.[25]

During the postwar generations whites remained convinced that the entire community of free blacks had succumbed to crime. Writing in Guilford County, North Carolina, the Reverend John Paris praised slavery's gentle control mechanisms. Slavery "watched over, and guarded against misconduct" by the blacks, Paris said. Since emancipation, however, crime had increased twenty times. An 1868 contributor to the *Land We Love* calculated an even higher increase of black misbehavior. As freedmen the blacks "commit more crimes every week than the aggregate crimes among them during the two hundred years of slavery."[26] Theft ranked foremost in the whites' catalogue of black wrongdoing.[27] Alabama planter John Horry Dent blasted emancipation for inciting blacks to steal from their employers. In his opinion, their wages only whetted the Negroes' "taste for money . . . and their want for money keeps ahead of their earnings, hence they resort to stealing to procure money." Writing in the 1870s, South Carolina merchant/planter Charles Manigault attributed the high frequency of black theft to Yankee education. "They took *special care*," noted Manigault, "while *corrupting* the *Negroes* to teach them *how to* steal at which the Negroes

soon became *great adepts.*'' Theft, however, represented the mere tip
of the iceberg to southern whites. While it could perhaps shrug off the
loss of a few chickens as the product of ''Negro character,'' the ruling
class could never quite cope with what it termed the severe upheaval
of racial etiquette and black behavior.[28]

Whites blamed emancipation for driving a wedge between the ex-
masters and their former slaves. They longed for the paternalism and
the give-and-take that reportedly had existed between patriarchal masters
and devoted servants during slavery days. They expressed their longing
for the mutual love and respect that marked race relations under the old
regime. John B. Baldwin, Speaker of the Virginia House of Delegates,
expressed this point most clearly in 1866:

I do not like the negro as well free as I did as a slave, for the reason that there
is now between us an antagonism of interest to some extent, while, before his
interest and mine were identical. Then, I was always thinking of how I could
fix him comfortably. Now I find myself driving a hard bargain with him for
wages; and I find that sort of feeling suggested directly by motives of interest
coming in between the employer and the employed.

Slavery, wrote Charles Manigault, developed ''mutual family interests
& kind personal feelings'' between blacks and whites. The latter sorely
missed the role of teacher, guardian, and friend. The blacks ''are *free
now*,'' moaned Manigault, ''their heads & hearts are turned against *us*
their former protectors & friends. They have now become lazy, improvident, & won't work efficiently.''[29]

While some whites no doubt missed reciprocal relationships with
slaves, most chafed under the loss of social and economic control over
what they deemed a barbaric, backward race in their midst. Without
the discipline provided by slavery, they envisioned chaos and disorder.
Many considered this the bitterest fruit of abolition.[30] They pointed to
the behavior of the freedmen as evidence not only of slavery's right-
eousness, but its absolute necessity for maintaining order in a biracial
society. Whites insisted that emancipation unleashed negative qualities
in blacks that had been kept under wraps by enslavement. The blacks,
wrote H. Rives Pollard of the Richmond *Southern Opinion*, ''tempo-
rarily crazed and blinded by their sudden transition from slavery to
liberty,'' had begun a reign of riot, ruin, anarchy, and death. Whites
identified every manner of disrespectful black deportment—by omission

and commission—all through the South. Violating prior racial etiquette, the blacks were labeled as surly, insolent, annoying, impertinent, impudent, indifferent, ungrateful, and, according to an author in the *Land We Love*, "puffed up." Whereas slavery had transformed Africans into a respectable and productive peasant class, free status allegedly converted them into a race of dirty, ignorant, brutal savages. A troubled, unhappy people, the freedmen reportedly lied, cheated, and broke their marriage vows. Sexual promiscuity and infidelity spread rampant. Daniel Heyward, owner of a large rice plantation on the Savannah River, summed up the prevailing image of the slave among postemancipation white southerners. The freedmen, he concluded, had gone "bad," had lost the positive traits that slavery had provided them. The mass of free blacks unmistakably were "lapsing, rapidly back to their ancestral state of savage life in Africa."[31]

## IV

As if these personal characteristics were not direful enough, whites also uniformly condemned both the quality and quantity of free black labor. Because emancipation had been too sudden, they said, blacks were unprepared to make a smooth transition into a free labor system.[32] Whites also argued that the freedmen failed to grasp the full meaning of emancipation. The ex-bondsmen would have to work harder than ever before. In Halifax County, North Carolina, Catherine Edmondston described the freedmen as wandering about in a daze, having no conception of their need to earn a living. Emancipation, she wrote, "is a terrible cruelty to them, this unexpected, unsolicited gift of freedom. . . . Their old moorings . . . rudely & suddenly cut loose, . . . they drift without a rudder into the unknown sea of freedom. God help such philanthropy." In Talladega County, Alabama, a planter reported that confusion reigned among the ex-bondsmen: "they . . . do not understand the importance of plenty of food, believe it will come whenever the appetite calls for it." According to North Carolina lawyer David Schenck, blacks misunderstood the very basis of freedom. "Every fool negro," complained Schenck in June, 1865, "thinks freedom consists in leaving his master and being idle as long as possible." The worst part of it, however, was that "while they are going through this preliminary enjoyment and finding out the realities of their dependence the crops are suffering."[33]

Whites concluded that, without compulsion, the blacks would continue not to labor. Writing from Paris in December, 1867, former Confederate diplomat John Slidell regretted that "even under the most favorable circumstances, we cannot expect from" the freedmen "anything like restrained & continuous industry, when left to factors uncontrolled, their natural instincts." Slidell and others believed that their former bondsmen truly were lost without slavery, confusing free status with freedom from work.[34] Almost every white southerner who expressed an opinion on the subject reasoned that blacks simply were too childlike, too inexperienced to comprehend the obligations of freedom. How, for example, could an ex-slave be expected to understand labor contracts? Although the government altered the black's legal status, Charles C. Jones, Jr., explained, the former bondsman would remain forever "ignorant of the operation of any law other than the will of his master." Whites commonly charged that freedom left the black man indolent, slothful to a fault. One writer observed, "When free, laziness is his master." Improvident and wasteful, the free black reportedly was transformed by emancipation into a totally unreliable and unmanageable worker. The black's apparent stubbornness and apathy toward his work convinced most whites that the experiment of free black labor was destined to fail miserably. By the summer of 1865, numerous planters began recording their impressions of how poorly the freedmen worked. With few exceptions they predicted an utter debacle. Again and again whites compared free labor unfavorably with the old slave system. Dr. J. R. Sparkman complained that freedpeople worked far less efficiently in South Carolina's rice and grain fields than slaves. In 1860, he explained, the Georgetown District produced a surplus of approximately one million bushels of grain. In 1866 its yield came to 150,000 bushels less than was required for home consumption. Much land lay idle because the freedmen refused to labor at tasks more than six hours per day. And black women now refused to perform field labor at all. As Sparkman and other whites were painfully aware, whereas the cast of characters remained essentially the same, the postwar agricultural world differed in important ways from that of the Old South.[35]

Immediately after the war, white planters and farmers devised new labor arrangements more or less satisfactory to themselves and to the freedmen.[36] In many cases these were supervised by Freedmen's Bureau agents. The labor contracts varied widely throughout the South—from region to region, county to county, and even from farm to farm. And regardless of locale, these arrangements also changed over time, as blacks and whites dickered over terms. Soon after Appomattox, various forms of sharecropping, share wages, and tenantry systems sprang up like patchwork quilts all across the South. Much experimentation resulted as whites sought to reach prewar levels of agricultural productivity and as blacks endeavored to establish themselves as free men in practice as well as name. Three questions dominated the negotiations between white employers and their black employees. How much control would the ex-master hold over the ex-slave? Which, if any, of the factors of production would the blacks possess? And how would the blacks be compensated for their work? Whites watched closely as the blacks tested their freedom. The freedmen desperately sought land and, ultimately, denied "forty acres and a mule," fashioned their rights and responsibilities as best they could as hired laborers.

Throughout the postwar decades southern whites idealized the agricultural performance of the slaves and held nothing but contempt for the work of the freedmen.[37] Whites blamed the poor quality of free black laborers on the loss of control over the former bondsmen. In June, 1865, for example, Edmund Ruffin, Jr., complained that U.S. military forces in Virginia would not allow whites to whip the freedmen: "hence they [the freedmen] are utterly lazy and negligent." Unwilling to grant the blacks a chance to prove themselves worthy of freedom, Ruffin and others concluded all too quickly that the freedmen were worthless and untrustworthy. White yeomen must replace them as the South's work force, they said. "The negro will never work to any profit for himself or any one else except as a slave," wrote North Carolinian A. M. McPheeters in June, 1865. Most agreed that the blacks refused to obey orders, required constant supervision, worked inefficiently, and labored far below their former level as slaves.[38]

Specific complaints punctuate the correspondence and diaries of planters throughout the South. In southwest Tennessee, for example, businessman/farmer John H. Bills jotted down his daily dissatisfactions with freed laborers. He found them "lazy in the extreme," "idle & disipated [sic]," often "pretending to work & really doing nothing." They seemed to revel in their freedom—dancing and drinking in excess. Bills, who owned one hundred slaves in 1860, objected in principle to the ownership of blacks. But in practice, Bills remained convinced that slavery was "the best state" for the black. Emancipation transformed once industrious bondsmen into ineffectual and lethargic paupers—"a trifling set of lazy devils who will never make a living without Masters to make them work." Two and one-half years of freedom had proven them "wholly improvident and unsuited for their situation." According to Bills, "*freedom* is anything but a blessing to most of them." Like Bills, South Carolinian Robert I. Gage doubted the willingness of the freedman to labor. "The nigger wont work," wrote Gage in 1866, and "will be a free nigger as free niggers always have been." He advocated colonization as the only true solution to the "Negro problem."[39]

For Mississippian Everard Green Baker, emancipation posed a management problem. How, he asked, could one organize free blacks to work most effectively? The planter complained that the blacks refused to enter the fields early or to work on Saturday evenings. And they demanded long dinner breaks. Gone was the steady, docile, disciplined labor of the slave. James Mallory, a farmer from Talladega, Alabama, complained that his cotton production had fallen after slavery because the free black hands he employed were unfaithful laborers, having "but little pride or ambition" in their work. Late in 1865, North Carolinian Catherine Edmondston sized up the condition of the freedmen. Most waxed indifferent, she said, shunning work in favor of dissipation. True, there were exceptions to the rule. Former slaves Owen and Dolly alone remained "faithful, cheerful, industrious & grateful." Refusing wages, they sought "only to live & to be treated for the future as they have hitherto lived & been treated." Mrs. Edmondston contrasted the two contented ex-bondsmen with Henry, their former slave foreman, who, like most emancipated blacks, "became moody, disappointed & grasping." The Edmondstons fired him because he refused to act in a subservient manner. Catherine considered Henry an unfortunate victim of freedom—"poor fellow," she wrote, "made worthless by emancipation!"[40]

In Alabama, John Horry Dent agreed with Mrs. Edmondston: management of a plantation with free black labor was more trouble than it was worth. The ex-slaves were, in his opinion, ungrateful, dissatisfied, "surly and disrespectful." They labored sloppily and frequently abused farm animals and equipment. The blacks, fumed Dent, considered "their remaining" on his plantation "an obligation on their parts confered, which should allow them privileges." In the midst of Dent's February, 1866 planting the freedmen exhibited what he diagnosed as symptoms of insubordination. They left work at will, fought among themselves, carried firearms, and argued with the black driver he employed. Most important, Dent failed to convince the blacks to take a personal interest in the crop. Repeatedly, Dent complained, the freedmen broke their contracts.[41]

The former slaves balked at laboring in gangs, working under white supervision, and being told when and how to cultivate the crop. And they refused to perform nonfield, "slave work"—fixing fences, chopping wood, clearing ditches, tending swine. Dent objected to the blacks' after-hours socializing, especially their leaving his plantation to visit friends or relatives on neighboring farms. "It is now evident," remarked the planter in April, 1866, that "few of the negroes know how to appreciate their freedom." Most considered freedom "liberty to do as they please." Dent judged that because the blacks held little interest in his crop, it took fifteen freedmen to complete the same amount of work performed previously by ten slaves. Free black labor, then, was both too unreliable and too costly. It would remain so, predicted Dent, until the blacks "could be bound to service in such a way they could not break their contracts." Disgusted by free blacks and convinced "that large plantations & freed men . . . are incompatible," Dent late in 1866 sold his Alabama lands. He purchased a small farm in Georgia with hopes of employing white men only, thereby never again having to wrangle with free blacks.[42]

## V

Like Dent, many white southern farmers and planters would have preferred to cashier the freedmen as their region's agricultural work force. In their opinion, the ex-slaves overestimated freedom's privileges and undervalued its responsibilities. No longer able to impose their will on the black, whites came to view their former bondsmen as antagonists. When they could no longer make blacks extensions of themselves, ex-slaveholders sought to oust black people from their world. But whites desperately needed black agricultural laborers, and thus were forced by necessity as well as habit to live and labor among them and to employ them. Anxious to maintain control over the large black population in their midst, white southerners moved quickly to institute new legal means and modes of white supremacy and caste hegemony over their former bondsmen. The Black Codes, vagrancy laws, enticement statutes, apprenticeship arrangements, game and stock laws, lien laws, sharecropping, farm tenantry, peonage—these became the surrogates of chattel slavery. When all else failed, whites resorted to violence to keep the freedmen in a state of dependence.[43]

Over the next twenty-five years, white southerners wrote often—in private correspondence, periodicals, religious journals, books, and newspapers—about slavery and the horrors of emancipation. Throughout the postwar years they focused minutely on slavery. The topic provided them with an ideological legacy, a crucial metaphor for the racial control they frantically sought to impose on blacks. Not only did it enable them to order their world; it allowed them to cling desperately to vestiges of their lost civilization. In these years no subject, except that of their beloved Lost Cause, captured the attention of white southerners as did slavery.[44] Again and again writers went on record contrasting the evils of emancipation with the beneficences of slavery. Proslavery ideologues relentlessly defended the institution from ongoing neoabolitionist attacks, arguing that in spite of emancipation, blacks still required white control. So heavily did white southerners dwell on the subject that in 1865 North Carolina journalist Joseph S. Cannon implored them to wipe it from their consciousness. The South, Cannon informed readers of the Raleigh *Standard*, must look forward, not backward, on the race question. He reminded southerners of what they already knew but wanted to forget: "Slavery . . . is dead forever. Not a few refuse to realize it. They think it may be resuscitated, or that necessity will at least compel the negro to a kind of serfdom or peonage, that will be a very good substitute for actual slavery. Their desire fathers the expectation." Such hopes, warned the editor, were now mere pipe dreams. The slavery question was settled. Preoccupation with renewing it would only lead to more trouble. "Slavery in name and fact, substance and shadow, principal and substitute, is destroyed, exterminated, annihilated, rubbed out, washed out, and positively, unconditionally, eternally gone." All, white and black, must accept abolition and get to work. Whites no longer could expect to be waited upon, explained Cannon. "Just throw away all the slave furniture . . . pull down the bells and wait on yourselves."[45]

But few whites listened to such appeals. During and after Reconstruction, slavery as a subject of inquiry and as an idea continued to play a vital role in American racial thought. Though no longer a legal entity, slavery and forms of neoslavery nevertheless helped determine the politics of Reconstruction. Southern white intransigence on slavery spirited the Radical Republicans forward in fashioning the constitutional amendments and civil rights legislation of these years. Much can be learned by examining the ways in which whites and blacks perceived slavery *after* the institution's demise. As sectional tensions gradually lessened, whites in all parts of the country welcomed the myth of slavery as a benign institution. The comical portrait of the happy slave became standard fare in late nineteenth-century literature, folklore, theater, and caricature. Although proslavery and antislavery forces continued to battle over the old questions throughout and following Reconstruction, the American public generally accepted a new consensus on slavery. Proslavery thought ultimately carried the day. Ironically, by the end of Reconstruction, white southerners had garnered in peace what had eluded them in war: the triumph of the old proslavery argument. The patriarchal, proslavery image of the slave popularized by novelist John Esten Cooke in 1876 appealed to whites in the North as well as in the South. Celebrating slavery in colonial Virginia, Cooke wrote that not only was the Virginia slave "well fed, and rarely overtaxed," but his master generally provided him with a garden patch to grow his own crops. The bondsman, wrote Cooke, "was a merry, jovial musical being," who, "when his day's work was over, played his banjo in front of his cabin, and laughed and jested and danced by the light of the moon." House servants, he said, "were looked upon very much as members of the family, whose joys and sorrows were their own too." According to Cooke, the blacks "were slaves in nothing but the word."[46]

Influenced by white racism—itself a key force of sectional reconciliation—few late nineteenth-century Americans assessed blame for slavery. Most described slavery as a mild, patriarchal institution, more a school than a system of coerced labor. "We make no apology whatsoever for slavery," argued the Reverend John Paris in 1877. The North Carolinian followed this remark with twenty-five handwritten pages eulogizing slavery's virtues and damning the horrors of emancipation. Responsibility for the peculiar institution was now placed on northerners as well as southerners. "It was not the crime of the South," argued the Reverend C. K. Marshall of Mississippi in 1880, "it was the crime of America; it was the fearful crime of England. It was the terrible and inexcusable transgression of the Achan of a sinister, impious and God-defying civilization."[47]

In 1876 the New Orleans *Daily Picayune* informed white southerners that they could keep their heads high on all sectional matters, including the slavery question. Yes, "The New South" had abandoned slavery and was loyal to the Union, exclaimed the editor. But, he added, "We forget nothing. We apologize for nothing. We simply take things as we find them, and make the best of them." Five years later the Atlanta *Constitution* summarized the various strains of proslavery thought that echoed in the post-Reconstruction American mind.

In its humane aspect and in the results that have followed, the system of slavery as it existed in the south never had and can never have its parallel in the history of the world. So far as the negro is concerned, it was the only field in which the seed of civilization could be sown. It was as necessary to his moral, mental and physical disenthralment as the primary school is to the child. It was the prerequisite of freedom and citizenship.

The institution of slavery had existed for almost two hundred and fifty years, and after the war white southerners found it virtually impossible to view blacks as anything but slaves. It required a major transformation of thought to alter this assumption. Few made the adjustment smoothly or comfortably. Most never made it at all.[48]

## NOTES

1. Ella Gertrude Clanton Thomas Diary, May, 1865, p. 20, Duke University; Spencer to Eliza, March 10, 1866, Letter Book vol. 1, Cornelia Spencer Papers, North Carolina Division of Archives and History; "A Plea for the Negro," Raleigh *Daily Standard*, January 23, 1866; Porter quoted in J. L. Tucker, *The Relations of the Church to the Colored Race* (Jackson, MS, 1882), 48.

2. Shreveport *Southwestern* quoted in *Southern Cultivator*, 25 (February, 1867): 41; Fulkerson, *The Negro: As He Was; As He Is; As He Will Be* (Vicksburg, 1887), 17; anon., "The African in the United States," *Southern Review*, 14 (January, 1874): 130, 156; anon., "Roanoke Valley," *Land We Love*, 2 (January, 1867): 181–182.

3. Anon., "Mistaken Sympathy, or Mistaken Figures," *Land We Love*, 1 (September, 1866): 351–355, 356; Eliza B. Tillinghast to David Ray Tillinghast, June 6, 1865, Tillinghast Family Papers, Duke University; "Memories of the War," *DeBow's Review*, a.w.s., 3 (March, 1867): 226; Robert I. Gage to sister, January 31, 1868, James M. Gage Papers, Southern Historical Collection, University of North Carolina at Chapel Hill; Fulkerson, *The Negro*, 23.

4. Wilson, *Baptized in Blood: The Religion of the Lost Cause, 1865–1920* (Athens, 1980), 68–69, 102–104, 106–109; "Ariel," *The Negro: What Is His Ethnological Status?* (Cincinnati, 1867), 45, 48, 46, 48. An anonymous south-

erner, "Optician," attacked "Ariel," denying that the slaveholders viewed the blacks as beasts and treated them inhumanely. See *Speculum for Looking into the Pamphlet Entitled "The Negro"* (Charleston, 1867), 6, 20.

5. "A Minister," *Nachash: What Is It? or, An Answer to the Question, "Who and What Is the Negro?" Drawn from Revelation* (Augusta, 1868), 42, 43, 44.

6. D. G. Phillips to W. R. Hemphill, December 31, 1868, Hemphill Family Papers, Duke University.

7. See William Stanton, *The Leopard's Spots: Scientific Attitudes toward Race in America, 1815–1859* (Chicago, 1960), vii, 160; John S. Haller, *Outcasts from Evolution: Scientific Attitudes of Racial Inferiority, 1859–1900* (Urbana, 1971), passim; George M. Fredrickson, *The Black Image in the White Mind* (New York, 1971), 55, 57, 60, 87, 277; William Coleman, *Biology in the Nineteenth Century: Problems of Form, Function, and Transformation* (New York, 1971), 89, 91.

8. See Forrest G. Wood, *Black Scare: The Racist Response to Emancipation and Reconstruction* (Berkeley, 1970); editorial, "Negroes, Dog-Days, and White Slavery," Chicago *Times*, July 7, 1865; anon., " 'American Slaveholders': The Founders of American Liberty," *Old Guard*, 6 (November, 1868): 837; "The Problem of the Races," ibid., 5 (May, 1867): 382–383.

9. Hayes, *Negrophobia "On the Brain," in White Men* (Washington, 1869), 12, 14, 16, 17, 25, 31.

10. Anon, " 'Abolition of Slavery' Forever Impossible," *Old Guard*, 3 (April, 1865): 176; "The Negro in America," ibid., 4 (December 1866): 729; John H. Van Evrie, *White Supremacy and Negro Subordination* (New York, 1867) passim; *Abolition Is National Death* (New York, 1866), 8–12, 18; *The Six Species of Men* (New York, 1866), 6, 12, 15; Harlow S. Orton, *The History and Development of Races* (Madison, 1869), 18; *Free Negroism; or, Results of Emancipation* (New York, 1866), 27; "Slavery under the Mosaic, the Roman, and the American Code," *Old Guard*, 3 (July, 1865): 323; Marcus M. Pomeroy, *Soliloquies of the Bondholder* (New York, 1866), 22; *Reconstruction Speech of Hon. James Brooks, of New York in the House of Representatives* (Washington, 1867), 4, *A White Man's Government: Speech of Hon. Andrew J. Rogers of New Jersey Delivered in the House of Representatives* (Washington, 1868), 11; anon., "White Supremacy and Negro Subordination," *Old Guard*, 3 (May, 1865): 199; anon., "Religious Inequality of Human Races," *Old Guard*, 7 (February, 1869): 85.

11. " 'Abolition of Slavery' Forever Impossible," 176, 181; anon., "Mongrelism," *The Democratic Almanac for 1867* (n.p., n.d.), 50–52; anon., "The Basis of American Civilization," *Old Guard*, 5 (August, 1867): 625, 631; "The Problem of the Races," 382–383.

12. Fredrickson, *The Black Image in the White Mind*, 92.

13. Anon., *Abolition Is National Death*, 7, 8, 12; "The Negro in America," 732; anon., "Different Laws for Different Races," *Old Guard*, 5 (January, 1867): 66.

14. Anon., "Northern Delusions about Negroes," *Old Guard*, 7 (May 1869): 330; Stetson, *The Southern Negro As He Is* (Boston, 1877), 15, 16; G. F., "Moral and Intellectual Characteristics of Savage Races," *Old Guard*, 6 (May, 1868): 375; C. H. H., "The Condition of the South," ibid. (March, 1868): 224, 226; anon., "The Effects of the Abolition Policy, As Far As Developed," *Old Guard*, 6 (December, 1868): 925.

15. Manigault, "The Decay of Religion in the South," *Land We Love*, 5 (July, 1868): 209, 214, 213; anon., "Negro Agrarianism," *DeBow's Review*, a.w.s., 5 (February, 1868): 136; anon., "Blunders of the Confederate Government," ibid. (May, 1868): 475; editorial, "The Negro Knows No Law," *Southern Opinion*, March 14, 1868; C. M. Vaiden, "The Labor Question," *Southern Cultivator*, 28 (April, 1870): 109; J. C. Delavigne, "The Troubles in the South," *Southern Magazine*, 16 (May, 1875): 518; J. L. Tucker, *The Relations of the Church to the Colored Race*, 5, 12; Ralls, *The Negro Problem* (Atlanta, 1877), 21.

16. Robert Toombs to Alexander Stephens, December 12, 1865, in Ulrich B. Phillips, ed., *The Correspondence of Robert Toombs, Alexander H. Stephens, and Howell Cobb* (Washington, 1911), 675; Henry Flanders, *Observations on Reconstruction* (Philadelphia, 1866), 23–25; G. I. Crafts to William Porcher Miles, April 13, 1867, William Porcher Miles Papers, Southern Historical Collection, University of North Carolina at Chapel Hill; G. Manigault, "The Future of Young Africa," *Land We Love*, 5 (October, 1868): 523–529; "Beauties of Negro Civilization," *Southern Opinion*, February 1, 1868; Charles Manigault, "Respecting Slavery," unpublished manuscript [1873?], Manigault Family Papers, Southern Historical Collection, University of North Carolina at Chapel Hill.

17. Nott, *The Negro Race: Its Ethnology and History* (Mobile, 1866), 9, 22. See also Stanton, *The Leopard's Spots*, 80–81, 149, 158–159, 160.

18. Grant, "The Southern Negro," *Scott's Monthly Magazine*, 2 (November, 1866): 856, 857; Lon Taylor to S. F. Patterson, February 12, 1866, Lindsay Patterson Papers, Southern Historical Collection, University of North Carolina at Chapel Hill; anon, "The Negro Problem," *DeBow's Review*, a.w.s., 5, (March 1869): 250; editorial, "Shall We Have a Negro War?" *Southern Opinion*, September 26, 1868; Ella Gertrude Clanton Thomas Diary, July 30, 1870.

19. Journal entry, January 7, 1865, in Robert M. Myers, ed., *The Children of Pride* (New Haven, 1972), 1244; Eliza B. Tillinghast to David Ray Tillinghast, June 3, 1865, Tillinghast Family Papers; Marcel, "Feeling of the South Carolinians," *Nation*, 1 (August 24, 1865): 237–239; A. M. McPheeters to R. L. Patterson, June 10, 1865, R. L. Patterson Papers, North Carolina Division of Archives and History.

20. See, for example, anon., "The Labor Question," *Southern Cultivator*, 24 (April, 1866): 87; E. T. Winkler, "The Negroes in the Gulf States," *International Review*, 1 (September, 1874): 584; A. R. Kilpatrick, "Original Correspondence," *Richmond and Louisville Medical Journal*, 14 (November, 1872): 606–623; E. T. Easley, "The Sanitary Condition of the Negro," *American Medical Weekly*, 3 (July 31, 1875). 49–51; "Early Syphilis in the Negro," *Maryland Medical Journal*, 1 (August, 1877): 135–146; F. Tipton, "The Negro Problem from a Medical Standpoint," *New York Medical Journal*, 43 (May, 1886): 569–572; Eugene R. Corson, "The Future of the Colored Race in the United States from an Ethnic and Medical Standpoint," *New York Medical Times*, 15 (October, 1887): 193–200; Horace W. Conrad, "The Health of the Negroes in the South," *Sanitarian*, 18 (1887): 502–510; James McIntosh, "The Future of the Negro Race," *Transactions of the South Carolina Medical Association*, (1891): 183–188; Robert Reyburn, "Type of Disease among the Freed People (Mixed Negro Races) of the United States," *Medical News*, 63 (December 2, 1893): 623–627; J. F. Miller, "The Effects of Emancipation upon the Mental and Physical Health of the Negro of the South," *North Carolina Medical Journal*, 38 (November 20, 1896): 285–294; E. A. Yates, "Effect of Emancipation upon the Mental and Physical Health of the Negro," *North Carolina Christian Advocate*, 42 (January 6, 1897): 2; J. T. Walton, "The Comparative Mortality of the White and Colored Races in the South," *Charlotte Medical Journal*, 10 (1897): 291–294; John Herbert Claiborne, "The Negro," *Virginia Medical Semi Monthly*, 5 (April 13, 1900): 3–6; J. Allison Hodges, "The Effect of Freedom upon the Physical and Psychological Development of the Negro," *Richmond Journal of Practice*, 14 (June, 1900): 161–171.

21. Nott, *The Negro Race: Its Ethnology and History*, 12, 26, 19; "The Problem of the Negro Race," Charlotte *Church Intelligencer*, 6 (June 21, 1866): 90; anon., "Easily the Negro Dies," *Land We Love*, 1 (July, 1866): 233. For a similar statement, see John Y. Lind to R. R. Hemphill, November 27, 1869, Hemphill Family Papers.

22. Anon., "The Enterprise and Energy of the South," *Land We Love*, 2 (February, 1867): 280. On blacks' birth and death rates, see "Editorial," *Land We Love*, 2 (January, 1867): 225; H. H. Goodloe, "The Negro Problem," *Southern Magazine*, 14 (April, 1874). 375.

23. Henry Watson, Jr., to Julia, December 16, 1865, Henry Watson, Jr., Papers, Duke University; Vance, "All about It," *Land We Love*, 6 (March, 1869): 367.

24. R., "My Experience with the Freedmen," *Southern Cultivator*, 24 (July, 1866): 162; "Editor's Note," ibid.; George Petrie, ed., "William F. Samford, Statesman and Man of Letters," *Transactions of the Alabama Historical Society, 1899–1903*, 4 (1904): 479; Josephus Anderson to Howell Cobb, September 8, 1866, in Phillips, ed., *The Correspondence of Robert Toombs, Alexander H. Stephens, and Howell Cobb*, 682.

25. John Paris, "The Moral and Religious Status of the African Race in the Southern States," unpublished manuscript [1877?], John Paris Papers, Southern Historical Collection, University of North Carolina at Chapel Hill; I. A. Maxwell, "Will the Negro Relapse into Barbarism?" *DeBow's Review*, a.w.s., 3 (February, 1867): 182–183; Charles Nordhoff, *The Cotton States in the Spring and Summer of 1875* (New York, 1876), 105; "Editorial," *Land We Love*, 6 (February, 1869): 345.

26. Paris, "The Moral and Religious Status of the African Race in the Southern States"; anon., "The Haversack," *Land We Love*, 6 (November, 1868): 83.

27. See, for example, Nimrod Porter Diary and Notes, August 5, 16, 1865, Southern Historical Collection, University of North Carolina at Chapel Hill; A. M. Wallace to William A. Graham, September 18, 1865, in Max R. Williams, ed., *The Papers of Alexander Graham, Volume IV, 1864–1865* (Raleigh, 1976), 363; A. H. Spence to W. R. Hemphill, May 6, 1867, Hemphill Family Papers; J. C. Delavigne, "The Troubles in the South," *Southern Magazine*, 16 (May, 1875): 514; Daniel Heyward quoted in Charles Manigault, "Respecting Slavery."

28. John H. Dent Plantation Journal, February, 1866, vol. 6, p. 145, Troy State University, Troy, Alabama; Manigault, "Some Things Relating to Our Family Affairs but Not to Go in Our Will," unpublished manuscript [1873?], Manigault Family Papers.

29. John W. Norwood to Thomas Ruffin, May 8, 1865 in J. G. de Roulhac Hamilton, ed., *The Papers of Thomas Ruffin*, 4 vols. (Raleigh, 1920), 3:451; Eliza B. Tillinghast to David Ray Tillinghast, June 3, 1865, Tillinghast Family Papers; N. S. Dodge, "A Charleston Vendue in 1842," *Galaxy*, 7 (January, 1869): 119–123; Baldwin testimony, February 10, 1866, in *Report of the Joint Committee on Reconstruction*, 39th Congress, 1st session, House of Representatives Report 30 (Washington, 1866), 109; Manigault, "Respecting Slavery."

30. James Mallory Diary, January 4, 1871, Southern Historical Collection, University of North Carolina at Chapel Hill; William H. Meadow, "A Fact from the History of the War," New York *Metropolitan Record*, May 20, 1866, in John Houston Bills Diary, Southern Historical Collection, University of North Carolina at Chapel Hill; anon., "The Africans' Evil Genius Pursues the Victim," *Southern Opinion*, September 7, 1867; anon., "Shall We Have a Negro War?" ibid., September 26, 1868; Charles Manigault, "Some Things Relating to Our Family Affairs."

31. Editorial, "The Cause and Duty of the South," *Southern Opinion*, June 15, 1867; Robert D. Graham to William A. Graham, July 22, 1865, in Williams, ed., *The Papers of William Alexander Graham*, 329; Ella Gertrude Clanton Thomas Diary, July 22, 1865, May 7, 1869; James Mallory Diary, May 29, 1868; Samuel A. Agnew Diary, December 5, 1865, Southern Historical Col-

lection, University of North Carolina at Chapel Hill; Cheveux Gris, "A Peculiar People," *Southern Magazine*, 13 (July, 1873): 173; Delavigne, "The Troubles in the South," 515; G. Manigault, "The Future of Young Africa," *Land We Love*, 5 (October, 1868): 528; Heyward quoted in Charles Manigault, "Respecting Slavery."

32. Tucker, *The Relations of the Church to the Colored Race*, 2; Dent Plantation Journal, vol. 7, p. 3; Ella Gertrude Clanton Thomas Diary, December 3, 1865; anon., "Memories of the War," *DeBow's Review*, a.w.s., 3 (March, 1867): 228; anon., "Education of the Freedmen," ibid. (February, 1867): 196; Cheveux Gris, "The Negro in His Religious Aspect," *Southern Magazine*, 17 (October, 1875): 502; Paris, "The Moral and Religious Status of the African Race."

33. Journal entry of May 13, 1865, in Beth G. Crabtree and James W. Patton, eds., *"Journal of a Secesh Lady": The Diary of Catherine Ann Devereux Edmondston, 1860–1866* (Raleigh, 1979), 711; James Mallory Diary, June 24, 1865; David Schenck Diary, June 7, 1865, Southern Historical Collection, University of North Carolina at Chapel Hill.

34. Kenneth Raynor to William Elder, September 20, 1865, in Raleigh *Daily North Carolina Standard*, November 1, 1865; Samuel A. Agnew Diary, November 8, December 12, 1865; editorial, "The Problem of the Negro Race," Charlotte *Church Intelligencer*, 6 (May 10, 1866): 66; G. Manigault, "The Future of Young Africa," 525, 528; Slidell to Edward G. W. Butler, December 2, 1867, Edward G. W. Butler Papers, Duke University.

35. Anon, "Mistaken Sympathy, or Mistaken Figures," *Land We Love*, 1 (September, 1866): 356; editorial, "Worshipping the Ebony Idol," *Southern Opinion*, June 29, 1867; Jones to Mrs. Mary Jones, July 28, 1866, in Myers, ed., *Children of Pride*, 1338; G. Manigault, "The Future of Young Africa," 523–529; Delavigne, "The Troubles in the South," 514–515; G. Manigault, "The Decay of Religion in the South," 214; David Schenck Diary, July 24, 1865; Heyward in "Respecting Slavery"; Cheveux Gris, "A Peculiar People," 173; Henry Watson, Jr., to James A. Wemyes, January 26, 1866, Watson Papers; Report of James Ellis, July 14, 1867, in George D. Humphrey, "The Failure of the Mississippi Freedmen's Bureau in Black Labor Relations, 1865–1867," *Journal of Mississippi History*, 36 (February, 1983): 36; Sparkman, "Results of Emancipation," *Land We Love*, 4 (November, 1867): 24–26; anon., "Northern and Southern Labor Compared," *Southern Cultivator*, 28 (June, 1870): 173.

36. See Oscar Zeichner, "The Transition from Slave to Free Agricultural Labor in the Southern States," *Agricultural History*, 13 (January, 1939): 22–32. For sample contracts, see *Smith College Studies in History*, 1 (April, 1916): 152–154; Rosser H. Taylor, "Post-Bellum Southern Rental Contracts," *Agricultural History*, 17 (April, 1943): 121–128; Arney R. Childs, ed., *Planters*

66                                                      The Old Arguments Anew

*and Business Men: The Guignard Family of South Carolina, 1795–1930* (Columbia, 1957), 106–108; Roger L. Ransom and Richard Sutch, *One Kind of Freedom: The Economic Consequences of Emancipation* (Cambridge, 1977), 58–59, 91, 124; Robert Higgs, *Competition and Coercion: Blacks in the American Economy, 1865–1914* (Cambridge, 1977), 43–44, 46, 50; John David Smith, "More than Slaves, Less Than Freedmen: The 'Share Wages' Labor System during Reconstruction," *Civil War History*, 26 (September, 1980): 256–266.

37. See, for example, William Porcher Miles Diary, December 8, 9, 31, 1872, Miles Papers; Jonathan W. Heacock to Sarah Bunting, October 13, 1867, Sarah W. Bunting Papers, Duke University; anon., "Education of the Freedmen," *DeBow's Review* a.w.s., 3 (February, 1867): 195; Nordhoff, *The Cotton States in the Spring and Summer of 1876*, 99; Bell I. Wiley, "Vicissitudes of Early Reconstruction Farming in the Lower Mississippi Valley," *Journal of Southern History*, 3 (November, 1937): 451–452.

38. Edmund Ruffin, Jr., to Thomas Ruffin, June 9, 1865, in Hamilton, ed., *The Papers of Thomas Ruffin*, 3:457; J. M. Pelot to Julia Pelot, June 10, 16, 1866, Lalla Pelot Papers, Duke University; A. M. McPheeters to R. L. Patterson, June 10, 1865, Patterson Papers; J. D. Collins to John A. Cobb, July 31, 1865, in Phillips, ed., *The Correspondence of Robert Toombs, Alexander H. Stephens, and Howell Cobb*, 666; Samuel A. Agnew Diary, September 19, November 9, 1865; David Schenck Diary, June 14, 1865; Mrs. Eva B. Jones to Mrs. Mary Jones, June 27, 1865, in Myers, ed., *Children of Pride*, 1276; anon., "Letter from Mississippi," New Orleans *Daily Picayune*, December 2, 1865.

39. Bills Diary, March 18, June 15, July 30, December 26, 1867, August 7, September 6, 1865, January 1, 1866; Gage to "My Dear Patterson," January 1, 1866, Gage Papers.

40. Everard Green Baker Diary and Plantation Notes, September 5, 1865, October 21, 1866, July 17, 1867, June 13, 1871, Southern Historical Collection, University of North Carolina at Chapel Hill; James Mallory Diary, January 16, September 12, December 18, 1866; Journal entries of December 29, 31, 1865 in Crabtree and Patton, eds., *"Journal of a Secesh Lady,"* 722–723, 724.

41. Dent Plantation Journal, April 20, 1866, vol. 6, p. 171.

42. Ibid., April 18, 1866, vol. 7 pp. 3, 5, 7, 22, 65. See Ray Mathis, *John Horry Dent: South Carolina Aristocrat on the Alabama Frontier* (University, AL, 1979), 216–218. For similar criticisms, see S. W., "The Labor Question," *Southern Cultivator*, 26 (May 1868): 133.

43. See Steven Hahn, "Hunting, Fishing, and Foraging: Common Rights and Class Relations in the Postbellum South," *Radical History Review*, 26 (1982): 44–45, 48, 51; Jay Mandle, *The Roots of Black Poverty* (Durham, 1978), chapters 1–3; John Q. Anderson, ed., *Brokenburn: The Journal of Kate Stone, 1861–1868* (Baton Rouge, 1955), 356, 368.

44. The literature on the Lost Cause virtually ignores the slavery theme. See, for example, Susan S. Durant, "The Gently Furled Banner: The Development of the Myth of the Lost Cause, 1865–1900" (Ph.D. diss., University of North Carolina at Chapel Hill, 1972), 298; Rollin G. Osterweiss, *The Myth of the Lost Cause*, (Hamden, CT, 1973); Timothy C. Jacobson, "Tradition and Change in the New South, 1865–1910" (Ph.D. diss., Vanderbilt University, 1974), 27; Thomas L. Connelly and Barbara L. Bellows, *God and General Longstreet: The Lost Cause and the Southern Mind* (Baton Rouge, 1982); Gaines M. Foster, "Ghosts of the Confederacy: Defeat, History, and the Culture of the New South, 1865–1913" (Ph.D. diss., University of North Carolina at Chapel Hill, 1982), 44–47, 296, 331, 415.

45. Raleigh *Daily Standard*, August 5, 1865. For a similar view, see "To the Planters and Farmers of North Carolina," Tarboro (NC) *Reconstructed Farmer*, 1 (May, 1869): 18–19.

46. Cooke, "Virginia in the Revolution," *Harper's New Monthly Magazine*, 53 (June, 1876): 2–3. On the development of proslavery images in the periodical literature of these years, see Arnold H. C. Pennekamp, "The Treatment of the Negro in the Literary Magazines of the South during the Reconstruction Period from 1865 to 1880" (M.A. thesis, University of North Carolina, 1936), and Rayburn S. Moore, "Southern Writers and Northern Literary Magazines, 1865–1890" (Ph D. diss., Duke University, 1956).

47. Paris, "The Moral and Religious Status of the African Race in the Southern States"; Marshall, *The Exodus: Its Effect upon the People of the South* (Washington, 1880), 8.

48. Editorial, "The New South," New Orleans *Daily Picayune*, May 12, 1876; editorial, "The Future of the Negro in the South," Atlanta *Constitution*, February 2, 1881.

# 3

## Antislavery Thought from Reconstruction to Reconciliation

### I

The adamant refusal of white southerners to accept abolition did not go unnoticed in the North. Proslavery propaganda only fueled the resurgence of northern antislavery thought during Reconstruction. Criticisms of slavery and the new forms of quasi-slavery appeared regularly throughout the North in these years.[1] Just as Appomattox had failed to silence proslavery theorists, abolitionists and other opponents of slavery kept alive their denunciations of the institution up through the 1890s and well into the new century. At that time a group of neoabolitionist historians and writers emerged to integrate antislavery ideas with the tenets of turn-of-the-century national reconciliation and "scientific" history. True, postwar criticisms of slavery lacked the moral intensity and immediacy of the earlier antislavery crusade. Most white northerners, no less imbued with antiblack phobias than their southern brethren, worried little over the human dimensions of neoslavery. They ignored the blatant discrimination of the Black Codes, peonage laws, and later, the legalized degradation so much a part of southern black life in the Age of Jim Crow. Yet some genuinely wished to remove the spirit of slavery from American life once and for all. These neoabolitionists realized just how strong a hold slavery had on southern white racial thought after emancipation. They renewed the slavery crusade to transform the ex-slaves into freedmen in spirit as well as in name.

With slavery removed as a legal institution, the tone as well as the argument of abolitionist rhetoric took on new meaning. As James M. McPherson has suggested, postwar abolitionist missionaries sustained their old interest in slavery. But they adopted a new formula in approaching slavery and the ex-slaves, one that fitted the special needs of blacks in the postemancipation age. Although by 1890 a majority of southern blacks had been born under freedom, their northern friends continued to charge "that the oppressive legacy of bondage still weighed heavily on the older generation and through them on their children." Perceiving the blacks "from a paternalistic, neo-Puritan perspective," they sympathized with them as "benighted, crippled" victims of southern repression. According to McPherson, "most abolitionists considered the freedmen potentially equal to whites but believed that slavery had dwarfed their intellects, degraded their morals, and crippled their ambition." In their opinion, slavery infantilized and emasculated the blacks. Throughout the postbellum decades, northern teachers, preachers, military men, and politicians did their part to expose slavery's horrors and underscore its vile bequest to blacks.[2]

During Reconstruction, neoabolitionists seldom missed an opportunity to inform northerners of the degraded condition of the freedmen. But in doing so they reinforced many of the racist images espoused by the new proslavery school. White abolitionists emphasized the deep, seemingly indelible scars left on black people by the peculiar institution. Whereas the new proslavery writers blamed emancipation for the blacks' apparent primitive religion, immorality, thievery, carelessness, and poor agricultural work habits, the new antislavery school attributed such behavior to slavery's malevolent influences. In 1869, for instance, Parker Pillsbury, once a militant disciple of abolitionist William Lloyd Garrison, identified a single cause for all the woes of the freedmen and the South. "Slavery was the one sole cause," he said, "of the terrible devastation and desolation under which the South reels to-day, and from which it cannot recover in a hundred years under any policy." Fourteen years later Pillsbury renewed his assault on "the desperate and deadly . . . monster," slavery. He called it "the sublimest scourge and curse that ever afflicted the human race." Slavery degraded and brutalized the blacks, wrote Pillsbury. It kept them ignorant and subjected the bondsmen to severe punishments and indiscriminate murder. Slaves lived in "torture-chambers" and were surrounded by the institution's "reeking, shrieking alters, and ghastly paraphernalia of whips, fetters, blood-hounds and red-hot branding irons." Pillsbury concluded that slavery "was wholesale, legalized, sanctified concubinage, or adultery, from first to last."[3]

Other abolitionists, old and new, employed the essential strategy "of telling the worst" about life among the freedmen "and blaming it on slavery." In their opinion, "slavery was even worse than abolitionists had realized; its vices persisted into freedom and would require long, hard work to overcome."[4] Numerous northerners wrote of the deep imprint slavery left on the ways black and white southerners viewed their worlds. In 1877, for example, a contributor to the *Northwestern Christian Advocate* condemned the manner in which slavery

degraded its victims. They have lost their manhood and self-respect. The bluster and self-assertion, which characterize so many of them, are but efforts to deny a truth that they do not wish to acknowledge. . . . Generations of oppression have poisoned their blood with the virus of inferiority, and nothing but independence and culture will ever antidote the poison.

Earlier that year, a missionary to the freedmen remarked that "The worst things abolitionists ever *wrote*, *spoke* or *thought* about slavery are not half the truth." He added, "No one knows the depth of degradation to which slavery has brought men that has never tried to lift up . . . one who has been a slave." Another neoabolitionist attacked white southerners' ongoing ethnological defenses of slavery. As late as 1875, explained a contributor to the *Methodist Quarterly Review*, whites still dragged out the wrongheaded scientific rationale for slavery. "The boldness of this assumption takes us back to the good old *ante-bellum* days, when we heard so much of the Negro's compressed *os frontis*, his curious shin, his protuberant heel, and, we blush to name it, his incipient tail. To handle the *debris* of so old a controversy is like stirring the ashes of a forsaken forest fire." And addressing a post of the Grand Army of the Republic in 1889, Senator William E. Chandler of New Hampshire denounced slavery as "the sum of all villanies." To these writers, slavery represented the consummate sin in the American past.[5]

Slavery's postwar critics reiterated the old antislavery positions but updated them within the context of postemancipation society. They condemned the peculiar institution on moral, religious, humanitarian, and legal grounds. The neoabolitionists emphasized slavery's exhausting labor conditions, exposed its cruel punishments, and damned the African and domestic slave trades. Following in the footsteps of slavery's defenders, they too impugned as treacherous and hypocritical New England's role in transporting the Africans to the Western Hemisphere in the first place.[6] Neoabolitionists extolled emancipation for removing blacks from the grips of vicious slaveholders. They complimented individual slaves who fought the system and thirsted for freedom.[7] Most were also optimistic, no matter how guardedly, about the future of the freedmen. They praised the newfound progress, the spirit of liberty among the South's blacks. Writing in 1870 from Charleston, a northern educator observed that the freedmen no longer were demoralized by the incubus of slavery. They even looked and dressed better, said J. W. Alvord, superintendent of education for the Freedmen's Bureau. The "linsey woolsey, ragged garments" of the bondsman were now replaced by "the costume of freedom, each choosing his or her dress, according to taste."[8] White neoabolitionists agreed that the former bondsmen, in spite of their backwardness and moral debasement, could be elevated. They would have to be uplifted to the ways of freedom.

Neoabolitionists were quick to note that southern whites also gained from emancipation. It freed them from violating God's laws because, as a Kansan expressed it, "slavery put its foot on christianity's neck. It strove to make Christ and his apostles accessories to the blackest crimes." On a more secular level, slavery's critics welcomed the fact that southern soil would no longer be damaged by what they believed were the slaves' careless agricultural practices. Slavery had degraded manual labor, discouraged white immigration to the South, and disheartened white artisans.[9] According to the New York *Daily Tribune*, under the free labor system

labor will no more be stigmatized . . . as the fit employment of "mud-sills" and mindless, benighted, degraded serfs. Had Slavery never crossed the Atlantic, the population of the South would have been double and her wealth at least treble what they are to-day. Common schools would have educated her children; manufactures diversified and enriched by her industry. Freedom of speech and of the press would have enlightened and elevated her masses.

Freed from the restrictions of slavery, said the New Orleans *Daily Picayune*, the South's postwar economy would burgeon.[10] More often than not, white neoabolitionists viewed slavery's demise as a boon to the nation's material progress. But few sympathized with the plight of the freedmen.

The neoabolitionists included none other than arch southern white supremacist Hinton R. Helper. In the postwar years, Helper continued to attack slavery on the same grounds that had made him one of his region's most ardent antebellum antislavery spokesmen. Slavery, charged Helper, artificially served to elevate the black man over the poor white. It undercut white caste solidarity. Blacks, Helper explained in 1867, were willing accomplices in the enslavement process. "To be a slave of the white man . . . exempt from the necessity of labor, has always been the ruling ambition of the negro." In his opinion, "the negro has but too generally succeeded in foisting himself, as a parasitical slave . . . upon white men." "In losing her slaves, the South lost nothing that was worth keeping," added Helper in 1868. "Had slavery only been abolished by law years ago, our whole country would be infinitely better off to-day." Helper regretted, however, that emancipation was not accompanied by forced colonization of the freedmen. Under "Radical misrule," southern whites still were degraded by "multitudes of sleek, stupid, foul-smelling, filthy, greasy, and grinning negroes . . . the curse-inflicting pets, alike of infatuated and folly-governed ex-slaveholders and Radicals." Like the proslavery writers, Helper blamed emancipation for the murders, robberies, rapes, and burnings allegedly committed by blacks. But in opposing slavery, he parted ways with other southern white racists. Emancipation, according to Helper, was but the first step "to the ultimate whitening up of all the Southern States."[11]

Helper's writings, of course, clashed with the view of slavery held by most white southerners during the immediate postwar years. The persistent proslavery actions and attitudes of these white southerners during Presidential Reconstruction played a major role in the failure of Andrew Johnson's program of reconstruction and in his overthrow by the Radical Republicans. Northerners in general and neoabolitionists in particular focused on the many remnants of slavery prevalent in the South in the years following Appomattox. "The old slavery ideas" die hard, proclaimed a clergyman in the New York *Christian Advocate* in 1866. Another contributor to that periodical disclosed that a prominent Tennessean "expected ere long to own and work his slaves in East Tennessee as aforetime." In language reminiscent of his prewar anti-slavery statements, Senator Charles Sumner wrote in 1866:

Slavery has ceased in name; but this is all. The old masters still assert an inhuman power, and now by positive statutes seek to bind the freedman in new

chains. Let this conspiracy proceed unchecked, and the freedman will be more
unhappy than the early Puritan, who, seeking liberty of conscience, escaped
from the "lords bishops" only to fall under the "lords elders." The master
will still be the master under another name. . . . Serfdom or apprenticeship is
slavery in another guise.

Six years later, Sumner damned efforts by white southerners to segregate
the races in public accommodations. He branded such acts mere surrogates for slavery. "Every such attempt," he said, "is an indignity
to the colored race, instinct with the spirit of Slavery. . . . It is slavery
in its last appearance." Livid at the South's Black Codes, antislavery
spokesmen asserted that southerners were bypassing the Thirteenth
Amendment and riveting new forms of slavery on the freedmen. Writing
in 1886, for example, former Congressman James G. Blaine underscored the similar wording and intent of the slave codes of the Old
South and the Black Codes of Presidential Reconstruction. The latter,
in his opinion, not only reenslaved the blacks but imposed "a form of
servitude . . . more heartless and more cruel than the slavery which had
been abolished. And years after emancipation, a North Carolinian remarked that many whites still viewed blacks "as so many dollars torn
by violence and with cruel insult from your hands."[12] White southerners' desperate grasping of slavery confirmed the worst suspicions of the
Radicals, who remained convinced that the ex-Confederates were un-
repentant, that Johnson and the Democrats would revive the slavocracy
to reestablish a southern power base, and that without congressional
intervention, blacks would continue to languish in servitude.

Neoabolitionists employed slavery as an important comparative model
to document the ways in which southern whites treated the freedmen.
Aghast at the level of Ku Klux Klan violence in Georgia, the Reverend
H. W. Pierson remarked that he had not observed such force against
blacks "in any five years of slavery as I heard and saw at Anderson,
Georgia" from December, 1868, to February, 1869. In *False Reconstruction; or, the Slavery That Is Not Abolished* (1870), Thomas Chapman emphasized the South's ongoing commitment to slavery, a
commitment other northerners maintained was a mere substitution of
serfdom for the peculiar institution. Slavery's new critics charged that
blacks continued to waste away in virtual slavery. After spending five
months in the South in 1880, a neoabolitionist declared that "slavery
is *not* dead. . . . Nothing is changed but the *legal* relation; the social and

domestic relations are infinitely deeper and more powerful, and these are still the same. All the forces and materials which went to make slavery are in vehement operation today as they were twenty years ago.'' Supreme Court Justice John Marshall Harlan agreed. In his famous dissent in the 1883 Civil Rights Cases, Harlan wrote that blacks consistently confronted ''class tyranny.'' Whites kept them ''in practical subjection'' by using arbitrary power ''to dole out . . . just such privileges as they may choose to grant.'' White southerners, concluded a minister in 1888, remained no less determined to keep blacks enslaved than they had been in 1865.[13]

## II

Such vituperative antislavery statements indeed played no small part in the tailoring of the bloody shirt. During Reconstruction slavery symbolized the inertia, the unwillingness, of white southerners to accept true freedom for blacks. For years the mere thought of slavery kept alive the smoldering coals of northern sectionalism and hatred of the South. The new forms of race control that replaced slavery provided Republicans with a constant source of ammunition to attack the Democrats and the South. Condemnation of slavery continued as a major Republican rallying cry during and after Reconstruction. In his *Observations on Reconstruction* (1866), Henry Flanders challenged the motives of Republican politicians. These men cared little for the black man, he insisted, but sought instead to keep slavery's image before the American voting public. ''Although slavery is dead,'' wrote Flanders, ''political anti-slavery is alive, and the imaginary wrongs of the negro in a state of freedom are as useful in the shifts of party as his real wrongs in a state of slavery.'' Whereas Flanders condemned the use of emancipation as a political tool by the Republicans, the Reverend George H. Hepworth assailed ex-slaveholders for manipulating the freedmen in order to capture their political support for the Democrats. ''Such a picture of patriarchal life is said to exist, that we should expect the whole assemblage to vote with unanimous force for the dear old master, who smiles on his former slaves so benignantly, and so politely asks for their influence in the name of the sweet memories of auld lang syne.'' To be sure, politicians squeezed every bit of utility out of the slavery question.[14]

In March, 1866, for example, Senator Lot M. Morrill of Maine spoke strongly in favor of altering the South's congressional representation. How, he asked, could the House of Representatives seat southerners "requiring no security for the protection of" the freedmen—"remanding them to the custody of their old masters, knowing that their object and their purpose is to hold them as an unprivileged and unprotected class?" In the 1868 presidential campaign, a Republican pamphlet endorsing Grant's supporters asked black voters if they believed "the Democrats [would] make slaves of the colored people again if they could?" The Union Republican Congressional Committee answered in the affirmative. "It is fair to presume that they [the Democrats] would, for they have opposed their [blacks'] freedom by every means, have always labored to extend slavery, and would now try to deprive them of the right to vote." Repeatedly the Republicans alleged that the Democrats would reenslave the blacks. During Grant's 1872 campaign, Frederick Douglass reminded black voters that Grant and his running mate, Henry Wilson, symbolized their emancipators; Horace Greeley and B. Gratz Brown represented their enslavers. Over the last forty years, railed Douglass, the Democratic party "existed almost entirely to make sure our slavery and degradation as a race." Slavery also entered into local political contests. In New Hampshire a Republican campaign document charged that "The South wish[es] to re-establish Slavery, and the Democratic party of New Hampshire and throughout the North are pledged to act with the South." If Greeley triumphed, the Republicans predicted, the Democrats most assuredly would "devise some system of legislation by which *without again reducing them* [blacks] *to slavery, they would be made to discharge the incumbent duties of a laboring class.*" The Republicans resurrected similar arguments, emphasizing peonage as a surrogate for slavery, long after Reconstruction. Condemnation of slavery remained a staple in Republican party strategy in the presidential campaigns of 1880, 1884, and 1888.[15]


## III

Andrew Johnson unwittingly provided the Republicans with the necessary ammunition to launch the new abolitionist campaign. His failure to vitiate slavery in spirit as well as in fact partly contributed to the collapse of his mild plan of reconstruction for the South. In July, 1865, the president sent General Carl Schurz, a critic of slavery "because of its effects on free institutions rather than its effects on the enslaved," on a fact-finding southern tour.[16] Johnson reportedly sought information that would enable him to monitor what he termed his "experimental" reconstruction policies. Most likely, Johnson hoped that Schurz would submit a report favorable to his belief that white southerners should rebuild their region and dictate the new order of race relations. After landing on Hilton Head Island, Schurz proceeded to Georgia, Alabama, Mississippi, and Louisiana before returning to Washington. Soon after the start of his mission, Schurz offered a glimpse of his later report. Having barely touched southern soil, the presidential envoy complained that "The new labor system is nowhere taken up with eagerness." Southern whites, wrote Schurz to his wife, "are unquestionably thinking of subjecting the negroes to some kind of slavery again."[17]

Schurz's report, published by Congress in 1865, totalled more than one hundred pages of narrative and accompanying documents. As Hans L. Trefousse has correctly noted, it "played an important role in furthering congressional Reconstruction" and underscored "the baleful influence of the president's policy upon race relations."[18] In his report, Schurz exposed the complete unwillingness of white southerners to accept the full implications of emancipation, to accommodate themselves to the new free labor system. He had met with innumerable planters, Schurz explained, and observed the South's first attempts to regulate blacks by alternatives to chattel slavery. Much to Johnson's consternation, Schurz openly charged white southerners with retaining as much of the nature of slavery as they could. Southerners accepted emancipation, he said, "only in so far as chattel slavery in the old form could not be kept up. But although the freedman is no longer considered the property of the individual master, he is considered the slave of society, and all independent State legislation will share the tendency to make him such." Race relations in the region, charged Schurz, still rested atop the infrastructure of slavery.[19]

In his report to Johnson, Schurz identified many of the new proslavery themes articulated by white southerners. Convinced that the freedmen would not labor without force, whites went on to identify emancipation with all the woes of their region. According to Schurz:

If negroes walked away from the plantations, it was conclusive proof of the incorrigible instability of the negro, and the impracticability of the free negro labor. If some individual negroes violated the terms of their contract, it proved unanswerably that no negro had, or ever would have, a just conception of the binding force of a contract, and that this system of free negro labor was bound to be a failure. If some negroes shirked, or did not perform their task with sufficient alacrity, it was produced as irrefutable evidence to show that physical compulsion was actually indispensable to make the negro work. If negroes, idlers, or refugees crawling about the towns, applied to the authorities for subsistence, it was quoted as incontestably establishing the point that the negro was too improvident to take care of himself, and must necessarily be consigned to the care of a master. I heard a Georgia planter argue most seriously that one of his negroes had shown himself certainly unfit for freedom because he impudently refused to submit to a whipping.

Months after Appomattox whites still held a glimmer of hope that slavery would be preserved. They invoked all manner of force and intimidation—whipping, hanging, shooting, drowning—to keep the blacks in a state of subjection.[20]

Emancipation, explained Schurz, united poor whites and planters in a manner impossible as long as slavery existed. The former "seemed to be more ardent in their proslavery feelings than the planters themselves, [and] are possessed by a singularly bitter and vindictive feeling against the colored race since the negro has ceased to be property." Whites continued to perceive themselves as masters, maintained Schurz. They looked upon slaveholding as their natural right. Citing local ordinances from Louisiana, Schurz impugned the Black Codes as mere extensions of the antebellum slave codes. He offered as an example a former master in Shreveport who agreed to allow Calvin, his ex-slave, "to hire to whom he pleases, but I shall hold him as my property until set free by Congress." Antivagrancy laws and other laws aimed at restricting blacks from working for employers of their choice. The laws, noted Schurz, bound the freedmen to their employers much as under slavery. Employers conspired to keep wages low and placed the freedmen under a vigilante martial law. The Black Codes subjected the blacks to the control of men "hardly fit to control themselves," he said, much less to regulate others.[21]

In marked contrast to the proslavery writers, Schurz noted genuine progress among the freedmen. Most worked hard and stayed on the plantations, he observed. If anything, their conduct "is far more submissive than anybody has a right to expect." In his opinion, whites were totally absorbed with retaining the etiquette of slavery. Unwilling to treat the blacks as freedmen, they demanded behavior that befitted bondsmen. "When southern people speak of the insolence of the negro," he explained, "they generally mean something which persons who never lived under the system of slavery are not apt to appreciate. It is but rarely what would be called insolence among equals." Because the blacks doubted that their freedom was complete, they distrusted the whites around them—and with good reason, Schurz emphasized. Throughout the South, ex-masters sought to replace conventional slavery with "systems intermediate between slavery as it formerly existed ... and free labor." Serfdom, peonage, apprenticeship—enforced by law and custom—would keep blacks forever under the thumb of the master class. Schurz implored Congress to deny readmission of the ex-Confederate states until they had truly emancipated the blacks in deed as well as in word.[22]

## IV

Schurz's oft-quoted report to Johnson set the tone for an avalanche of northern criticism of slavery and the new forms of quasi-slavery. This criticism appeared regularly during the months following emancipation. Such neoabolitionist ideas continued unabated in government documents, books, articles, and tracts all the way up to the 1890s. From June to November, 1865, for example, the New York *Daily Tribune* hammered away at vestiges of slavery in the South. Outraged by Governor William L. Sharkey's policies in Mississippi, the paper charged that "Sharkey evidently believes, with [Roger B.] Taney's revolutionary patriots, that negroes have no rights which white men are bound to respect; and it will take a very keen observation, a nice discernment, to discover the difference between Slavery and the condition of the Mississippi negroes under his unchecked sway." Outraged by white Floridians' treatment of the freedmen, the paper's Jacksonville correspondent proclaimed, "They know not how to bring any influence to bear upon the negro but authority and coercion." Livid at the South's Black Codes, the editor judged the Codes of Tennessee and South Carolina worthy of special condemnation. In the former state, he charged, black children were liable to be apprenticed by "any slave-loving local judge . . . to any slave-hankering friend." The journalist reminded white Tennesseans "that, when Slavery died, all things pertaining to Slavery died with it. When we proclaimed emancipation, we did not remove one set of shackles that you might replace them with another." The *Tribune* found South Carolina's Codes so repressive, it declared that under them "involuntary servitude will exist for the punishment of no crime except the old crime of having a black skin."[23]

Numerous northern observers wrote of the deep imprint slavery left on the ways in which white southerners viewed their world. They marveled at the lengths to which southerners would go to retain every last shred of slavelike behavior in their ex-bondsmen.[24] Among the many U.S. Army officers stationed in the South during Reconstruction, Major Benjamin C. Truman provided one of the most perceptive and critical analyses of the legacy of slavery. Truman spent thirty-one weeks in eight ex-Confederate states in late 1865 and early 1866. As late as April, 1866, he identified in Texas "the substance of slavery . . . in the form of the bondage of custom, of fear, and of inferiority." Throughout the South, whites persecuted the freedmen, obstructed their free movement, and demanded slavelike deference. Truman censured slaveholders for failing to provide for the blacks' mental and moral growth. At best, they had looked after the slaves' present needs and, consequently, the blacks were unprepared for freedom. True, most blacks in 1866 were paid for their work,

but, as a general thing, the freedmen are encouraged to collect about the old mansion in their little quarters, labor for their former master for set terms, receiving, besides their pay, food, quarters, and medical attendance, and thus continuing on in their former state of dependence. The cruelties of slavery, and all of its outward forms, have entirely passed away; but, as might have been expected, glimmerings of its vassalage, its subserviency, and its helplessness, linger.

Truman wrote disparagingly of persistent southern white attitudes toward slavery. Southern whites still believed that the black man belonged somewhere "between the human race and the animal," he said. Consequently, ex-slaveholders and poor whites alike "regard it as a real misfortune to him that he should be stripped of a protector."[25]

Observing daily contact between the ex-masters and their former slaves, government officials noted that southerners seriously doubted that the federal government possessed the power to emancipate slave property. Writing in July, 1865, John H. Pilsbury, a Treasury Department agent, explained that Charlestonians retained "a lingering hope . . . that although African slavery is abolished, the States may yet so legislate as to place the negro in a state of actual peonage and submission to the will of the employer.'' In the same month, Colonel J. L. Haynes wrote that the Vicksburg, Mississippi, newspapers argued that the Emancipation Proclamation had been unconstitutional all along and that manumission was the exclusive province of the states. "Nowhere that I have been," remarked Haynes, "do the people generally realize the fact that the negro is free.'' In Shreveport, Louisiana, planters employed a strategy—casting off elderly and sick ex-slaves—designed to embarrass the government and force it to restore slavery. "A majority of the planters desire to prevent the success of the free-labor system,'' wrote Lieutenant W. B. Stickney, "that they may force Congress to revive slavery, or, what is more, a system of peonage.''[26]

One northerner after another condemned the brutal and unjust treatment heaped upon the freedmen by their former masters. Writing from Raleigh, North Carolina, in August, 1865, General Thomas H. Ruger recorded that murders and other "acts of unlawful violence towards the freedmen are becoming more frequent. The first effect on the mind of the people . . . is . . . wearing off, and, the apparent apathy and stupor resulting from the changed condition of things, is replaced in the minds of those who give up Slavery with reluctance, by feelings of hostility to the freedmen." Later that month a Unionist in Sampson County, North Carolina, reported that ex-slaveholders there employed "all means to repossess themselves of the negroes again." County police used dogs to scour the countryside for errant freedmen. Blacks unwilling to serve their former masters "were hung by the thumbs until they promised to do so.'' This practice reportedly was "more common now than it was when they were slaves.'' [27]

White violence directed at the freedmen knew no bounds. In Mobile, for example, white policemen reputedly raped freedwomen, reported General Thomas Kilby Smith in September, 1865. "These men, having mostly been negro drivers and professional negro whippers, were fitting tools for the work at hand.'' Other blacks received all manner of harassment—whippings, robberies, murders, beatings—as their masters sought to keep them in chains. In western Mississippi, whites meted out corporal punishment to coerce blacks to labor as slaves. According to one officer: "In portions of the northern part of this district the colored people are kept in slavery still. The white people tell them they were free during the war, but the war is now over, and they must go back to work again as before.'' A random sample of complaints registered by blacks against their ex-masters in Beaufort, Pitt, and Hyde counties,

North Carolina, for October, 1865, reveals that 45 percent of the cases involved whippings, beatings, and shootings.[28]

Such violence and abuse identifiable with slavery persisted in the months after ratification of the Thirteenth Amendment. In 1866, for instance, John Johnson and four other ex-slaves were convicted of larceny by the Anne Arundel County, Maryland, Circuit Court. The local judge ordered that each was to be sold to the highest bidder at auction in Annapolis. That same year a Freedmen's Bureau official sent a dispatch that summarized well the conditions of the freedpeople in Osceola County, Mississippi: "I have released three colored persons from slavery . . . having been held for the last three years without any pay or agreement for pay." One of the black women was threatened with murder if she left. Beaten and horsewhipped, she elected to remain enslaved rather than experience any further the fruits of freedom. Also in 1866, a Virginian recounted that whites were so enraged against the freedmen that blacks might just face mass extermination. According to George S. Smith, the whites "always have been the negro's masters; they controlled him; they never acknowledged that he had any rights; he had no rights more than a beast had; I was a slaveholder myself, and I know it. When you come to give the negro his rights, it is very galling to men educated in that way. They cannot yield to the negro those rights that they can to the white man." By December, 1866, a Freedmen's Bureau official in South Carolina warned that the physical coercion of blacks by whites had reached crisis proportions. Without protection from the military, the freedmen would "gradually revert back to a condition differing little from their former slavery—save in name." And as late as December, 1867, a Freedmen's Bureau officer reported that white North Carolinians placed so many obstacles in the way of the freedmen that the blacks were "almost as much within the grasp of their former owners as in the days of slavery."[29]

Northerners fumed at the unwillingness of southerners to accept the blacks as freedmen. "Wherever I go," explained Colonel Samuel Thomas, Freedmen's Bureau assistant commissioner for Mississippi, "the street, the shop, the house, the hotel, or the steamboat—I hear the people talk in such a way as to indicate that they are yet unable to conceive of the negro as possessing any rights at all." So embedded was slavery in their consciousness that many southerners disavowed the reality of emancipation. Whites, judged Thomas, "esteem the blacks their property by natural right, and however much they may admit" that the war ended slavery, "they still have an ingrained feeling that the blacks at large belong to the whites at large." According to an officer in the Fiftieth U.S. Colored Infantry, "They have preached it, talked it, spoken it so long, that free labor would be a failure in the south, (and especially negro labor) that it seems they have made themselves believe it, and very many act as though they were bound to make it so, if it was not going to be the natural result." Testifying before the Joint Committee on Reconstruction, General Rufus Saxton concluded "that the former slaveholders, even if they earnestly destined it, could not be just to the former slaves, for they do not know what justice to the negro means." Another officer informed General O. O. Howard of the blatant proslavery sentiment around Clinton, Mississippi. In the words of one planter in July, 1865, "These niggers will all be slaves again in twelve months. You have nothing but Lincoln proclamations to make them free." Some whites sought to organize politically to revive the peculiar institution. Colonel H. R. Brinkerhoff informed General Howard that in Mississippi he had uncovered "a secret rebel, anti-emigration, pro-slavery party formed . . . whose present policy appears to be to labor assiduously for a restoration of the old system of slavery, or a system of apprenticeship, or some manner of involuntary servitude, on the plea of recompense for loss of slaves." Its organizers hoped to match the presence of northern school teachers and the free labor system with systematic intimidation of blacks and with cruelty. Generals Edward Hatch and Wager Swayne identified similar schemes in Tennessee and Alabama, respectively. White Tennesseans, said Hatch, fantasized that "by some kind of legislation they can establish a kind of peonage; not absolute slavery, but that they can enact such laws as will enable them to manage the negroes as they please—to fix the prices to be paid for his labor." Swayne discovered in Alabama's legislature "a formidable party, determined to enjoy the unpaid labor which slavery had allowed, without even the obligations of maintenance which that system had imposed."[30]

Such attitudes, noted slavery's critics, made military presence in the postwar South all the more crucial. Many agreed that should the Freedmen's Bureau and the army leave the region, the blacks would inherit a fate more heinous than slavery. Even with the army on the scene, whites brutalized them, subjected them to legal and extralegal restraints, and conspired to keep blacks working for their ex-masters at pitifully low wages. Testifying before the Joint Committee on Reconstruction,

General Christopher C. Andrews, a Minnesotan, warned that if the Freedmen's Bureau ceased operations:

The freedmen would undoubtedly be worse off than they were as slaves. They would be subjected to great restraint and would not have the friendly protection which they had from their masters. There is no doubt that the white and black races in the south are not friendly. . . . It was a common thing [after the war] for the masters to say to the blacks, "Now you are made free; you are free and can go wherever you please. Go, if you choose, immediately; but if you remain with me you must remain and do just as you have done heretofore, and I will treat you just as I have heretofore." The consequence was that a great many of the freed people were obliged to remain still in a state of slavery or wander off exposed to various hardships and dangers. And I would further say, that there was an understanding among those who had formerly been slave owners that the colored people should not be employed without the consent of their former masters.

In March, 1868, Freedmen's Bureau official Jacob F. Cline pinpointed the manner in which whites attempted to reestablish the working conditions of slavery. He rejected a labor contract brought before him that had been made between a North Carolina planter and his black employees. The "price of labor" paid the blacks, Cline judged, was "even below the price paid for slave labor before the war." Such contracts, he added, "when the land-owner undertakes to control the personal liberty of the laborers, are utterly foreign to free institutions."[31]

## V

No one sensed the lingering spirit of slavery in the South more than the freedmen themselves. Impassioned testimony by blacks in the throes of their liberation underscored the determination of white southerners to cling to the old racial order. Throughout Reconstruction and well up to the end of the century, blacks emphasized the horrors of enslavement and the persecution of neoslavery. Their outrage with slavery and reverence for freedom made a mockery of the new proslavery argument. "We were not born to wear the yoke," exclaimed the Reverend Henry H. Garnet in 1865. For the black man, he insisted, "death is a thousand times more preferable than slavery."[32] Ex-slaves and northern free blacks alike damned slavery's vile legacy of racial hatred and oppression.[33] In 1882 the Reverend Isaac McCoy Williams took exception to the proslavery arguments of white clergymen. He criticized slavery because it "kept us in a semi-barbarous condition" and slowed black intellectual growth. A year later black diplomat John M. Langston, himself a former bondsman, denounced slavery's "barbarous torture." So atrocious was slavery that it denied the black man control over his own body, the right to protect his family, the ability to acquire possessions. Even when emancipated, charged Langston, the black's freedom has been . . . a mockery, because he has been deprived of those civil and political powers which render enfranchised manhood valuable and its dignities a blessing."[34]

Immediately upon emancipation, the freedmen began shedding their slavelike behavior. They sought to carve out an identity apart from the slave experience, and demanded land and assistance from the government—weapons with which to combat whites who sought to keep them helpless and dependent.[35] The blacks moved quickly to reorder their lives. Many searched for long-lost relatives. Writing in July, 1865, for instance, ex-slave James Smith informed another freedman that now that "the lord has broken the slavery chain I hope you may get to see your wife."[36] Blacks in Richmond complained loudly that both the civil and military governments there perpetuated the etiquette of slavery.[37] Black Virginians demanded full recognition by whites of their new status. They refused to be controlled, closely supervised, and subjected to the tortures incident to slavery. They resisted the remnants of bondage by ceasing labor or simply not showing up for the next day's work. To whites, such "wandering" behavior connoted black retrogression in the absence of slavery's guardianship. To blacks, freedom of movement represented their only real weapon against the omnipresent shadow of slavery. Reenslavement loomed as a real fear for blacks throughout the South. Should representatives of the old master class return to Congress, warned ex-slave Richard R. Hill, "the condition of the freedman would be very little better than that of the slaves, and . . . their old laws would still exist by which they would reduce them to something like bondage." Writing soon after attaining her freedom, Charlotte Ann Jackson recalled: "When i was liveing with White People i was tide down hand and foot and they tide me to the Post and whip me till i Could not stand up and they tide my Close over my head and whip me much as they want. . . . But the light has come the Rebles is put down and Slavry is

dead God Bless the union Forever more. . . . i hope slavly shall be no
more.'' Such painful recollections of bondage remained fresh long after
black emancipation.[38]

Postbellum black writings on slavery provided a vital, firsthand dimension to postwar antislavery thought. Many blacks found little difference between chattel slavery and the new conditions of life and labor
confronting them after the war. Addressing a group of blacks on St.
Helena Island in July, 1865, Martin R. Delany, one of the Union army's few black commissioned officers, warned the freedmen that
whites sought to keep them in chains. ''Yankees from the north . . .
come down here to drive you as much as ever . . . before the war. Its
slavery over again northern, universal U.S. slavery.'' Blacks, implored Delany, must resist the snakelike grip of slavery. Whites would
seduce them with kind words, then exploit them—''its slavery over
again as much as ever it was.'' In October, 1865, for example, a black
soldier was arrested in Larue County, Kentucky, for trying to rescue
his family from slavery. Two months later a black Virginian complained that ''never was wee any more treated Like slaves then wee
are now in our Lives.'' A black soldier in Mississippi also informed
the Freedmen's Bureau commissioner that his people were subjected
to extreme violence—''outraged beyound humanity''—by whites.
Robbed, murdered, and driven from their homes, the blacks possessed no rights that whites were bound to respect. ''Some are being
knocked down for saying they are free, while a great many are being
worked just as they ust to be when Slaves, without any compensation.
. . .'' White Mississippians ''are doing all they can to prevent free
labor, and reasstablish a kind of secondary slavery.'' And in May,
1866, six black soldiers petitioned President Johnson on behalf of their
families back in Kentucky, explaining that their kinsmen remained in
virtual slavery. Blacks had willingly joined the army, wrote the soldiers, to liberate themselves and their descendants. While they were
away from home, however, their families were abused: ''turned out
of Doors . . . they has no Place to lay thire heads and we has no way
to healp them.'' In their opinion, the freedmen stood helpless and vulnerable to the wrath of the whites. ''I would like to Know how,'' asked
one of the blacks, they were to ''go about takeing cire of thire Selfs
and Children. . . . the old Servent has Spent the best of his days in
Slavery. then must these Poore Creatchers be Suffered to lye out of
Doors Like Beast or sum brute''?[39]

## VI

The intensity of such appeals kept antislavery images alive during Reconstruction and well up through the turn of the century. Slavery's postwar critics played an important role in reminding the American public that the Civil War had indeed concluded as a struggle for black liberation. They argued correctly that slavery remained firmly entrenched in southern white racial thought. Writing, for example, in June, 1865, a missionary to the freedmen noted that "slavery still exists in the interior and is spending its last moments in the old abominations of whipping and punishing. Of course it is nearly dead,—the people know they are free and the masters have to own it,—but the ruling passion is strong in death." Old abolitionists such as Wendell Phillips continued to harp upon the fact that southern blacks remained enslaved in every way except legally. Race subordination and white supremacy, Phillips informed a Boston audience in October, 1865, survived the war as the ordering principle in the South. "State rights, subordination of labor, the impracticability of the two races living equally together the principles upon which the South went out—upon these principles she returns." Throughout the 1870s, 1880s, and 1890s, neoabolitionists underscored slavery's cruelties and blamed the institution for the contemporary "Negro problem." Slavery not only had dragged the nation into a horrible internecine war, but had left a skeleton of race hatred in its wake. Speaking before the House of Representatives in 1876, George F. Hoar of Massachusetts complained that white southerners never truly accepted emancipation and equal treatment of the freedmen. The ruling class in the South, charged Hoar, concocted "a concerted, crafty scheme to reduce the negro to a system of peonage which degraded him below the condition of slavery, but imposed no corresponding obligation upon the master."[40]

In their important writings, Albion W. Tourgée and George Washington Cable disseminated these antislavery themes to a popular, though not always appreciative, audience. Espousing unwelcome causes in North Carolina and Louisiana, respectively, the two writers clearly identified postwar southern racism with the then deceased peculiar institution. The egregious horrors of slavery remained embedded in both authors' minds. They agreed that in spite of the Thirteenth Amendment, white southerners continued to expect slavelike deference and behavior from blacks.

Writing in 1884, for instance, Tourgée explained that "the boundary-line of servitude marked also the distinction of race. Only the white man had the right to freedom in the South." In his fiction, the North Carolina carpetbagger stressed the many ways in which slavery victimized blacks and whites. Aside from its well-known physical cruelties, slavery remained engraved on the souls of former masters, bondsmen, and poor whites. Tourgée elaborated in 1888:

Slavery as a condition of society has not yet become separable, in the minds of our people, North or South, from slavery as a political idea, a factor of partisan strife. They do not realize that two centuries of bondage left an ineradicable impress on master and slave alike, or that the line of separation between the races, being marked by the fact of color, is as impassable since emancipation as it was before, and perhaps even more portentous. They esteem slavery as simply a dead, unpleasant fact of which they wish to hear nothing more, and regard any disparaging allusion to its results as an attempt to revive a defunct political sentiment.

Tourgée also chided whites for failing to meet their obligations to blacks. "For every dollar of unrequited toil that went into our wondrous aggregate of wealth," he noted, the black "has a right to claim a just and fair equivalent in intelligence and opportunity." And Tourgée regretted that whites in the New South worked so feverishly to keep blacks dependent and helpless. They conspired to retain the labor of blacks "upon terms as nearly on a level with the condition of slavery as possible."[41]

Cable surpassed Tourgée in his social criticism of southern institutions in general and of what he termed the remnants of slavery in particular. After the mid-1880s Cable championed full civil rights for the freedmen in his many books, articles, and lectures. He deplored the racial injustice of the Gilded Age. Repeatedly Cable employed slavery as a metaphor to blast exploitation of black labor, segregated schools, Jim Crow legislation, disfranchisement, and especially the convict lease system. He branded these "the debasements of slavery and semi-slavery." For example, in his commencement address at the University of Mississippi in 1882, Cable linked postwar sharecropping to slavery. "The plantation idea is a semi-barbarism. It is the idea of the old South with merely the substitution of a negro tenantry for negro slaves. It is a pathetic and senile sentiment for the maintenance of a landed aristocracy in a country and in times that have outgrown that formidable error in political economy." Writing three years later in *The Silent South*, Cable implored white southerners to combat slavery's legacy.

The problem before us is the green, rank stump of that felled Institution. Slavery in particular—the slavery of the individual man to his one master . . . is by the law abolished. Slavery in general—the subordination of a fixed rule to a fixed ruling class—the slavery of *civil caste*, which can only in part, and largely cannot, be legislated away, remains. Sad will it be for our children if we leave it for their inheritance.

In Cable's opinion, slavery left white southerners dictatorial in spirit, prone to lynching and political corruption. "It made our master caste a solid mass," he wrote, "and fixed a common masterhood and sub-serviency between the ruling and the serving race." Cable sympathized with the ex-slave, "brought here by cruel force, and with everybody's consent except his own." The bondsman's descendants remained impoverished peasants, surrounded by "the remaining vestiges of an incompletely abolished slavery."[42]

Cable's brilliant antislavery polemics notwithstanding, conditions for blacks worsened in the 1890s. One southern state after another followed Mississippi's lead and passed segregation laws in these years. The crop lien system, peonage laws, and disfranchisement solidified the subordinate status of black southerners in custom and law. As the repressive grip of Jim Crow tightened on southern blacks, another generation of critics—politicians, educators, reformers—stepped forward to counter the new defenses of slavery. Enraged by the conditions of neoslavery of the New South, these writers illustrate well the strong continuity of antislavery thought from Reconstruction to reconciliation.

In 1893, for example, Representative Eugene J. Hainer of Nebraska demanded that federal regulation of elections in the South continue. Without such assistance, he predicted, white southerners most assuredly would return the blacks to some form of quasi-slavery. Another politician warned that blacks had to be protected from the constant spectre of reenslavement, recalling that during Reconstruction whites had steadfastly refused to admit that the blacks were free. Even when confronted with the reality of black elected officials, they "still sullenly believed they owned their legislators." In a similar vein, speakers at the Second Mohonk Conference on the Negro Question also impugned slavery and its vestiges. They lamented that enslavement had denied the blacks fundamental education, imbued them with disrespect for property rights, and degraded black womanhood. Editor Oswald Garrison Villard charged that white southerners were determined to keep blacks in "servitude for all time." The ruling class in the South, he informed the National Negro Business League, insisted that blacks remain "hopeless inferiors whose social position is fixed by iron bonds of caste and prejudice."[43]

These late nineteenth-century neoabolitionists expressed disbelief that a new proslavery argument had arisen at all. How, they asked, could anyone at the turn of the century still defend slavery? How could the nation allow black southerners to be returned to a slavelike status? William Goodell Frost, for instance, president of Kentucky's Berea College, complained in 1899 that "it is now the fashion to varnish slavery." Scores of teachers and missionaries who had worked among the freedmen knew better, he said. The plantation myth simply was erroneous. Under slavery, explained Frost in 1904, the blacks were denied any semblance of family life. "Slavery was a school of laziness, deception, suspicion and theft. . . . [It] removed the natural motives to ambition and self-improvement," inflicting severe psychological scars upon the race. According to Frost, those who glossed over slavery's cruelties simply failed to grasp its pathological impact on the black race.[44]

Early in the new century novelist Caroline H. Pemberton of Philadelphia voiced similar disgust. She balked at the resurgence of apologies for slavery so prevalent in American racial thought. Daughter of distinguished chemist Henry Pemberton and niece of Confederate General John C. Pemberton, she descended from a long line of Pennsylvania Quakers. This aristocrat-turned-reformer championed virtually all of the social and economic causes of her day. For example, Pemberton opposed American imperialism with the same vigor that she crusaded in favor of organized labor and black rights. In her attacks on lynching, anti-miscegenation laws, and the sharecropping and peonage systems, Pemberton combined theories of class and racial oppression. Writing in 1903 to W. E. B. Du Bois, she explained that whites concealed their "class hatred" toward blacks under the guise of "race hatred." She continued: "I do not say that race hatred does not exist separate & apart from class hatred,—but the fact that the white man wants your unrecompensated toil is largely the reason of his race prejudice,—the reason why he hates the sight of an educated colored man,—a colored teacher or doctor or lawyer. It is just one more prisoner escaped from the stockade of unrequited toil!'' Pemberton, assistant secretary of the Pennsylvania state committee of the Socialist Party, also took a bold stand against segregationist practices within the ranks of the Socialists themselves. According to Philip S. Foner, Pemberton's writings on race "made everything else by Socialists of this period on the Negro question look superficial by comparison."[45]

Writing in January, 1900, Pemberton argued that contemporary whites resurrected the same arguments to defend lynching as had earlier proponents of slavery. Then as now, she explained, whites viewed blacks as mere animals, depraved and contemptible, unworthy of equal justice before the law. In both periods whites blamed the degeneracy of blacks for white lawlessness. Pemberton implored readers of the *Arena* not to forget

that the Southern slaveholder justified slavery exactly on this basis. He pleaded as eloquently as his sons and daughters are now pleading that the negro was a brute, and could never rise to man's estate. Slavery was excusable because the slave was too degraded and vicious to be permitted to take care of himself. He needed a master to keep him in the position of a beast of burden.

Because the white southerner "must always justify his historic past," Pemberton wrote, he continued to view blacks as property. She asked her readers to put themselves in the place of one whose " 'lost cause,' for which you and yours had fought, bled, and died only thirty-five years ago, still existed before your eyes in the immediate presence of eight million of beings whose parents and grandparents you had bought and sold like cattle, and over whom you still exercised the control that the owners of the soil possess over the ignorant tillers." Pemberton, as passionately as any of the neoabolitionists, condemned white racism and its by-product—what she termed "the lingering echo of the slaveholder's argument."[46]

Soon afterward, Pemberton lashed out against the proslavery statements of Charles Dudley Warner, president of the American Social Science Association. No race-baiting southern reactionary, Warner was a respected New England editor and leader in the cause of social progress. What prompted Pemberton's ire were Warner's statements pertaining to slavery in an address on black education. Much like Booker T. Washington, Warner innocently praised slavery as a vocational school, an institution that transformed the black "into an industrial being, and

held him in the habit of industry for several generations.'' Outraged by
this remark and the entire body of proslavery rhetoric of her age, Pemberton responded in the Springfield, Massachusetts *Republican*. First,
she inquired,

may I ask whence comes this rose-tinted reassuring picture of slavery and its
effects on the slave? Is it not a resetting of the old slaveholders' argument in
defense of their cherished institutions? In the soft twilight of bygone days,
fading year by year from memory, even our old-time abolitionists are pleased
to speak of the ''beneficent influences of slavery'' in almost the same language
that the pro-slavery advocates used before the war.

In Pemberton's opinion, Warner and other ''old-time friends'' of the
blacks distorted slavery. Blacks had never perceived it as ''a blessing
in disguise.'' Rather, the peculiar institution constituted an indelible
stain on the fabric of American civilization, ''an accursed and monstrous
system of legalized wrong.''[47]

Pemberton went on to use the *Republican*'s columns as a forum from
which to damn slavery's negative effects on black southerners past and
present. She admitted that the conditions of slave life had not yet been
studied objectively. Nevertheless, Pemberton wrote confidently that at
best antebellum plantation society resembled ''a very barbaric kind of
splendor.'' Unlike Washington or Warner, she doubted whether many
bondsmen received mechanical training at all. She emphasized slavery's
physical cruelties and the barbarities of slave breeding and the domestic
slave trade. Most slaves, Pemberton insisted, labored in the fields under
the supervision of brutal overseers. Having only recently traveled in
the rural South, she assured readers that conditions for blacks in 1900
differed little from those of the antebellum period. Chattel slavery had
given way to new forms of servitude—the convict lease, farm tenancy,
and sharecropping. Education remained the blacks' only hope for rising
from slavery. Pemberton feared that blacks would remain trapped by
the incidents of servitude as long as whites viewed the past in romanticized, sentimental terms.[48]

No neoabolitionist better represents the continuity of antislavery thought
than Carl Schurz. In 1903 the old critic of slavery charged that the
''reactionary spirit'' of bondage still haunted white southerners. Like
Pemberton, he identified offensive sentiments in southern newspapers
and political speeches that ''bear a striking resemblance to the proslavery arguments . . . heard before the Civil War.'' Citing Mississippi

governor James K. Vardaman as an example, Schurz argued that many whites sought to ensnare blacks in a "permanent condition of serfdom." All of this, he complained, was too reminiscent of slavery times. Once again whites believed that they knew what was best for the blacks. Once again white racism prevented freedom of inquiry below the Mason-Dixon line. Schurz warned New South "reactionists"—who sought to straddle blacks with some alternative form of slavery—of the dire consequences of such actions for their section of the country. Just as slavery had "numbed" and "stupefied" antebellum southern progress, so too would steps aimed at keeping contemporary blacks in "some sort of semi-slavery." As long as whites required submissiveness and obedience from the blacks, they would remain "the slaves of slavery . . . the victims of their failure to abolish slavery altogether."[49]

Schurz's 1903 remarks bring to mind his 1865 report to Andrew Johnson. Throughout the four decades following Appomattox, Schurz and other neoabolitionists fought the traces of slavery that remained in the South with the zeal of their antebellum forebears. They made many accurate observations concerning the impact of slavery on the freedmen during Reconstruction and concerning the legacy of neoslavery in the New South. Their portrayal of slavery as an oppressive institution whose victims deserved compassion and help served diverse humanitarian and partisan ends. Even so, politicians in Washington, as well as missionaries, teachers, and federal officers living in the South, often tended to perceive the ex-slaves through what James M. McPherson has described as a paternalistic, neo-Puritan lens. "They probably exaggerated the 'Sambo' syndrome in the black personality," explains McPherson. "They generalized too easily about the universally corrupting impact of slavery from the worst examples in their own experience; and their culture-bound perceptions inhibited an understanding of the positive values of some facets of black culture, especially the church."[50] All the same, the neoabolitionists recognized that the spirit of slavery remained shamelessly alive in the South. Slavery's postwar critics had closed ranks to meet the new proslavery argument head-on. They established an important ideological base for those historians who continued to advocate antislavery themes well into the new century.

## NOTES

1. See, for example, anon., "Revival of Slavery," *National Anti-Slavery Standard*, 26 (August 12, 1865): 1; anon., "The Substitute for Slavery," ibid.

(September 16, 1865): 1; editorial, "Southern Temper," ibid. (December 30, 1865): 2; anon., "Undoing Emancipation," ibid., 28 (January 25, 1868): 1; A. L. Robinson, "Slavery in Kentucky," ibid., 29 (January 23, 1869): 1; Samuel Johnson, "Anti-Slavery Work Not Ended," ibid. (February 13, 1869): 2; Gilbert Haven, "The Slavery That Is Not Yet Abolished," ibid. (February 13, 1869): 1; John T. Sargent, "Caste and Color Prejudice—the Stalking Curse of Slavery!" ibid. (April 3, 1869): 1; editorial, "Prejudice against Color," ibid., 30 (June 26, 1869): 2; A. B. S., "Life in Virginia," ibid., n.s., 2 (November 18, 1871): 2.

2. McPherson, *The Abolitionist Legacy: From Reconstruction to the NAACP* (Princeton, 1975), 184–185, 66, 79, 185.

3. McPherson, *The Abolitionist Legacy*, 57; Pillsbury, *Acts of the Anti-Slavery Apostles* (Concord, NH, 1883), iii, 47, 49, 70, 71, 58, 55.

4. McPherson, *The Abolitionist Legacy*, 62, 59–60.

5. Henry Colman, "That Wicked Color-Line," *Northwestern Christian Advocate*, 25 (September 19, 1877): 1; Robert F. Markham, May, 1877, quoted in McPherson, *The Abolitionist Legacy*, 185; anon., "The Negro," *Methodist Quarterly Review*, 4th ser., 27 (January, 1875): 85; Chandler, *Decoration Day Address of William E. Chandler* (Concord, NH, 1889), 4.

6. Anon., "Charleston, S.C.: The Slave Mart," *National Freedman*, 1 (April 1, 1865): 85; "Items," *Freedman's Journal*, 1 (April, 1865): 15; George H. Moore, *Notes on the History of Slavery in Massachusetts* (New York, 1866), 68 and passim. Pillsbury described Moore's important book as "one of the most surprising volumes ever issued by the American press." See *Acts of the Anti-Slavery Apostles*, 72.

7. Anon., "Davy Jones," *Freedman's Journal*, 1 (May, 1865): 17; anon., "For Christ's Sake," ibid., 1 (November, 1865): 41.

8. Alvord, *Letters from the South, Relating to the Condition of the Freedmen* (Washington, 1870), 7, 17; "From Miss Barnes," *National Freedman*, 1 (April 1, 1865): 75; anon., "Colored Laborers in Louisiana," *Freedman's Journal*, 1 (April, 1865): 15; anon., "A Voice from the South," *Northwestern Christian Advocate*, 25 (May 30, 1877): 1.

9. William Reynolds to Jonathan Worth, January 3, 1866, Jonathan Worth Papers, North Carolina Division of Archives and History; William C. Richards, *Thanksgiving for Peace: A Sermon* (New York, 1866), 31–32; Jo. Bean, "The Old and New South," *South-Atlantic*, 4 (June, 1879): 145–146, 152.

10. Editorial, "The South Victorious," New York *Daily Tribune*, October 27, 1865; editorials, "Capital Wanted," New Orleans *Daily Picayune*, October 28, 1865, "State Legislation and the Freedmen's Bureau," ibid., December 13, 1865.

11. Helper, *Nojogue: A Question for a Continent* (New York, 1867), 193, 205, 284; idem, *Negroes in Negroland* (New York, 1868), xiii, 243, 250.

12. J. Miley, "The Southern Labor Question," New York *Christian Advocate*, 41 (March 29, 1866): 97; Thomas H. Payne to the editor, April 7, 1866, ibid. (April 26, 1866): 130; Sumner, *The Equal Rights of All: The Great Guarantee and Present Necessity* (Washington, 1866), 28; idem, speech in U.S. Senate, January 15, 1872, *Congressional Globe*, 42nd Congress, 2nd session (Washington, 1872), 383; Blaine, *Twenty Years of Congress*, 2 vols. (Norwich CT, 1886), 2:96, 97; *Speech of Hon. Henry R. Low, on the Right of Congress to Determine the Qualification of Its Members* (Albany, 1866), 13; *Abolition of Slavery: Speech of Hon. John A. Kasson of Iowa* (Washington, 1867), 1; Andrew P. Peabody, *Lessons from Our Late Rebellion* (Boston, 1867), 3–4; *"Northern Radicals and Southern Radicals": Speech of Hon. Henry Wilson, of Massachusetts* (Washington, 1868), 5, 7; Cornelia P. Spencer, "The Young Ladies' Column," *North Carolina Presbyterian*, August 31, 1870.

13. Chapman, *False Reconstruction; or, The Slavery That Is Not Abolished* (Saxonville, MA, 1876), 5, 14, 18, 23; D. D. Whedon, "Southern Methodist Press on Negro 'Intimidation,' " *Northwestern Christian Advocate*, 25 (January 17, 1877): 1; H. W. Pierson, *A Letter to Hon. Charles Sumner, with "Statements" of Outrages upon Freedmen in Georgia* (Washington, 1870), 20; E. B. Emery, *Letters from the South, on the Social, Intellectual, and Moral Condition of the Colored People* (Boston, 1880), 9; *U.S. Supreme Court Reports Vol. 109* (Rochester, 1885), 856; E. W. S. Hammond, "The New Epoch in the Elevation of the Negro," *Southwestern Christian Advocate*, 23 (January 12, 1888): 1.

14. Flanders, *Observations on Reconstruction* (Philadelphia, 1866), 8n; Hepworth, *Oration Delivered before the City Council and Citizens of Boston, July 4, 1867* (Boston, 1867), 23.

15. Morrill, *Apportionment of Representation* (Washington, 1866), 2, 14; *The Party of Freedom and Its Candidates: The Duty of the Colored Voter* (Washington, 1868), 2; *Shall Capital Own Labor? The Rebel Democracy the Enemy of the People: Seymour and Blair's Nomination Means Revolution, Repudiation and Slavery!* (Washington, 1868), 2–3, 8; Douglass, *U.S. Grant and the Colored People* (Washington, 1872), 8; anon., *The Record of the Democratic Party* (Concord, NH, 1872), 10; Jay A. Hubbell, *The Overshadowing Issue! The True "Inwardness" of the "Solid South!"* (Washington, 1880); J. B. Gordon to the editor, New York *Commercial Advertiser*, November 21, 1884; D. McD. Lindsey, *The Wrongs of the Negro—the Remedy* (Boston, 1888), 4–5, 6–7, 9, 12; William E. Chandler, "Our Southern Masters," *Forum* 5 (July, 1888): 517.

16. Michael Burlingame, "Schurz, Carl," in John A. Garraty and Jerome L. Sternstein, eds., *Encyclopedia of American Biography* (New York, 1974), 972.

17. Schurz to Margaret Meyer Schurz, July 30, 1865, in Joseph Schafer, ed., *Intimate Letters of Carl Schurz, 1841–1869* (Madison, 1928), 345.

18. Trefousse, "Carl Schurz's 1865 Southern Tour: A Reassessment," *Prospects*, 2 (1976): 306.

19. Trefousse, *Carl Schurz: A Biography* (Knoxville, 1982), 154–158; Schurz, "Report of Carl Schurz on the States of South Carolina, Georgia, Alabama, Mississippi, and Louisiana," in *Message of the President of the United States*, 39th Congress, 1st session, Senate Executive Document 2 (Washington, 1865), 45. The latter source hereafter cited as Schurz Report.

20. Schurz Report, 17, 18, 19.

21. Ibid., 20, 21, 22–23, 24.

22. Ibid., 29, 30, 31, 32, 35, 36, 38, 39.

23. Editorials, "Sharkey—Mississippi," "From Florida," "Reconstruction—How Not to Do It," "South Carolina Re-Establishing Slavery," New York *Daily Tribune*, June 15, 20, 23, November 14, 1865.

24. Whitelaw Reid, *After the War: A Tour of the Southern States, 1865–1866* (Cincinnati, 1866), 45n, 51, 95, 151, 218; Sidney Andrews, *The South since the War: As Shown by Fourteen Weeks of Travel and Observation in Georgia and the Carolinas* (Boston, 1866), 21, 27, 387, 395–398; J. T. Trowbridge, *The South: A Tour of Its Battle-Fields and Ruined Cities, a Journey through the Desolated States, and Talks with the People* (Hartford, 1866), 367, 368, 391, 393, 409, 427, 485, 489, 576; John Richard Dennett, *The South As It Is: 1865–1866* (New York, 1965), 15, 71, 78, 84, 91, 163, 177, 212, 220, 222, 307, 311, 272, 293, 318, 352; Edward King, *The Great South* (Hartford, 1875), 159, 182, 427–435, 599, 717, 773; John W. DeForest, "The Man and Brother," *Atlantic Monthly*, 22 (September, October, 1868): 337–348, 414–425.

25. Truman, *Report of Major Benjamin C. Truman to President Andrew Johnson*, 39th Congress, 1st session, Senate Executive Document 43, (Washington, 1866), 9, 10, 8.

26. John H. Pilsbury to Carl Schurz, July 24, 1865, Haynes to B. F. Morey, July 8, 1865, Stickney to Thomas W. Conway, August 1, 1865, in Schurz Report, 51, 75, 91.

27. Thomas H. Ruger to W. W. Holden, August 1, 1865, and Extract of J. C. Williams to Holden, n.d., in Ruger to J. W. Ames, August 14, 1865, Governors' Papers, William W. Holden, North Carolina Division of Archives and History.

28. Smith to Carl Schurz, September 14, 1865, Charles H. Gilchrist to W. A. Gordon, September 17, 1865, W. A. Poillon to Wager Swayne, July 29, 1865, J. H. Weber to Samuel Thomas, September 28, 1865, in Schurz Report, 58, 69, 73, 78; R. K. Scott to O. O. Howard, November 1, 1866, in *Letter of the Secretary of War, . . . Reports of the Assistant Commissioners of Freedmen, and a Synopsis of Laws respecting Persons of Color in the Late Slave States*, 39th Congress, 2nd session, Senate Executive Document 6, 2 vols. (Washing-

ton, 1867), 1:112 (hereafter cited as *Letter of the Secretary of War*); Monthly Return of Cases Heard, October, 1865, by Lieutenant I. G. Holt, Case Files Relating to the Administration of Justice, 1865–1868, Records of the Assistant Commissioner for the State of North Carolina, Bureau of Refugees, Freedmen, and Abandoned Lands, Record Group 105, National Archives and Records Service.

29. *Abolition of Slavery: Speech of John A. Kasson of Iowa*, 4; Report of Lt. Mix, October 31, 1866, quoted in *Freedmen in Arkansas: Letter from General E. O. C. Ord, in Relation to the Treatment of Freedmen in Arkansas*, 39th Congress, 2nd session, House Miscellaneous Document 14 (Washington, 1867), 2; Robert K. Scott to O. O. Howard, December 18, 1866, Nelson A. Miles to Howard, December 4, 1867, quoted in John A. Carpenter, "Atrocities in the Reconstruction Period," *Journal of Negro History*, 47 (October, 1962): 239, 241. See also Scott to Howard, November 1, 1866, *Letter of the Secretary of War*, 1:112.

30. Thomas to Schurz, n.d., Charles H. Gilbert to W. A. Gordon, September 17, 1865, in Schurz Report, 80–81, 69; Saxton testimony, February 21, 1866, Hatch testimony, January 25, 1866, in *Report of the Joint Committee on Reconstruction*, 39th Congress, 1st session, House of Representatives Report 30 (Washington, 1866), part 3, p. 101, part 1, p. 108 (hereafter cited as *Report of the Joint Committee on Reconstruction*); H. R. Brinkerhoff to Howard, July 8, 1865, in Schurz Report, 76; Swayne to O. O. Howard, October 31, 1866, in *Letter of the Secretary of War*, 1:4–5. On child apprenticeship as a form of neoslavery, see Rebecca Scott, "The Battle over the Child: Child Apprenticeship and the Freedmen's Bureau in North Carolina," *Prologue*, 10 (Summer, 1978): 101–113.

31. Scott to O. O. Howard, December 18, 1866, in Carpenter, "Atrocities in the Reconstruction Period," p. 239; Testimony of Christopher C. Andrews, March 13, 1866, W. H. H. Beadle, April 4, 1866, Edward Hatch, January 25, 1866, in *Report of the Joint Committee on Reconstruction*, part 3, pp. 148–149, part 2, p. 269, part 1, p. 108; Cline to W. K. Ruffin, March 19, 1868, in J. G. de Roulhac Hamilton, ed., *The Papers of Thomas Ruffin*, 4 vols. (Raleigh, 1920), 4:196.

32. "A Visit to a Former Slave-House," *Freedman's Journal*, 1 (October, 1865): 38.

33. *Equal Suffrage: Address from the Colored Citizens of Norfolk, Va., to the People of the United States* (New Bedford, MA, 1865), 2–7; anon., *Why the Colored People in Philadelphia Are Excluded from the Street Cars* (Philadelphia, 1866), 23; I. H. Putnam, *The Review of the Revolutionary Elements of the Rebellion, and of the Reconstruction* (Brooklyn, 1868), 8.

34. Williams in J. L. Tucker, *The Relations of the Church to the Colored Race* (Jackson, MS, 1882), 30; Langston, "Citizenship and the Ballot," *Freedom and Citizenship* (Washington, 1883), 99.

35. Claude F. Oubre, *Forty Acres and a Mule: The Freedmen's Bureau and Land Ownership* (Baton Rouge, 1978), 53.

36. Randall M. Miller, ed., "Freedom Time, 1865: An Ex-Slave Writes Home," *Negro History Bulletin*, 38 (April/May, 1975): 382.

37. "An Appeal from the Richmond Negroes for Protection," New York *Daily Tribune*, June 7, 1865; "The Richmond Negro Delegation in Washington," Richmond *Republic*, June 17, 1865.

38. John W. Turner testimony, January 23, 1866, Richard R. Hill testimony, March 3, 1866, in *Report of the Joint Committee on Reconstruction*, part 2, pp. 5, 56; Jackson in Henry L. Swint, ed., *Dear Ones at Home: Letters from Contraband Camps* (Nashville, 1966), 252. This is a literal transcription of Jackson's letter.

39. Ira Berlin, Joseph P. Reidy, Leslie S. Rowland, eds., *Freedom: A Documentary History of Emancipation, 1861–1867: Series II* (Cambridge, 1982), 739–740, 750, 725, 754–755, 756, 780–781. I have retained the literal transcription of these documents followed by the editors.

40. William C. Gannett to ?, June 9, 1865, in Elizabeth W. Pearson, ed., *Letters from Port Royal, 1862–1868* (Boston, 1906), 309; Phillips, "The South Victorious," *National Anti-Slavery Standard*, 26 (October 28, 1865): 2; Charles Stearns, *The Black Man of the South, and the Rebels; or, The Characteristics of the Former, and the Recent Outrages of the Latter* (New York, 1872), 112–118; Hoar, *Political Condition of the South* (Washington, [1876]), 12–13. See also "The Freedmen," *Methodist Quarterly Review*, 4th ser., 29 (July, 1877): 462–463, 481.

41. Tourgée, *An Appeal to Caesar*, quoted in Otto H. Olsen, *Carpetbagger's Crusade: The Life of Albion Winegar Tourgée* (Baltimore, 1965), 30, and see 214–226; Tourgée, "The South as a Field for Fiction," *Forum*,6 (December, 1888): 404; idem, "Shall We Re-Barbarize the Negro?" *Congregationalist and Boston Recorder*, 74 (December 5, 1889): 1; idem, "Our Semi-Citizens," *Frank Leslie's Illustrated Newspaper*, 69 (September 28, 1889): 122. For criticisms of slavery in Tourgée's fiction, see *A Fool's Errand: A Novel of the South during Reconstruction* (New York, 1879), 86–87, 91, 96, 140; idem, *Bricks without Straw* (New York, 1880), 27, 46, 89.

42. Cable, "The Convict Lease System in the Southern States," *Century Magazine*, 27 (February, 1884): 582–599; idem, *The Silent South* (New York, 1889), 48; idem, "The Freedman's Case in Equity," *Century Magazine*, 29 (January, 1885): 414; Arlin Turner, "George W. Cable's Revolt against Literary Sectionalism," *Tulane Studies in English*, 5 (1955): 22; Cable, *The Silent South*, 106; idem, "My Politics," in Turner, ed., *The Negro Question* (Garden City, 1958), 20; "The Freedman's Case in Equity," 411, 409; idem, *The Negro Question* (New York, 1888), 26. See also Turner, *George W. Cable: A Biography* (Durham, 1956), 93–94, 195, 215, 253, 260, and Louis D. Rubin,

Jr., *George W. Cable: The Life and Times of a Southern Heretic* (New York, 1969), 81–85, 111, 119, 158, 170.

43. Hainer, *Election Laws. Southern Rule a Fraud. Negro Domination a Myth. Maintenance of Law, the Patriot's Watchword* (Washington, 1893), 6–7, 26–27; S. V. White, *Address of Hon. S. V. White, upon the Race Question in the South, Delivered at Salisbury, N.C.* (n.p., [1890]), 9; Isabel C. Barrows, ed., *Second Mohonk Conference on the Negro Question Held at Lake Mohonk, Ulster County, New York* (Boston, 1891), 8, 9, 28, 29, 117; Villard, *The Negro and the Domestic Problem* (Boston, n.d.), 4–5. For similar themes, see Moorfield Storey, *Negro Suffrage Is Not a Failure: An Address before the New England Suffrage Conference* (Boston, 1903), 5–7, 10, 11.

44. Frost quoted in McPherson, *The Abolitionist Legacy*, 185.

45. Pemberton to Du Bois, December 12, 1903, W. E. B. Du Bois Papers, University of Massachusetts, Amherst; Pemberton to Thomas H. Ruiggold, November 20, 1904, Leon Gardiner Collection, Historical Society of Pennsylvania; Foner, "Caroline Hollingsworth Pemberton: Philadelphia Socialist Champion of Black Equality," *Pennsylvania History*, 43 (July, 1976): 245–246; John David Smith, "Caroline H. Pemberton: Critic of the New Proslavery Argument," *Negro History Bulletin*, 45 (October–December, 1982): 113–114.

46. Pemberton, "The White Man's Problem: The Barbarization of Civilization," *Arena*, 23 (January, 1900): 5–6, 7, 14.

47. Warner, "The Education of the Negro," *Journal of Social Science*, 38 (December, 1900): 7–8; Pemberton, "The Negro in Slavery and Now," Springfield *Republican*, May 15, 1900. Sections of Pemberton's letter also appeared in *Literary Digest*, 11 (May 26, 1900): 630.

48. Pemberton, "The Negro in Slavery and Now."

49. Schurz, *Can the South Solve the Negro Problem?* (n.p., [1903]), [15, 13, 12, 14].

50. McPherson, *The Abolitionist Legacy*, 66.

# The Formative Period of American Slave Historiography

# PART TWO

## The Formative Period of American Slave Historiography

# 4

# The Nationalist Historians and the Continuance of the Abolitionist Tradition

As the first three chapters have argued, during the post–Civil War decades black slavery remained a salient metaphor for the ways in which white Americans, especially southerners, viewed race relations. Whites could not free themselves from viewing blacks as slavelike figures. They longed for the better days "before the war" when the inferior, subordinate status of the black man was codified both de jure and de facto. Black slavery cropped up repeatedly as a comparative model in late nineteenth-century discussions of southern black labor and racial control. It ran like a leitmotif through postbellum conversations on the "Negro problem." Planters and politicians, reformers and racists, focused on slavery. To be sure, few whites, even the most rabid Negrophobes, imagined that reenslavement was feasible. Yet slavery served as a constant, a touchstone for white southerners as they pondered such solutions to the race question as colonization or mass deportation.[1]

Though emancipation had ended slavery as a legal entity once and for all, slavery as an idea lingered in American racial thought from Appomattox to Versailles. In the 1890s white southerners put theory into practice, reestablishing hegemony over blacks in their region by legal, political, and terrorist means. The Jim Crow legislation of these years provided whites with what Alan F. Westin described as "a paler substitute for the chattel ownership" denied them by the Thirteenth Amendment. Outraged by the new forms of racial oppression under which blacks lived and labored, Supreme Court Justice John Marshall

Harlan in 1896 condemned segregation as itself a form of quasi-slavery. A decade later he argued that proscriptions on black laborers reinstituted "the badges and incidents of slavery."[2] Slavery as a metaphor represented more than a romantic look backward for southern apologists, or a pole from which northern critics could wave the bloody shirt. Antebellum slavery symbolized a tried and true mode of racial control. The assertiveness of postwar blacks—their unflagging demands for land, schools, the ballot, participation in politics, equal treatment—convinced white conservatives of the necessity of keeping their former bondsmen in their place. Many white southerners remained convinced that some variant of the old institution held the key to racial order in the New South.

# I

It was within this context that slavery assumed another important role in American thought in these years. In the late nineteenth century slavery gradually emerged as a leading topic of historical inquiry. Few topics received as much attention from professional as well as amateur historians. Writing in 1880, an anonymous reviewer in the *Nation* observed that now "Slavery takes its turn with other fossil remains in adorning our cabinets of curiosity and of science, and in being studied under the microscope." The avalanche of scholarship on slavery caused another reviewer in 1901 to remark how "unusually fertile" had been the last decade of the century in works about slavery. Ten years later, so much had been written on the subject that William T. Laprade, America's first student of slave historiography, marveled at the preoccupation among historians with the topic. "Of making many books on American slavery there does not seem to be any prospect of an end in the immediate future," he explained. Laprade went on to note, however, that in spite of "the perennial interest which seems to attach to the subject . . . some of the most fundamental questions with regard to slavery in America still await authoritative answers."[3]

Who were these pioneer students of the peculiar institution? And why did they choose to study slavery? The earliest historians to examine slavery belonged to what Stanley M. Elkins has termed the Nationalist school of historians of slavery. This group of historians, composed of both amateurs and German-trained Ph.D.'s, first appeared in 1876 with the publication of Hermann Eduard von Holst's *Constitutional and Po-*

*litical History of the United States.* In subsequent years the histories of Holst, James Schouler, John Bach McMaster, James Ford Rhodes, and Albert Bushnell Hart contributed important neoabolitionist interpretations of slavery. Among American historians, Rhodes became recognized as the first real authority on slavery. Consequently his background and his contribution on the peculiar institution deserve the most detailed assessment. Though professing objectivity and scholarly rigor, Rhodes and these other historians actually disseminated a partisan, antislavery point of view—one designed to challenge the proslavery opinions so prevalent in American thought from Reconstruction through World War I. Starkly critical of slavery, the Nationalist historians contradicted the new proslavery ideology point by point. But in spite of their neoabolitionism, the Nationalist historians shared little of the commitment to black rights of such antislavery polemicists as Carl Schurz, Caroline H. Pemberton, or W. E. B. Du Bois. They brought virtually no sense of immediacy or of social concern to the task of untangling the history of slavery. They seemed immune, indeed insensitive, to the pernicious racism that resulted from two centuries of black slavery in America. And their writings contributed, albeit unwittingly, to the racist caricature of blacks that became the norm among almost all whites in the Age of Jim Crow.[4]

White racism in fact played a crucial role in the shift from viewing slavery as a contemporary, partisan concern to a historical issue. By 1900, explained Paul H. Buck, a national consensus on the "Negro problem" had emerged. Antiblack sentiment smoothed the national road to reunion between North and South. Dominant forces in both sections agreed that white southerners should be free to construct their own racial superstructure—an edifice built upon the foundation of white supremacy. According to Buck:

The unchanging elements of the race problem had become apparent to most observers and the old impatient yearning for an immediate and thorough solution had passed away. Once a people admits the fact that a major problem is basically insoluble they have taken the first step in learning to live with it. The conflicting elements of the race problem had dropped into a working adjustment which was accepted and rationalized as a settlement. Imperfect as it was, it permitted a degree of peace between North and South hitherto unknown, [and] gave to the South the stability of race relations necessary to reconcile her to the reunited nation.

With a modus operandi for contemporary racial matters thus established, the Nationalist historians were all the more encouraged to study past racial questions with a spirit of fairness and candor. But resembling many white critics of slavery before them, they too combined open censure of the peculiar institution with virtually no sense of the day-to-day degradation of slave life.[5]

Slavery surfaced as such a popular subject of inquiry in part because of the forces of nationalism and scientism then current in western Europe and the United States. Americans around the turn of the century found bitter sectional antagonism increasingly unattractive. They prided themselves on turning their backs on past hostilities and welcoming a national consensus based on shared economic and racial attitudes. American imperialism, itself the result of a belief in the cultural and racial supremacy of white people, added yet another nationalizing force. In speeches delivered early in the new century, two white southerners placed slavery within the nationalist context of their day. Addressing a meeting of southern educators in 1904, Bishop Charles B. Galloway of the Methodist Episcopal Church, South, declared:

It is time for us to cease discussing who is most responsible for American slavery. Present duty has been neglected in an acrimonious wrangle of history. For, after all, the only difference between the South and the North on the slavery question is the difference between father and grandfather. My father was connected with slavery, and so was their grandfather.

New South publicist Henry W. Grady made much the same point. Speaking before a Boston audience in 1889, Grady explained: "The slave-ships of the Republic sailed from your ports—the slaves worked in our fields. You will not defend the traffic, nor I the institution." And three years earlier, when delivering his famous "The New South" speech before New York's New England Club, the Atlanta journalist reminded his northern audience "that the chattel in human flesh ended forever in New England when your fathers—not to be blamed for parting with what didn't pay—sold their slaves to our fathers—not to be praised for knowing a paying thing when they saw it."[6]

The Nationalist historians tended to mouth these ideas. Caught up in the spirit of sectional reconciliation that reached its apogee during the Spanish-American War, they viewed slavery as reprehensible, but as a national and not a sectional tragedy. These historians deemphasized blame and interpreted the peculiar institution as *the* cause of a national problem, the bloody Brothers' War. In their opinion, a thorough, dispassionate understanding of slavery would not only heal old wounds but foster American patriotism, itself a vital nationalizing force.

As Elkins has explained, times were ripe in the late Victorian period for the systematic examination of the peculiar institution. By the last quarter of the nineteenth century it had become "possible for the idea of 'American' history to operate on men's minds as something more than an abstraction, as something comparable to the former concreteness of 'North' and 'South.' "[7] Put another way, by the late nineteenth century, American scholars believed that they could distance themselves from the old sectional debate over slavery and the Civil War. That conflict had launched postbellum America into an industrial revolution of untold proportions. The "new" immigration of these years transformed America's booming urban centers into heterogeneous ethnic communities. Management and control of "inferior" people, both at home and abroad, posed new problems for American politicians. White southerners were already well on their way to establishing a repressive apartheid system in their region, where rigid segregation would serve as the mode of racial control. Certainly there were contemporary lessons to be learned from the history of slavery. Historians reasoned that enough time had lapsed for Americans to step back and assess the peculiar institution coolly, calmly, scientifically.

The Nationalist historians, as well as other scholars of their day, examined slavery during a period when science had triumphed in American thought. "To be 'scientific' was the great desideratum," explains W. Stull Holt. "The very word was a fetish." Actually, Europeans began espousing the "objective" approach to the past as early as the middle of the nineteenth century in a realistic protest against the romanticism of amateur historians. The "scientific" view also grew out of the reverence Victorians held for Charles Darwin's dramatic findings in the natural sciences. Historians of these years became obsessed with the idea of applying the "scientific" method to their craft. They amassed "facts" with an eye toward enunciating historical "laws." Writing, for example, in 1910, Albert Bushnell Hart explained that historians should draw upon

the fortunate analogy of the physical sciences: did not Darwin spend twenty years in accumulating data, and in selecting typical phenomena, before he so much ventured a generalization? . . . In history, too, scattered and apparently unrelated data fall together in harmonious wholes; the mind is led to the discovery of laws; and the explorer into scientific truth is at last able to formulate some of those unsuspected generalizations which explain the whole framework of the universe. That is the way in which Darwin came upon his universally guiding principle of natural selection; is it not the way in which historians must work?

"To be scientific," wrote historian Carl L. Becker of the University of Kansas, "was to assume, in respect to historical events, the objective and detached attitude of mind with which the scientist regarded natural phenomena." Whereas students of history had up to this time sat in judgment of men and measures, "scientific" historians emphasized the evolution of institutions such as slavery.[8]

The Nationalist historians of slavery devoted themselves to the "scientific" method. In their opinion this approach would equip them with the objectivity, the impartiality, necessary to grapple with as volatile a historical question as black slavery. Armed with the detachment of the natural scientist, they would escape the pitfalls of previous writers—proslavery and antislavery polemicists as well as historians—who always seemed to link slavery to sectional chauvinism. Most earlier historians of the United States had been Brahmins, New England amateur scholars, lawyers, clergymen, or businessmen. These "romantic" historians viewed the past as a literary art form. They used history to foster American nationalism and to teach broad moral lessons. Slavery, not surprisingly, clashed with their understanding of progress and morality. They criticized it soundly but, characteristic of their age, found few positive qualities in blacks. Predominantly northerners, historians such as Richard Hildreth and George Bancroft tended to avoid writing about the slaves as human beings. They focused instead—and in a rather abstract fashion—on the horrors of enslavement. According to George H. Callcott, early American historians approached slavery more "as publicists rather than historians on the issue, few scholars or textbook authors could refrain from at least a veiled attack on the institution." In 1849, for example, Hildreth described Virginia's first slaves as an "objectionable species of population," whose importation contributed "enduring and disastrous effects upon . . . the United States." A decade later, Bancroft criticized America's "anomaly of negro slavery in the midst of liberty."[9]

The New England patricians lacked both professional training in history and virtually any sense of perspective regarding the peculiar institution. Consequently their comments regarding slavery illumine little of its history. Fortunately, graduate education modeled after that offered in German universities became one of the identifying characteristics of the new "scientific" history in America. In 1876 Professor Herbert Baxter Adams, himself schooled in Germany, began teaching graduate students in his historical "seminary" at The Johns Hopkins University in Baltimore. Among the Nationalist historians, though, only Holst and Hart possessed the requisite training, the earned doctorate in history, that marked them as "scientific" historians. Nonetheless, each of the Nationalist historians subscribed to the creed of the "scientific" historian. "They schooled themselves," explains Bert James Loewenberg, "to look at both sides, discarded pejorative symbols, and gave up the simplistic theories of causation."[10] Enamored of the German historical method, these scholars sought detachment and "objectivity" by immersing themselves in original sources. They were committed to positivism and viewed the past through the lens of institutional development—as an evolving, organic whole. Slavery, a complex legal institution that had developed for over two centuries in America, posed an ideal challenge for these "scientific" historians. They sought to dissect it, test its suppositions, and analyze its impact on the lives of white Americans. Generally unconcerned with blacks as people possessing human needs and sensibilities, these scholars all but ignored the human dimension of the peculiar institution. Their disregard for the impact of slavery on blacks reinforced these historians' vision of slavery as essentially a legal institution. Their favorite source materials—legal codes, antebellum statutes, and antislavery travel accounts—added to this one-dimensional view of slavery. Shunning polemics in favor of accumulating "facts," the Nationalist historians became America's first serious students of black slavery. Their writings on slavery underscore the persistence of antislavery thought in these years. They also reveal the serious limitations of "scientific" methodology when applied to a subject as charged with emotion and passion as slavery.

## II

Holst, for example, failed to restrain himself in what amounted to a total repudiation of slavery. He ripped into slavery with the subtle force of a tornado. Writing American history from the vantage point of the "scientific" European researcher, he dominated American historical scholarship on slavery in the 1870s and 1880s. A native of Russia, Holst later became a German resident, and his love for German liberalism matched his hatred of Russian absolutism. His clashes with czarist despotism left permanent scars. Trained in German historical method by Heinrich von Sybel at the University of Heidelberg, Holst completed his dissertation in 1865 on the subject of Louis XVI and absolutism. Soon afterward Holst devoted his energies to the study of American history and became Europe's most renowned specialist on the subject. Through years of studying America's past he came to champion democracy in the United States with the zeal of the convert. Dogmatic, insistent, and fiercely moralistic, Holst identified slavery as the logical antithesis of democracy. He condemned it repeatedly and unmercifully, refusing to disassociate slavery as a historical force from slavery as an ethical force. So consumed was Holst with the peculiar institution that, according to Bert James Loewenberg, it became for him "the standard of judgment of forces, of events, and of men. The moral principles violated by slavery were transcendental principles." In Holst's opinion, slavery represented "the purely moral element in the irrepressible conflict." A critic once grouped Holst's views of slavery with those of the "narrowminded, fanatical, New England Abolitionists." When assessing slavery in his multivolume history or in other writings, Holst cast aside those qualities of "scientific" and "objective" history so dear to the German scholar.[11]

Holst saw slavery as a genuinely "peculiar" institution—"a curse and . . . a frightful blot upon the civilization of the nineteenth century." His disdain for slavery as *the* force opposing American democracy pervades Holst's seven-volume *Constitutional and Political History*. The German historian focused not on the institutional but on the political aspects of slavery. Throughout the volumes Holst lectured to his readers about the evils and aggressive policies of the slave barons who corrupted antebellum American politics in their selfish efforts to preserve slavery. In his opinion, slavery suppressed the development of small farms, demoralized white laborers, and dissuaded immigrants from entering the region. It forced upon the South an aristocratic-landed ethos—one that discouraged manufacturing. According to Holst, slavery also created a society closed to ideas that were hostile to the institution. Establishing a pattern that would become identifiable with the work of the

Nationalist historians, Holst paid little attention to the slaves themselves. Referring to the bondsmen almost as abstractions—"adult children who lived only for the moment"—he viewed the blacks as passive actors in the plantation tragedy. They suffered, Holst said, because white southerners held absolute hegemony over them. Writing, for example, about the conditions of slave life, he explained: "Food, clothing, shelter, the kind and amount of labor,—these depended solely on the will of the masters. Although as a rule, interest demanded the longest preservation of the living capital . . . in both big and little things, less care would be shown for the slaves than the free workmen of the north showed for themselves." In Holst's opinion, slavery lay at the root of everything that was bad in the Old South.[12]

Schouler and McMaster shared Holst's disdain for slavery, but their multivolume histories softened the tone of his antislavery nationalism. Schouler, a Civil War veteran and lawyer-turned-historian, descended from New England abolitionist stock. His father had helped to establish the Republican Party in Massachusetts in the 1850s. After graduating from Harvard, Schouler developed a lucrative law practice, published legal texts, and lectured at Boston and Johns Hopkins universities on constitutional history. This subject became the emphasis of his seven-volume *History of the United States of America under the Constitution*. In volumes 1 and 2, published in 1880 and 1882, respectively, Schouler concurred essentially with Holst: slavery stained every inch of the fabric of American civilization. But unlike Holst, Schouler sympathized with the white southerners. American slavery, he wrote, differed from previous forms of bondage—it existed "purely as a race institution." The South's slaves were neither debtors nor defeated enemies, rather "an alien, uncouth-looking people, whom the Caucasian could hardly regard without mirth and contempt." Schouler agreed that the peculiar institution was wasteful and unprofitable. But, he insisted, manumission seemed totally incomprehensible to a people "whose capital was employed in raising crops to which negro labor appeared indispensable."[13]

Schouler emphasized slavery's ill effects on the morals of the blacks. In doing so, he exhibited his own racial bias and utter disregard for black family and community life. In his opinion, masters were waited upon by "handsome mulatto girls" clad in loose dresses, "girt round the waist too carelessly to conceal other than temptingly those charms which modesty should have hidden." Schouler described slave marriage as "a sort of concubinage at will." He charged that the bondsmen were encouraged to breed offspring much as were plantation cattle. "Loose sexual contact" between the two races, wrote Schouler, resulted from what he described as a totally immoral environment. Only the inherent qualities of the black man, he said, his "innate patience, docility," and almost "canine" attachment to his master made enslavement tolerable. Outraged by the cruelties endemic to slavery, Schouler remarked that slave treatment was "at least lenient enough to make a dog's life happy."[14]

McMaster, a civil engineer by training, pioneered social history as genre and taught history for many years at the University of Pennsylvania's Wharton School of Finance and Commerce. Historians generally credit him with infusing life into the dry-as-dust "scientific" history of the period by drawing upon newspapers as sources. In 1883 McMaster published the first volume of *A History of the People of the United States from the Revolution to the Civil War*. Adhering closely to the antislavery views of Holst and Schouler, McMaster damned the "pitiable" conditions of slavery and the "brutal" slave codes under which the bondsmen lived and labored. Slaveholders worked to keep their bondsmen "as ignorant, as superstitious, as devoted worshippers of sticks and stones, as their most remote ancestors." Because the average field hand "was but an instrument of production," masters pared down their maintenance costs by feeding and clothing the blacks at subsistence levels. "Nowhere was the yoke of slavery easy," McMaster declared. Perhaps his most original contribution was McMaster's statement, based on antebellum newspaper accounts, that a large proportion of bondsmen reared in the border states died before being acclimated in the lower South. In the tradition of the old abolitionists, he criticized slave breeding and the separation of families by sale. Yet in spite of such criticism, McMaster was among the first scholars to acknowledge that masters frequently provided their slaves with poultry and allowed them to cultivate garden truck patches. Eggs and vegetables, he suggested, supplemented the slaves' bland diet of corn and pork. While much of his evidence pertaining to slavery was gleaned from antebellum newspapers, McMaster in fact never examined the newspaper files. Virtually all of the newspapers he cited appeared in a secondary source published in 1839 by the American Anti-Slavery Society. According to Stanley M. Elkins, McMaster's writings on slavery depended so heavily on the work of James Ford Rhodes that "his treatment is an actual plagiarization of Rhodes's."[15]

## III

Other scholars also incurred heavy debts to Rhodes's path-breaking analysis of slavery. Paradoxically, Rhodes emerged as one of the outstanding historians of slavery during the era of professional and "scientific" history, even though the Cleveland ironmaster turned Boston historian qualified neither as a professional historian nor as a "scientific" scholar. With virtually no academic training as a historian, but equipped with ample time and finances to support his research, Rhodes included an eighty-page chapter on slavery in volume 1 of his *History of the United States from the Compromise of 1850*, published in 1892. In this chapter, Rhodes presented what in his day became the most influential Nationalist interpretation of slavery as an institution in the Old South.[16]

The son of an Ohio Copperhead, Rhodes never earned a college degree because he was obliged to manage the iron and coal business he had inherited from his father. Rhodes worked until 1884 to amass a fortune substantial enough to allow him to retire and become a "historian without portfolio." On one occasion Rhodes explained to the Harvard History Club his unusual preparation for the work of a historian:

I was immersed in business between the ages of twenty-two and thirty-seven. After three years of general and special preparation I began my writing at forty. The businessman has free evenings and many journeys by rail, as well as summer vacation, when devotion to a line of study may constitute a valuable recreation. Much may be done in odd hours in the way of preparation for historical work, and a business life is an excellent school for the study of human character.

Shortly after his retirement, Rhodes began to study the last decade before the Civil War, which later served as the subject of his first two volumes. According to Rhodes, that period was "about the most interesting epoch" in American history. He recognized that "if one does not make an account of it interesting the fault is in the writer and not in the events." He began writing the volumes in 1888 with the assistance of Henry and Edward Bourne, two brothers who taught at Western Reserve University. Edward held a Ph.D. in history. A spirit of collective work pervaded Rhodes's instructions to the Bournes. In one instance, Rhodes cited an 1856 quotation from a Tennessee newspaper; it described how the fear of a slave insurrection had caused the rapid sale of bondsmen out of the state. Rhodes desired material on this panic, wondering if it had spread to other states. "Do you find much of anything in this?" Rhodes asked. "And if you have the material, construct a graphic account." The historian later recalled how Edward was "especially attracted" to and provided careful revision of the important chapter on slavery in the first volume.[17]

Rhodes completed the first two volumes of the *History* in 1891 and later that year moved from Cleveland to Cambridge. He sought acceptance to Boston society and to the research facilities of Harvard's library and the Boston Athenaeum. Rhodes quickly gained entree into the inner circles of both the Boston gentry and the historical profession. The favorable response to the publication of his volumes skyrocketed the coal and iron magnate into the ranks of America's premier historians. In 1898, for instance, Rhodes was elected president of the American Historical Association. His *History* garnered Rhodes other accolades as well, including the Pulitzer Prize in 1918 and ten honorary degrees. Rhodes's Nationalist interpretation of slavery and the Middle Period won him friends in the North and the South. Despite a reaction against his later volumes, Rhodes's reputation as a trusted historian remained essentially intact into the 1930s.[18]

Several factors influenced the way Rhodes viewed history in general and the subject of slavery in particular. In many ways he represents the literary tradition of the gentleman historian. Affluence enabled Rhodes to study history as well as hire research assistants and acquire an extensive personal library. Rhodes esteemed his membership in the productive wealthy class—unlike other men, he said, who gave "themselves up to a life of calculated luxury and unbridled sensuality." But Rhodes smacked of elitism: he found capitalists "a lot sight better than the proletariat." His move to Boston in 1891 indicated an attempt to join a people "whose good manners and cultivation give them a distinction rarely seen elsewhere." Rhodes revealed his mugwumpery in opposing a variety of causes and groups of the times: soft money, tariff protection, "the Bryan crowd," annexation of the Philippines, organized labor, socialists, and even the Boers. He favored civil service reform. Politically, Rhodes supported Grover Cleveland, William McKinley, and Theodore Roosevelt because he believed they would best serve the "cultivated" class.[19]

Rhodes the patrician-historian lived an epicurean life. When not researching or writing, he vacationed at Bar Harbor, Maine, enjoying novels and the sea, or he traveled abroad. In Hamburg, Germany, Rhodes found "the cuisine . . . delicate, the attendance excellent, [and] the wines ausgezeichnet." In 1910 he invited Frederick Jackson Turner to be his guest at Boston's prestigious Wednesday Evening Club. "The men come together at half past nine," explained Rhodes, "supper is served at ten and there is talkee-talkee until midnight." On the eve of World War I, Rhodes enjoyed himself in France. "We ate, drank, and were merry," he informed Thomas S. Perry, "but no champagne—white burgundy for luncheon, red bordeaux for dinner and I must confess . . . 1811 brandy after our coffee." His close personal rapport with such influential Americans as Secretary of State John Hay, Justin Winsor of Harvard, and Presidents McKinley and Roosevelt had a strong impact on Rhodes's historical work. These men provided him with insights that enabled Rhodes to write the history of America since 1850 "as a partial contemporary." They also reaffirmed his perception of the past through the lens of the white, elite capitalist class.[20]

Rhodes overcame his lack of professional historical training by hard work and determination. Few college professors read as widely as he did, and he modeled himself after Holst and the other "scientific" historians. Throughout his famous chapter on slavery, Rhodes mentioned his search for the "true" picture of the peculiar institution. He warned against writers who marshal evidence simply to support a preconceived thesis. Attempting to be "scientific," Rhodes repeatedly mentioned his concern with being impartial and fair. When discussing miscegenation, for example, he denied being a "moralist." His concern, Rhodes explained, was "simply with the facts." Regardless of his illusions of objectivity and impartiality, Rhodes's moralistic, antislavery tone resembled more the rhetoric of the Garrisonian Abolitionists than it did the "scientific" monographs produced at Johns Hopkins University under Herbert Baxter Adams. Many of Rhodes's judgments were quickly challenged by the more analytical scholars then emerging from the graduate history departments.[21]

One such historian, Frederic Bancroft, who earned his Ph.D. at Columbia University in 1885, assessed Rhodes's background and personality accurately. Bancroft, both Rhodes's friend and sharp critic, concluded that Rhodes's career as a businessman explained his strengths and weaknesses as a historian.

The business quality of his mind is one of the most remarkable phenomenon that I know of in historical writing. Genius, and imagination, and even a fair literary style, are wholly lacking; yet his seriousness, his command of facts, his labored researches for parallels and ancient incidents, and a certain gravity, not to say pompousness, in his language, impress nine readers out of ten so favorably that they do not realize that any of the requirements are lacking.

Bancroft added that, because Rhodes's mind was so "sluggish" and "materialistic," he naturally avoided abstract problems. After studying Rhodes's life and thought, Robert Cruden agreed. In his opinion, Rhodes possessed a "pedestrian . . . mind which shied away from analysis and especially from contending with intangibles."[22]

But none of Rhodes's characteristics more strongly influenced his writing on slavery than his racial views. He accepted without challenge his generation's prevailing belief in white supremacy. Blacks, he wrote authoritatively, formed "one of the most inferior races of mankind." Confident in the affirmations of Anglo-Saxon superiority espoused by Charles Darwin and Louis Agassiz, Rhodes believed that most blacks remained barbarians, and he steadfastly opposed conferring social equality upon them. Rhodes, in fact, found little in blacks, slave or free, that appealed to him. Female slaves, he said, lacked "chaste sentiment" and were "yielding without objection, except in isolated cases, to the passion of their masters." When describing slave laborers at work, Rhodes employed pejorative terms that were more racist than antislavery in origin. He noted, "The besotted and generally repulsive expression of the field hands; their brute-like countenances, on which were painted stupidity, indolence, duplicity, and sensuality; their listlessness; their dogged action; the stupid, plodding, machine-like manner in which they labored, made a sorrowful picture of man's inhumanity to man." On different occasions, Rhodes referred to the newly emancipated slaves as "a mass of childishness." He condemned the architects of Radical Reconstruction because they "showed no appreciation of the great fact of race" and succumbed to "trying to make negroes intelligent by legislative acts." And his view of contemporary race relations reinforced Rhodes's interpretation of the past. "If the negroes stop committing rape on white women," wrote Rhodes in 1905, lynchings would soon cease and the "Negro problem" be partially solved. According to the historian, American democracy could be developed into the best type of government only under the direction of "the Teutonic race." He found "our task . . . made difficult enough by Cuffee."[23]

Rhodes never questioned that blacks were inferior to whites. After meeting with Roosevelt in 1905, he wrote of how the president had remarked that the blacks were "200,000 years behind" the whites. Rhodes retorted that Roosevelt's figure was too low. "I suggested a million," explained Rhodes, "an amendment which he accepted." Although he had only limited exposure to black people, Rhodes's attitude toward Booker T. Washington and his relationship with George A. Myers reveal much about his racism. Washington "and men of his kind" appealed to Rhodes because they were "the only ones who can save the negro from being forced to the wall in competition with the whites." Myers's ties to Rhodes went back to Cleveland, where Myers served as the historian's barber at the Hollenden Hotel. Myers continued to correspond with Rhodes after the historian's move to Massachusetts. Indicative of the paternalistic relationship between them was Rhodes's lifelong custom of sending Myers his discarded neckties. On several occasions Myers urged Rhodes both to include more material on blacks in his *History* and to soften his condemnation of alleged black corruption during Reconstruction. In 1917–1918 Myers unsuccessfully encouraged Rhodes to revise his volumes in light of criticisms leveled in the *Journal of Negro History* by the Mississippi black politician John R. Lynch. Myers informed Rhodes that Rhodes would never appreciate the blacks' perspective "because you have never been discriminated against." But the historian cared little about the woes of blacks. In 1920 Rhodes remarked casually that he would gladly exchange black enfranchisement for the repeal of prohibition.[24]

As much a part of Rhodes's writing as his racial views was his nationalistic interpretation of slavery and the coming of the Civil War. He prided himself on de-emphasizing southern blame and acquired a reputation for his "sense of fairness." Though he soundly condemned slavery as a moral wrong, Rhodes viewed the peculiar institution as a national rather than a sectional sin. It resulted, he said, as much from the greed of New England shippers who carried the blacks from Africa as from that of southern planters who purchased them. Again and again in Rhodes's volumes he celebrated "our common human nature North and South." He looked upon sectional harmony with a sense of mission, considering "no work    holier than one directed to bringing together the South and the North." Historian William E. Dodd singled out Rhodes's volumes for contributing to the turn–of–the–century sectional rapprochement. Thanks to Rhodes, an intellectual climate existed in which "the differences of 1861–65" no longer aroused passions or

symbolized the "red rags" of partisanship. So influential was Rhodes's
*History* that Henry Steele Commager asserted that it set northerners on
the "road to reunion with the South."[25]

## IV

The overriding theme of Rhodes's first five volumes was the struggle
for nationality between two distinct civilizations, the North and the
South, over slavery. In Rhodes's opinion, slavery was the most significant cause of the division of an otherwise united population into
hostile sectional camps. Rhodes's first volume focused on the peculiar
institution, and unmistakably from the antislavery perspective. Rhodes
assessed many aspects of slavery, including the Atlantic slave trade,
the origins of slavery in colonial America, slavery in the North, plantation crops, and the cotton gin. Early in the narrative he summarized
his major assumption: that by 1850 slavery had captured the attention
of the entire country. The topic was debated "in the city mart, the
village store, and the artisan's workshop." Rhodes set the volume's
tone with the remarkably "unscientific" declaration that "the historian
whose sympathies are with the anti-slavery cause . . . can most truly
write the story" of slavery. Recognizing his limitations, Rhodes admitted that it was "quite easy for one of Northern birth . . . to extenuate
nothing; more care must be taken to set naught in malice." In chapter
4, devoted entirely to the peculiar institution, Rhodes interpreted slavery
as a complex force—one that left an indelible mark on southerners black
and white.[26]

Rhodes's famous chapter emphasized the cruel treatment and poor
care slaves received from their masters. Legally the bondsmen were
chattels—transferable like horses or cattle—and subject to the whims
of their masters. White southerners treated the slaves as property, not
people. For most slaveholders, Rhodes insisted, the bondsmen meant
little more than a profit or loss in a ledger book. True, house servants,
"naturally brighter" than their comrades who labored in the fields, were
awarded superior food, clothing, and training. And Rhodes believed
that the blacks' "imitative faculty" served as a sort of education in
itself. But he reminded his readers that the idealized picture of happy
house servants waiting eagerly for the return of their masters clashed
with reality. More typical, he said, was the harsh and often brutal
existence endured by most bondsmen. Relying heavily on antebellum

travel accounts, Rhodes cited cases in which slaves were overworked to the point of injury or death. During picking season in cotton country or grinding time in sugar districts, slaves frequently toiled longer than the sixteen hours per day set as a limit by southern slave codes. Rhodes described the slaves as being treated much like animals, and he quoted Harriet Martineau as an expert witness. She had found "a walk through a lunatic asylum . . . far less painful than a visit to the slave quarters."[27]

Slaveholders, Rhodes explained, whipped their bondsmen because they considered them mere children in need of discipline. While he concluded that corporal punishments were common during slavery, Rhodes admitted that "wanton cruelty did not rule." The worst excesses in the system resulted, he said, from the "unrestrained power" available to whites in the master-slave relationship. Much like the abolitionists before him, Rhodes damned overseers as those responsible for the most treacherous outrages meted out to the slaves. According to Rhodes: "They were generally ignorant, frequently intemperate, always despotic and brutal. Their value was rated according to the bigness of the cotton crop they made, and, with that end in view, they spared not the slave. The slave always worked under the lash." Rhodes also perpetuated the abolitionist view of the black driver as "a stout negro . . . whose qualification . . . depended upon his unusual cruelty." This man followed the slaves in the field, his loud voice and whip offering them constant stimulus to work.[28]

Rhodes challenged the proslavery argument that the slaves received better food, clothing, and lodging than free laborers in the North. Drawing heavily on Frederick Law Olmsted's *The Cotton Kingdom* (1861) as his source, he asserted that even northern convicts subsisted on better rations than the slaves. Slave masters cut costs at every turn, Rhodes insisted. They sought only the cheapest food and clothing available, disregarding "decency and health." No wonder visitors to the plantations recoiled at the slaves' "ragged, unkempt, and dirty appearance." On large plantations, Rhodes explained, "economy in feeding these human cattle was studied with almost scientific precision." Again citing Olmsted's travel accounts, Rhodes averred that Louisiana planters spent an average of only thirty dollars annually per slave. Of this total, clothing accounted for one-third and food the remainder. On a meager food budget of five cents per day, masters provided the bondsmen mostly with cornmeal. Although some slaves regularly received bacon and molasses to supplement their daily rations, Rhodes charged that for most others these items constituted a luxury. He found additional support for this interpretation in J. D. B. DeBow's estimate that the food allowance for slaves on cotton plantations amounted to slightly over two cents per day. In spite of the slaves' limited diet, Rhodes ran across few instances of slaves actually going hungry. But slave housing was another matter. After carefully weighing the evidence, Rhodes concluded that slave cabins generally were "foul and wretched." He conceded, though, that the poor condition of the slave quarters stemmed as much from the blacks' "indolent and filthy habits" as from "the plantation parsimony" of the masters.[29]

For those cotton, sugar, and rice planters who watched their pennies closely, concluded Rhodes, slaves proved a profitable investment. During the colonial period, slaves produced an abundance of rice and indigo to pay for their initial cost. "They were a profitable investment," Rhodes declared, but "the temptation was to work them beyond their physical endurance." Given the great worldwide demand for cotton, he explained, during the antebellum years southwestern planters were able to reap tremendous fortunes. Intelligent plantation management— careful reinvestment in fresh land and more slaves—enabled some masters to possess as many as five hundred bondsmen and earn an annual profit of $100,000. Yet Rhodes the former industrialist criticized "the ignorant newly-rich" of Mississippi who, like the nouveaux riches of New York, handled their money poorly. Some, driven by dreams of "enlarged gains and greater social considerations," overextended their means and accumulated large debts to cotton factors. Hinting at Ulrich B. Phillips's later thesis, Rhodes argued that too often planters' "profits were laid out in more land and negroes," leaving the South's economy shy of capital and undiversified. Rhodes deemed slavery unprofitable in grain and tobacco cultivation. He asserted that agricultural production in the South since emancipation had proven that free black workers outdistanced slave laborers across the board.[30]

Slavery's repressive grip, Rhodes wrote, prevented the blacks from bettering themselves. Because state laws in the South forbade teaching slaves to read or write, few slaves emerged from thralldom with the basic skills necessary for citizenship. Rhodes suggested that masters who educated their slaves did so to "make the slave useful without making him restless." Apart from the exceptional slaves who became literate, most received some religious education. According to Rhodes, slave owners provided spiritual training in order to render their blacks more submissive to the hardships of life on earth. Of course, Rhodes remarked, religion did not mean the same thing to the black slave as to his white master, because the former failed to grasp the relationship between religion and morality. "An entire lack of chastity among the women, and an entire lack of honesty among the men," charged the historian, "did not prevent their joining the church and becoming, in the estimation of their fellow-slaves, exemplary Christians." White southerners, in Rhodes's opinion, used slave religion to reinforce their social system. Masters were careful to preach neither "honesty to men who did not own their labor, nor chastity to women who did not own their bodies."[31]

The tragedy of slavery, Rhodes emphasized, lay in the fact that the slaves held virtually no control over their own destinies. To illustrate this point, he singled out the domestic slave trade for special censure. By the 1850s, according to Rhodes's estimate, at least 25,000 bondsmen were transported annually from the border slave states to the "cruel doom" of the sugar and cotton districts of the lower South. Slave breeding became a vital source of income, an economic survival mechanism for Virginia planters. Rhodes noted that fluctuations in slave prices had a direct correlation to the price of southern staples. Apart from its economic implications, he branded slave breeding "the most wretched aspect" of a despicable institution, and condemned the slave traders who profited from the sale of human flesh. In Virginia, charged Rhodes, fertile black females were treated much as "brood mares," and masters bragged of their "breeders." Aghast at the separation of slave families by sale, Rhodes modified this element of the old abolitionist argument. Though such "separations were not infrequent," he wrote, "they were not the general rule." Rather:

There was a disposition, on the score of self-interest, to avoid tearing asunder of family ties, for the reason that if slaves pined on account of parting from those to whom they had become attached, they labored less obediently and were more troublesome. Humane masters would, whenever possible, avoid selling the husband apart from the wife, or young children away from the mother. The best public sentiment frowned upon an unnecessary separation of families.

Rhodes parted ways with the abolitionists when he questioned whether much of the sympathy for the slave family had not been misdirected after all. Perhaps, he reasoned, William Lloyd Garrison and Harriet

Beecher Stowe had "unconsciously vested the negroes with their own fine feelings, and estimated the African's grief at separation from her family by what would be their own at a like fate." Again and again Rhodes employed such condescending terms to describe the bondsmen. Slave women, he argued, naturally were inclined to lose their chastity at an early age, hoping that pregnancy would result in a lighter work load. They yielded freely to their white captors because they were proud to bear offspring of the "ruling class." In Rhodes's opinion, enslavement so thoroughly emasculated black males that the slave husband "felt little or no displeasure when the fancy of the master chanced to light upon his wife." A later generation of scholars would have to sharpen the focus of Rhodes's vision of the unstable, disjointed black family.[32]

Rhodes held slavery accountable not only for bringing out the worst characteristics in blacks but for its direful effect on whites as well. He wrote confidently that the peculiar institution kept the slave states less prosperous than their free counterparts. While Rhodes personally admired the social attributes of the plantocracy, he charged that slavery caused class conflict among white southerners. It left the mass of non-slaveholding whites in utter poverty and ignorance, and Rhodes emphasized repeatedly that these people lived on a scale worse than northern laborers did. Too often the poor whites "asserted the aristocracy of color" by lashing out against the only class beneath them—the blacks. Skin color, explained Rhodes, represented the yeoman's only claim to superiority. Fear of slave revolt, especially after Nat Turner's bloody 1831 insurrection, led white southerners to pass repressive laws aimed at protecting slavery at all costs. Whites behaved as if they lived with a constant enemy in their midst, and they transformed their region into an armed camp. Their denial of free speech, Rhodes concluded, placed a stigma of anti-intellectualism upon the South. In short, Rhodes endorsed Henry Clay's dictum that slavery was "a curse to the master and a wrong to the slave."[33]

## V

Rhodes's treatment of slavery received high marks from both the contemporary literary world and the historical profession. The *Nation* praised his chapter's honest and judicious results and complimented Rhodes on his understanding of slavery's broad institutional role in the

Old South. In *Historische Zeitschrift*, the usually critical Holst lauded Rhodes's treatment of slavery as "a very sound accomplishment . . . one of the best which the country has produced to date." The German scholar welcomed Rhodes's reconciliationist tone and predicted quite patronizingly that Rhodes would continue to "grow with his work." Other trained Ph.D.'s, Frederic Bancroft and Charles McLean Andrews, commended the thoroughness and balance of Rhodes's chapter. Andrews judged it "as interesting to read as a romance." Rhodes's analysis of slavery constituted a veritable oasis of "fairness and toleration" amid the partisan post-Civil War literature on the peculiar institution.[34]

But Rhodes's pioneer work on slavery encountered criticism, some of it severe. Holst identified numerous contradictions in Rhodes's chapter, weaknesses that he attributed to the author's lack of professional, "scientific" training in history. Holst also faulted Rhodes for failing to underscore slavery's moral dimensions. "Not that his own ethical position . . . is lukewarm," said Holst, "but he [Rhodes] underestimates the weight which the ethical factor has . . . in . . . historical development." Bancroft chided Rhodes for failing to consult southern news papers as sources and for ignoring slavery in the border states and the cities. Contrary to Holst, Bancroft argued that Rhodes unduly emphasized slavery's harshness. Several scholars—David E. Spencer, C. H. Smith, and John William Burgess—broadened this criticism. Spencer, who taught at the University of Michigan, charged that Rhodes wrote "as if but for the slavery question we should have had no history worth the writing." Burgess, a Tennessean on the faculty of Columbia University, regretted that in Rhodes's chapter "the abolitionist assumes . . . the historian's place." According to Burgess, Rhodes included only the "sensational and exceptional" and omitted the "regular and ordinary" sides of slavery. An ex-slaveholder from North Carolina, Patrick Henry Winston shared Burgess's dissatisfactions. Winston insisted that the slaves he had known in his youth, unlike the bondsmen portrayed in Rhodes's volume, were "physically comfortable and mentally happy."[35]

Professor Woodrow Wilson of Princeton University made the harshest attack on Rhodes's treatment of slavery. Referring in an unsigned review to Rhodes's volumes as "a superior sort of antislavery pamphlet," Wilson exposed Rhodes's unwarranted emphasis on and distorted picture of slavery. When writing about the South, Rhodes reportedly lacked knowledge and objectivity. He relied almost totally on rumor and speculation and, as a result, approached the region as "a foreign country, whose condition and sentiments he learns piecemeal and at intervals from travelers.'' Instead of a balanced and consistent evaluation of slavery, Rhodes first listed "the evils of slavery in black catalogue" and later "suddenly . . . and smilingly" noted its more benign features. Writing three years later, Wilson again emphasized Rhodes's unfamiliarity with the South and his overreliance on travel accounts. He lamented that when writing about the South, northern historians like Rhodes "almost always" quoted travelers, "just as I would describe Kamchatka, a place to which I did not intend to go and did not hope to go.'' Wilson objected to the method—"matching this traveler's tale with that traveler's tale"—that Rhodes employed when writing about slavery.[36]

Wilson's strictures of Rhodes actually masked the future president's own conservative, antiblack, proslavery interpretation.[37] But they correctly identified serious deficiencies in Rhodes's chapter on slavery. Rhodes perceived himself as the first northern historian to treat the slavery question fairly. He believed that he understood the South and its past, basing his confidence on trips to the region in 1868, 1869, and 1872 while investigating iron and coal deposits. Visits to North Carolina, Georgia, Tennessee, and Louisiana, he said, had brought him "in close contact with the ruling 'carpet-bagger' and the 'unreconstructed rebel.' " But, as historian William P. Trent correctly concluded, these brief excursions hardly qualified Rhodes as an authority on the South.[38] As a matter of fact, Rhodes failed to recognize the great diversity of agriculture, geography, and culture in the Old South. He conveyed the false impression that large plantations dominated the landscape and culture. Rhodes all but ignored the many small slave owners, yeoman farmers, and poor whites. He further neglected to mention the various settings in which slaves labored as well as the different ways of organizing their labor. According to Raymond C. Miller, "No one who knew the South at all and had Rhodes's earnest desire to serve truth could have written the famous slavery chapter in Volume I."[39]

Rhodes not only lacked firsthand knowledge of the South, but relied almost wholly on antebellum travel accounts as sources. He considered travel narratives valuable primary sources and cited them in much the same way later students of slavery would employ plantation records. A source analysis of his footnotes on slavery reveals that eight of the twenty sources Rhodes cited most frequently fall into this category. Harriet Martineau, Jean Jacques Ampère, Charles Mackay, Alexis de

Tocqueville, and Frederick Law Olmsted dominate the sources used. Among these, almost one-quarter of the footnotes for his chapter on slavery refer to Olmsted's volumes, with three-quarters of the citations drawn from Olmsted's *The Cotton Kingdom*, the 1861 edition of his earlier travel narratives. Olmsted wrote *The Cotton Kingdom* after the start of the Civil War, with an eye toward marshaling English public opinion against slavery and the Confederacy. Whereas in earlier writings, notably *A Journey in the Seaboard Slave States*, Olmsted had described the slaves as "better off then the starving Irish, the English poor . . . or the struggling Northern workers," in the later volume he stressed the severity of the peculiar institution and its economic and social drawbacks. Rhodes thus relied most heavily upon a highly biased version of Olmsted's observations.[40]

In most cases Rhodes's source materials reinforced his antislavery perspective. He generally ignored the inherent bias of many travel accounts—the specious evidence and limited experiences of the narrators—and failed to discriminate in his use of abolitionist pamphlets and reminiscences. Rhodes freely took material on slavery from the polemical literature, usually without noting its obvious partisan slant. And though handicapped by the scarcity of manuscripts and plantation records, Rhodes could have conducted research in antebellum southern newspapers or, like Frederic Bancroft, interviewed black and white southerners. Unlike the graduate students studying slavery in the 1880s and 1890s at Johns Hopkins, Rhodes neglected to search out diaries, state documents, and other primary sources. His lack of professional training and his patrician orientation placed Rhodes more in the tradition of the literary historians of the early nineteenth century than of the new "scientific" scholars. He remained content to use the sources in his personal library and to make a priori moral judgments on slavery. And his examination of the economics of slavery was woefully thin: he neglected to calculate on a cost basis the price of slaves, plantation expenses, and slave productivity. Such an analytical approach was beyond the methodology of Rhodes or the travelers upon whose accounts he relied.

Even so, Rhodes worked at a time when plantation records and other primary sources were only beginning to be systematically collected by libraries.[41] He overcame the paucity of sources and he revised interpretations of slavery that harkened back to the abolitionists. For example, Rhodes concluded that the abolitionists had exaggerated the frequency of both slave whippings and the division of slave families for sale. He also hinted at a diversity of attitudes among slaveholders regarding slave education and religion, thus suggesting that the nature of slavery varied throughout the South. With his midwestern industrialist background, Rhodes was a most unlikely student of slavery. Nevertheless, he became the first historian to study the various aspects of slavery as an institution. Devoting sections of his chapter to plantation management, the domestic slave trade, miscegenation, and other subjects, Rhodes outlined the topics that later scholars would investigate. According to Elkins, Rhodes's institutional approach to slavery "did much to establish the pattern for whatever would subsequently be written on the subject."[42]

## VI

Rhodes's famous chapter on slavery indeed influenced many later scholars, but perhaps none as significantly as Albert Bushnell Hart. In *Slavery and Abolition, 1831–1841* (1906), Hart built upon the institutional themes Rhodes had identified, but expanded and synthesized them into an important monograph for scholar and layman alike. Writing to Hart soon after the book's publication, Rhodes explained: "Having gone over the same ground I can see how much more thoroughly you have done it. This from your great industry." Hart's book, explained Rhodes, epitomized the Nationalist historians' approach to slavery. "I doubt whether a more severe indictment of slavery exists and its severity is heightened by your calmness and reasonableness and your power of putting yourself in the Southerner's place. It is remarkable I think for one brought up in an Ohio Abolitionist family." "Harvard and Germany and von Holst are factors of course," added Rhodes, "but your travel, residence and acquaintance at the South have made many pages more vivid than otherwise could have been."[43]

Rhodes's assessment of Hart's background and scholarship was accurate indeed. Born in Pennsylvania in 1854, Hart was reared in Ohio's Western Reserve in an environment openly hostile to slavery. His father attended the 1848 Free Soil Party convention and throughout the sectional crisis steadfastly supported the causes of Union and emancipation. After graduating from Harvard, Hart studied under Holst at the University of Freiburg, where he received his Ph.D. in 1883. A superior organizer and planner, Hart edited the first important monographic series in American historiography, *The American Nation: A History*. In 1884 he helped draft the American Historical Association's charter. While serving on the Harvard faculty from 1883 to 1926, Hart trained many historians, including W. E. B. Du Bois. He recognized as well as any scholar the difficulties confronting "a son and grandson of abolitionists" in treating slavery impartially. Yet in the best traditions of the "scientific" and Nationalist historians, Hart emphasized slavery's complexities and sought fairness in his analysis. His background for this task was strengthened, he said, by extensive trips to the South and "personal impressions gained from association with southern whites . . . [and] descendants of slaves." For years he included lectures on plantation slavery in his Harvard classes.[44]

Significantly, Hart dedicated *Slavery and Abolition* to Rhodes, claiming to have been inspired by his friend's chapter on slavery, which he described as "one of the best brief accounts" of the subject. Not surprisingly, the two men held similar views not only on slavery but on class, race, and contemporary race relations as well. Hart, for instance, shared Rhodes's belief in inherent black inferiority. He described the bondsmen as indolent, shiftless, "ignorant men"—"coarse and unattractive in appearance." According to the Harvard professor, postwar blacks had progressed little since emancipation. The race, he insisted, still lacked "self-control" and "personal morality." Like Rhodes, Hart also envisioned no long-range solution for the "Negro problem." In his opinion, slavery had left a "terribly long road to retrace." He held guarded optimism for economic progress by twentieth-century blacks who, Hart said, surpassed the average annual productivity of their slave forebears.[45]

*Slavery and Abolition* is one of the more important works on slavery written during these years. It investigated the various institutional features of slavery popularized by Rhodes, yet the monograph surpassed Rhodes's chapter in scope, detail, and interpretation. Still, in many ways Hart's analysis of slavery closely paralleled Rhodes's. Both viewed the peculiar institution as a force undermining southern prosperity and morality. By itself it had caused the disastrous Civil War. Like Rhodes, Hart also avoided evaluating the profitability of slavery on a cost basis. Instead, he simply concluded that in the long run the institution "did not pay." On the final page of *Slavery and Abolition* Hart wrote the murky statement that slavery was "a profitless method of organizing labor." His central argument, however, was that slavery hurt southern economic advancement. It proved unadaptable, he wrote, to diversified crops and restricted the South to those staple crops lending themselves to cultivation by "rude labor in large gangs." In good years, Hart speculated, cotton production was profitable. But he considered it a "moot question whether the south would not have found a greater profit in other crops." Hart's discussion of slave housing, overseers, and the domestic slave trade also followed Rhodes's. On the topics of the slave family, slave religion, and slave law, Hart essentially adopted Rhodes's point of view but expanded the discussion by adding considerable detail.[46]

Yet Hart also examined aspects of slavery not considered by Rhodes. In doing so he not only broke fresh ground but anticipated the focus of modern scholars. In an effort, for instance, to offer a balanced view of the institution, Hart presented both proslavery and antislavery opinions. "On good plantations," he wrote, "there was indeed little suffering and much enjoyment." Although he concluded that slavery was wrong and cruel, Hart recognized that generalizations about slavery were difficult because bondsmen lived under a variety of conditions. The Harvard historian also revised two traditional assumptions concerning slaves. First, in his judgment, house slaves were not the "refined or well-kept" servants portrayed in romanticized plantation accounts. Second, many slaves "showed intellectual qualities" that permitted them to become educated by illegal "secret schools" established by plantation mistresses and children. Hart further credited the slaves with creating their own subculture, especially the large corpus of black folk stories and songs. Hart's research further uncovered that slaves plied many skilled trades. They labored, he said, on river steamboats, in factories, and in mines. Some produced naval stores, while others served as blacksmiths, carpenters, and mechanics. Especially talented slaves were allowed to hire themselves out. In this "milder form of servitude," Hart concluded, the bondsman frequently was able to purchase his own freedom.[47]

Hart pioneered discussion of still other dimensions of the slave experience. For instance, he rescued the topic of slave medicine from obscure antebellum journals and described the ailments most frequently fatal to slaves. His examination of the slaves' diet, along with McMaster's, ranks among the first scholarly treatments of the subject. Hart mentioned that many bondsmen were allowed to cultivate garden truck patches and to keep bees, chickens, and pigs. Anticipating later writers who asserted that slaves sabotaged equipment on the plantation, Hart characterized slaves as neglectful and abusive to their masters' farm animals. Hart all too briefly touched on other topics—urban slavery, slave recreation, and "negro foremen"—ignored by previous students of slavery. He even discussed the different varieties of whips used to punish the bondsmen. Hart concluded that masters preferred the lash over other forms of slave punishment because, he wrote sardonically, "imprisonment was no penalty for a slave."[48]

Hart's *Slavery and Abolition* dominated general treatments of slavery until the publication of Ulrich B. Phillips's *American Negro Slavery* in 1918. Well into the 1920s it remained the most important antislavery antidote to Phillips's proslavery writings. Taken as a group, the Nationalist historians played an important role in countering the new proslavery argument that surfaced after Appomattox. But despite the value of their work, especially that of Hart and Rhodes, the Nationalist historians ultimately played at best a limited role in the development of the historiography of slavery. Their affirmations of "scientific" history notwithstanding, Holst, Schouler, and McMaster wrote more in the tradition of New England patricians Hildreth and Bancroft than of the legendary German "scientific" scholar Leopold von Ranke. Each tended to view history as a sweeping pageant, and all three wrote in moralistic terms. Unlike the students who studied slavery under Herbert Baxter Adams at Johns Hopkins, the Nationalist historians missed source materials that would have fallen within the grasp of more thorough researchers. But like the vast majority of white writers of their day, they wrote the history of slavery with little or no concern for the plight of the bondsmen themselves. Resembling the postwar neoabolitionist writers who preceded them, the Nationalist historians succumbed to writing the history of slavery with an ideological axe to grind. They belong unmistakably in the antislavery camp, having failed utterly to liberate themselves from the old sectional debate. Yet to their credit, in their famous multivolume histories the Nationalist historians popularized research on slavery and amassed a vast quantity of detailed material on the topic. Despite his elitism, racism, and methodological weaknesses, among the Nationalist group Rhodes made the most significant contributions to the historiography of slavery. He posed the essential questions, establishing the basic institutional features of slavery that would become standard fare for scores of later scholars. Still, a neoabolitionist bias remains Rhodes's and the Nationalist historians' most identifiable legacy. The strong antislavery tone of their writings affirms that the embers of slavery and sectionalism remained dimly lit, ready to be sparked anytime by a gust of wind from the past.

## NOTES

1. See, for example, E. T. Winkler, "The Negroes in the Gulf States," *International Review*, 1 (September, 1874): 581–588; Edward P. Humphrey, *The Color Question in the United States* (Washington, 1877); Charles K. Marshall, *The Exodus: Its Effect upon the South; Colored Labor Not Indispensable* (Washington, 1880); Carlyle McKinley, *An Appeal to Pharaoh: The Negro Problem and Its Radical Solution* (Columbia, 1889); Francis G. Ruffin, *White or Mongrel? A Pamphlet on the Deportation of Negroes from Virginia to Africa* (Richmond, 1890); John Temple Graves in *Race Problems in the South: Report of the Proceedings of the First Annual Conference Held under the Auspices of the Southern Society for the Promotion of the Study of Race Conditions and Problems in the South* (Richmond, 1900), 54, 56, 57, and "The Problem of the Races," in *The Possibilities of the Negro in Symposium* (Atlanta, 1904), 10, 23, 28; William P. Calhoun, *The Caucasian and the Negro in the United States: They Must Be Separate* (Columbia, 1902), 7; Paul B. Barringer to Woodrow Wilson, August 28, 1915, Paul B. Barringer Papers, University of Virginia.

2. Westin, "John Marshall Harlan and the Constitutional Rights of Negroes: The Transformation of a Southerner," *Yale Law Journal*, 66 (April, 1957): 637, 688, 699, 704.

3. Review of Joel Chandler Harris, *Uncle Remus: His Songs and His Sayings*, in *Nation*, 31 (December 2, 1880): 398; anon., "On the History of Slavery," *Publications of the Southern History Association*, 5 (July, 1901): 304; Laprade, "Some Problems in Writing the History of American Slavery," *South Atlantic Quarterly*, 10 (April, 1911): 134. See also Laprade, "Newspapers as a Source for the History of American Slavery," *South Atlantic Quarterly*, 9 (July, 1910): 230–238.

4. See Elkins, *Slavery: A Problem in American Institutional and Intellectual Life* (Chicago, 1959), 5–8; I. A. Newby, *Jim Crow's Defense: Anti-Negro Thought in America, 1900–1930*, (Baton Rouge, 1965), 52–82.

5. Buck, *The Road to Reunion, 1865–1900* (Boston, 1937), 308–309.

6. Galloway, *The South and the Negro* (New York, 1904), 5; Grady, "The Boston Banquet Speech" and "But What of the Negro?" in *The Possibilities of the Negro in Symposium*, 39, 57. Notwithstanding Grady's nationalist statements, in the first of the speeches quoted here he went on to praise slavery. "I do hereby declare," he explained, "that in its wise and humane administration, in lifting the slave to heights of which he had not dreamed in his savage home,

and giving him a happiness he has not yet found in freedom—our fathers left their sons a saving and excellent heritage'' (''The Boston Banquet Speech,'' p. 39).

7. Elkins, *Slavery*, 6.

8. Holt, ''The Idea of Scientific History in America,'' *Journal of the History of Ideas*, 1 (June, 1940): 352; Hart, ''Imagination in History,'' *American Historical Review*, 15 (January, 1910): 232–233; Becker, ''Some Aspects of the Influence of Social Problems and Ideas upon the Study and Writing of History,'' *Publications of the American Sociological Society*, 7 (1912): 9; John David Smith, ''The Formative Period of American Slave Historiography, 1890–1920'' (Ph.D. diss., University of Kentucky, 1977), 1–29. See also Richard Heath Dabney, ''Is History a Science?'' *Papers of the American Historical Association*, 5 (July, 1891): 266; Colyer Meriwether to William E. Dodd, September 15, 1902, William E. Dodd Papers, Manuscript Division, Library of Congress; Meriwether, ''Scientific History,'' *Publications of the Southern History Association*, 11 (September–November, 1907): 300–305; John Higham, ''Scientific History: The American Orthodoxy,'' *History: Professional Scholarship in America* (Princeton, 1965), 93–94.

9. Richard Hofstadter, *The Progressive Historians: Turner, Beard, Parrington* (New York, 1968), xvi, 13, 14; Callcott, *History in the United States, 1800–1860: Its Practice and Purpose* (Baltimore, 1970), 167–168; Hildreth, *The History of the United States of America*, 6 vols. (New York, 1849–1852), 1:119; Bancroft, *History of the United States from the Discovery of the American Continent*, 8 vols. (Boston, 1859–1860), 1:172–173.

10. Loewenberg, *American History in American Thought: Christopher Columbus to Henry Adams* (New York, 1972), 317.

11. Holst, review of James Ford Rhodes, *History of the United States from the Compromise of 1850*, in *Historische Zeitschrift*, 77 (1896): 337–340; idem, review of Woodrow Wilson, *Division and Reunion*, in *Educational Review*, 6 (June, 1893): 89; idem, *John C. Calhoun* (Boston, 1882), 57; Loewenberg, *American History in American Thought*, 482–485, 486–487; anon., ''The Late Professor Von Holst,'' *Bookman*, 19 (March 1904): 17. On Holst see Charles R. Wilson, ''Hermann Eduard von Holst,'' in William T. Hutchinson, ed., *The Marcus W. Jernegan Essays in American Historiography* (Chicago, 1937), 60–83; Eric F. Goldman, ed., ''Importing a Historian: Von Holst and American Universities,'' *Mississippi Valley Historical Review*, 27 (September, 1940): 267–274, and Goldman, ''Hermann Eduard von Holst: Plumed Knight of American Historiography,'' ibid., 23 (March, 1937): 511–532.

12. Holst, *The Constitutional and Political History of the United States*, 7 vols. (Chicago, 1876–1892), 4:239, 289; 3:566; 1:342, 344; 3: 582, 568, 580–581; 1:344–345; 2:97; 1:354.

13. Lewis Ethan Ellis, ''James Schouler,'' in Hutchinson, ed., *The Marcus*

W. *Jernegan Essays in American Historiography*, 85, 89; Loewenberg, *American History in American Thought*, 501–504; Schouler, *History of the United States of America under the Constitution*, 7 vols. (New York, 1880–1913), 1: 4, 7, 257.

14. Schouler, *History of the United States of America*, 1:259; 2:262, 263, 264.

15. William T. Hutchinson, "John Bach McMaster," in Hutchinson, ed., *The Marcus W. Jernegan Essays in American Historiography*, 123–125, 139; Goldman, *John Bach McMaster—American Historian* (Philadelphia, 1943), 139; McMaster, *A History of the People of the United States from the Revolution to the Civil War*, 8 vols. (New York, 1883–1913), 2:18; 7:239, 237, 238, 240–243, 246–247; Smith, "The Formative Period of American Slave Historiography," 79, 345n; Elkins, *Slavery*, 8n.

16. Rhodes's work appeared in nine volumes, 1892–1922. It will hereafter be cited as *History*, with the appropriate volume and page numbers.

17. Rhodes to William E. Dodd, January 11, 1905, Dodd Papers; Rhodes to Andrew Dickson White, May 17, 1900, Andrew Dickson White Papers, Cornell University; Wendell Phillips Garrison to Rhodes, January 5, 1894, in *Letters and Memorials of Wendell Phillips Garrison* (Cambridge, 1908), 104; Rhodes, "The Profession of Historian," *Historical Essays* (New York, 1909), 79; Robert Cruden, *James Ford Rhodes: The Man, the Historian, and His Work* (Cleveland, 1961), 20; Rhodes to Mr. Bourne, August 2, 1890 and undated note, James Ford Rhodes Papers, Massachusetts Historical Society; Rhodes, "Tribute to Edward Gaylord Bourne," Massachusetts Historical Society *Proceedings*, 3rd ser., 1 (March 1908): 405.

18. Rhodes to Frederic Bancroft, October 15, 1892, Frederic Bancroft Papers, Columbia University; William A. Dunning to Rhodes, June 17, 1893, Rhodes Papers; Rhodes to William E. Dodd, January 25, 1907, Dodd Papers; Frederic Bancroft to Allan Nevins, January 17, 1932, Allan Nevins Papers, Columbia University.

19. Rhodes to Theodore Roosevelt, March 16, 1907, Theodore Roosevelt Papers, Manuscript Division, Library of Congress; Rhodes to John T. Morse, Jr., August 11, 1923, in Mark A. DeWolfe Howe, *James Ford Rhodes: American Historian* (New York, 1929), 345; Rhodes to M. A. DeWolfe Howe, February 15, 1909, Mark Anthony DeWolfe Howe Papers, Houghton Library, Harvard University; Rhodes to Andrew Dickson White, February 13, 1900, White Papers; Rhodes to Edward A. Atkinson, December 4, 1898, Edward A. Atkinson Papers, Massachusetts Historical Society; Rhodes to Theodore Roosevelt, May 18, 1908, Roosevelt Papers; Rhodes to Carl Schurz, May 11, 1893, Carl Schurz Papers, Manuscript Division, Library of Congress; Rhodes to Robert Grant, March 3, 1912, Robert Grant Papers, Houghton Library, Harvard University.

20. Rhodes to Gallatin Riddle, May 25, 1893, Gallatin Riddle Papers, Western Reserve Historical Society; Rhodes to Thomas R. Lounsbury, November 13, 1910, Thomas R. Lounsbury Papers, Beinecke Library, Yale University; Rhodes to Andrew Dickson White, June 23, 1900, White Papers; Rhodes to Turner, November 8, 1910, Frederick Jackson Turner Collection, Henry E. Huntington Library; Rhodes to Perry, July 13, 1914, James Ford Rhodes Papers, Duke University; Rhodes to the Misses Norton, October 25, 1908, Norton Family Papers, Houghton Library, Harvard University; Rhodes to George W. Julian, February 3, 1898, Joshua R. Giddings and George W. Julian Papers, Manuscript Division, Library of Congress; Rhodes to Miss Gilman, February 9, 1909, Gilman Family Papers, Yale University Library; Rhodes to Andrew Dickson White, April 14, 1900, White Papers; Rhodes to Roosevelt, January 5, 1909, Roosevelt Papers; Rhodes to William L. Cross, December 19, 1909, *Yale Review*, Correspondence, Beinecke Library, Yale University.

21. Rhodes, *History*, 5:485; 1:355, 342; Rhodes to George A. Myers, April 19, 1916, in John A. Garraty, ed., *The Barber and the Historian* (Columbus, 1956), 42–43; unidentified correspondent to Charles H. Haskins, January 13, 1901, American Historical Association Papers, Manuscript Division, Library of Congress; Rhodes to Literary Editor, Charleston *News and Courier*, March 7, 1905, Hemphill Family Papers, Duke University; Rhodes to William Garrott Brown, October 9, 1905, William Garrott Brown Papers, Duke University.

22. Bancroft's Washington Notebook, unpublished manuscript, vol. 2: 172–173, vol. 4:350, Bancroft Papers; Cruden, *James Ford Rhodes*, 262.

23. Cruden, *James Ford Rhodes*, 44; idem, "James Ford Rhodes and the Negro: A Study in the Problem of Objectivity," *Ohio History*, 71 (July, 1962): 129–137; Rhodes, *History*, 1:309–310, 372, 335; 5:556; 6:36; 7:39, 168; Rhodes to Hilary A. Herbert, March 4, 1905, Hilary A. Herbert Papers, Southern Historical Collection, University of North Carolina at Chapel Hill; Rhodes, "Negro Suffrage and Reconstruction," *Massachusetts Historical Society Proceedings*, 2nd ser., 18 (December, 1904): 466; Rhodes to Theodore Roosevelt, February 17, 1905, Roosevelt Papers; Rhodes to Thomas Wentworth Higginson, October 24, 1905, Thomas Wentworth Higginson Papers, Houghton Library, Harvard University; Rhodes to Carl Schurz, October 15, 1893, Schurz Papers.

24. Memorandum of visit with Roosevelt, November 16, 1905, quoted in Howe, *James Ford Rhodes*, 120; Rhodes to Nancy Toy, May 13, 6, [1906], Myers to Rhodes, September 23, 1915, Rhodes Papers; Myers to Rhodes, January 8, 1918, Rhodes to Myers, January 16, 1918, in Garraty, ed., *The Barber and the Historian*, 77–79; Lynch, "Some Historical Errors of James Ford Rhodes," *Journal of Negro History*, 2 (October, 1917): 345–368; idem, "More about the Historical Errors of James Ford Rhodes," ibid., 3 (April, 1918): 139–157; Rhodes to Barrett Wendell, November 15, 1920, Rhodes Papers.

25. James Schouler to Rhodes, November 28, 1909, James Schouler Papers, Massachusetts Historical Society; Thomas J. Pressly, *Americans Interpret Their Civil War* (Princeton, 1954), 174–175, 178; William P. Trent to Rhodes, April 8, 1901, Rhodes Papers; Rhodes to Trent, April 10, 1901, William P. Trent Papers, Columbia University; Rhodes to Hilary A. Herbert, November 12, 1904, Herbert Papers; Dodd to Rhodes, February 22, 1907, February 28, 1908, Rhodes Papers; Commager, "The Eighteen Nineties: A Watershed in American History," New York *Times Book Review*, October 6, 1946, p. 7.

26. *History*, 1:2, 152, 322, 362.

27. Ibid., 308–309, 317–318, 333–334, 308, 310.

28. Ibid., 325–326, 306–309.

29. Ibid., 305–307.

30. Ibid., 4, 303–304, 311–314.

31. Ibid., 327–333.

32. Ibid., 315–317, 323–324, 318–319, 322, 310, 311, 335–342.

33. Ibid., 56, 61, 377–379, 344–345, 350–351, 352, 303.

34. Anon., "Rhodes's History of the United States," *Nation*, 55 (December 29, 1892): 499–500; Holst in *Historische Zeitschrift*, 337, 338; Bancroft, "A New History of the United States," *Critic*, 19 (February 18, 1893): 93; Andrews, "Rhodes's History of the United States," *Christian Union*, 47 (February 25, 1893): 382–383.

35. Holst in *Historische Zeitschrift*, 337, 338, 340; Bancroft, "A New History of the United States," 93; Spencer, "The Irrepressible Conflict," *Dial*, 14 (May 1, 1893): 280–281; Smith in *Yale Review*, 2 (May, 1893): 108; Burgess in *Political Science Quarterly*, 8 (June, 1893): 342–343; Winston to Rhodes, October 22, November 15, 1901, Rhodes Papers.

36. [Wilson], "Anti-Slavery History and Biography," *Atlantic Monthly*, 72 (August, 1893): 272–274; idem, "Remarks by Prof. Woodrow Wilson," *Annual Report of the American Historical Association for the Year 1896*, 2 vols. (Washington, 1896), 1:294–295. See also John David Smith, "James Ford Rhodes, Woodrow Wilson, and the Passing of the Amateur Historian of Slavery," *Mid-America*, 64 (October, 1982): 17–24.

37. Wilson, *Division and Reunion, 1829–1909* (New York, 1893), 105, 125–128.

38. Rhodes to Edward A. Atkinson, June 3, 1897, Atkinson Papers; Rhodes, "Remarks," Massachusetts Historical Society, *Proceedings*, 2nd ser., 18 (February, 1904): 237; Frederic Bancroft, "James Ford Rhodes," *Harper's Weekly*, 36 (December 17, 1892): 1219; Howe, *James Ford Rhodes*, 25; R. D. W. Connor to Rhodes, July 13, 1912, Trent to Rhodes, March 21, 1893, Rhodes Papers.

39. "James Ford Rhodes," in Hutchinson, ed., *The Marcus W. Jernegan Essays in American Historiography*, 175–176.

40. Rhodes, *History*, 1:304; Harvey Wish, ed., *The Slave States* (New York, 1959), 22, 90, 241, 266; Rhodes to Frederic Bancroft, March 16, 1893, Bancroft Papers; Broadus Mitchell, *Frederick Law Olmsted: A Critic of the Old South* (Baltimore, 1924), xvn.

41. See John David Smith, " 'Keep 'em in a fire-proof vault': Pioneer Southern Historians Discover Plantation Records," *South Atlantic Quarterly*, 78 (Summer, 1979): 376–382.

42. Elkins, *Slavery*, 7.

43. Rhodes to Hart, November 4, 1906, Albert Bushnell Hart Papers, Manuscripts and Archives Division, New York Public Library.

44. Carol F. Baird, "Albert Bushnell Hart: The Rise of the Professional Historian," in Paul Buck, ed., *Social Sciences at Harvard, 1860–1920* (Cambridge, 1965), 129–142, 132, 154; Hart, *Slavery and Abolition, 1831–1841* (New York, 1906), xv, xiv.

45. Rhodes to Hart, November 4, 1906, Hart Papers; Hart, *Slavery and Abolition*, 325, 93, 94; idem. "Why the South Was Defeated in the Civil War," *New England Magazine*, n.s., 5 (November, 1891): 375; idem, "The Outcome of the Southern Race Question," *North American Review*, 188 (July, 1908): 51; Hart to William E. Dodd, July 11, 1905, Dodd Papers; Hart, *The Southern South* (New York, 1910), 138.

46. Hart, *Slavery and Abolition*, 56, 57, 61, 162, 101–102, 119, 123–135, 102–107, 110–118, 169, 323.

47. Ibid., pp. 120–121, 144, 167, 114, 136, 97, 94–95, 96–97, 131.

48. Ibid., pp. 107–108, 100, 105, 94, 105, 111, 120, 113, 112.

# 5

# The Study of Slavery at Johns Hopkins

I

While Rhodes, Hart, and the other Nationalist historians worked to counterbalance the rhetoric of the post-Civil War proslavery spokesmen, a movement was under way to remove partisanship from slavery scholarship altogether. Trained in the new "scientific" history of their day at The Johns Hopkins University and other pioneer graduate schools, young historians began to take a dim view of antebellum writings on slavery. They frowned, too, on the blatant chauvinism exhibited by both sides in the postwar slavery debate. At Johns Hopkins in particular, graduate students and faculty alike worked to produce what they perceived to be detached, unemotional studies of slavery. In the process they greatly advanced the level of scholarship on the subject and left amateurs like Rhodes forever in their wake.

The students of slavery at Johns Hopkins challenged the preexisting canons of American historiography. Despite Rhodes's genuine contributions to the literature of slavery, his work fell clearly in the tradition of the "romantic" historian George Bancroft and the utilitarianism of Richard Hildreth. The new generation of "scientific" historians at Johns Hopkins worked to abandon anything that smacked of sectional, partisan history. Significantly, Rhodes, Holst and their fellow Nationalist historians also had dedicated themselves to the tenets of "scientific" history. But when they approached the emotion-laden subject of black slavery, these scholars ultimately abandoned that ideal. How would the students at Johns Hopkins avoid the pitfalls of historical chauvinism? How would they successfully apply the "scientific" method to the study of slavery when others had failed? Professor Herbert Baxter Adams led them, carefully guiding the graduate students at Johns Hopkins through the treacherous eddies inherent in the study of slavery. Adams's approach to history—tracing the evolution of legal institutions such as slavery—smoothed their path. He implored his students to cleanse their writings of identification with any sect, section, or political philosophy. As a result of his brilliant training, his students contributed important monographs and gained for their institution a reputation as the leading research center on slavery.[1]

Adams, trained at the University of Heidelberg in the 1870s, imported German "scientific" history to Johns Hopkins in 1876. He considered his seminars there "laboratories where books are treated like mineralogical specimens." Armed with primary, nonpartisan sources as evidence, "scientific" historians eschewed value judgments. Yet, according to Professor William P. Trent of the University of the South, objectivity on the slavery question was at best a pipe dream. "How is a Southerner, or a Northerner," Trent asked in 1895, "to approach any portion of our history involving the subject of slavery and the late war without a *parti pris*?" Nevertheless "scientific" historians at Johns Hopkins, in their determined quest for objectivity, went about their business under Adams's direction. They traced black slavery's generic origins principally on the colonial and state levels.[2]

Adams realized that the availability of primary materials on slavery held the key to the success or failure of the new "scientific" research on slavery. Many practitioners of "scientific" history believed that the records of the past should be allowed to speak for themselves. Respecting the integrity of documents, they insisted, would guarantee impartial, unbiased history. They failed to consider the natural bias that investigators bring to every historical problem. And they ignored the methodological dilemmas involved with sorting and marshaling evidence selectively. Nonetheless, armed with this faith in historical objectivity, historians at Johns Hopkins canvassed the South in search of the records of slavery—especially statutes, pamphlets, plantation records, newspapers, and diaries. These became the analytical tools, the test tubes, of the "scientific" historians of slavery.

As the case of Rhodes illustrated, serious problems confronted the historian of slavery who never left his study on Beacon Street in Boston. Primary sources on slavery were so widely scattered at this time that major difficulties awaited even the most disciplined "scientific" scholar. Adams and his colleagues worked hard to acquire slavery-related materials at Johns Hopkins. In 1891, for example, the school accessioned the Birney and Scharf Collections. The former contained over one thousand books and pamphlets on the peculiar institution gathered by General James G. Birney, including Jesse Torrey's rare *Portraiture of Domestic Slavery* (1817). At the time, the Birney Collection was judged to be the largest and most complete group of sources on slavery in existence. Soon afterwards Colonel Thomas Scharf of Baltimore donated an immense collection of manuscripts, newspapers, and pamphlets to Johns Hopkins. These materials established the school's strong holdings in southern history, "thus doing for the South what Harvard and Yale have done for the New England States." Such acquisitions enabled the Johns Hopkins librarian to report in 1892 that the university held about three thousand volumes on the South—"a collection of much importance, especially in the subject of slavery."[3]

Equipped with the necessary research tools, Adams attracted a surprisingly large number of graduate students to Baltimore to study slavery. There came together a group of men destined to emerge as important historians of slavery, including Jeffrey R. Brackett, John Spencer Bassett, James C. Ballagh, John H. Russell, and Harrison A. Trexler. Their training, largely in seminars, was supplemented by frequent guest lecturers. In 1895, for example, historian Frederic Bancroft, an early student of the domestic slave trade, presented a series of lectures on slavery. These included "Slavery in Maryland," "What Became of the Northern Slave?" "The Last Fugitive Slave," and "The Negro in Politics." After completing his doctorate at Johns Hopkins in 1894, Bassett returned to his alma mater as a visiting lecturer on the subject of slavery. Bassett's notes offer a glimpse of the breadth of his presentations.

I expect to begin with the decay of slavery in the later Roman empire and deduce the lessons for us who by a process somewhat different . . . have still to decide how we shall develop a servile population into a state of reliable freedom. I desire to find out what there is in the negro, what he has done, and what he can and will do. I do not see how the most blinded "Bourbon" can object to such a treatment, and if he will but follow it through I think his eyes ought to be opened somewhat.

A later lecturer, Professor George Petrie of Alabama Polytechnic Institute at Auburn, shared with the Johns Hopkins students the fruits of his research on slavery in Alabama.[4]

Slavery came to dominate the discussions in Adams's graduate seminar. Meeting on Friday evenings, the Seminary, as it was officially named, served as a forum for the presentation of papers by students, faculty, and guests. In 1883 Hermann Eduard von Holst, the famed German scholar, gave an address entitled "The Study of Slavery as an Institution." Holst urged the students to examine slavery in its broadest context—as a historic, economic, and social factor in southern life. He pointed out that no attempt to that time had been made to prepare a suitable "scientific treatise" on slavery. While works on the political side of the slavery controversy were plentiful, slavery as a "historic institution" remained unexamined. Holst believed that the men at Johns Hopkins were best suited to the task.

Students from the South [explained Holst], trained to a knowledge of scientific methods, should take up the history of slavery—the peculiar institution. Study the slaveholders as such, study their position, occupations, modes of life, their intercourse with the outside world. . . . Such inquiries would show to some extent the character of southern civilization. No individual can complete this great task. It will be a work for the coming century.

Inspired, no doubt, by Holst's encouragement, students in Adams's seminar energetically began investigations of black slavery. Their papers focused on slavery in the North and the South as well as in the District of Columbia.[5]

In 1885, one of Adams's graduate students, Jeffrey R. Brackett, presented his initial findings on the institutional history of slavery in Maryland at the annual meeting of the American Historical Association. This was the first paper on the peculiar institution delivered before that organization. Brackett's "Report on Certain Studies in the Institution of African Slavery in the United States" implored scholars of slavery to abandon polemics in favor of institutional, especially legal, investigations. He urged them to examine slavery in microcosm by using court records, legislative journals, newspapers, and "testimony of reliable whites and blacks."[6] Back in Baltimore, Brackett also prepared seminar papers—in 1885, 1887, and 1888—on the Annapolis slaveholders convention of 1841, the introduction of slavery in Georgia, and on patterns of slave crime and punishment, respectively. According to the graduate student, where slavery was concerned, economic factors always triumphed over humanitarian considerations. In Oglethorpe's colony, for instance, Georgians forbade slavery, explained Brackett, until direct competition with the cheap labor of South Carolina forced them, too, to employ bondsmen. Brackett's essay on the legal side of slavery later became a chapter in his important dissertation on slavery in Maryland.[7]

Brackett and his fellow graduate students at Johns Hopkins were among the first historians to conduct field research on slavery throughout the South. Most historians restricted their investigations to a single colony or state. One student, Shirley C. Hughson, wrote Professor Adams from South Carolina in 1893, informing him that he was "hard at work on the negro." Hughson, who was researching the slave trade in South Carolina, reported to his mentor that he was finding a wealth of "wholly new material" in Charleston's "confused and uncatalogued libraries." He hoped to unearth other previously untapped records at the state capitol in Columbia. Another student, James C. Ballagh, scoured the libraries of Virginia for materials for his pioneer research on slavery in that colony and state. After receiving his doctorate in 1895, Ballagh joined Adams on the history faculty and lectured to the graduate students on slavery, especially "its broad institutional character." Ballagh carefully examined the interrelation of slave law and the social effects of slavery. He underscored the importance of grasping both sides of slavery's contradictory nature—its cruel and its benevolent dimensions. Looking back in 1900 over the research on slavery and southern history conducted at Johns Hopkins, Adams praised it as "nonpartisan" and "objective." He remarked with pride how "Yale and Harvard have followed in its lead."[8]

In 1901, the year of Adams's death, Ballagh assumed responsibility for training historians of slavery at Johns Hopkins. For more than a decade he continued to offer advanced work in southern history and, not surprisingly, devoted considerable attention to slavery. In his course "History of American Slavery," Ballagh required the students to compare the institutional development of bondage in North America with forms of servitude in ancient, medieval, and modern Europe. This method—what twentieth-century scholars later would label "comparative slavery"—was not totally unfamiliar to historians of Ballagh's day. And his graduate students tackled various other aspects of slavery as well. In 1898, for example, William S. Drewry prepared a seminar paper on slave resistance in Virginia. It served as the core of his 1900 doctoral dissertation. The bulk of the students, though, examined the legal status of the slaves, free blacks, and slavery in the various colonies and states. Typical projects included Douglas Southall Freeman's paper on free blacks in Georgia, F. G. Holmes's investigation of slavery in South Carolina, and William T. Laprade's work on bondsmen in the nation's capital. Johns Hopkins offered these students and others an intellectually exciting and dynamic environment within which to study the peculiar institution.[9]

## II

Certainly *The Johns Hopkins University Studies in Historical and Political Science* served as one attraction of studying history at that institution. It provided graduate students and faculty with an outlet for publication of their dissertations and monographs. Established by Adams in 1883, the *Studies* published works on a variety of topics—the development of local government, law, taxation, commerce, education—all falling within the broad realm of institutional history. Given Adams's and Ballagh's keen interest in slavery, that subject quickly made its way into the *Studies*. Indeed, from 1889 to 1914 the *Studies* published fifteen monographs dealing with slavery. Several examined slavery in the North, the antislavery movement, white servitude, and slave laws in individual states. Seven of the *Studies*, however, dealt specifically with slavery in the South.[10]

These monographs initiated the minute examination of slavery on the state level. Determined not to judge the peculiar institution, the young authors hoped to free themselves from partisanship, to uncover slavery's origins, and to explore its institutional evolution over time. By necessity, each of the works on slavery that appeared in the *Studies* covered some similar material. And on most aspects of slavery, despite differences from state to state, they reached similar conclusions. All of the authors, with their "scientific" detachment, still supported the benign view of slavery set forth so often by the proslavery ideologues of the postwar years. For instance, all of the authors interpreted slavery as patriarchal, emphasizing how the fortunate bondsmen received lessons in civilization from kind masters. Almost uniformly they characterized the blacks as contented servants, the recipients of adequate food, clothing, and shelter. They credited the slaves with holding certain privileges, including access to religious instruction, garden plots, and the ownership of draft animals. Unlike Rhodes and the neoabolitionists, the Johns Hopkins writers agreed that masters bred and sold slaves reluctantly. And only rarely, they said, were slave families divided for sale.

Jeffrey R. Brackett contributed the first volume on slavery to appear in the Johns Hopkins *Studies*. A Massachusetts native, he graduated from Harvard in 1883. After receiving his doctorate from Johns Hopkins in 1889, he lectured on philanthropy and social work and headed Baltimore's Department of Charities and Corrections. From 1904 to 1920 Brackett chaired the School for Social Workers at Simmons College in Boston. An outspoken proponent of the application of "science" to history, Brackett interpreted the past as "an orderly process: with lessons for today." In his historical work he strived for an "exact record," stressing accurate observations, just inferences, and contrary opinions. To broaden himself in the ways of the South, while in Baltimore Brackett traveled throughout the rural areas of Maryland and Virginia. Like most white historians of his generation, this "child of New England Puritans" ultimately came to defend slavery and the slaveholders.[11]

Brackett presented his thoughts on slavery in his dissertation, *The Negro in Maryland* (1889), as well as in an extended essay on the legal status of slaves published the same year, and in *Progress of the Colored People of Maryland* (1890). All focused on slave law, and this became the trademark of the Johns Hopkins *Studies*. Brackett listed court cases and laws so profusely that his narrative became almost a litany, "act on act, judgment on judgment, report on report." Dedicated to viewing slavery dispassionately, he shunned "the controversial literature of the abolition school" and strove "to put himself . . . in the place of the conscientious Southern planter." Brackett's sources were models of impartiality for the 1880s: a variety of state and county records, slave court cases, newspapers, records of the Society of Friends, and the papers of Governor Robert Dinwiddie of Virginia.[12]

Such source materials limited Brackett's focus to slavery's legal growth and disinclined him from treating blacks as anything more than legal entities. In his opinion, Maryland's slave laws evolved sui generis under the indirect impetus of English mercantile policy. They received little influence from slave jurisprudence of ancient societies or even from the slave system of eighteenth-century Barbados. Different laws for blacks and whites, Brackett said, were uncommon until the eighteenth century, when large numbers of slaves, "brutal, very ignorant and very imitative," entered the colony along with numerous English felons. Separate statutes began to appear, Brackett explained, to curb the habits that the slaves acquired from the dregs of English white society. In the next century economic competition with Baltimore tradesmen led to a ban on bondsmen hiring themselves out.[13]

Brackett's essay on the legal status of the slaves contrasted slavery in the colonial North and South. Expanding a theme from his dissertation, he maintained that before 1700 slaves in the colonies of both regions received justice equal to that accorded free whites. Brackett's research suggested that "negroes were punished at first, very much as white servants were." This anticipated a theme later developed by James C. Ballagh in his volumes that appeared in the *Studies*. Much like the proslavery authors, Brackett argued that southern slave codes exhibited a degree of flexibility—"usually the exact nature of the punishment was left to the discretion of the court, with the provision that it be so administered as to deter other slaves from like crimes." He concluded that by 1789 the principles of the Revolution and the North's decreasing slave population led to moves for abolition in that section. But in the South the burgeoning slave population caused increased restrictions on the slaves.[14]

Going beyond Brackett's scope, John Spencer Bassett contributed two monographs on slavery to the *Studies*. A native North Carolinian and a graduate of Trinity College in Durham, Bassett became perhaps the best known of all the authors of the Johns Hopkins school. His many later publications include *The Middle Group of American Historians* (1917), *The Southern Plantation Overseer as Revealed in His Letters* (1925), and the six-volume *Correspondence of Andrew Jackson* (1926–1935). In 1902 he founded the prestigious *South Atlantic Quarterly* as a medium for critical and independent southern thought. Bassett held an unusually keen interest in slavery and race relations. More than any other trained white historian in these years, Bassett sympathized openly with blacks. He suggested that masters actually provided their slaves with sparse clothing and paid little attention to the marriage relation among their bondsmen. He disapproved, too, of the miscegenation that slavery caused. Bassett found it increasingly difficult to write history after his return to North Carolina in 1894 as a history professor at Trinity College. The ultraconservative racial mood prevalent in the state, he said, discouraged free thinking, even on the old slavery question.[15]

As early as 1897 Bassett advocated tolerance toward scholars whose interpretations clashed with southern sensitivities. "We must recognize," implored the historian, "that we cannot treat an author whose opinion is contrary to ours as we used to treat a slave whom we did not consider to have opinions." Trained in Adams's seminar to be impartial and critical, Bassett balked at the unjust cries of black misrule in North Carolina when a coalition of whites and blacks voted into power a Populist administration. And, though he was advanced for his day on the race question, Bassett still retained much of his generation's racism. An enlightened paternalist, he urged his fellow whites to remember that

The white people of America brought the negro here for the good of their own pocket-books. To reap gold in dollars out [of] fields of tobacco and cotton they undertook to put up with his barbarism. They probably did not see how the inferior leaven would leaven their own life. . . . They thought that slavery would keep barbarism down; but they didn't understand that side of the problem . . . and now are coming to realize how they lost in the whole transaction. They don't realize that it is going to take an immense amount of patient training and a long period of development before the effects of the old inferiority are wiped out of the negro race.

Bassett advocated vocational training for most of the blacks and higher education for the black talented tenth. He considered black suffrage "nauseating."[16]

In spite of such cautious and conservative disclaimers, Bassett's views were far too liberal for most white North Carolinians of the period. He infuriated southerners at large by predicting future racial equality and, in a famous remark, rating Booker T. Washington as the greatest southerner next to Robert E. Lee. This comment released an avalanche of criticism upon Bassett, and he nearly lost his teaching position at Trinity College because of it. Historian Walter Lynwood Fleming interpreted the comment as typical of Bassett's "martyrological, superior, new Southern, jackassical attitude . . . toward all things of the 'Old South.' " According to historian William E. Dodd, the "Bassett Affair" was "tantamount to saying that free speech shall not be permitted in our section of the country." Bassett eventually became convinced that he no longer could "write history and direct public sentiment too." In 1906 he departed North Carolina for what he judged to be the less restrictive intellectual environment of Smith College in Massachusetts.[17]

Bassett's sympathy toward blacks never prevented him from identifying certain redeeming features in slavery. For example, he described the Africans brought to American shores as "untamed, degraded, superstitious and dull." Slaves belonged, Bassett insisted, to a race prone to "sensuality" and "animal emotions" expressed in "impetuous fear, joy, or sorrow." Although he blamed slavery for thwarting black development, he praised it for keeping in check "the lowest tendencies of the negro." "Whites ought not to expect too much" from blacks, wrote Bassett in 1905, but should instruct and encourage them toward self-elevation.[18]

Bassett's *Slavery and Servitude in the Colony of North Carolina* and *Slavery in the State of North Carolina* appeared in 1896 and 1899, respectively. True to the Johns Hopkins form, the treatment of slavery in both monographs adhered to the legalistic/institutional mode. Yet in contributing a long chapter to slave religion, Bassett paid more careful attention to this subject than any previous investigator had. Drawing heavily on the Baptist Association Reports and Minutes of the Methodist Church for North Carolina, Bassett explained how religion served masters as a double-edged tool—both as a form of discipline and as a reward. Though a few independent slave congregations existed, he said, most bondsmen worshipped in special galleries at the same time or attended a later service. Bassett wrote that the ignorant slaves eagerly accepted the simple doctrine of Baptist and Methodist missionaries, a creed that transformed North Carolina blacks into submissive laborers. But he cited ex-slave Lunsford Lane's 1842 narrative to prove that some slaves, at least, realized how religion served to tighten their chains. This minority of blacks "in their hearts never accepted the institution of slavery." On this point Bassett anticipated later historians' use of black testimony, and their recognition of religion as a tool both of racial control and slave resistance.[19]

Bassett also broke fresh ground by making several other important observations regarding slavery in North Carolina. In 1898 he praised as "a triumph of humanity" the North Carolina case *The State vs. Will* (1834). That celebrated case established the slave's right to defend himself against threats upon his life by a white man.[20] In addition, Bassett noted that although white servitude and slavery coexisted in colonial North Carolina, slavery ultimately emerged as the predominant labor system. Africans, he said, more readily adapted than white Europeans to the climate and rigor of field work. Bassett called this a prime example of "the survival of the fittest." From the reminiscences of planters he concluded that slavery proved profitable in rice, cotton, and turpentine production. Under ideal conditions, he noted, a slave employed in the naval stores industry might produce annually up to one thousand dollars beyond the amount necessary to feed and clothe himself. This lone reference to the economics of slavery set Bassett apart from most of his fellow contributors to the Johns Hopkins *Studies*, who simply ignored the subject. Economics received little consideration in institutional studies of slavery until the publication of *American Negro Slavery* by Ulrich B. Phillips in 1918.[21]

No member of the Johns Hopkins school did more to shape the institutional orientation of the *Studies* than did James C. Ballagh. The son of an antislavery clergyman, one of America's first Protestant missionaries to enter Japan, Ballagh was born in Virginia's Shenandoah Valley in 1867. Before enrolling at Johns Hopkins he studied at the University of Virginia and at Washington and Lee University. After receiving his Ph.D. in 1895, Ballagh remained at Johns Hopkins; following Adams's death, he alone determined the direction of slave studies at the school. Altogether Ballagh wrote or edited six books. In all of them he advocated a strictly "objective" approach to history in general and slavery in particular. On the one hand, Ballagh encouraged the study of slavery because, he said, it rested at the basis of American history since the 1850s. Yet he complained that too many scholars had given slavery a disproportionate share of attention, slighting the role of the tariff and public lands. Influenced by the New South ideology of Henry W. Grady, Ballagh urged his students neither to defend nor attack the peculiar institution, but to look forward to a prosperous "New South" as "the willing daughter of the Old." Yet in 1913 Ballagh abandoned the South. He left Baltimore to teach political science at the University of Pennsylvania's Wharton School of Finance and Commerce.[22]

Ballagh's legacy, beyond training students of slavery and editing the *Studies*, lies in two areas. First, he made salient contributions to our understanding of the origins of slavery in North America. Years before Oscar Handlin, Carl N. Degler, and Winthrop Jordan battled over this issue, Ballagh already had staked out the boundaries of the debate. All three acknowledge Ballagh's central importance to the controversy. According to Jordan, for the early twentieth century, Ballagh's thesis represented a "new and different interpretation."[23] Actually, Ballagh's argument concerning slavery's growth in Virginia represents just one part of his larger interpretation of slavery's institutional features in the state.

In his dissertation, *White Servitude in the Colony of Virginia* (1895), Ballagh argued that white servants and black slaves shared a similar legal status through much of the seventeenth century. Both were considered chattels personal before the law and thus were judged taxable property. But Ballagh observed that there were legal distinctions between the two classes of laborers. White servants possessed privileges denied black slaves, including provisions for religious and secular instruction. White Virginians favored white indentured servants over blacks on moral and social grounds. But in an uncharacteristic economic interpretation, Ballagh went on to explain that "from a purely economic point of view," blacks proved superior, and slowly black slavery replaced white servitude as the preferred system of labor. Still, argued Ballagh, white servitude paved the way "both legally and practically" for slavery in Virginia. Soon afterward, in 1897 and again in 1898, Ballagh further refined his argument. Slavery, he maintained in a book review, did not become clearly distinguishable as Virginia's labor system until the eighteenth century. And in a paper delivered before the Johns Hopkins Historical and Political Science Association, Ballagh stressed that in a purely legal sense, Massachusetts and Connecticut had established slavery prior to Virginia.[24]

Ballagh incorporated these findings into his classic *A History of Slavery in Virginia* (1902), an expanded version of two articles on slavery that had appeared in the *Conservative Review*. This volume best represents the Johns Hopkins institutional approach to studying the history of slavery. First of all, Ballagh's source materials surpassed those employed by Rhodes or, for that matter, any previous investigator. They included sixteen manuscript collections, the records of numerous county courts, and papers and letter books from the Virginia State Library and the Library of Congress. *A History of Slavery in Virginia* contained all of the elements that characterized its genre: it was "objective" in the contemporary sense of the term, it was strongly legalistic in method and tone, and it highlighted the various institutional components of slavery, with the notable exception of slave economics.[25]

Second, Ballagh stressed the evolutionary nature of slave law in Virginia. The blacks who landed at Jamestown in 1619, he argued, were not legally slaves. Having been captured by pirates, they were protected by international law. As "colony servants" they worked for limited durations on public lands. Other blacks imported into Virginia in the mid-seventeenth century also were servants—subject to the same legal restraints as white indentured servants—with limited terms of service. Such a system of black and white servants proved unsatisfactory, Ballagh maintained, until 1661, when the first differentiation between white and black servants appeared in Virginia statute law. This differentiation resulted, said Ballagh, from the failure of white servants to compete economically with the increasing number of inexpensive black laborers. Gradually special restrictions based on skin color were placed on blacks, completing their transformation in status from servant to slave. The tenure of the black no longer was restricted but became perpetual—a necessity if the blacks were to be made "socially safe." The conception of property in laborers also changed from that of buying a worker's service to purchasing his person.[26]

Like Rhodes, Ballagh depended heavily on Olmsted's travel accounts for his analysis of slave treatment. But Ballagh's benign portrait of slave society reveals just how two authors relying on the same source can reach radically different conclusions. Unlike the neoabolitionists, Ballagh argued that speculation in slave property was rare and never was practiced until the late antebellum period. And even then, he explained, only unruly bondsmen were sold. Most masters preferred to suffer a financial loss, he said, by keeping too many bondsmen rather than selling them. This attitude, according to Ballagh, grew from the sense of "mutual attachment" shared by masters and their slaves. In exchange for the slave's loyalty and service, the slave owner assumed the roles of "playmate, pedagogue, brother, exemplar, friend and companion." In such a relationship, insisted Ballagh, unrestrained whippings occurred rarely, and chaining was "more apparent than real." While he admitted that cruel masters existed under slavery, Ballagh deemphasized this dimension of master/slave relations. In the tradition of slavery's old defenders, and anticipating the later theses of Ulrich B. Phillips and Eugene D. Genovese, Ballagh underscored paternalism as the vital ingredient of the slave regime.[27]

Ballagh found little in slave life that was depressing. Because most Virginia slaves lived on small farms, "bad treatment" was exceptional and often was confined to slaves hired out by their masters. Laughter and music emanated from the slave quarters, he argued, and the plantation black possessed many qualities found in his master. According to Ballagh, the slave was

cheerful, polite, and respectful to his superiors . . . without sycophancy and without fawning. He was well-bred like his master, and his manners were rather those of a person accustomed to liberty by the reign of law and order than to servile oppression. He often showed a dignity and self-respect that brought into striking contrast the pert inquisitiveness and false pride of the lowest stratum of the laboring whites.

Again, Ballagh simultaneously revived elements of the old proslavery rationale and prefigured the work of Phillips. For example, he praised the plantation system for developing the slaves into the South's master workmen. Field hands learned skills from observing house servants and plantation craftsmen alike. Carpenters, smiths, cobblers—"the black aristocracy of skilled laborers"—had ample free time to practice their crafts off the plantation and to apply their earnings toward emancipation. Bondsmen also learned trades when hired out for labor on public works, on ships, and in mines. Slave religion, said Ballagh, was still another aspect of slavery that benefited the bondsmen. Masters cared for their slaves' moral and spiritual needs by providing Sunday schools and allowing the blacks to attend white churches. Although slaves usually were seated in separate galleries, Ballagh maintained that in the Old South "The color line was political and social, not religious." His interpretations of slavery for the entire antebellum period assumed that blacks retained an element of their seventeenth-century status: in day-to-day affairs they were "servants." They were "slaves" only before the law.[28]

Just as Ballagh's volumes surpassed in quality those of Brackett and Bassett, the Johns Hopkins students who succeeded Ballagh contributed institutional analyses of slavery that outdistanced his own. In 1913, John H. Russell of Allegheny College completed an important dissertation that both reinforced and revised Ballagh's writings. Russell's *The Free Negro in Virginia* credited Ballagh with first recognizing that the earliest blacks brought to Virginia were servants, not slaves. Russell also acknowledged that white servitude was the base upon which slavery later evolved. But he made better and more extensive use of Virginia

county court records than Ballagh had. Russell stated that slavery orig-
inated in Virginia by customary law, but disagreed with Ballagh by
asserting that slavery was sanctioned by court decisions prior to the
1661 statutory recognition of slavery. In the period 1640–1660, some
blacks labored as servants and others as slaves. Yet most blacks after
1640, he emphasized, were imported as bondsmen. Basing another
observation on additional research in county records and petitions in
the Virginia State Library, Russell remarked that "the period of the
existence of the black master was conterminous with the period of the
existence of slavery." This last point remains virtually unexplored even
by today's historians of slavery.[29]

But the most noteworthy volume in the *Studies*, Harrison A. Trexler's
*Slavery in Missouri*, appeared in 1914. Born in Illinois in 1883, Trexler
entered Johns Hopkins after earning a Ph.B. from Hastings College and
beginning graduate study at the University of Chicago and the University
of Bonn, Germany. Many years later historian Frederic Bancroft cited
Trexler as an example of a historian from the North who, though well
received in the South, was "able to retain his critical faculty." Trexler
spent much of his long teaching career at Southern Methodist University.
His study of Missouri slavery became the last of the Johns Hopkins
*Studies* to examine slavery as an institution. It represents the culmination
of years of research conducted at Johns Hopkins on the peculiar
institution.[30]

Trexler's monograph transcended the other volumes in the *Studies* in
thoroughness and interpretation. More than any of the others, it broke
fresh ground in research and methodology. Encouraged by Professor
John M. Vincent to emphasize the economic side of slavery in Missouri,
Trexler made this the focus of his dissertation without omitting the usual
legal or social questions. Following in the footsteps of earlier Hopkins
students, Trexler conducted extensive field research. During the summer
months of 1912 and 1913 he traversed Missouri's length and width in
search of primary sources on the peculiar institution, and his industry
paid off. In obscure county seats and local libraries Trexler uncovered
vast riches, including probate records, tax returns, assessment lists, and
city directories. In September, 1912, he wrote enthusiastically of his
progress: "I got a list of old settlers and newspapermen and have their
statements. I also ran down many old slaves. I found the tax books and
probate records in all counties, except Platte, more or less complete."
The graduate student also discovered a mine of official and private

manuscripts pertinent to his subject at the Library of Congress, at the Missouri Historical Society, and in private hands. To supplement these materials Trexler interviewed ex-slaves as well as white Missourians who had personal recollections of slavery days. Trexler thereby established himself as a pioneer in applying oral history testimony to the study of slavery.[31]

When Trexler began his study he was determined to assess the profitability of slavery in Missouri. He no doubt recognized the virtual absence of this sort of inquiry from the works completed by his predecessors at Johns Hopkins. But upon finishing his own dissertation, Trexler had to admit that his efforts along this line had also been "disappointing." There were several impediments, he noted, to analyzing the economics of slavery. First, discrepancies between county and federal tax returns made it difficult even to determine the actual number of slaves in the state at any one time. Also, because bondsmen often were assessed at rates lower than market value, local officials lacked uniform standards for rating them. Trexler argued that there were so many variables in Missouri that "to generalize" on the value of slave labor at different periods "would be most misleading."[32]

Another methodological problem Trexler identified was the difficulty of comparing slavery as a system with free labor. To accomplish this, he explained, would necessitate contrasting the account books of hundreds of Missouri slaveholders and nonslaveholding farmers with similar documents from farmers in free territory. Trexler concluded quickly that this task was impossible because few farmers in Missouri, or elsewhere, kept systematic records, and he uncovered virtually none of these records himself. A final stumbling block in determining slavery's profitability concerned Missouri's constant shortage of white labor, which created an artificial demand for slaves. Confronted with these obstacles, Trexler concluded that the profitability of slavery in Missouri could not be "mathematically settled." "The amount of data is so enormous," he warned, "and at the same time so incomplete and so contradictory that one is not justified in drawing conclusions."[33]

Despite these caveats, Trexler cautiously argued that under certain circumstances slavery in Missouri showed a profit. For instance, he believed that "the healthy western Missouri negro must have been a profitable investment as a hemp cutter and breaker." Concerning Saline and Marion counties, areas well suited to slave labor, Trexler supposed that the institution had thrived. But, he added, large sections of the state were unadaptive to slavery, and as Ulrich B. Phillips would later note, slave ownership proved risky even for the most ardent supporter of the peculiar institution. Masters confronted "the ever-threatening danger of escape" as well as losses incurred by supporting slaves who were too young or too old to be productive. Many slaveholders also complained that they often lacked work for their slaves and were forced to hire them to others. Eighty percent of the "old slaveholders" Trexler interviewed on the question of the profitability of slavery judged slavery in Missouri to be unprofitable. Still, Trexler recognized that profitability depended heavily on the "personal equation"—the managerial skills of the individual farmer.[34]

Trexler wrote more confidently on noneconomic aspects of Missouri slavery. He joined most white writers of these years in describing slavery as "patriarchal." This proved especially true in Missouri, he said, because the institution never became established on a large scale, being restricted mainly to general farm rather than to plantation agriculture. Even though a few large slaveholdings existed along the Missouri River, most slave owners held only a few bondsmen. Many slaves served as domestics or as "all around laborers," not as field hands. Only for hemp production in western Missouri did overseers and gangs of slaves predominate. Trexler maintained that slave life was milder in this northernmost slave state than in the lower South. Thus his conclusions differed from those of earlier contributors to the Johns Hopkins *Studies*. For example, Missouri never legally distinguished between servant and slave status. It also failed to tighten its slave laws after Nat Turner's revolt. Because slaves at no time constituted more than one-fifth of the state's population, whites held little fear of insurrection.[35]

## III

The Johns Hopkins *Studies* on slavery, from Brackett's first volume to Trexler's final work, received enthusiastic comments from contemporary reviewers. Frederic Bancroft credited Brackett's study with initiating consideration of the "actual conditions" of slavery. Another critic complimented both Brackett and Bassett for their use of "trustworthy original sources" in presenting "the actual facts of slavery as a concrete institution." He especially welcomed Bassett's treatment of slave religion. A reviewer judged Ballagh's dissertation a "model paper" for its day, and the applause awarded his monograph on slavery in Virginia in the *Critic* must certainly have proved gratifying to him. According to the reviewer, *A History of Slavery in Virginia* was "rigidly scientific" in method and "purely objective" in spirit. Black scholar W. E. B. Du Bois, not prone to withholding criticisms of authors, black or white, called the volume "the best local study of American slavery" then available, despite the author's racism. Solon J. Buck lauded Trexler's volume in the *Mississippi Valley Historical Review*, especially its use of county records. Bancroft found many "special merits" in *Slavery in Missouri*, a volume he characterized as thorough, impartial, and remarkably fair.[36]

The studies elicited some sharp criticism as well. Bancroft argued that Brackett's book fell short because the author failed to digest his evidence fully. The book resembled more "a collection of the raw materials of intellectual subsistence" than a flowing narrative. But Ballagh's monograph on slavery incurred the severest criticism of any of the volumes in the *Studies*. Du Bois attacked its apologetic tone, finding Ballagh's argument that England forced slavery on Virginia "a little far-fetched." Bassett disagreed with Ballagh's thesis on the origins of slavery in North America. Bassett maintained that blacks were sold in perpetual slavery by customary law before 1661. He also noted that Ballagh's "feelings are conservatively sympathetic with the slave holders." An unidentified reviewer in the *Publications of the Southern History Association* stung Ballagh acutely, accusing him of departing from the high standard established by previous authors in the Johns Hopkins series. He considered Ballagh's work too legalistic, too narrow. He said it overemphasized slavery's institutional features.[37]

Recent critics also tend to view the Johns Hopkins *Studies* with disfavor. In 1959 Stanley M. Elkins set the tone for these appraisals. In his opinion, the *Studies* started off on the wrong foot by failing to ask the right questions.

The emphasis was genetic, with an effort toward total objectivity; the question was not so much whether the institution was good or bad, or how it worked, but simply, How did it get started? The result was that these studies . . . having no polemical, moral direction, appeared to have no direction at all. The price of detachment, ironically, was that the work—much of it admirably detailed— had little positive impact on other scholars; it could not really become a part of the conversation on slavery. The Johns Hopkins monographs were widely used, though principally as stepping-stones for more polemics, rather than as models of method.

Other scholars, notably Bennett H. Wall and Burton M. Smith, virtually parroted Elkins's remarks. Clarence L. Ver Steeg, Robert W. Fogel, and Stanley L. Engerman have questioned the volumes' overt legal emphasis, the latter two scholars saying the works lacked a sense of the "material or psychological conditions of the slaves." Most recently, sociologist Orlando Patterson dubbed the Johns Hopkins *Studies* the "theoretical dead-end" of slave historiography. They existed in "a theoretical vacuum," he said.[38]

To be sure, the Johns Hopkins *Studies* on slavery contained serious deficiencies. Each author portrayed blacks in the racist stereotypes current in late nineteenth-century America, and all but one of them focused far too narrowly on legal themes. They listed statutes, cases, and regulations in endless profusion. Rarely did they assess whether or not the various laws were enforced, and if so, why. Generally the graduate students described but failed to analyze the slave codes. They focused so minutely on the colonial period that, with Trexler as a notable exception, the antebellum period virtually was ignored. No one integrated race as a factor in the origin and growth of the peculiar institution. Economic questions played a minimal role at best in their thinking. All of the authors relied heavily on "traditional" sources for their discussions of slavery's nonlegal features. In this sense, they were no more "scientific" than Rhodes or the postwar polemicists.

Specifically, Brackett omitted consideration of the impact of the domestic slave trade on Maryland's economic fortunes. Bassett's volumes, despite the author's concern with slave religion, slighted interpretation. Ballagh ignored the role of slave prices in slavery's evolution and tended to assume that slavery in Virginia typified the institution for the entire South. Like Ballagh, Russell was vague on the role of color prejudice in establishing the legal status of blacks. Even though Trexler conscientiously attempted to tackle the economics of slavery, he failed to calculate the profitability of slavery on a cost basis. Moreover, the Johns Hopkins writers never succeeded in their quest for objective, "scientific" history. They, like the vast majority of whites of their generation, agreed that blacks had benefited from slavery's tutelage. Unable to distance themselves from their own biases and preconceptions, the Johns Hopkins authors contributed significantly to the image of slavery as a patriarchal, benevolent institution.

The tone of the Johns Hopkins *Studies* smacked of the old proslavery rationale. True, their institutional framework and legalistic approach tended to gloss over this overall bias. These characteristics made their chauvinism less pronounced than that of more openly partisan writings. But careful dissection of the *Studies* reveals the skeleton of proslavery ideology never laid to rest. The authors, for example, maintained that overseers were not as brutal as the abolitionists had portrayed them. They interpreted slave laws as generally humane—with the mutual interests of slave and master of uppermost concern. The graduate students deemphasized slave insurrections. Revolts, they said, existed more in the whites' fears than in reality. And they charged that slave laws were at best enforced irregularly. Individual masters generally were fair and generous in their treatment of their bondsmen.

But despite their biases and weaknesses, the Johns Hopkins monographs remain important. They were the first volumes to evaluate slavery systematically on the state level. By employing new sources—government records, manuscripts, newspapers—they departed from the previous dependence on travel accounts. Their legal emphasis may actually have resulted as much from the abundance of legal documents as from an interest in the legal development of slavery. Strongly institutional in character, the Johns Hopkins *Studies* expanded and treated in much greater detail the categories identified by Rhodes in 1892. Although the authors sympathized with the slaveholders, they carefully noted slavery's long-range negative moral and social effects on southerners of both races. Describing the evolution of various elements of slavery, not judging them, the Johns Hopkins students naturally were less partisan than previous writers. In their sheer volume and in the detailed attention that they gave slavery, the volumes brought a new scholarly dimension to the study of the peculiar institution.

Elkins and those historians who have accepted his critique fail to place the Johns Hopkins volumes within the context of their day. The authors of the *Studies* shared the contemporary devotion to "scientific" history. Following the German ideal of historianship, they examined slavery as an evolving institution and honestly believed that their role was to allow the "facts" to speak for themselves. If anything, students at Johns Hopkins asked the correct questions. The contributors to the *Studies* assiduously avoided polemics, purposely concentrating on slavery's legal side. In their minds this side of servitude was the least vulnerable to special pleading and distortion. That these queries fail to satisfy later historians suggests a common dilemma in historiography: presentism. Further, for years historians have relied heavily on the Johns

Hopkins dissertations on slavery. Scholars as diverse in outlook as W. E. B. Du Bois and Ulrich B. Phillips, or Kenneth M. Stampp and Eugene D. Genovese, have acknowledged their debts to the series. Phillips, for example, included in *American Negro Slavery* (1918) twenty references to the *Studies*.

Finally, the Johns Hopkins volumes indeed served as models for later students of slavery. In both the quality of their research and their method, the dissertations towered above much of the other scholarship. Students throughout the country looked to them as guides for scope, organization, and source materials. As careful as these "scientific" scholars at Johns Hopkins were to avoid value judgments, they ultimately failed to transcend the proslavery ideas prevalent in their age. Yet it must be remembered that the students at Johns Hopkins were the first historians to devote all of their scholarly attention to slavery, contributing the first monographs exclusively on the topic. Their efforts popularized graduate training, research, and publication on slavery. In so doing, the Johns Hopkins *Studies* established an important prototype. Others would try to improve the model.

## NOTES

1. James Schouler, *Historical Briefs* (New York, 1896), 54; James A. Woodburn, "Promotion of Historical Study in America following the Civil War," *Illinois State Historical Society Transactions*, 29 (1922): 45–46; Frederick W. Moore et al., "The Teaching of History in the South," *Vanderbilt University Quarterly*, 3 (January, 1903): 23; Adams to Samuel A. Green, February 26, 1882, Samuel A. Green Papers, Massachusetts Historical Society; James C. Ballagh, "The Johns Hopkins University and the South," *Johns Hopkins University Circulars*, 20 (January, 1901): 23.

2. Adams, *The Study of History in American Colleges and Universities* (Washington, 1887), 175; Wendell Holmes Stephenson, "Herbert B. Adams and Southern Historical Scholarship at the Johns Hopkins University," *Maryland Historical Magazine*, 42 (March, 1947): 8–9; Trent, "The Study of Southern History," *Vanderbilt Southern History Society Publications*, 1 (1895): 5.

3. William K. Boyd, "Southern History in American Universities," *South Atlantic Quarterly*, 1 (July, 1901): 240; [John M. Vincent], "The Birney Collection of Books on Slavery," *Johns Hopkins University Circulars*, 10 (February, 1891): 56; William Birney to Herbert Baxter Adams, January 12, 1891, Herbert Baxter Adams Papers, Johns Hopkins University; *Sixteenth Annual Report of the President of the Johns Hopkins University* (Baltimore, 1891), 14,

16; "Abstract of the Report of the Librarian," *Seventeenth Annual Report of the President of the Johns Hopkins University* (Baltimore, 1892), 85; Ballagh, "The Johns Hopkins University and the South," 12.

4. Adams to Bancroft, March 5, 1885, Frederic Bancroft Papers, Columbia University; Bassett to Adams, December 16, 1898, June 21, 1899, October 23, 1899, December 7, 1900, Adams Papers; *Report of the President of the Johns Hopkins University* (Baltimore, 1908), 59.

5. "Dr. von Holst's Lectures on the Relation of History to Politics, etc.," *Johns Hopkins University Circulars*, 3 (January, 1884): 43; Johns Hopkins University Historical Seminary Records, vol. 1 (1877–1892), 124, 493–495, vol. 2 (1892–1901), 15, 23, 173, Johns Hopkins University.

6. Brackett, "Report of Certain Studies in the Institution of African Slavery in the United States," *Papers of the American Historical Association*, 1 (September, 1885): 436, 437.

7. Johns Hopkins University Historical Seminary Records, vol. 1, pp. 281, 409, 493–495; *Johns Hopkins University Circulars*, 4 (March, July, 1885): 66, 122.

8. Hughson to Adams, July 9, 1893, Adams Papers; Hughson, "Carolina Slave Laws," New York *Evening Post*, March 18, 25, April 8, 1893; Johns Hopkins University Historical Seminary Records, vol. 2, pp. 345–346, 378, 402, 412.

9. *Twenty-third Annual Report of the President of the Johns Hopkins University* (Baltimore, 1898), 64; *Report of the President of the Johns Hopkins University* (Baltimore, 1908), 59; *Report of the President of the Johns Hopkins University* (Baltimore, 1909), 57; *Report of the President of the Johns Hopkins University* (Baltimore, 1910), 59, 61; *Report of the President of the Johns Hopkins University* (Baltimore, 1912), 54–55; Johns Hopkins University Historical Seminary Records, vol. 2, pp. 15, 23, 173, 183, 345–346, 378; Laprade, "The Legal Status of the Negroes in the District of Columbia Previous to the Abolition of Slavery" [1911], William Thomas Laprade Papers, Duke University Archives.

10. The following volumes in the Johns Hopkins University *Studies* either treat slavery in the North or touch upon slavery in the South in only a superficial manner. Consequently, they are excluded from this analysis: Bernard C. Steiner, *History of Slavery in Connecticut* (1893); James Alton James, *English Institutions and the American Indian* (1894); Edson L. Whitney, *Government of the Colony of South Carolina* (1895); Henry S. Cooley, *A Study of Slavery in New Jersey* (1896); Stephen B. Weeks, *Southern Quakers and Slavery* (1896); Eugene I. McCormac, *White Servitude in Maryland, 1634–1820* (1904).

11. Brackett, "History" and "The Passing of the Southern Cavalier," unpublished manuscripts, Jeffrey R. Brackett Papers, Simmons College; Katharine D. Hardwick et al., *Jeffrey Richardson Brackett: Everyday Puritan* (Boston,

1956), 25–31; John David Smith, "Jeffrey Richardson Brackett," in Walter I. Trattner, ed., *Biographical Dictionary of Social Welfare in America* (forthcoming). Unless otherwise indicated, information on the Johns Hopkins historians is drawn from J. M. Vincent et al., eds., *Herbert B. Adams: Tributes of Friends* (Baltimore, 1902), and Norman Brown, *Johns Hopkins Half Century Directory* (Baltimore, 1926).

12. Brackett, *The Negro in Maryland—A Study of the Institution of Slavery* (Baltimore, 1889), 263 and passim; idem, review of John Kells Ingram, *A History of Slavery and Serfdom*, in *American Historical Review*, 1 (October, 1895): 154.

13. Brackett, *The Negro in Maryland*, 2, 147n, 42, 118, 119, 66–67, 106–107.

14. Brackett, "The Status of the Slave, 1775–1789," in J. Franklin Jameson, ed., *Essays in the Constitutional History of the United States in the Formative Period, 1775–1789* (Boston, 1889), 270, 277, 309.

15. Bassett to William E. Dodd, December 10, 1911, William E. Dodd Papers, Manuscript Division, Library of Congress; Wendell Holmes Stephenson, "The Negro in the Thinking and Writing of John Spencer Bassett," *North Carolina Historical Review*, 25 (October, 1948): 427–441.

16. Bassett, "History as It Relates to Life," *Methodist Review*, 45 (July–August, 1897): 355; Bassett, "Two Negro Leaders," *South Atlantic Quarterly*, 2 (July, 1903): 272; "Stirring Up the Fires of Race Antipathy," ibid. (October, 1903): 301, 304; Bassett to Oswald Garrison Villard, November 17, 1905, Oswald Garrison Villard Papers, Houghton Library, Harvard University; Bassett to Herbert Baxter Adams, November 15, 1898, Adams Papers.

17. Bassett to Charles Francis Adams, November 3, 1911, John Spencer Bassett Papers, Massachusetts Historical Society; Fleming to J. G. de Roulhac Hamilton, October 22, 1902, J. G. de Roulhac Hamilton Papers, Southern Historical Collection, University of North Carolina at Chapel Hill; Dodd to Edwin Mims, November 23, 1903, Edwin Mims Papers, Joint University Libraries, Nashville; Bassett to Dodd, May 7, 1907, John Spencer Bassett Papers, Duke University Archives.

18. Bassett, *Slavery and Servitude in the Colony of North Carolina* (Baltimore, 1896), 13; idem, "The Negro's Inheritance from Africa," *South Atlantic Quarterly*, 2 (October, 1903): 299; Bassett to Oswald Garrison Villard, November 17, 1905, Villard Papers. For an excellent statement of Bassett's view of slavery and race, see "Is the Southern Position Anglo-Saxon?" *Colored American Magazine*, 17 (July, 1909): 56–59.

19. Bassett to Herbert Baxter Adams, July 31, 1895, Adams Papers; Bassett, *Slavery in the State of North Carolina* (Baltimore, 1899), 47, 48, 52, 53, 51, 50.

20. Bassett, "The Case of the State vs. Will," *Historical Papers Published by the Trinity College Historical Society*, ser. 2, (1898): 20.

21. Bassett, *Slavery and Servitude in the Colony of North Carolina*, 15, 60; idem, *Slavery in the State of North Carolina*, 86.

22. "James Curtis Ballagh," *Old Penn*, 12 (October 4, 1913): 41, in James C. Ballagh Biographical File, University of Pennsylvania Archives; George D. Fairborn, "Men and Things," Philadelphia *Bulletin*, August 6, 1936; Johns Hopkins University Historical Seminary Records, vol. 2, pp. 345–346, 378, 402, 463; Ballagh, review of Albert B. Hart, *Slavery and Abolition*, in *American Historical Review*, 12 (July, 1907): 903–904; idem, "Introduction to Southern Economic History—the Land System," *Annual Report of the American Historical Association for the Year 1897* (Washington, 1898), 105; idem, "Southern Economic History: Tariff and Public Lands," *Annual Report of the American Historical Association for the Year 1898* (Washington, 1899), 234; Ballagh to Herbert Baxter Adams, September 17, 1897, Adams Papers.

23. Jordan, "Modern Tensions and the Origins of American Slavery," *Journal of Southern History*, 28 (February, 1962): 18; Handlin, "Origins of the Southern Labor System," *William and Mary Quarterly*, 3rd ser., 7 (April, 1950): 203; Degler, "Slavery and the Genesis of American Race Prejudice," *Comparative Studies in Society and History*, 2 (October, 1959): 50. See also Joseph Boskin, *Into Slavery: Racial Decisions in the Virginia Colony* (Philadelphia, 1976), 102.

24. Ballagh, *White Servitude in the Colony of Virginia* (Baltimore, 1895), 64, 67, 68, 91, 68; idem, review of Philip A. Bruce, *Economic History of Virginia in the Seventeenth Century*, in *Citizen*, 3 (May, 1897): 69; idem, "The Introduction of Slavery into North America," *Johns Hopkins University Circulars*, 17 and 18 (December, 1898): 31.

25. Ballagh, "The Institutional Origin of Slavery," *Conservative Review*, 2 (August, 1899): 47; idem, "The Social Condition of the Ante-Bellum Negro," ibid., 3 (March, 1900): 211; advertisement in *Johns Hopkins University Circulars*, 21 (April, 1902): 56; Ballagh, *A History of Slavery in Virginia* (Baltimore, 1902), 149; Ballagh to Adams, June 24, July 28, 1895, Adams Papers.

26. Ballagh, *A History of Slavery in Virginia*, 28, 29n, 30–39, 40, 63; idem, "The Institutional Origin of Slavery," 64.

27. Ballagh, *A History of Slavery in Virginia*, 100, 102, 97, 98, 99, 101, 106.

28. Ibid., 107, 108, 106, 113, 114, 115.

29. Russell, *The Free Negro in Virginia, 1619–1865* (Baltimore, 1913), vii, 17, 18–19, 25–28, 29, 31, 33, 36–37; idem, "Colored Freemen as Slave Owners in Virginia," *Journal of Negro History*, 1 (July, 1916): 242.

30. Bancroft to Charles S. Sydnor, May 3, 1930, Charles S. Sydnor Papers, Duke University Archives.

31. Trexler, *Slavery in Missouri, 1804–1865* (Baltimore, 1914), vii; Trexler to James C. Ballagh, February 6, 1912, John M. Vincent Papers, Johns Hopkins

University; James M. Breckenridge, *William Clark Breckenridge: Historical Research Writer and Bibliographer of Missouriana* (St. Louis, 1932), 65, 66; Trexler, "My Recollections of William Clark Breckenridge," *Missouri Historical Review*, 22 (July, 1928): 543–546.

32. Trexler, *Slavery in Missouri*, 53n, 13, 14, 44, 37. See also Trexler, "The Value and the Sale of the Missouri Slave," *Missouri Historical Review*, 8 (January, 1914): 69–85.

33. Trexler, *Slavery in Missouri*, 54, 56.

34. Ibid., 24, 55, 33, 29, 54, 53.

35. Ibid., 46, 13, 19, 18, 16–17, 21, 23, 22, 28, 58, 70, 82. See also Trexler, "Slavery in Missouri Territory," *Missouri Historical Review*, 3 (April, 1909): 179–197.

36. Bancroft in *Political Science Quarterly*, 5 (December, 1890): 688; anon., in *American Historical Review*, 5 (October, 1899): 169; Lyon G. Tyler in ibid., 1 (October, 1895): 158; anon., in *Critic*, 41 (November, 1902): 480; Du Bois in *American Historical Review*, 8 (January, 1903): 356; anon., in *Nation*, 75 (October 16, 1902): 311; Buck in *Mississippi Valley Historical Review*, 2 (December, 1915): 450; Bancroft to Charles S. Sydnor, January 7, 1932, Bancroft to Trexler, August 15, 1918, Bancroft Papers.

37. Bancroft in *Political Science Quarterly*, 5 (December, 1890): 689; Du Bois in *American Historical Review*, 8 (January, 1903): 356, 357; William H. Glasson and Bassett, "Two Recent Books on the Negro," *South Atlantic Quarterly*, 2 (January, 1903): 84, 85, 87; anon., "Two Recent Books on Slavery," *Publications of the Southern History Association*, 6 (November, 1902): 515–516.

38. Elkins, *Slavery: A Problem in American Institutional and Intellectual Life* (Chicago, 1959), 8–9; Wall, "African Slavery," in Arthur S. Link and Rembert W. Patrick, eds., *Writing Southern History, Essays in Honor of Fletcher M. Green* (Baton Rouge, 1965), 185; Smith, "A Study of American Historians and Their Interpretation of Negro Slavery in the United States" (Ph.D. diss., Washington State University, 1970), 56; Ver Steeg, "Historians and the Southern Colonies," in Ray Allen Billington, ed., *The Reinterpretation of Early American History* (San Marino, 1966), 83, 97; Fogel and Engerman, *Time on the Cross: Evidence and Methods* (Boston, 1974), 178–179; Patterson, "The Theory of Slavery and Slave Society," unpublished paper, 1974, p. 2, copy in University of Kentucky Library; idem, "Slavery," *Annual Review of Sociology*, 3 (1977): 413.

# 6

# Institutional Studies of Slavery

The Johns Hopkins University *Studies* not only set a scholarly standard for institutional monographs on slavery, but served to establish slavery as one of the most popular subjects of inquiry for graduate students and other investigators. But after the turn of the century, Johns Hopkins began to lose its dominance in the field of Southern history in general and slave studies in particular. Courses in Southern history soon were offered at the University of Wisconsin, Columbia University, and the University of Chicago. In 1902, for example, Frederick Jackson Turner hired young Ulrich B. Phillips to teach Southern history at Wisconsin. Turner noted that the Madison campus possessed excellent research facilities for studying the history and culture of the South. "We desire to understand the South," wrote Turner, "and to have its history treated here impartially and fully." Even before Phillips arrived, such student theses as "Economic Characteristics of Slavery in 1850" and "The Anti-Slavery Movement in Kentucky prior to 1849" had begun to emanate from Wisconsin's seminars.[1]

At Columbia, students flocked to work with John William Burgess and William A. Dunning, whose Ph.D.'s in turn offered similar fare to another generation. In 1906, for example, Walter Lynwood Fleming began offering a course "Slavery in America" at West Virginia University in Morgantown. In this seminar Fleming stressed the evolution of slavery worldwide—in the Orient, Europe, and England. His students juxtaposed slavery in different places and at varying times with comparative free labor systems. They evaluated American slavery as a broad sectional, economic, and social force with long-range effects on blacks and whites alike. Fleming's course syllabus, "History of Slavery," suggests the professor's view of slavery as a fluid and diversified labor system. Elsewhere, others such as Professors J. Franklin Jameson and William E. Dodd also taught specialized courses in the history of slavery.[2]

This flurry of interest in slavery resulted in the publication of hundreds of obscure theses, monographs, and articles on the topic. To be sure, some of these added next to nothing to the slavery debate even in those years. Today they stand as curiosities of an earlier day. At the very most they illustrate the varieties of proslavery or neoabolitionist thought still current as late as 1918. But many of the lesser-known scholarly and popular writings on slavery made important contributions. They transcended the narrow confines of the Johns Hopkins dissertations and began to provide the necessary detail for broader interpretive studies. Influenced strongly by the work already completed at Johns Hopkins, these writings tended to mirror in method and sources much of the research begun in Baltimore. They adoped the institutional framework first introduced by Herbert Baxter Adams—examining the evolution of different elements of an institution over time. Several of the authors discussed in this chapter broke fresh ground and established new avenues in the study of the peculiar institution. They began to occupy, but far from filled, glaring gaps in the literature. All in all, these institutional writings attest to the persistent interest in slavery throughout the late nineteenth and early twentieth centuries. And they suggest the breadth of the literature on slavery even in its seminal years.

# I

Because of the widespread availability of published slave codes, legal digests, statutes, and court proceedings, slave law remained the most popular subject for students of the peculiar institution. A virtual flood of writings, often thin in substance and hackneyed, dominated writings on slavery in these years. So common were studies of slave law that at least two scholars called for fresh approaches to the topic. In 1911 Professor William T. Laprade of Trinity College complained that previous writings simply listed slave statutes at random. They ignored the interplay of custom and racial etiquette in the enforcement of these laws.[3] According to Robert E. Park of the University of Chicago, so much attention was paid to slave jurisprudence that "the more intimate and human side . . . the relations between the races . . . has been neglected." Students of slavery, insisted Park in 1915, were misled by relying too heavily on law codes as sources.[4]

But the topic of slave law continued to hold great appeal. For many white students it reinforced the distant, impersonal, formal, and legalistic way most white Americans viewed blacks in general during the age of Jim Crow. As late as 1918, an Alabama newspaper published an article that underscored white southerners' satisfactions with the old system of slave laws. Slave justice, the article explained, consisted of two tribunals. On the one hand, slave courts protected the bondsmen from abuse. Masters, on the other hand, fashioned their own regulations to suit the needs of plantation discipline. According to the Montgomery *Advertiser*:

There were very few violations of the law on the part of these slaves, and their conduct was such that the time of the courts was rarely ever taken up with cases against them. Whereas, now the time of the courts is almost altogether occupied in trying offenders for violations against their free brothers, as the chain-gangs, jails, coal mines and penitentiary will testify.

The more whites pondered contemporary race relations, the more convinced they became of the correctness and magnanimity of white justice under the slave regime.[5]

Whites in these years overwhelmingly perceived blacks as inferiors, a people who, despite the Reconstruction amendments, were unworthy of American citizenship. The 1883 Supreme Court ruling in the Civil Rights Cases and its decision in *Plessy vs. Ferguson* (1896) had sounded the call: the federal government would neither protect blacks against discrimination by private acts nor nullify state segregation statutes. The Court decided that racial discrimination in itself did not constitute "incidents" or "badges" of slavery. In the case of the 1883 decision, all but one justice declared that "it would be running the slavery argument into the ground to make it apply to every act of discrimination which a person may see fit to make as to the guests he will entertain, or as to the people he will take into his coach or cab, or admit to his concert or theatre, or deal with in other matters of intercourse or business." A separate legal sphere for blacks quickly translated into unequal conditions of life across the board.[6] In the last decade of the nineteenth century one southern state after another revised its legal code to deny blacks full participation in American economic, educational, and political life. The "badges" of servitude adorned the fabric of race relations throughout the Southland. With the legal status of contemporary blacks under such careful scrutiny, students naturally cast a backward glance to understand the origins of racial distinctions in American law.

In 1889, for example, Mary Tremain, a graduate student at Nebraska State University, began work on her thesis concerning slavery in the District of Columbia. In her study, almost totally a recitation of Virginia and Maryland slave laws, she condemned the legislation but questioned the degree to which the slave statutes actually were enforced. Tremain suspected that in practice they may have been softened by custom. A year later Gerald Montgomery West completed his Ph.D. dissertation at Columbia, "The Status of the Negro in Virginia during the Colonial Period." This study drew almost totally on William W. Henning's *Statutes at Large* (1819–1823) and presented no interpretation or analysis whatsoever.[7] These early studies illustrate the undigested nature of most of the verbatim presentations of slave law undertaken in these years. One student after another adopted a formula that usually included compiling a virtual catalog of slave laws, crimes, and punishments. Few authors tried to explain the cause or significance of the slave legislation or to show how it evolved over time. And rarely did anyone assess the degree to which the various slave laws were enforced. Instead, each student sketched in minute detail the nature of the slave as legal entity. Slave children followed the status of their mothers. Bondsmen could not absent themselves from the farm or plantation without leave, and laws prevented them from assembling freely. There were also restrictions on the slaves' ability to own and sell property. The authors agreed that stealing was the most common slave crime. While masters were required to treat their slaves humanely, in almost every southern state they received compensation for the loss of a bondsman executed for a capital crime. In what almost became a litany of slave laws, each writer listed the various punishments allowable under law, the details of the patrol system, and the fine points of trial procedure for slave cases.[8]

Several of the earliest authors clearly belong in the neoabolitionist camp. They used the study of slave law to attack the peculiar institution. In 1893 Shirley C. Hughson, an Episcopal clergyman, criticized whites in colonial South Carolina for passing strict slave laws in response to imaginary slave restiveness. Their paranoia led the whites to abuse the bondsmen and to disregard "the human nature that dwelt in the breast of every slave, savage though he might have been." Six years later, Walter C. Clephane, the son of an antislavery leader, openly sympathized with slaves who had resided in the District of Columbia. Slave laws in the District, he said, were too harsh—so severe that "a slave could hardly be called a man under the law." The code, for example, prohibited emancipating slaves over forty-five years old, even if the manumission had been specified in a will. If a slave struck a patrol officer, the black was subject to having his ears cropped. Sensitive to the many legal hardships experienced by Washington slaves, Clephane asserted that "to be born black seems to have been . . . a misfortune which no power known to man could overcome."[9]

In 1917 John M. Mecklin of the University of Pittsburgh blamed the South's slave codes for curbing the slaves' self-development. These codes served "to negate the personality of the slave and to fix his status as a part of an industrial system." Anticipating in part the later thesis of Stanley M. Elkins, Mecklin faulted slave law for keeping the black man forever a child. The slave "lived perpetually in an atmosphere of fawning and flattery," said Mecklin, one certainly not "conducive to the development of independent manhood." Mecklin judged the "negation" of the slave's "personality" most tragic. The bondsmen behaved according to the expectations of their white owners, or in Mecklin's words, "solely in terms of the social mind of the white." Two years later William Lloyd Imes censured parts of Tennessee's brutal slave code, a code that left the bondsman in limbo—"at once being slave and man, property and human being." Slave statutes held little force, though, in East Tennessee, said Imes. Drawing heavily on the testimony of former slaves, he identified significant violations of laws against interracial mixing. Liaisons between slave males and Scotch-Irish, yeoman-class females were frequent. The bondsmen and mountain whites violated social custom as well by engaging in such social activities as quilting, husking, and barn raising.[10]

In spite of these critical remarks, the vast majority of the legal studies defended slavery as a just, benign legal institution. In studies on slave law in Mississippi, Louisiana, the District of Columbia, South Carolina, and Georgia, the authors emphasized the safeguards protecting the bondsmen from abuse. Alfred Holt Stone, an unabashed proslavery theorist and planter, maintained that masters held genuine affection for their slaves. Few would have subjected them to mistreatment, he said. What on the eve of the twentieth century appeared as harsh laws, continued Stone, were acceptable at a time when medieval punishments still were inflicted on free persons throughout the world. "So far from being a creature with no legal status," the slave "was surrounded by all the protection which just laws, humanely administered, could afford." Another Mississippian, lawyer and banker W. W. Magruder, wrote in a sarcastic, antinorthern tone. He affirmed that insubordinate slaves received "reasonable chastisement," but that the bulk of the bondsmen were "happy, contented, well fed, well clothed people." He even judged slave marriages more stable than those of the Mississippi black population in 1901. Defending Louisiana's slave laws, James J. McLoughlin linked them to the state's then current Jim Crow statutes. He justified the former as "an expression of an innate necessity of nature to keep the races pure." The latter served just as indispensable a role: to maintain a social distance between the superior and inferior races. In 1911 Professor William T. Laprade of Trinity College argued that masters in the District of Columbia evaded slave laws in ways that benefited the bondsmen. They provided the slaves "privileges which were not warrantable under the law," wrote Laprade, "and in few cases was the letter of the law enforced."[11]

South Carolina historians Edward McCrady and William A. Schaper also found little to criticize in the slave laws. The first author in fact praised Carolinians for the spirit of their 1740 slave code revision. In the aftermath of the Stono Revolt, he said, they chose to ameliorate the condition of the blacks rather than to make slave legislation more severe. Schaper, a recipient of a Ph.D. from Columbia, stressed the flexible nature of slave control. Slave statutes in South Carolina permitted a "very wide latitude" in the management of bondsmen. In a similar vein, Herschel P. Cobb, a member of the Savannah Bar, extolled the protection that Georgia slave laws afforded the blacks. Although they appeared severe on paper, he said, in practice the most drastic laws never were implemented. Under most circumstances the administration of slave law was "informal." Like innumerable proslavery theorists since emancipation, Cobb countenanced slavery for pounding "civilized ideas into the thick skull of the barbaric African."[12]

Fortunately one writer in these years, Howell M. Henry, examined slave law with the scholarly rigor and detachment of the Johns Hopkins students. Born in Newberry, South Carolina, in 1879, Henry received his Ph.D. in 1913 from Vanderbilt University. He studied under Professor St. George L. Sioussat, himself trained at Johns Hopkins and a contributor to its *Studies*. Henry's *The Police Control of the Slave in South Carolina* (1914), which had been his dissertation, became the most important examination of slave law of its day. Despite the book's racist underpinnings, old-fashioned method, and legalistic tone, it remains important to the historiography of slavery. In an effort to be fair and judicious in his assessment, Henry delved deeply into manuscript court records, local ordinances, county records, and, most impressively, hard-to-find newspapers. For example, in order to determine to what degree slave laws were enforced, he examined the manuscript records of nine districts representing every section of South Carolina. He also gleaned valuable data on slave trial procedure from criminal court records contained in the various Sessions Journals.[13]

Alone among historians of these years, Henry examined *why* the various slave laws were passed and *which* ones were enforced. He argued that most slave restrictions evolved from expediency, not as a result of a fixed theory of slave treatment. Statutes were written for emergencies such as insurrections; masters rarely consulted them for daily plantation routine. Laws against slaves trading with white merchants were established "as occasion demanded." Such laws, as well as prohibitions against importing slaves and hiring bondsmen out, generally were ignored. Only rarely were slaves punished for attending religious gatherings, dances, corn shuckings, or logrollings, or for swearing, smoking, and loitering—yet all these things were outlawed by specific slave ordinances. Similarly, the laws for the punishment of whites guilty of killing or excessively punishing slaves went into effect only when evidence indicated a blatant violation.[14]

Henry insisted, however, that the Seamen Acts and the restrictions against slave stealing never were evaded. The latter crime, according to the author, was considered an even more heinous offense than murdering a slave. Such was the unbridled power of the master class in antebellum South Carolina, wrote Henry. Killing a slave while correcting him was justifiable, he added, under the accepted legal and social mores of owning chattel personal. Slave stealing, on the other hand, threatened "the entire stability of the whole system and was subversive of the interests of society." The slave stealer became in the mind of the South Carolina planter "the anarchist of Southern serfdom."[15]

Henry argued that sectional differences within the Palmetto State played a major role in influencing slave legislation. In the upland regions, with a low concentration of bondsmen, farmers made few demands for rigid slave laws. Their low-country neighbors, however, the affluent Carolina planter elite, required strict slave regulations because of the large black population in their districts. Throughout his monograph, Henry stressed the strength of the planter class in shaping South Carolina's slave codes. Planters, he insisted, favored slave laws designed to keep the bondsmen laboring at their highest efficiency, but nonslaveholding whites also favored their passage. According to Henry, "Slavery was not only an economic and industrial system . . . but more than that, it was a gigantic police system, which the poor man in the up-country as well as the wealthy planter in the lowlands did not know how to replace." Much like Hughson before him, Henry charged that most slave legislation resulted from an unwarranted fear of slave violence. Yet Henry's own evidence regarding the Stono Revolt of 1739 and Denmark Vesey's 1822 plot suggests that Carolinians indeed had reason to fear their captives. In the wake of the Vesey plot, whites took action to tighten their bonds of power. They ousted free blacks from their state, prohibited new manumissions, and passed the Seamen Acts—the latter to restrict black seamen aboard ships docked in South Carolina ports.[16]

In his discussion of slave law, Henry offered important insights into the workings of South Carolina's slave patrol system. Dating back to 1686, the patrol guarded against the free movement and insubordination of slaves. Patrollers served as an unofficial statewide police force to keep the bondsmen in line. Henry identified two problems with the patrol system. First, masters often allowed their slaves—in direct violation of the law—to visit friends on neighboring farms and plantations. Second, masters genuinely feared the mishandling of their chattels by nonslaveholding patrollers who "looked upon the patrol as the guarantee of . . . safety from evils often perpetrated by the black race." Henry judged the abuse of slaves by patrollers "the greatest evil of the system." Slave patrols gave police power over the blacks to "unscrupulous persons" rather than to "the better class."[17]

Henry recognized two additional aspects of slave law generally ignored by previous writers. Anticipating the later work of Richard C. Wade, he explained how Charleston's urban environment posed serious impediments to effective police control of bondsmen.[18] City slaves, often skilled craftsmen, enjoyed privileges denied their comrades on the plantations and farms. They often hired themselves out and had ample opportunity to associate with free blacks. Such a situation, noted Henry, required flexible slave laws and police enforcement. In the rural areas, day-to-day law enforcement tended to rest with the plantation overseer. South Carolina's 1712 slave code required every absentee master to have a white man present on his plantation. The overseer thus became a virtual "plantation quasi–police officer," supervising not only agricultural production but slave discipline as well. Unfortunately, wrote Henry, the average plantation supervisor was "a misfit, a makeshift," who rarely accepted his "middle position in society" or completely satisfied his employer. Low wages and the nature of the job ("stern necessity . . . forbade even a tendency toward kindness") often made the overseer cruel, "coarse and brutal." He provided the bondsmen with little moral direction. Most men of this class perceived overseeing as "a step to nothing." "In a sense," concluded Henry, the overseer "like the slave he controlled, found no hope or ambition in the system."[19]

In 1916, two years after his book appeared, Henry applied the same methodology he had used for South Carolina to slave law in Tennessee. He identified many similar characteristics of slave jurisprudence in the two states. Slave discipline frequently depended on extralegal conditions determined by community standards. Local slave courts, often manned by nonslaveholders, made "hasty" decisions that infuriated masters. Henry reminded historians that they must judge slave treatment "by the standards of a time when the slave was little better than a savage." He praised the Tennessee Supreme Court for insisting upon humane treatment for bondsmen, the court "often appearing to strain the law to do so." Henry also observed the effects of similar geographic and social cleavages on slave law in Tennessee as on slave control in South Carolina.[20]

*The Police Control of the Slave in South Carolina* contained two of the flaws inherent in the Johns Hopkins *Studies*. Henry failed to relate slave law to economic aspects of the peculiar institution. And by emphasizing the infrequent enforcement of slave laws, he also argued implicitly that slavery in his native state was benign. But Henry's study surpassed in thoroughness, interpretation, and scope all of the Johns Hopkins dissertations except for Harrison A. Trexler's study of slavery in Missouri, also published in 1914. Henry's careful examination of slave law viewed the institution in South Carolina as a complete system. Henry incorporated William T. Laprade's 1911 mandate that historians of slavery contrast the enforcement of statutes pertaining to slavery with the actual laws.[21] In so doing, Henry examined previously unexplored aspects of slavery, including special slave courts and the legal status of hired slaves. Significantly, his observation that white mechanics in Charleston protested the competition of skilled slaves anticipated the later work of Robert S. Starobin.[22] Whereas other investigators ran aground in the mire of slave law, Henry took the subject out of the statute books and placed it clearly in the workaday world of master, overseer, and slave.

## II

Appearing simultaneously with the works on slave law was a group of state and local studies on the peculiar institution that paralleled, and to some degree surpassed, those completed at Johns Hopkins. This genre consisted of two broad groups: writings that openly espoused the new proslavery attitude current in these years, and less polemical works that helped fill the holes in the growing literature on the peculiar institution. These latter studies provide important micro views of little-explored aspects of slave life. Whereas the first group generally added little to the ongoing slavery debate, the second unearthed fresh insights, yet more often than not also retained the tone of the slavery apologist.

Robert A. Brock's early essays on slavery in Virginia typified the lingering proslavery rationale. In 1887 Brock, librarian of the Virginia Historical Society, argued that even though slavery retarded southern economic growth, it contributed to "a patriarchal . . . social system"— well worth the price of any monetary loss or lasting regional back- wardness. On another occasion he wrote with even more assurance that "the condition of the negro as a slave in the Southern States was infinitely for his betterment, mentally, spiritually, and physically." Some years later A. R. H. Ranson, a former Virginia slave owner and Confederate staff officer, offered a practical explanation for the kind- hearted treatment accorded the bondsmen. It was in the best self-interest of the owner to attend to his slave's needs, wrote Ranson. "He took care of his slave because it was money in his pocket to do so, and money out of his pocket if he did not. . . . That the negro was better housed, better fed, better clothed, and better looked after in sickness than now, was simply because the owner had money at stake." Jennie

C. Morton, editor of the *Register of the Kentucky State Historical Society*, justified slavery within a broader context.

The negroes were cared for in slavery as no other poor people of any nation were ever cared for in the world before or since. . . . They were given an industrial education, the best in the world for them. They were, what it seems impossible to make them in Africa, a people; trained to peaceful pursuits in the common but no less essential industries of farm and domestic life, their native barbarity controlled and suppressed, if not eliminated by discipline and authority, their labor was made advantageous to the South on the plantations and to Kentucky on the farms.

Slavery, then, provided broad benefits that bettered Kentucky slaveholders and bondsmen alike.[23]

Dunbar Rowland, who organized Mississippi's Department of Archives and History in 1902, wrote one of the classic defenses of slavery on the state level. His "Plantation Life in Mississippi Before the War" appeared in 1900 and eulogized all of slavery's good points. Couching his images of slavery in terms reminiscent of Sir Walter Scott's novels, he mourned the loss of a social system where "princely" masters protected their contented plantation serfs. He romanticized "the chivalrous, courtly, courageous Southern gentleman . . . the grandest embodiment of the most superb manhood that ever graced a forum or died upon a battlefield." The master/slave relationship "was humane, generous, loving and sympathetic." Mississippi bondsmen received abundant food, suitable clothing, and commodious housing. On the latter point Rowland asserted that every slave cabin included "a large front room," and that all slaves were provided a garden truck patch for their use. What basis, he asked, did the abolitionists and neoabolitionists have for their condemnations of slavery? Rowland was convinced that the slaves were satisfied because they constantly sang. The Mississippian wrote, apparently in all seriousness, "All men and women who sing while they toil are happy." Virtually parroting Rowland, in 1913 Ruth B. Hawes lauded Mississippi slavery as "beneficent plantation life such as the world can never see again."[24]

Fortunately, a talented amateur historian and a number of graduate students went beyond such romanticized views of slavery on the state and local level. In 1895 Philip Alexander Bruce published the best early work on the economic and social sides of slavery in the colonial period.

Unlike most of his peers, with or without portfolio, Bruce refused to shy away from the question of slavery's profitability. Important but long forgotten dissertations on Kentucky slavery by William Reynolds Vance and Ivan E. McDougle first analyzed the elements that set slavery in the Commonwealth apart from the institution in her sister southern states. Meriwether Harvey and James K. Turner conducted even more minute grass roots research on slavery in Auburn, Alabama, and Edgecombe County, North Carolina, respectively. One investigator after another probed the inner workings of slavery. Yet the proslavery assumptions of their day blinded these investigators, no matter how thorough or "scientific." The new proslavery argument remained embedded even in the best of these scholarly works.

Bruce came by the proslavery interpretation naturally: he was plantation born and bred. His earliest writings on slavery gave little indication of Bruce's later achievement as a historian of the peculiar institution. This scion of a long line of Virginia plantation aristocrats embodied the values and symbols of the Old South. The influential proslavery novelist Thomas Nelson Page and James A. Seddon, Confederate secretary of war, ranked among Bruce's Virginia relatives. Bruce grew to manhood surrounded by numerous bondsmen and lived on a five-thousand-acre tobacco plantation in Charlotte County. According to his biographer, in this environment Bruce "early absorbed the romantic notions and visions of a grandiose age." Educated at the University of Virginia and Harvard Law School, he succeeded first as a Baltimore lawyer, then as manager of Richmond's Vulcan Iron Works, and finally as a journalist. Like Rhodes, Bruce eventually chose to abandon industrial capitalism for the life of the gentleman scholar. In the years 1895–1910 he contributed three major works on the economic, social, and institutional history of his native state in the seventeenth century. During these years Bruce also published a popular study on the "Negro problem," *The Plantation Negro as a Freeman* (1889), and an important work in the Henry Grady tradition, *The Rise of the New South* (1905).[25]

Slavery assumed a major place in Bruce's thought. Whether writing about the Old South or the New, he retained the notion of white domination over a class of incestuous black wards. In *The Plantation Negro as a Freeman* he wrote glowingly of the black man as slave.

There is no record of any agricultural laborer who excelled the negro as such when he was a slave. Docile, obedient, cheerful, unresentful, of remarkable strength and unusual powers of endurance, he lacked no quality which a tiller of the soil should have, except that it was more or less necessary that he should always be carefully overlooked; but under such supervision, . . . he had few, if any, deficiencies.

Yet emancipation transformed the black into an indolent thief, an obsessive rapist of white women. "There is something strangely alluring and seductive to them [black men] in the appearance of a white woman; they are aroused and stimulated by its foreignness to their experience of sexual pleasures, and it moves them to gratify their lust at any cost in spite of every obstacle." Bruce waxed pessimistically on the depths of black moral and social decline without the helping hand of slavery. He complained that when denied the discipline of enslavement, blacks regressed toward savagery, that they were incapable of functioning without white control. But departing from the standard proslavery line, Bruce admitted that slavery had not lessened black lasciviousness, but only stabilized and "restrained" it. There was no cure, he said, for the black man who would remain a perennial child in emotions, morals, and capacity. In Bruce's opinion, even slavery had not succeeded in upgrading the savage black's loose morals. "Marriage under the old regime," he wrote, "was very like unlawful cohabitation under the new, only that the master . . . compelled the nominal husband and wife to live together permanently." Emancipation served only to degrade the blacks further, he said. Their "character and conduct" had deteriorated immensely since manumission. Like so many other white Americans, Bruce lamented slavery's departure, for slavery alone had ensured racial harmony between two such unequal peoples. As slaves the blacks proved to be "faithful, cheerful, and submissive to their fate." As freedmen they dragged whites down to what Bruce judged to be their miserable level. Not surprisingly, Bruce defended disfranchisement, endorsed segregation, and espoused mass deportation of blacks.[26]

His racist diatribes aside, Bruce longed for what he deemed the simple race relations of the colonial period. In 1895 he published the two-volume *Economic History of Virginia in the Seventeenth Century*. Exhaustively researched, this work and Bruce's two-volume *Institutional History of Virginia* (1910) compared favorably with the Johns Hopkins *Studies* in quality of research and interpretation. In the first study, Bruce added a new defense to his earlier praise of slavery as a necessary social institution. Not only did the peculiar institution guarantee racial peace, he said, but it gave seventeenth-century white Virginians a profitable alternative labor source to indentured Europeans. Slavery promoted "the extension of the [tobacco] plantation by cheapening labor to the lowest point." Blacks adapted quickly to Virginia's climate and, as lifelong servants, required lower expenditures than white servants, who were provided supplies upon completion of their indentures. Blacks, calculated Bruce, were cheaper to keep because they accepted "plainer fare" and "humbler lodgings." He also observed how the bondsmen were "docile and tractable"—"totally devoid of power to resist." Bruce found little difference, except in the most skilled trades, in the quality of work performed by white colonists and black slaves. But his most significant contribution to the literature on slavery was Bruce's argument that slavery provided a more profitable labor system than white indentured servitude. He reached this conclusion at a time when most historians virtually ignored the question.[27]

Convinced that blacks retained the sexual instincts of their African forebears, Bruce focused on the question of miscegenation in colonial Virginia. He explained that widespread racial mixing resulted from whites working in the tobacco fields alongside the blacks. Although such intercourse was prohibited by statute and by church laws, it occurred openly throughout the seventeenth century. White indentured females, said Bruce, succumbed to miscegenation because, coming from England, they were "comparatively free from the race prejudice that was so likely to arise upon close association with the African." Unfortunately, he explained, these degraded white women never acquired a "repugnance to association with Africans upon a footing of social equality."[28]

Anticipating James C. Ballagh's later theme, Bruce also explained that under colonial laws, black slaves and white indentured servants held similar legal status. Despite the later dominance of slave labor, Bruce insisted that white colony servants, not blacks, met seventeenth-century Virginia's labor needs. Not until the next century were transportation facilities available to satisfy the colony's demand for slaves. Only then, Bruce continued, did slavery begin to shape Virginia's economic and social life. Exhibiting a marked difference from later students of slavery, Bruce insisted that as an institution, slavery changed little between its inception in 1619 and its collapse in 1865. He failed to recognize slavery as a fluid and diversified institution. The history of slavery in the Old Dominion as a record of adaptation to changing land

and labor needs escaped his attention. Rather, Bruce interpreted slavery in Virginia as an uninterrupted record of blacks receiving adequate clothing, housing, and light work assignments. Few were overtasked. Masters exhibited "just and humane" treatment, most of them demanding their bondsmen to work shorter days than did contemporary English husbandmen. In each category of labor sustenance, however, white servants consistently received better care than blacks. In Bruce's mind this added force to his argument: slaves cost less to maintain than white freemen.[29]

Reviewing Bruce's volumes for the *Yale Review*, Johns Hopkins-trained historian Stephen B. Weeks remarked that "Perhaps never in the history of any Southern State have the original sources . . . been used to a larger extent." Weeks's comments hit the mark squarely. Never before had a historian of slavery relied so heavily on manuscript records to document his work. For example, in order to obtain information on the comparative value of slaves to other types of property, Bruce drew on the McDonald Papers at the Virginia State Library. He consulted the Ludwell Papers at the Virginia Historical Society to document his argument on slave housing. Bruce also employed numerous wills and property inventories hidden away in Virginia's court and county records. These identified slave naming practices and provisions for privileged bondsmen, as well as providing such detailed information on slave life as the variety of utensils and furnishings found in slave cabins. His systematic examination of slave prices logged in county records enabled Bruce to conclude that slave prices climbed throughout the seventeenth century despite the increased number of fresh Africans imported. Not until Ulrich B. Phillips began publishing his work early in the new century would a historian match Bruce's mastery and use of the primary sources on slavery.[30]

Illustrative of the sort of institutional studies that followed Bruce's works were the Vance and McDougle dissertations on slavery in Kentucky. Vance completed his dissertation at Washington and Lee University in 1895. Vance's study remains among the more obscure examinations of slavery of the period because its author never joined the historical guild. Vance taught law instead at several schools, including Yale University and the Universities of Michigan and Chicago. Drawing heavily on informal statements by ex–Kentucky bondsmen, Vance sketched a benign picture of slave life in Kentucky. If in theory the bondsmen were policed tightly, in practice they "were controlled by patriarchal rule, each master regulating his own slave household, making his own by-laws, and taking cognizance in his own way of any misdemeanors committed by his slaves." Blacks enjoyed as much freedom as they wished, asserted Vance, as long as they performed their work well in Kentucky's hemp and tobacco fields. On the rare occasions when blacks received corporal punishment, the slaves accepted their correction with characteristic good humor. Whipping left no emotional scars on the blacks, said the future jurist.

The negro did not have the spirit of the freeman that revolts at a blow, but accustomed from his infancy to the patriarchal rule of his master, he felt the lash only on his back. If the punishment by stripes was effective in checking the negro's inclination to commit misdemeanors, it was certainly a wise and better system of punishment than that which now fills our jails and penitentiaries.

Vance clearly adhered to the post–Civil War idea common to whites— that slavery, after all, provided the ideal mode of racial control of blacks.[31]

In Vance's opinion, white Kentuckians actually retained the institution for this purpose, long after it had proved itself economically moribund. They feared enlarging the Commonwealth's class of free blacks, according to Vance, "a miserable class of beings, ill-fitted to maintain themselves in the struggle for existence." Beyond their constant fear of racial control, white Kentuckians held a genuine humanitarian concern for "their" slaves. Having redeemed them from savage Africa, they upgraded the blacks with the teachings of Christianity and fortified the slaves with "wholesome food, comfortable clothing and quarters." Vance disagreed with neoabolitionist charges that Kentucky served as a breeding ground for the domestic slave trade. The close interpersonal relations bred by the peculiar institution gave the lie to such accusations, proclaimed Vance. Slavery encumbered white Kentuckians and became a yoke around their necks, he concluded, but served as the only means of reconciling peacefully "two totally dissimilar and unequal races."[32]

McDougle's 1918 dissertation, completed at Clark University, built atop and expanded the scope of Vance's earlier study. Kentucky slavery, McDougle declared, was "a comparatively mild form of servitude." Slave life in Kentucky outdistanced that in other states because most Kentucky bondsmen resided on small farm units. They labored alongside their masters growing produce, usually corn or tobacco, not a dominant staple crop. McDougle agreed with Vance that slavery generally proved unprofitable to white Kentuckians. Again, this unprofitability did not render the Commonwealth the slave breeding and trading center described by abolitionists and neoabolitionists alike. Farm paternalism reigned in Kentucky, McDougle insisted. Public opinion steadfastly opposed a commercial, "heartless traffic in slaves." McDougle praised Kentucky's slave statutes because, alone among equivalent laws in the other slave states, they did not prohibit slaves from learning to read and write. Yet the author's research in local newspapers tended to weaken this argument. In examining newspaper advertisements for 350 Kentucky runaway slaves, McDougle identified few bondsmen who were described by their masters as literate. To his credit, he was the first student of slavery to exploit the rich Kentuckiana materials in the University of Chicago's Durrett Collection. McDougle examined at least sixty files of obscure Kentucky newspapers and scores of city directories and commercial journals as well. These served as the basis for his proslavery conclusions regarding the internal slave trade in the Commonwealth. He also was among the first investigators to employ manuscript church records as historical sources on slavery. For him they established without a doubt that white Kentuckians placed few restrictions on slaves attending religious services with their white masters.[33]

The essays by Meriwether Harvey and James K. Turner remain important because they represent the type of micro research on slavery that still cries out to be written. Harvey, a student at Alabama Polytechnic Institute at Auburn, made the most detailed examination of the period of slavery in any one locale. He focused on slavery in Auburn, in 1860 a small cotton-producing community of one thousand whites and seven hundred blacks. Most white families in the community owned plantations of between five hundred and one thousand acres, and held from thirty to sixty bondsmen. So detailed was Harvey's analysis that he described the doors, ornaments, floors, and even the size of the planks used in the construction of slave cabins. He also listed the ample foods provided Auburn's slaves and the variety of after-hour diversions available to them. Slaves of both sexes chewed and smoked tobacco, and all enjoyed such plantation folk activities as corn shucking and logrolling. Some slave men earned extra money by splitting rails and burning charcoal. Slave discipline, noted the student researcher, usually was administered by slave foremen, not overseers. The "worst whippings'' on area plantations were meted out, he said, by slave parents to their children.[34]

Turner's essay on Edgecombe County cast fewer insights into day-to-day slave life than Meriwether's did. Located in eastern North Carolina, Edgecombe County had seven thousand white and ten thousand slave residents in 1860. Although slaves principally cultivated cotton, the area also produced turpentine and other naval stores. Handicapped by a scarcity of primary sources, Turner nevertheless made several important observations. He noted, for example, that Edgecombe slaves who had experienced baptism generally received more lenient treatment before slave courts than those who had not entered the church. Prohibited by state law from establishing their own places of worship, the slaves joined white congregations, with whom they shared equal rights in religious instruction and communion. They sat, however, in segregated galleries and were denied any role in congregational polity. Unlike many white writers of his day, Turner took seriously the slave marriage rite. After the master of both bondsmen had approved the match, the slave groom presented his bride with some toy or trinket to complete the ceremony. Unfortunately, said Turner, slave marriages often ended in forced separations. Masters demanded that their slave women bear offspring, refusing to tolerate childless unions. Slaveholders, like other nineteenth-century capitalists, sought to turn a profit.[35]

## III

Not until Ulrich B. Phillips began to churn out his important writings in the first years of the new century would writers begin to assess the economic dimensions of slavery. The few available analyses of this important subject were woefully inadequate. Economic issues almost uniformly escaped inquiry by the Johns Hopkins authors as well as those who followed in their wake. Historians in these years frequently expressed concern over this void in the literature. In 1907, for example, Guy S. Callender, editor of the *Yale Review*, lamented that so little was known of the cost of plantation operations in Virginia. "Just what was the economic condition of slavery in Va. before the extension of slavery into the southwest?" he asked historian William E. Dodd. "Was it a real burden at that time to most of the planters? How many of them were embarrassed by over stocked plantations? Is it true as the travelers had declared that most of them were?" Planter/historian Alfred Holt

Stone posed many questions pertaining to slave economics as well. He wrote in the *American Historical Review* in 1908 that "The time has come when we must study slavery as an economic institution without regard to its ethical or political aspects." A year later J. Franklin Jameson, director of historical research at the Carnegie Institution, declared that the economic side of the peculiar institution still was "crying aloud to be written."[36]

The complexity of the subject and what was believed to be a dearth of sources discouraged students from examining slave economics. While these impediments did not dissuade Phillips, they contributed to what must be judged a disappointingly thin crop of economic studies before the appearance of his pioneer work. For example, in 1902 John G. Haskell barely scratched the economic surface in his analysis of the profitability of slavery in western Missouri. He concluded that early in its history slavery proved unprofitable because of that section's distance from markets and because of a short growing season. After the Mexican War, however, "the profitableness of slavery . . . marvelously increased" and "western Missouri offered as fine a field upon which to exploit the advantages of slavery as the cotton-raising states." In another study, geographer F. V. Emerson of the University of Missouri investigated the influence of the South's diversified physiography and climate on slavery's evolution. But he waffled on the slave profitability question. On the one hand, Emerson admitted that bondsmen were "cheaply maintained" and proved profitable in tobacco, rice, and cotton production. Yet he charged that "in the long run" the slaves' poor agricultural methods proved too "expensive" to their masters.[37]

Meyer Jacobstein's 1907 Columbia dissertation in economics, *The Tobacco Industry in the United States*, placed the profitability question on a higher plane. His emphasis on slavery's economic benefits was based largely on statistics gleaned from *American Husbandry*. Like Bruce before him, but unlike Phillips who followed him, Jacobstein concluded that colonial tobacco planters reaped genuine profits by employing black slaves instead of white servants. Some masters earned annually a 20 percent profit on their total capital investment per slave, he said. Slave labor lowered the cost of production and in turn lowered the price of tobacco and stimulated further consumption and cultivation. According to Jacobstein, the slaves' "unscientific" methods of farming hardly hindered tobacco production because the crop "did not require more skill than the negro possessed." And, he added, slaves were available all year round to perform "secondary occupations" (mending, repairing, foraging) after the tobacco crop had been harvested and shipped. Jacobstein limited his important conclusions, though, to large plantations and to slavery in the colonial period.[38]

Others, however, found less evidence to support the profitability argument. In two studies published in 1897, economist Matthew B. Hammond of the University of Illinois outlined two critical dimensions of the issue. His research indicated that on the South's large cotton plantations slaves did cost less to support than white hands did. But on a day-to-day basis the blacks proved less efficient workers. Hammond explained:

Slave labor probably cost absolutely, though not relatively, less than free labor, and the owner had the advantage of absolute control over the laborer's services. But this was more than offset by the lack of interest which the slave took in his work. His low cost of maintenance did not make up for his waste of his master's property. The slave learned methods of agriculture slowly, and he therefore worked best when employed in cultivating only one crop.

The dependence on one staple that resulted from slavery contributed, said Hammond, to long-range weaknesses in southern agriculture. These continued to haunt the region long after Appomattox. Slavery discouraged crop rotation and diversification and led to the rapid depletion of soils. Hammond's argument was challenged by one reviewer, who charged that "like so many who are dissatisfied with Southern progress, he makes slavery the scapegoat of ills and sins, and unmercifully piles on that poor beast the blame for nearly all the industrial short-comings of the South." But another historian, Walter Lynwood Fleming, found Hammond's thesis on the mark. Writing in *The South in the Building of the Nation*, Fleming also blamed the peculiar institution for severely handicapping the South's economy. Slavery absorbed too large a percentage of the region's scarce capital. Concentration of the region's investments in human flesh, explained Fleming, denied the South the means to develop its water and mineral resources as well as its manufacturing and transportation facilities.[39]

Economist and sociologist Gustavus W. Dyer also found "no special advantage" in slaves over free laborers. A faculty member at Vanderbilt University, in 1905 Dyer published *Democracy in the South before the Civil War*. He asserted that the Old South exhibited more democratic than aristocratic leanings. Foreshadowing the later emphasis of Frank L. Owsley and his Vanderbilt students, Dyer championed the yeoman farmers, not the planters, as the dominant characters in the antebellum South. Carefully examining census records, Dyer maintained that slavery neither prevented growth of manufacturing in the South nor hindered yeomen from obtaining suitable farmland. By suggesting that slaveholders held few advantages over nonslaveholders, Dyer indirectly portrayed the slave system as more costly, or at least more speculative, than free labor. He wrote, for example, that planters incurred large expenses and assumed many risks in owning bondsmen. The slaves had to be maintained both during peak periods and times of economic depression. And, Dyer continued, blacks had inherent weaknesses as laborers: their labor was inflexible; their morals and standards of behavior were suspect. Although not examining specifically the profitability question, Dyer intimated that in many cases slaves were considerably more expensive than their free counterparts.[40]

When most writers of this period addressed slave economics, they generally focused more on the various occupations at which the bondsmen labored than on the debate over profitability.[41] In one of the most thoroughly researched articles in these years, "Slavery and the Beginnings of Industrialism in the American Colonies," Marcus W. Jernegan of the University of Chicago prefigured many of the conclusions reached by Robert S. Starobin in *Industrial Slavery in the Old South* (1970). Late in the seventeenth century, Jernegan explained, southern slaves labored in a variety of nonagricultural jobs. The shortage of imported manufactures necessitated their work as artisans in colonial shops and factories. Over the next century the use of industrial slaves expanded both in plantation industries and in the production of goods for commercial sale. Jernegan pointed out, like Howell M. Henry and Julia Flisch before him, that white mechanics objected to the competition presented by these slave craftsmen. Yet he argued that skilled slaves played a fundamental role in the South's economic development, allowing colonial planters to diversify and expand their operations into such areas as tanning, woodworking, and butchering. Drawing heavily on rich files of colonial newspapers, not biased reports of the royal governors, Jernegan listed twenty-eight different crafts at which slaves labored. He concluded that their important role as colonial craftsmen proved the "skill and intelligence" of the black slaves. So vital was this labor that Jernegan doubted whether the eighteenth-century plantation "could have survived if the negro slave had not made his important contributions as an artisan, in the building and other trades, calling for skill in transforming raw materials into manufactured articles."[42]

With the exception of William K. Boyd's pioneer essay on the proponents of ad valorem slave taxation in North Carolina,[43] few historians except Phillips dug deeply into the nature of the economics of slavery and the plantation system. Students in these years paid remarkably little attention, for instance, to the domestic slave trade. An understanding of this topic would have thrown considerable light on the question of slavery's profitability. When the early writers did examine the slave trade, they invariably emphasized the origins of slavery in North America or the dimensions of the African trade in bondsmen. Some also continued to hurl the charges (left over from the Reconstruction period) concerning New England's role as an accessory in the crime of slave trading.[44]

Only Winfield H. Collins's *The Domestic Slave Trade of the Southern States* (1904) grappled directly with the problem of the interstate exchange in bondsmen. A fierce white supremacist, an open advocate of lynching, and a proponent of black colonization, Collins hardly represented the typical "scientific" investigator of his generation. He mourned the loss of the "old-time Negro" because this Negro's successors were "abnormally criminal," inefficient, shiftless, and diseased. Writing as late as 1918, Collins charged that "it is as natural for the Negro to sit in idleness, or shoot crap, to go on marauding expeditions or connive at insurrections, as it is for the white man to establish courts, collect libraries, and found schools." He praised "the restraining influence of slavery" and cursed "harebrained preachers and teachers" from the North for freeing blacks for a life of dissipation.[45]

Approaching the slave trade with this ideological bent, Collins, not surprisingly, proved loath to condemn it. He admitted that after 1815 a heavy traffic in slaves existed between the upper and lower slave states. But, he insisted, three-fifths of those blacks emigrating to the Deep South accompanied their masters. They had no direct connection to the internal slave trade. And while Collins acknowledged that some planters bred slaves specifically for sale, he again softened this old abolitionist accusation. According to his research in border state newspapers and the census, slave breeding on a large scale was "very improbable." One factor that worked against it was that "the prolific negro race'' multiplied rapidly even without stimulation from the master class. Collins also maintained that if the border states had genuinely served as a breeding ground for slaves, that section of the South therefore would have annually had a larger proportion of young slaves than the alleged slave-buying states. His close examination of the census for 1830–1860, however, revealed that the border states had fewer slaves under age ten than did the latter. Collins therefore concluded that the border states were "not only practically freed from the charge of multiplying slaves and raising them for market as a business, but that, as a rule, they did not sell their slaves unless compelled to do so by pecuniary or other embarrassments." Collins overturned yet another of what he termed abolitionist myths when he challenged the view that slaves dreaded the "cruel doom" of being sold to the lower South. Actually, wrote Collins, the slaves' apprehensions were caused by the prospect of having to move to a strange environment, not from fear of inhumane treatment. Still, Collins did not minimize the harsh effect of the slave trade on slave family life. Before the eventual repudiation of his major arguments by Frederic Bancroft in 1931,[46] Collins's monograph influenced such works as Beverly B. Munford's 1909 general account of slavery and secession in Virginia, McDougle's state study on Kentucky, and Phillips's classic *American Negro Slavery* (1918).[47]

## IV

Despite the volume of institutional studies on slavery, three themes— slave religion, miscegenation, and slave resistance—received surprisingly little attention from late nineteenth-century writers. The scant regard paid these topics stemmed from several complex factors. First, each suffered from a scarcity of available source materials. True, church records, demographic data, and recollections of ex-slaves could have been tapped by industrious researchers even earlier than the turn of the century. But few libraries or archives collected such materials, and their acquisition remained sporadic at best. Further, given the historical method and biases of the day, few would have sought them out.

The handful of writings on slave religion generally adhered to the defensive, proslavery position adopted by most white writers after Appomattox. According to a recent student of the religion of the Lost Cause, postwar southern "clergymen restated the argument that slavery was a God-ordained, spiritual institution." Southern denominational assemblies also "were concerned enough with the issue to justify slavery long after its demise."[48] The racial milieu of Jim Crow America encouraged few whites to embark on research on the subjects of interracial mixing or slave revolts. Few people during these years, white or black, wrote or spoke openly of sexual matters pertaining to slavery. Americans writing during the age of segregation almost uniformly judged interracial sex a taboo. Former slaveholders fell conspicuously quiet on this theme, the South's large mulatto population underscoring their silence. Discussion would not only have exposed their crimes against black females, but would have exposed slavery as exploitative and immoral. But whites were quick to condemn, in what became a ritual of blind hate, what they perceived as the moral decline of blacks since emancipation. Whereas the moral degeneracy argument appeared throughout Reconstruction, by the end of the century it was nudged aside by the dominant southern white fantasy of the day: the black male as rapist.

Finally, few whites studied slave resistance, because to do so would overturn the vital ingredients of proslavery theory. Concentration on the resistance of blacks to enslavement would have contradicted the image of the contented slave and shattered the stereotyped view of the passive and hapless black. Almost all whites viewed slave revolts in their antebellum context—as crimes. Residents of the Old South lived in perpetual fear of slave uprisings. Their descendants employed new tactics to control the freedmen and their offspring. Determined to maintain racial hegemony, whites spoke rarely of slave revolts. The mere idea of social equality with blacks angered most whites, and images of their former bondsmen with guns and knives no doubt would have turned some to rage. In their minds insurrections symbolized social disorder and chaos. How could a generation of writers convinced of slavery's merits admit that the bondsmen seethed with restiveness and worked constantly to break their chains?

As a result, in these years slave religion never received scholarly monographic treatment. Some studies examined the role formal religious bodies played in bringing the alleged benefits of Christianity to the bondsmen. But no white researcher analyzed the place of religion in the daily lives of the slaves. With the exception of one or two folklorists, none explored African or Caribbean influences on the bondsmen's religious thought. W. E. B. Du Bois assumed these tasks in *The Souls of Black Folk* (1903). Most scholars simply acknowledged that masters allowed their chattels to attend some kind of religious service. Or they agreed with sociologist Robert E. Park's 1919 remark that except in isolated pockets of the South "the plantation Negro's religion was a faithful copy of the white man's." And even then, few writers credited the blacks with absorbing the white man's faith. Edward McCrady summarized the prevailing opinion that "the fruits" of missionary activity among the slaves were "very small and inconsiderable."[49]

William Pope Harrison and Joseph Butsch contributed accounts celebrating missionary work among the slaves by the Methodist Episcopal and Roman Catholic churches. Harrison's highly partisan *The Gospel among the Slaves* (1893) smacked of the old proslavery rationale. He defended slavery and praised white southerners for spending nearly two million dollars for evangelizing the bondsmen. Missionaries, he said, combed the South promoting religion to a people who often retained "the sins and vicious nature which belong to . . . [their] people." Harrison argued that Methodism served both races well. Whereas it provided masters more tractable laborers, it pointed the slaves in the direction of civilization. Not an apologist for slavery, Butsch stressed the considerable humanitarianism of Catholic priests toward the slaves. In Louisiana and Maryland they worked to baptize the blacks and offer them the rudiments of religious instruction. Butsch asserted that Louisiana's relatively moderate Code Noir was "inspired by Catholic teaching and practice."[50]

Marcus W. Jernegan, author of the impressive article on industrial slavery, also wrote far and away the best study of slave religion to appear in these years. In "Slavery and Conversion in the American Colonies," he assessed the numerous stumbling blocks that prevented missionaries from reaching more than a small minority of the bondsmen. According to Jernegan, with few exceptions masters never seriously encouraged the religious conversion of their slaves. Despite encouragement from the Crown and the various religious sects, Christianity never reached most blacks in the colonial South. Jernegan explained that the vast majority of slaveholders feared that religious education might deter the slaves from their work at hand, and at the same time give them a sense of equality. Many of the southern whites, he added, were themselves indifferent to religion and reluctant at best to bring their bondsmen under the tutelage of missionaries. Reflecting the bias of his day, Jernegan charged that many blacks, because of "mental incapacity, lack of knowledge of the English language, or disinclination to accept a new religion in place of their heathen rites," failed to grasp the religious instruction available to them. In contrast to Harrison and Butsch, Jernegan concluded that few missionaries to the slaves held a genuine commitment to converting the slaves. The small number of dedicated clergymen could barely dent the spiritual needs of the South's widely dispersed slave population.[51]

Unfortunately, no comparable book or article on miscegenation surfaced during these years—and not because writers totally ignored the subject. Neoabolitionists like Rhodes openly criticized the wanton abuse of slave women by masters. For obvious reasons the proslavery apologists disregarded the issue or argued that it had been exaggerated by the abolitionists. The vast majority of writers, including those trained at Johns Hopkins, simply buried the topic. They listed it amid the various antebellum state laws prohibiting interracial marriages and describing the legal restrictions on mulatto progeny.

One author, however, sociologist Edward B. Reuter of the University of Illinois, did confront what he termed the "mongrelization" of the races. In *The Mulatto in the United States* (1918), Reuter charged that miscegenation resulted not from slavery but from "the simple fact . . . that the women of the lower races everywhere seek sex relations with the men of the superior race or caste." Applying this idea to the Old South, Reuter implied that slave women encouraged liaisons with their masters. In his opinion they sought offspring fathered by whites and were "enormously proud of their light-skinned, half-caste children." If anything, said Reuter, slavery worked not to encourage miscegenation but "to lessen the amount of intermixture by separating and restraining the vicious elements, and so preventing an indiscriminate sexual relation." He went on to assert that the mulatto surpassed in intelligence the "full-blooded" black as slave and as freedman. His message was unmistakably clear: the accomplishments of gifted blacks were attributable to their mixed (white) blood. Reviewers in both sociological and historical journals uniformly condemned Reuter's overtly racist book. They denounced his blatant attack on black females and countercharged that white males and females were fully as responsible for miscegenation as blacks. Distinguished black novelist Jessie Fauset railed against Reuter's "comparatively valueless . . . biased, unreliable and unscientific" volume, and other critics agreed. The book rivaled even the crudest proslavery tract in its racist poison.[52]

The only two studies of slave revolt written in these years also could have been mistaken for proslavery propaganda. Both authors, Stephen

B. Weeks and William Sidney Drewry, received Ph.D. degrees in history from Johns Hopkins. They examined Nat Turner's 1831 insurrection but broadened their conclusions to apply to the topic of slave resistance for the entire South. In addition to their common historical training, both scholars shared a disdain of black Americans. Weeks, for example, expressed candidly that he and his fellow whites never would allow black domination of the United States. Drewry maintained that if the black man became "conscious of his inferiority," and rejected all aspirations for political office, then and only then could the two races live together in peace. Otherwise he advocated their mass deportation "beyond the limits of the United States."[53]

Weeks completed his degree in 1891, writing his dissertation on the development of church and state in his native North Carolina. That study and another work, *Southern Quakers and Slavery* (1896), appeared in the Johns Hopkins *Studies*. Weeks joined the Trinity College faculty in 1891 and thereby assumed the first distinct chair of history in any southern educational institution. He amassed the most outstanding collection of primary materials on southern history of his day but ultimately became discouraged by the regional apathy toward his work. In 1891 Weeks published his influential article on the Nat Turner rebellion in the *Magazine of History*. This piece established the interpretation of that slave revolt that historians would accept for almost fifty years. In Weeks's opinion, four factors made slaves reluctant to rise up against their masters. They stood in fear of capital punishment. By nature, he said, the race was docile. Separated from one another on farms and plantations, the slaves also lacked the requisite organization. Finally, because the bondsmen received such humane treatment, for all but the most dissatisfied slave freedom would be out of the question, a backward step. Only a "demon" like Nat Turner, wrote Weeks, could have inspired the blacks of Southampton County, Virginia, to massacre their white neighbors. Weeks described Turner as an intelligent slave preacher—"restless, inquisitive, observant." Yet the black insurrectionist "wrapped himself in mystery." Playing upon the credulity and superstitions of his fellow blacks, Turner convinced them that he was their prophet, willed by God to lead them in a war against their captors. In Weeks's judgment, contemporary observers greatly exaggerated the size of Turner's "army of liberation." Actually, he said, not more than ten blacks performed the bloody murders. Weeks noted that although the slaves were inspired to their deadly deeds by drams of brandy, they butchered but did not torture their victims. "The actors," he concluded, "were perhaps appalled by the very success of their hideous enterprise."[54]

Drewry completed his training at Johns Hopkins in 1900. Probably only the narrow focus of his dissertation precluded its publication in the *Studies*. A native Virginian, he received his early education in Southampton County. No doubt Drewry became intrigued as a youth with the Turner revolt. For years he listened to accounts of the rebellion by local residents who remembered those frightful days of August, 1831. In *Slave Insurrections in Virginia* (1900), Drewry cited oral history testimony—interviews with twenty-one whites and nine blacks who had been alive at the time of Turner's insurrection. Like Weeks, Drewry placed the blame for the uprising on its "wild, fanatical" instigator. Certainly, he argued, slaves in southeastern Virginia had little warrant to rebel. Slave life there was at its patriarchal best, he said. Slaves and masters shared such a common bond, marveled Drewry, that it was "impossible to describe the ease, happiness and sense of security felt by all" at the time of the gory revolt.[55]

Only Turner's fanaticism and his religious mysticism, Drewry explained, could have led him to rebel against his kind and indulgent master. Virginia slavery, the author emphasized, was "an institution which nourished the strongest affection and piety in slave and owner, as well as moral qualities worthy of any age of civilization." Yet "the Prophet" secretly launched his holy war, murdering his master and the master's family, brutally killing approximately sixty whites and sacking fifteen homesteads. In retaliation, local whites savagely murdered 120 innocent blacks. Drewry's narration of the insurrection, from its planning stage until its conclusion on the gallows, closely paralleled Weeks's earlier account, albeit in greater detail. Both scholars relied heavily on the authentic "confessions" compiled by Turner's defense counsel, Thomas R. Gray. Drewry sought objectivity, and he praised the behavior of both the majority of Southampton's slaves and the county's white population during the revolt. He credited the blacks' deportment to the "obedience and contentment" bred in them by slavery. The whites' merciful reaction, he added, was shaped by more than mere humanitarian concern. The whites realized full well that masters would not receive compensation from the state for slaves killed by mob rule. Such was the perspective of the historian writing in an age when lynch law still controlled blacks in the South.[56]

As with virtually every one of the studies discussed in this chapter,

Weeks and Drewry also ignored the point of view of the slave. They overemphasized Turner's mysticism and undervalued the conditions of slave life that bred unrest. Neither scholar recognized any pattern whatsoever of slave resistance. They perceived slave revolts in isolation—as extraordinary events—showing no grasp of their relation to pent-up hostility or day-to-day slave dissatisfactions. Their antiblack and proslavery perspective blinded these white authors as well as their entire generation. They failed to grasp the psychological and sociological implications of prolonged and institutionalized degradation. They almost totally ignored slavery's human dimension. When describing enslavement these writers seemed oblivious to the complex factors that determined slave care. They almost never compared bondage in America with forms of servitude at different times and in different places in the world. American writers, complained J. Franklin Jameson in 1916, examined slavery as narrowly as if it "had never existed in other lands and other times." He called for them to broaden their focus, to consider "the history of slavery as a whole."[57] Lacking a comparative perspective to draw upon, most whites envisioned the bondsman as little more than a passive, mindless, and controllable extension of his master's will.

## NOTES

1. Turner to William K. Boyd, [1902], William K. Boyd Papers, Duke University Archives; Boyd, "Southern History in American Universities," *South Atlantic Quarterly*, 1 (July, 1902): 244.

2. *West Virginia University Catalogue for 1904–1905* (Morgantown, 1905), 83; Fleming, "History of Slavery," in Walter Lynwood Fleming Papers, Manuscripts and Archives Division, New York Public Library; Dodd to Frederic Bancroft, January 17, 1909, November 2, 1910, Frederic Bancroft Papers, Columbia University; W. Alexander Mabry, ed., "Professor William E. Dodd's Diary, 1916–1920," *John P. Branch Historical Papers of Randolph-Macon College*, n.s., 2 (March, 1953): 13; Wendell Holmes Stephenson, "A Half Century of Southern Historical Scholarship," *Journal of Southern History*, 11 (February, 1945): 27n, 28n.

3. Laprade to John M. Vincent, February 13, 1911, John M. Vincent Papers, Johns Hopkins University; idem, "Some Problems in Writing the History of American Slavery," *South Atlantic Quarterly*, 10 (April, 1911): 136–140; idem, "The Legal Status of the Negroes in the District of Columbia

Previous to the Abolition of Slavery, 1800–1862,'' unpublished manuscript [1911], pp. 1–5, William Thomas Laprade Papers, Duke University Archives.

4. Park, review of Carter G. Woodson, *The Education of the Negro Prior to 1861*, in *American Journal of Sociology*, 21 (July, 1915): 119.

5. "Code of Laws for Slaves Governed Each Southern Plantation in Early Days," Montgomery *Advertiser*, August 28, 1918, Slavery File, Tuskegee Institute.

6. Henry M. Turner, *The Barbarous Decision of the United States Supreme Court Declaring the Civil Rights Act Unconstitutional and Disrobing the Colored Race of All Civil Protection* (Atlanta, 1893), 20; *U.S. Supreme Court Reports, Vol. 109* (Rochester, 1885), 844; Arthur Kinoy, "The Constitutional Right of Negro Freedom," *Rutgers Law Review*, 21 (Winter, 1967): 388, 412; G. Sidney Buchanan, "The Quest for Freedom: A Legal History of the Thirteenth Amendment," *Houston Law Review*, 12 (October, 1974–March 1975): 1–34, 334, 378, 596.

7. Tremain, *Slavery in the District of Columbia* (New York, 1892), 38, 54; West, "The Status of the Negro in Virginia during the Colonial Period" (Ph.D. diss., Columbia University, 1890).

8. John V. Denson, "Slavery Laws in Alabama," *Alabama Polytechnic Institute Historical Studies*, 3rd ser. (1908): 1–47; Jacob Trieber, "Legal Status of Negroes in Arkansas before the Civil War," *Publications of the Arkansas Historical Association*, 3 (1911): 175–183; E. M. Violette, "The Black Code in Missouri," *Proceedings of the Mississippi Valley Historical Association for the Year 1912–1913*, 6 (1913): 287–316; Mark A. Candler, "The Beginnings of Slavery in Georgia," *Magazine of History*, 13 (July, 1911): 351, 345; Lester G. Bugbee, "Slavery in Early Texas," *Political Science Quarterly*, 13 (September, December, 1898): 404, 409, 661.

9. Hughson, "Carolina Slave Laws," New York *Evening Post*, March 18, 25, April 18, 1893.

10. Mecklin, "The Evolution of the Slave Status in the American Democracy," *Journal of Negro History*, 2 (April, 1917): passim, and (July, 1917): 246, 247, 248, 250; Imes, "The Legal Status of Free Negroes and Slaves in Tennessee," *Journal of Negro History*, 4 (July, 1919): 257, 258n, 271, 272.

11. Stone, "The Early Slave Laws of Mississippi," *Publications of the Mississippi Historical Society*, 2 (1899): 134, 135, 144, 136, 141, 144; Magruder, "The Legal Status of Slaves in Mississippi before the War," *Publications of the Mississippi Historical Society*, 4 (1901): 142, 136, 137, 135, 141; McLoughlin, "The Black Code," *Proceedings of the Mississippi Valley Historical Association for the Year 1914–1915*, 8 (1916): 210–213, 214, 216; Laprade, "The Legal Status of the Negroes in the District of Columbia Previous to the Abolition of Slavery, 1800–1862," 119.

12. McCrady, "Slavery in the Province of South Carolina, 1670–1770,"

*Annual Report of the American Historical Association for the Year 1895* (Washington, 1896), 657; Schaper, "Sectionalism and Representation in South Carolina," *Annual Report of the American Historical Association for the Year 1900*, 2 vols. (Washington, 1901), 1:307, 315, 314; Cobb, "Old Slave Laws of Georgia," *Case and Comment*, 23 (June, 1916): 8, 10, 9.

13. See John David Smith, "Neglected but Not Forgotten: Howell M. Henry and the 'Police Control' of Slaves in South Carolina," *Proceedings of the South Carolina Historical Association* (1980): 94–111.

14. Henry, *The Police Control of the Slave in South Carolina* (Emory, VA, 1914), 6, 7, 79, 20, 108, 99, 79, 145, 141, 119, 48, 74.

15. Ibid., 125, 108, 113, 114, 108.

16. Ibid., 56, 57, 154–155, 145–151, 152, 153, 154.

17. Ibid., 30–32, 28, 38, 39, 40.

18. Wade, *Slavery in the Cities: The South, 1820–1860* (New York, 1964).

19. Henry, *The Police Control of the Slave in South Carolina*, 44–45, 46, 47–50, 21, 18, 22.

20. Henry, "The Slave Laws of Tennessee," *Tennessee Historical Magazine*, 2 (September, 1916): 181, 183, 185, 186, 202–203, 192.

21. Laprade, "Some Problems in Writing the History of American Slavery," 136–138; idem, "Newspapers as a Source for the History of American Slavery," *South Atlantic Quarterly*, 9 (July, 1910): 231.

22. Henry, *The Police Control of the Slave in South Carolina*, 101–102; Starobin, *Industrial Slavery in the Old South* (New York, 1970).

23. Brock, "Prefatory Note, Exhibiting the Past Relation of Virginia to African Slavery," *Collections of the Virginia Historical Society*, n.s., 6 (1887): 2, 32; idem, in *Southern Historical Society Papers*, 30 (1902): 355; Ranson, "Plantation Life in Virginia before the War," *Sewanee Review*, 21 (October, 1913): 432; Morton, "Life in Kentucky in the Days of Negro Slavery," *Register of the Kentucky State Historical Society*, 5 (January, 1907): 45.

24. Rowland, "Plantation Life in Mississippi before the War," *Publications of the Mississippi Historical Society*, 3 (1900): 85, 91, 87, 89; Hawes to Franklin L. Riley, March 29, [1910], Franklin L. Riley Papers, Southern Historical Collection, University of North Carolina at Chapel Hill; Hawes, "Slavery in Mississippi," *Sewanee Review*, 21 (April, 1913): 233, 234.

25. William S. Powell, "Philip Alexander Bruce, Historian," *Tyler's Quarterly Historical and Genealogical Magazine*, 30 (January, 1949): 169; Lyman M. Simms, Jr., "Philip Alexander Bruce: His Life and Works" (Ph.D. diss., University of Virginia, 1966); idem, "Bruce, Philip Alexander," in David C. Roller and Robert W. Twyman, eds., *The Encyclopedia of Southern History* (Baton Rouge, 1979), 156; idem, "Philip Alexander Bruce and the New South," *Mississippi Quarterly*, 19 (Fall, 1966): 171–183; Darrett B. Rutman, "Philip Alexander Bruce: A Divided Mind of the South," *Virginia Magazine of History*

*and Biography*, 68 (October, 1960): 388–406; Herbert G. Gutman, *The Black Family in Slavery and Freedom, 1750–1925* (New York, 1976), 531–538; Bruce, "Recollections of My Plantation Teachers," *South Atlantic Quarterly*, 16 (January, 1917): 1–13.

26. Bruce, *The Plantation Negro as a Freeman* (New York, 1889), 175, 83, 16–17; idem, "The Negro Population of the South," *Conservative Review*, 2 (November, 1899): 270–273, 275; idem, "Social and Economic Revolution in the Southern States," *Contemporary Review*, 78 (July, 1900): 59; idem, "The American Negro of Today," ibid., 77 (February, 1900): 286; idem, "Race Segregation in the United States," *Hibbert Journal*, 13 (July, 1915): 867.

27. Bruce, *Economic History of Virginia in the Seventeenth Century*, 2 vols. (New York, 1895), 2:58, 62, 60, 59.

28. Ibid., 59, 65, 405, 570, 109, 110, 212.

29. Ibid., 65, 575, 57, 573, 104–106, 107, 105.

30. Weeks in *Yale Review*, 5 (May, 1896): 94; Bruce, *Economic History of Virginia in the Seventeenth Century*, 2:572, 90.

31. Vance, "Slavery in Kentucky" (Ph.D. diss., Washington and Lee University, 1895), 28–68, 25, 56, 54.

32. Ibid., 41, 45, 70, 52, 60, 62, 68, 66, 67, 70.

33. McDougle, *Slavery in Kentucky, 1792–1865* (Washington, 1918), 93, 78, 87, 25, 85–86, 8, 26–27, 22, 18, 73, 76, 43, 79, 81.

34. Harvey, "Slavery in Auburn, Alabama," *Alabama Polytechnic Institute Historical Studies*, 3rd ser. (1907): 1, 2, 4, 6, 12, 16.

35. Turner, "Slavery in Edgecombe County," *Historical Papers Published by the Trinity College Historical Society*, 12th ser. (1916): 9, 15, 18, 26, 32, 28.

36. Callender to Dodd, February 9, 1907, William E. Dodd Papers, Manuscript Division, Library of Congress; Stone, *Material Wanted for an Economic History of the Negro* (Washington, n.d.), 1–16; Stone to Dodd, July 10, 1907, Dodd Papers; idem, "Some Problems of Southern Economic History," *American Historical Review*, 13 (July, 1908): 779; John David Smith, "Alfred Holt Stone: Mississippi Planter and Archivist/Historian of Slavery," *Journal of Mississippi History*, 45 (November, 1983): 266–269; Jameson to Morgan P. Robinson, March 10, 1909, in Elizabeth Donnan and Leo F. Stock, eds., *An Historian's World: Selections from the Correspondence of John Franklin Jameson* (Philadelphia, 1956), 121.

37. Haskell, "The Passing of Slavery in Western Missouri," *Transactions of the Kansas State Historical Society*, 7 (1902): 32, 33, 36; Emerson, "Geographic Influences in American Slavery," American Geographical Society *Bulletin*, 43 (January, 1911): 14, 15, 24, 16, and (February, 1911): 111, 115.

38. Jacobstein, *The Tobacco Industry in the United States* (New York, 1907), 18, 19, 26, 37.

39. Hammond, "The Cotton Industry—an Essay in American Economic History," *Publications of the American Economic Association*, n.s., 1 (December, 1897): 36, 37, 40, 46–47, 63, 94, 95, 98–99, 109; idem, "The Southern Farmer and the Cotton Question," *Political Science Quarterly*, 12 (September, 1897): 455–456; anon., in *Publications of the Southern History Association*, 2 (April, 1898): 189; Fleming, "The Slave-Labor System in the Ante-Bellum South," in Julien A. C. Chandler et al., eds., *The South in the Building of the Nation*, 12 vols. (Richmond, 1909), 5:116, 120.

40. Dyer, *Democracy in the South before the Civil War* (Nashville, 1905), 45, 89–90, 40, 44–45.

41. See, for example, Edward Ingle, *Southern Sidelights: A Picture of Social and Economic Life in the South a Generation Before the War* (Boston, 1896), 75, 77, 78; Hollis B. Frissell, "Negro Education," *New World*, 9 (December, 1900): 626–627; James L. Watkins, *King Cotton: A Historical and Statistical Review, 1790 to 1908* (New York, 1908), 128, 172, 256; Julia A. Flisch, "The Common People of the Old South," *Annual Report of the American Historical Association for the Year 1908*, 2 vols. (Washington, 1909), 1:139–140. Flisch noted the resentment by white laborers at slave domination of jobs in the "mechanical arts."

42. Jernegan to J. Franklin Jameson, October 19, 1919, *American Historical Review* Editorial Correspondence, Manuscript Division, Library of Congress; idem, "Slavery and the Beginnings of Industrialism in the American Colonies," *American Historical Review*, 25 (January, 1920): 222, 224, 227, 228, 230, 239.

43. Boyd, "Ad Valorem Slave Taxation, 1858–1860," *Historical Papers Published by the Trinity College Historical Society*, 5th ser. (1905), 31–38.

44. See Charles A. Stakely, "Introduction of the Negro into the United States," *Magazine of American History*, 26 (November, 1891): 349–363; William L. Scruggs, "How England Forced the Slaves upon America," ibid., 28 (July, 1892): 32–41; John R. Spears, *The American Slave-Trade—an Account of Its Origins, Growth and Suppression* (New York, 1900). W. E. B. Du Bois's important work on the African slave trade is discussed in chapter 7.

45. Collins, *The Truth about Lynching and the Negro in the South* (New York, 1918), 32, 41, 58, 70, 140, 141–142, 159.

46. Bancroft, *Slave Trading in the Old South* (Baltimore, 1931).

47. Collins, *The Domestic Slave Trade of the Southern States* (New York, 1904), 62, 63–66, 70, 72, 77, 73, 76–77, 79, 104–105, 103; Munford, *Virginia's Attitude toward Slavery and Secession* (New York, 1909), 148.

48. Charles R. Wilson, *Baptized in Blood. The Religion of the Lost Cause, 1865–1920* (Athens, 1980), 102, 103.

49. Park, "The Conflict and Fusion of Cultures with Special Reference to the Negro," *Journal of Negro History*, 4 (April, 1919): 123; McCrady, "Slavery in the Province of South Carolina, 1670–1770," *Annual Report of the American Historical Association for the Year 1895* (Washington, 1896), 660.

50. Harrison, *The Gospel among the Slaves* (Nashville, 1893), 3, 99, 150, 298, 318; Butsch, "Catholics and the Negro," *Journal of Negro History*, 2 (October, 1917): 401–402, 403. For a proslavery account of the role of Methodist missionaries and the slaves, see Fletcher Walton, "What We Did for the Negro before the War," *Methodist Review*, 51 (November–December, 1902): 897–905.

51. Jernegan to J. Franklin Jameson, December 2, 1914, *American Historical Review* Editorial Correspondence; Jernegan, "Slavery and Conversion in the American Colonies," *American Historical Review*, 21 (April, 1916): 504, 508–509, 516, 517, 518, 519, 525.

52. Reuter, *The Mulatto in the United States* (Boston, 1918), 5; Reuter to the editor, *Survey*, 42 (April 19, 1919): 125; Reuter, *The Mulatto in the United States*, 92, 93, 174, 177, 197; Fauset in *Survey*, 41 (March 8, 1919): 842, 843; [Carter G. Woodson?] in *Journal of Negro History*, 4 (January, 1919): 106. Two critical reviews of Reuter's book by blacks include Kelly Miller in *American Journal of Sociology*, 25 (September, 1919): 218–224, and Carter G. Woodson in *Mississippi Valley Historical Review*, 7 (September, 1920): 175–176.

53. Weeks, "The Slave Insurrection in Virginia, 1831, Known as 'Old Nat's War,' " *Magazine of American History*, 25 (June, 1891): 448; Drewry, *Slave Insurrections in Virginia, 1830–1865* (Washington, 1900), 194.

54. Weeks to Thomas M. Pittman, December 24, 1899, Thomas Merritt Pittman Papers, Southern Historical Collection, University of North Carolina at Chapel Hill; Weeks, "The Slave Insurrection in Virginia," 448, 449, 450, 453, 454.

55. Drewry, *Slave Insurrections in Virginia*, 18, 22, 23.

56. Ibid., 44, 158, 95, and passim.

57. Jameson, preface to Agnes M. Wergeland, *Slavery in Germanic Society during the Middle Ages* (Chicago, 1916), viii.

# 7

## A Different View of Slavery: Blacks Confront the New Proslavery Argument

### I

Although the paternalistic interpretation dominated views of slavery during the postemancipation generation, blacks refused to let the new defenses of the peculiar institution go unchallenged. Continuing the assault on slavery leveled by blacks during Reconstruction, many late nineteenth-century blacks also proved unwilling to accept a romanticized version of slavery. Together with the white neoabolitionists, they formed a vanguard in the battle against vestiges of slavery in American law and custom. Slavery provided black civil rights activists with a historic link to the origins of racism in America. The spirit of slavery lingered so pervasively, wrote journalist John E. Bruce in 1890, that it colored every aspect of America's race problem. He concluded that this situation would not change until the full force of the law began to guarantee blacks their hard won liberty.[1] Not surprisingly, many of the blacks proved more articulate and forceful in their denunciations of slavery than their white brethren. They grasped slavery's importance both as a symbol of past oppression and as a crucial metaphor for contemporary racism. Throughout these years a broad range of black writers—clergymen, educators, social scientists, editors—joined a handful of trained black historians in interpreting slavery. Black intellectuals from diverse walks of life thus assumed the role of historian.

Regardless of pedigree, the black students of slavery brought a very personal perspective to the task, one that contrasted sharply with that of their white colleagues. For them slavery obviously held a more immediate meaning. In most cases they interpreted the peculiar institution in terms completely incomprehensible to whites. Blacks described the slaves as exceedingly able but discontented laborers. They focused their studies directly on the bondsmen, not on the masters; and they pointed to slave insurrections not as crime, but as proof that blacks were men, not fawning inferiors. Indeed, several of the black writers knew slavery all too well—from painful firsthand experience. Many held slavery accountable for what they considered the continued backwardness of their race. All had felt the stares born of prejudice, intolerance, and discrimination. Slavery remained alive in their thoughts as they observed with disgust the proscription and inequalities that surfaced after the demise of Radical Reconstruction. Disfranchisement, segregation by law and by custom, and finally the exclusion of blacks from Progressive Era reforms convinced many blacks to look backward to slavery to explain black degradation in America. They considered an understanding of the peculiar institution necessary to guard future generations from reenslavement.

Blacks used slavery—their special history—as a tool to lash out against the racism so prevalent around them. In the process they prefigured the focus and conclusions of much recent scholarship. Blacks dwelt upon slavery because it constituted the most recent, best known, and most controversial aspect of their history. Unless the story of slavery was told by blacks, they reasoned, generations born since emancipation would not learn fully of its horrors.[2] Blacks also noted the parallels between slavery and the conditions of black life in post-Reconstruction America—Jim Crow and peonage laws,[3] the crop lien and convict lease systems,[4] industrial capitalism and industrial education,[5] American imperialism,[6] and the antiblack policies of the Wilson administration.[7]Ex-slave Ida B. Wells, for example, judged the widespread lynching of blacks merely the "last relic of barbarism and slavery"—the ultimate form of intimidation of the freedmen. "Slavery is no more," wrote the editor of the Indianapolis *Freeman* in 1892, "but in its stead stalks race, caste, business and commercial ostracism, civil oppression and debarment, political persecution and all the brood of evils that survived the demise of the parent evil." Life in Jim Crow America, observed black Bishop Lucius H. Holsey, was a constant battle against "the always forging links and lengthening chains of a second form of old slavery."[8]

Again and again in these years blacks underscored slavery's ill effects on contemporary American life. In 1890 William S. Scarborough, a classics scholar and president of Wilberforce University, criticized whites for continuing to keep blacks in "a state of servile subjugation." Another black, Lafayette M. Hershaw, hit the nail right on the head: "while slavery no longer exists in this country as a legal institution, it does exist in the opinion, the sentiment, and the practices of the people." In 1913 Dean Benjamin G. Brawley of Morehouse College denounced slavery because it ingrained in both races an utter "contempt for industrial effort"—one so severe that it plagued the South five decades following Appomattox. And in his 1917 report on economic cooperation among blacks, Professor Thomas I. Brown of Atlanta University held the "blighting effects" of slavery responsible for the blacks' inability to work together. These black writers agreed that the dark cloud of slavery continued to loom over blacks as well as whites.[9]

The slavery theme, more than any other, dominated black historical writing in the years 1890 to 1918. To be sure, it assumed an important place even earlier, as shown by the publication in the 1880s of general histories of black Americans by George Washington Williams and William T. Alexander. In his two-volume *History of the Negro Race in America from 1619 to 1880* (1882), Williams challenged the proslavery argument head-on. He denied that Noah's curse translated into a divine prophecy against blacks and celebrated the high stature of ancient African culture. Drawing on numerous primary sources, he depicted slavery as harsh and inhumane. "The Hydra of slavery," wrote Williams, engulfed both bondsmen and master. Slaves received thoughtless and cruel treatment and wasted away in utter ignorance. Alexander's *History of the Colored Race in America* (1887) reproved slavery as unjust and brutal—"harsher and viler" than any previous system of servitude. He blamed it for a variety of the South's ills, from discouraging immigration to degrading white laborers. With these writings as a foundation, slavery came to assume a prominent position in the thinking of blacks all the way up through World War I. For example, it was the subject of many of the documents, reviews, and articles in the first five volumes (1916–1920) of the *Journal of Negro History*, edited by Carter G. Woodson, a Harvard-trained Ph.D. Almost uniformly, the black authors denounced slavery as the consummate sin in American history. It was the task of black historians, wrote bibliophile Arthur A. Schomburg, to "restore what slavery took away, for it is the social damage of slavery that . . . must [be] repair[ed] and offset."[10]

As on other questions, black thought regarding slavery was not a monolith, but rather a maze of inconsistencies and contradictions. For example, many blacks stressed the importance of slavery for comprehending the contemporary "Negro problem." But others urged members of their race to deemphasize slavery—to look forward to a bright future, not backward to a sordid past.[11] Blacks disagreed on other slavery-related questions as well. Were blacks inherently inferior? How advanced was ancient African civilization? Was slave treatment cruel? How did the slaves react to captivity? Such influential writers as Booker T. Washington, George L. Knox, Kelly Miller, William H. Councill, and Paul L. Dunbar offered seemingly contradictory statements regarding slavery, concurrently denouncing it soundly as an evil[12] yet finding benefits[13] in it for the bondsmen. Miller, for example, often attacked slavery's treacheries yet also proclaimed that under it the black man became "domesticated, if not educated in the University of slavery, whose diploma admitted him to practice in the wide arena of the world's work." In much of his fiction, Dunbar adhered to the plantation myths popularized by white Negrophobe Thomas Nelson Page. Dunbar's slave characters in *Folks from Dixie* (1898) and *Strength of Gideon* (1900), for example, revive sentimental images of slave life. His bondsmen revoke their manumission rather than face the ambiguities of freedom; they betray their fellow bondsmen in order to retain the good graces of their masters. Yet in at least two of his short stories, Dunbar openly attacked slavery.[14]

In 1899 black novelist Sutton E. Griggs used two of his characters to portray these contrary images of slavery. Bernard Belgrave, president of Griggs's imaginary Imperium in Imperio, rails against slavery in no uncertain terms.

For two hundred and forty-four years the Anglo-Saxon imposed upon the hapless, helpless negro, the bondage of abject slavery, robbed him of the just recompense of his uneasing toil, treated him with the utmost cruelty, kept his mind shrouded in the dense fog of ignorance, denied his poor sinful soul access to the healing word of God, and, while the world rolled on to joy and light, the negro was driven cowering and trembling, back, back into the darkest corners of night's deepest gloom.

Belgrave's more conservative antagonist, however, Belton Piedmont, assumes just the opposite position. He praises slavery because it compensates the bondsmen with training "in the arts of civilization, a knowledge of the English language, and a conception of the one true God and his Christ." In words remarkably similar to those employed by Booker T. Washington, Griggs's fictional character asserts that "when we calmly survey the evil and the good that came to us through American slavery, . . . we find more good for which to thank God than we find evil for which to curse man."[15]

Similarly, in these years the *Southern Workman*, organ of Hampton Institute, frequently pointed out how slavery's short-term evils matched its long-range beneficences. Black Negrophobe William Hannibal Thomas also found redeeming qualities in slavery, a system that he censured as a "monstrous iniquity."

Despite its barbarities, slavery wrought a salutary transformation in the negro race. It made rational men out of savage animals, and industrious serfs out of wanton idlers. It found the negro rioting in benighted ignorance, and led him to the threshold of light and knowledge. It clothed nakedness in civilized habiliments, and taught a jungle idolater of Christ and immortality.

Statements by blacks favorable to slavery played into the hands of those white racists determined to keep blacks in their place. According to Robert Bone, these statements suggest the brute strength of white coercion in these years. White supremacy dragged even forward-looking blacks into "the sterile fantasies of a nation engaged in a hollow ritual of self-justification."[16] Because of Booker T. Washington's importance in black thought and action in the Age of Jim Crow, his proslavery remarks merit special examination.

## II

When early twentieth-century white Americans envisaged an "acceptable" black man, their thoughts invariably turned to Booker T. Washington. Most whites, north and south, viewed him as the only black spokesman of these years who had the necessary moderation to discuss slavery fairly and without malice. In 1898 the editor of the conservative *Southern States Farm Magazine* praised Washington as "the greatest negro that this country has produced. He is head and shoulders above the mass of ecclesiastics and politicians who have in their selfish self-seeking misled and misrepresented their people for more than a generation. There is hope for his race, because he has become its wise, skilled and unwearingly faithful leader." Born a slave in Franklin County, Virginia, in 1856, Washington went on to work his way through Hampton Institute and finally became principal of the black vocational school at Tuskegee, Alabama. From these humble beginnings, he later emerged as the most influential black American in the latter nineteenth and early twentieth centuries. So successfully did he mask his intentions and his strategies that the complex Washington remained an enigma not only to his contemporaries but to generations of historians as well. Thanks to Louis R. Harlan's two-volume biography, we now can place Washington's seemingly contradictory remarks, including those regarding slavery, into proper perspective. As Harlan has so ably demonstrated, on the race question Washington frequently camouflaged his true attitudes, utilizing "weasel words that his critics said vitiated his purposes, but he contended . . . were necessary to gain any hearing at all from whites."[17]

Despite his numerous accommodationist statements, Washington never wavered from his long-range goal, the "complete and unqualified integration of the Negro into American society." But Washington was a realist; he recognized that his race must take gradual steps toward reaching its goal. Consequently, he encouraged blacks to make economic independence and security their first attainment. With an economic front once established, reasoned Washington, blacks eventually could obtain full acceptance into all areas of American life. In simple, pleasing, Christian terms, Washington thus appealed for cooperation among the races and urged blacks to accept the Jim Crow laws as a temporary expedient. Dedicated to achieving the economic and educational self-elevation of American blacks, Washington placated white supremacists by de-emphasizing racial equality. In exchange, he received their support for vocational training for blacks. Northern philanthropists showered their largesse upon him. For them he represented a dark-skinned Horatio Alger.[18]

Washington urged blacks to develop "race pride and race consciousness." He also ranked among the first of the black writers to employ anthropologist Franz Boas's findings to challenge the myths of African backwardness and white supremacy.[19] But Washington's complex personality included an even more telling element—his behind-the-scenes activism against antiblack legislation, disfranchisement, and any and all black critics who disavowed his conciliatory policies and leadership. According to Claude H. Nolen, Washington mystified his contemporaries because he "gave a deceptive appearance of freely bowing to Southern demands by repeating much of the white man's propaganda." Harlan portrays Washington as a surreptitious manipulator, a ruthless opponent, a wizard at strategy and deception. The Tuskegean secretly backed politicians and editors who espoused his philosophy of black progress, but quickly withdrew his support at the first hint of disloyalty. Washington "was forced from childhood to deceive, to simulate, to wear the mask," writes Harlan. "With each subgroup of blacks or whites that he confronted, he learned to play a different role, wear a different mask."[20]

Washington frequently used history, either his own autobiography or the story of his race, to communicate his messages of racial self-help and accommodation. His speeches, essays, and books constantly referred to slavery, generally in the form of some homespun didactic tale selected for its illustrative value. As an ex-slave, Washington often wove his personal experiences with slavery into whatever point he was trying to make. Not a trained historian, his statements regarding slavery suffer from inadequate documentation, oversimplify complex issues, and minimize the evils of white racism. To complicate matters, Washington employed outside researchers and writers to prepare many of his writings. T. Thomas Fortune, S. Laing Williams, Max Bennett Thrasher, Robert E. Park, and Monroe N. Work served as his ghostwriters. "But," writes Emma Lou Thornbrough, "there is no reason to think that the ideas and opinions expressed were not Washington's own."[21]

Washington wrote often concerning slavery because he considered it a major influence on the postwar race problem. And he put forth some valuable insights into the peculiar institution. He argued, for example, that conditions under slavery varied from plantation to plantation or from section to section within the region. The ex-slave also recognized that day-to-day slave life depended heavily on local custom. Yet Washington stopped short of anything more than a surface appraisal of slavery. Why? Despite his many references to it, Washington actually agonized over slavery. At one point he even remarked, "I sometimes fear that in our great anxiety to push forward we lay too much stress upon our former condition.'' His usual approach was to present one of the two conflicting views of slavery. Like a chameleon Washington adapted his view of slavery to the audience at hand, concurrently portraying slavery both as a curse and a blessing to blacks.[22]

Outright condemnation of slavery ran counter to Washington's optimistic outlook. Nevertheless, in several instances he attacked the peculiar institution with the vehemence of the abolitionist. His references to slavery as a curse and a yoke restraining blacks conveyed the impression that Washington subscribed to the antislavery school. Writing early in his career, for instance, he declared that ''no one who has . . . made the struggle and . . . freed himself would go back for any consideration into the old slavery.'' In Washington's opinion, the slaves worked ''under circumstances that were calculated to do anything but teach them to see the dignity, beauty, and civilizing power of intelligent labor.'' Bondage left the blacks unprepared to govern themselves, to control money, and even to raise their own children. Emancipation finally ''made us men instead of property.'' Years later Washington blasted the destructive effect slavery had on the black family. Masters ruthlessly dissolved slave marriages on a whim, he said.[23]

In 1898 Washington wrote sarcastically that, unlike the European immigrant, the African traveled to America ''*by special invitation*, in ships provided for him.'' Once settled in his new home, however, the black ''was forcibly restrained in any desire he may have had to return to his fatherland.'' In Washington's opinion both blacks and whites suffered injuries because of slavery. For the blacks, ''the whole machinery of slavery was not apt to beget the spirit of love of labour.'' Rather, slavery encouraged the dependence of blacks upon their masters and instilled in them a disrespect for property. Washington blamed slavery for ingraining in blacks an apathetic attitude toward manual labor. He bemoaned this apathy as one of the major obstacles facing black leaders in the New South. At Tuskegee, Washington often told his students that they must grasp the ''vast difference between working and being worked.'' Slavery also weakened white southerners because, in Washington's view, it made labor for the master class ''a badge of degradation, of inferiority.'' To a large degree, concluded Washington, slavery ''took the spirit of self-reliance and self-help'' from the whites and injured them as much as it did their black neighbors.[24]

Washington drew a parallel between slave control mechanisms, especially the patrol system, and postwar white modes of race control. The Ku Klux Klan evoked in his mind images of mounted slave patrollers hunting down errant bondsmen at night. He also condemned the poor care provided the bondsmen, pointing out that masters allowed their chattels few opportunities to maintain a stable family, or to acquire an education, property, or "character." Recalling his own boyhood as a slave, Washington referred to his "miserable, desolate, and discouraging surroundings," but he added quickly that his master represented the type that ruled by kindness, not by the whip. He retained vivid memories of his "bed of rags," insufficient food and clothing, slave patrols, slave songs, and cruel punishments. The blacks received their rations, remembered Washington, en masse—"very much as dumb animals get theirs." Still fresh in his mind in 1900 was the coarse flax "tow" shirt that he wore as a young slave. According to him such garments themselves became "quite an institution during slavery." But his most lasting reminiscence was the sight of his uncle being strapped to a tree and whipped. In the midst of this punishment, the slave rebelled against his captor by crying "Pray master! Pray master!" Washington's autobiography contains many references to slavery's degrading influences.[25]

Still, Washington paid equal, if not more, attention to what today seems almost a defense of slavery. In 1900 he complained when the American Publishing House falsely included his name as one of the coauthors of *A New Negro for a New Century* (1900). This volume contained a chapter entitled "Slavery Unmasked," by another writer— an extremely harsh antislavery account. Washington most likely objected to this strong antislavery position because it might weaken his image as the moderate spokesman of his race. Southern white legislators and northern philanthropists disliked extreme statements from uppity black folks. "He was a man schooled to repress his feelings," notes Harlan. So the Tuskegean not only held his tongue but balanced his criticisms of slavery with remarks more typical of the proslavery apologist.[26]

Washington recognized the irony of an ex-slave and national black leader admitting slavery's positive qualities. "As with every other human thing," he wrote, "there is more than one side to slavery, and more than one way of looking at it." Although he declared he "would be the last to apologize for the curse of slavery," many of Washington's statements in fact indicate tolerance for the institution. Writing in 1896, he explained that slavery was part of a divine plan for black progress. "We went into slavery pagans, we came out Christians. We went into slavery a piece of property, we came out American citizens. We went into slavery without a language, we came out speaking the proud Anglo-Saxon tongue. We went into slavery with the slave chains clanking about our wrists, we came out with the American ballot in our hands." Slavery, then, introduced Africans to the basics of civilization. It taught blacks to worship Christ, to speak the English language, to wear clothes, and to live in a house—in Washington's words, "no inconsiderable step in the direction of morality and Christianity." In 1909 Washington explained that "there was much in slavery besides its hardships and its cruelties; much that was tender, human, and beautiful." On another occasion he recalled the pleasant festivities on the plantation, where the bondsmen enjoyed seasonal folk celebrations such as corn-shucking bees. These images could have appeared in the plantation fantasies of Thomas Nelson Page.[27]

In line with his faith in the gospel of work, Washington declared that blacks profited most from the economic training offered by slavery. It provided them their "first lesson in anything like continuous, progressive, systematic labor." In *The Future of the American Negro* (1899) he explained that during the 250 years under slavery, "God . . . prepared the way for the redemption of the Negro through industrial development." Slaves, Washington continued, held a virtual monopoly on the Old South's skilled work force. The peculiar institution afforded vital hands-on apprenticeships for black craftsmen as diverse as carpenters, masons, and bridge builders. He cited Lewis Adams, an ex-slave who advised Washington in construction work at Tuskegee, as a prime example of a bondsman who received vocational education while enslaved. As a slave mechanic, Adams studied the trades of shoemaking, harness making, and tinsmithing and, thanks to the school of slavery, even learned to read and write. True, acknowledged Washington, masters trained their chattels "for selfish purposes." But this education, no matter how harsh, outfitted his race with both the long-range "business contact" and the technical skills necessary to compete in industrial America.[28]

Washington's conservative philosophy of patience caused him to identify virtues in the slave system that no doubt sickened other leaders of his race. He asserted, for example, that for many blacks the hardships experienced under slavery served to instill a "strength of mind and a clearness of vision." Slavery worked "to strengthen and form" the black man's character. "Notwithstanding the cruelty and moral wrong of slavery, the ten million Negroes inhabiting this country, who themselves or whose ancestors went through the school of American slavery, are in a stronger and more hopeful condition, materially, intellectually, morally and religiously, than is true of an equal number of black people in any other portion of the globe." Drawing upon his own experience as a slave, Washington made the ridiculous statement that had he not been enslaved he would have missed the opportunity "to learn nature, to love the soil, to love cows . . . pigs . . . trees . . . birds . . . and creeping things." Also, much like the white proslavery ideologues, he argued that under slavery "the two races had become bound together in intimate ways that people outside of the South could not comprehend." He even sympathized with those masters who had abused their slaves. In committing such depredations, reasoned Washington, the whites injured themselves more than they hurt their bondsmen. All in all, Washington concluded that "the black man got barely as much out of slavery as the white man did."[29]

While such statements infuriated less conservative blacks, whites welcomed them with open arms. In 1905, for example, a reviewer noted approvingly that the program of vocational training espoused by Washington was itself based on "no other than the system of slavery." Always a pragmatist, Washington, according to Eugene D. Genovese, "tried to meet the legacy of slavery on its own terms." By necessity he "had to protect a large constituency in the South." Others with less political capital at stake, notably W. E. B. Du Bois, were freer to speak their minds on slavery's overwhelming defects. Washington's statements on slavery fit into his overall strategy for black advancement. With slavery no longer a force in American law, the Tuskegean thereby was free to use "soft" images of the institution in his fight for things that mattered most to him: equal opportunities for blacks in the form of jobs, schools, and political appointments, and long-range victories against discrimination and proscription.[30]

To a lesser extent, Washington's inconstant position on slavery also resulted from his background. As a child he experienced slavery on a small farm in western Virginia. Because he was the son of a slave cook and one of only seven bondsmen on the farm, his enslavement was relatively mild. He once admitted, for example, that "although I was born a slave, I was too young to experience much of its hardships."

Yet in later life, the black leader encountered many ex-slaves who had lived under a much harsher brand of slavery. These contrary perceptions of slavery bred in Washington a certain ambivalence, an ambiguity that marked virtually every element of his personality and public persona. Washington's attitudes were further complicated by his genuine belief that slavery had provided blacks with basic skills and lessons in survival. The slave curriculum, he noted in 1896, taught the blacks patience, tolerance of oppression, and the ability to right wrongs by faith in ultimate justice. The bondsmen would make the most of their opportunities when they finally gained their freedom. Such ideas bolstered Washington's work ethic—the belief that the chance to direct his own labor and advance was the black's greatest victory from the Civil War. And as the early black students of slave folklore noted, the bondsmen resorted to guile when forbearance proved inadequate. The Wizard of Tuskegee remembered those lessons especially well. Commenting on the "moral insensitivity" of Washington's cutthroat tactics, Harlan explains that "having started in slavery and poverty," Washington "would gag at almost nothing that promised dominance."[31]

In the end, Washington employed slavery as a tool—a comparative model—to illustrate to whites just how far blacks had progressed since emancipation. It was a severe system, he said, but one that blacks ultimately came to fashion to their own special needs. He often praised the manner in which blacks had risen in spite of slavery's bonds, the way they had used the training slavery provided in their efforts to establish themselves in the free market economy.[32] Ever careful to strike an apt balance between criticism of whites and sycophancy, Washington skillfully manipulated his statements on slavery. According to Professor Harlan:

A lifetime of experience with white southerners gave him . . . an ability to see through the white stereotypes to the realities of southern society. When he himself employed the white stereotypes in his utterances, one assumes that he did so deliberately, to further a purpose of his own. Sometimes that purpose was his own influence and security, but it was more often an effort to buy social peace at the cost of concessions to the southern social order of segregation.

Washington's public comments regarding slavery reminded whites of their guilt, encouraged blacks to be proud of their past strength, and spurred blacks on to greater heights. The legacy of slavery served

Washington well in his campaign to establish an economic beachhead in enemy territory in the racially tense New South.[33]

## III

If Washington's back-door, slippery statements on the merits of slavery confused readers, W. E. B. Du Bois left no room for doubt about his attitudes. Just as Du Bois denounced Washington's conservative leadership in favor of higher education and full political rights for blacks, his knife-edged critique of slavery illustrates yet another dimension of their disagreement. Du Bois blasted slavery in no uncertain terms. Unlike Washington, he refused to compromise with what he considered slavery's all-encompassing wrongs. Du Bois inveighed against slavery so forcefully because in his opinion it "spread more human misery, inculcated more disrespect for and neglect of humanity, a greater callousness to suffering, and more petty, cruel, human hatred than can well be calculated. We may excuse and palliate it, and write history so as to let men forget it; it remains the most inexcusable and despicable blot on modern human history." Throughout Du Bois's many writings, his tone remained unmistakably antislavery. For him slavery symbolized "crushing repression," the seed of national tragedy, misunderstanding, and ridicule. Whereas Du Bois held southern whites and slavery accountable for the contemporary "Negro problem," Washington invariably placed the onus on the blacks themselves. Du Bois's numerous discussions of slavery established him as the most fiery and important black student of slavery in the pre–World War I period. More than any other writer, he linked slavery to the exploitation of free labor. He sensed the omnipresent legacy of slavery and led the black assault on the new proslavery argument. Such, he said, was life under the malignant veil of racism.[34]

Du Bois was born in western Massachusetts in 1868, and his New England free black origins rocketed him into an orbit completely beyond that of Washington. Schooled as a historian at the University of Berlin (1892–1894) and at Harvard (Ph.D., 1895), Du Bois understood "scientific" historical method as well as any graduate of Herbert Baxter Adams's seminar. Previous students of slavery, he charged, had been too hasty, superficial, unsystematic, uncritical, and fragmentary. They had assumed—without evidence—"that the docility of Africans made slave insurrections almost unknown, and that the Negro never developed in this country a self-conscious group life before 1860." Du Bois pleaded with historians to abandon their singular view of the slaves—from the perspective only of the masters. He sought an entirely new conception of the bondsmen, one that would take special note of the "social evolution and development among them."[35]

Du Bois correctly appraised the bulk of the writings on slavery when in 1898 he described their content. He probably had in mind the Johns Hopkins *Studies* when he wrote that first

the slave code of a state is given, the progress of antislavery sentiment, the economic results of the system and the general influence of man on master are studied, but of the slave himself, of his group life and social institutions, of remaining traces of his African tribal life, of his amusements, his conversion to Christianity, his acquiring of the English tongue—in fine, of his whole reaction against his environment, of all this we hear little or nothing, and would apparently be expected to believe that the Negro arose from the dead in 1863.

In Du Bois's opinion, such an approach to slavery shortchanged the blacks. It completely ignored any sense of social evolution among them.[36]

As a black American, Du Bois sensed slavery's broad pathological impact on both races. It left a legacy of mistrust and hate, of ignorance and suspicion. Du Bois attributed many characteristics of blacks to the peculiar institution. For example, he held slavery accountable for the lax morals, poor hygiene habits, and frivolity of Philadelphia ghetto blacks who had served as bondsmen in the upper South. In his study of blacks in the Georgia black belt, Du Bois concluded that the blacks farmed exhausted soil, lived in squalor, and more often than not lived apart from their spouses. These direful conditions, he said, resulted from "long custom, born in the time of slavery." Black tenant farmers and sharecroppers also remained in "the slavery of debt" to white landlords and cotton factors. "A slave ancestry and a system of unrequited toil," argued Du Bois, made these blacks resemble "all ground-down peasantries"—ripe for "crime and a cheap, dangerous socialism."[37]

On another occasion, Du Bois branded the South's crop lien and convict lease systems "the direct children of slavery and to all intents and purposes . . . slavery itself." The latter method of procuring laborers, especially popular in the Gulf states, outraged Du Bois because so large a percentage of southern convicts were black. He said the system contained all "the worst aspects of slavery without any of its redeeming features." Similarly, in an interview published in the Cincinnati *Times-Star*, Du Bois charged that the peonage existing throughout the South offered yet another example of how slavery persisted in twentieth-century America.[38]

Du Bois insisted that slavery explained still other negative aspects of black life in the New South. The bondsmen, he said, were taught to live degraded lives as slaves. Not surprisingly, many of their descendants became criminals. Slavery encouraged ignorance and fostered "timidity, lack of a sense of personal worth and inability to bear responsibility," explained Du Bois. It also instilled in blacks a certain carelessness and laziness. He judged most grievous the lasting cleavage slavery caused within the South's working class—that is, its black and nonslaveholding poor white population. On a more positive note, Du Bois credited slavery with at least providing some bondsmen "the habit of work, the English language, and the Christian religion." And, reminiscent of Washington, Du Bois noted that no substitute had arisen since Appomattox for "that finer sympathy and love between some masters and house servants."[39]

But unlike Washington, Du Bois in no way justified slavery, and he used every opportunity to condemn it with all his literary might. He held the planter class fully accountable for slavery's "oppression, cruelty, concubinage, and moral retrogression." In 1905 Du Bois excoriated novelist Thomas Nelson Page and the planter class that Page so idealized.

It is as inaccurate to call Southern slavery barbarous as it is to call the modern wage system ideal; but it is not inaccurate to say that Southern slavery fostered barbarism, was itself barbaric in thousands of instances and was on the whole a system of labor so blighting to white and black that probably the only thing that saved Mr. Page's genius to the world was the Emancipation Proclamation,— the very deed that allows the present reviewer the pleasure of criticizing Mr. Page's book instead of hoeing his cotton.

In Du Bois's opinion, the planters "debauched, destroyed, and took from" the African "the organized home." They wrenched apart the slave family and left its members passive characters—"owned," "spoken for," accorded mere "contemptuous forgetfulness"—in the plantation tragedy. Slavery precluded the emergence of "growth or exception" on the part of blacks, leaving them enslaved physically and to the "slavery of ideas and customs." The peculiar institution left such deep scars on blacks that it bred in them utter "contempt for themselves."[40]

In addition to his brilliant polemics against slavery, Du Bois the historian made salient contributions to specific aspects of slave historiography. These fall into the areas of the Atlantic slave trade, slave religion and folk culture, African survivals among the bondsmen, and slave housing and family life. As early as 1891 Du Bois presented a paper—the first black to do so—before the then lily-white American Historical Association. The Harvard graduate student argued that more than 250,000 Africans were imported illegally into the United States between the 1808 enactment of the congressional prohibition on slave importations and 1862. He charged American officials "with negligence, if not fraud" in their lax enforcement of the slave trade regulations. "If slave labor was an economic god, then the slave trade was its strong arm; and with Southern planters recognizing this and Northern capital unfettered by a conscience it was almost like legislating against economic laws to attempt to abolish the slave trade by statutes. Northern greed joined to Southern credulity was a combination calculated to circumvent any law." Du Bois regretted that financial gain had triumphed over moral considerations.[41]

Five years later Harvard published Du Bois's *The Suppression of the African Slave-Trade to the United States of America, 1638–1870*, which had been his doctoral dissertation. In it the black scholar continued to upbraid American officials, north and south, for succumbing to economic self-interest. Whites never were dedicated to halting the transatlantic traffic in slaves, he said. Consequently, the 1808 prohibition was "probably enforced as the people who made it wished it enforced." Coastal slave patrollers performed their task loosely, especially late in the antebellum period, when some southerners clamored for the reopening of the African trade. Du Bois interpreted the entire issue as typical of America's constant "bargaining, truckling, and compromising" with slavery. Too moralistic in tone, he also overestimated the number of slaves smuggled into the South and undervalued the high natural rate of reproduction among American bondsmen. Even so, Du Bois's monograph surpassed in breadth and quality any of the Johns Hopkins dissertations on slavery. He paid particular attention to slave resistance and, alone among scholars, emphasized the widespread fears generated in the United States by Toussaint L'Ouverture's 1791 Haitian slave revolt. Students of slavery continue to heap praise upon Du Bois's path-breaking work.[42]

Having established himself as an authority on the Atlantic slave trade, in *The Souls of Black Folk* (1903) Du Bois probed the minds of the slaves. This masterful analysis of black identity in a white world unleashed Du Bois's "impassioned polemics against compromise, incisive irony at hypocrisy, sensitive brooding over the dilemmas of democracy, and affirmation of race pride and solidarity." In this book he exhibited his almost mystical identification with blacks worldwide. Filled with emotion and despair at the tragedy of the black diaspora, Du Bois nevertheless interpreted black sorrow as sweetness. Africans survived abuse at the hands of the Caucasians, strengthened themselves, and left a magnificent cultural legacy.[43]

Du Bois's analysis of slave religion in *The Souls of Black Folk* first appeared in the *New World* and remains today among the most important examinations of this subject. Not until the publication of Eugene D. Genovese's *Roll, Jordan, Roll* (1974) would a historian delve as deeply into slave religion as Du Bois. He maintained that despite the veneer of Christianity given slave religion by masters and missionaries, for more than a century it retained the imagery and superstitions of the African forest. Bondsmen, declared Du Bois, drew upon "the resources of Heathenism"—exorcism, witchcraft, Obi worship, spells, and blood sacrifices—to resist their captivity. His religion served as the bondsman's weapon against a bondage that the black envisioned as "the dark triumph of Evil over him." By the middle of the eighteenth century, however, planters succeeded in indoctrinating their slaves with Christianity. Passive submission soon replaced the fresh Africans' active resistance. With their tribal rites removed, the blacks slipped into what Du Bois termed a "deep religious fatalism." In his opinion, the slaves' new Christian "religion of resignation" resulted in better, more docile laborers, but ones more prone to indulgence and crime.[44]

Du Bois recognized years before other scholars just how harsh a "social revolution" the Africans experienced in their removal to America. The slave preacher became a vital link with their past as well as a leader to help direct their future. He quickly emerged as "the most unique personality developed by the Negro on American soil." More than a spiritual leader, the slave preacher functioned as politician, intriguer, idealist, "boss," and medicine man.

He early appeared on the plantation and found his function as the healer of the sick, the interpreter of the Unknown, the comforter of the sorrowing, the supernatural avenger of wrong and the one who rudely but picturesquely expressed the longing, disappointment and resentment of a stolen and oppressed people. Thus, as bard, physician, judge and priest, within the narrow limits allowed by the slave system, rose the Negro preacher, and under him the first Afro-American institution, the Negro church.

The slaves also depended heavily on their culture, especially music, to withstand the horrors of enslavement. Du Bois found special meaning in the slave melodies, "that sometime, somewhere, men will judge men by their souls and not by their skins." Beautiful but sad, articulate yet veiled, in Du Bois's judgment the spirituals reflected the day-to-day features of slave life. Few of the songs dealt with happiness or love. When they mentioned members of the slave family, the melodies excluded the father—in Du Bois's opinion the emasculated and tragic figure of slave society. Still, the bondsmen sang of hope for ultimate justice.[45]

Throughout his writings on slavery Du Bois never lost sight of the African origins of the bondsmen. His deep emotional commitment to Africa and his sense of kinship toward Africans resulted, he said, from the "social heritage of slavery." Du Bois advanced Pan-Africanism and praised African culture long before Melville J. Herskovits published his important studies of African survivals in the Western Hemisphere. Du Bois felt obligated to repudiate the widespread misconceptions about Africa, to stress Africa's rich contributions to American life. In his spirited popular volume *The Negro* (1915), Du Bois summarized the achievements of past and contemporary Africans in art, industry, political organization, and religion.[46]

Depending heavily not only on the writings of Franz Boas but on those of anthropologists William Z. Ripley, Joseph Deniker, and Friedrich Ratzel as well, Du Bois simultaneously revised attitudes toward Africa and attacked slavery. As early as 1899 he noted that "with all its shortcomings," the powerful, polygamous, "strictly guarded savage home life of Africa" offered more protection for women than "the promiscuous herding" of the slave plantation. Nine years later Du Bois again charged slavery with "crushing out . . . the African clan and family life" of American blacks. "No more complete method of reducing a barbarous people to subjection," he said, could be devised than to destroy the ancient African conception of family. True, Du Bois admitted, traces of African family institutions persisted. But in the main, the bondsmen "were raped of their own sex customs and provided with no binding new ones. Slavery," Du Bois added, "gave the monogamic family ideal to slaves but it compelled and desired only the most imperfect practice of its most ordinary morals." Du Bois asserted that, paradoxically, "the greatest social effect" of slavery was the replacement of the polygamous black home with one "less guarded, less effective, less civilized."[47]

In addition to an orderly and established family life, Du Bois argued that Africans also possessed a long and rich history of economic cooperation. As agriculturists, herders, artisans, and craftsmen, the slaves' forebears developed intricate village marketing systems, trade routes, and road caravans. Du Bois credited the Africans with contributing iron smelting to the world and praised their early weaving of cotton cloth. Seizure and enslavement, however, destroyed or stifled many of the Africans' creative efforts and their affinity for economic organization. Still, under slavery the blacks applied their genius for organization in the formation of black churches, in planning revolts, in running away, and in diverse forms of resistance. They also revealed their organizational skill in establishing slave beneficial and burial societies. All of these, Du Bois said, had their roots in Africa.[48]

So did slave housing and family life. Du Bois's keen observations on these aspects of slavery still demand attention from scholars. He uncovered important connections between African buildings and the first homes of American bondsmen. They shared an essential form: they were windowless huts with woven walls and thatched roofs fashioned around four posts. Such homes, reasoned Du Bois, could be kept clean and shady. But as "the cold brutality of slavery" increased, slave cabins began to reflect the harshness of the institution. "The homes of the slaves became dirty one-room lodges," he said, "where, crowded like cattle, men slept in dreamless stupor after endless hours of forced and driven toil." Du Bois identified spatial patterns in slave housing that reflected regional variations and the changing nature of slavery over time. In Virginia, for example, slaves tended to live in one-room log cabins with stone chimneys and board floors. Positioned according to the feudal model, the cabins sat close to the big house, and slaves and masters had relatively close contact. In Du Bois's opinion, however, the mere imposition of European housing arrangements crushed the

Africans' ancient customs and diminished the Africans' self-respect. As slavery became more a commercial enterprise, especially on the large plantations of the lower South, the nature of slave housing changed accordingly. Absentee owners frequently placed their bondsmen under the care of overseers. In Du Bois's view, this system widened the distance between slave and master, and the slaves lost the whites as models upon which to shape their habits and behavior. As a result, the slave quarters became "filthy hovels" with "no family life, no meals, no marriages, no decency." Du Bois judged more favorably the housing arrangements for black slaves in the cities. These people enjoyed considerable freedom, he said, and lived in small one- or two-room homes adjacent to their masters' houses. In Du Bois's opinion urban slaves experienced one major disadvantage: exposure to the "sexual looseness" learned by the blacks through close association with the whites.[49]

Du Bois concluded that the housing conditions under slavery contributed to the instability of the black family in the post–Civil War South. Slave homes lacked even the most basic comforts and elements of hygiene. Having few possessions as slaves, the blacks gained little appreciation for thrift as freedmen. They became conditioned to live in poverty and squalor. And the absence of strong paternal leadership plagued them as slaves as well as citizens. Slave mothers spent long hours in the fields, complained Du Bois, and had little time to attend to their children. Fathers lacked authority to govern their families. Their wives and daughters stood vulnerable to sexual abuse by the whites, and any member of the family could be sold at the master's whim. Tragically, lamented Du Bois, the emasculated slave husband became a "male guest in the house, without respect or responsibility." Lacking unity, permanence, or a sense of direction, the slave family languished. It served as little more than a temporary, disjointed "agglomeration of atoms" devoid of force or pride. According to Du Bois, such living conditions typified the dehumanizing and destructive effect of slavery on the Africans.[50]

## IV

Most blacks in these years, of course, lacked Du Bois's historical training and his unique opportunities to conduct field research among both ghetto and rural blacks. And few whites or blacks in any age have possessed his brilliant insights into the mood and manner of his race.

Nevertheless, an unusually large number of blacks in this period focused clearly on the slavery theme. They brought varied backgrounds and perspectives to the subject but shared many of Du Bois's emphases. Postemancipation black thought on slavery overwhelmingly attacked the new proslavery argument. Blacks judged America's peculiar institution the severest form of bondage in world history. With the zeal of the abolitionists, turn-of-the-century blacks leveled the new defenses of slavery and the racism upon which they rested. In doing so they expanded the parameters of slavery scholarship and established a solid foundation for subsequent researchers.

In 1895, for example, Frederick Douglass cursed slavery as "a system of unmitigated, legalized outrage." Its new generation of defenders cloaked the goal of racial control under the banner of "the Negro as rapist." These men, Douglass wrote bitterly,

glory in the good old times when the slaves were under the lash and were bought and sold in the market with horses, sheep, and swine. It is another way of saying that slavery is better than freedom; that darkness is better than light, and that wrong is better than right; that hell is better than heaven It is the American method of reasoning in all matters concerning the Negro.

In 1907 Professor John W. Work of Fisk University challenged proslavery statements in a manner remarkably similar to that of Caroline H. Pemberton in 1900. Work found incomprehensible "all this latter day talk about the happiness and contentment of the slave." The new proslavery rhetoric was "either inexcusable ignorance," he said, "or a culpable effort at gross deception; for slavery was horrible in every aspect." Black novelist John Wesley Grant agreed. "There are too many scarred bodies of living slaves to bear testimony to its truthfulness," wrote Grant in 1909. Along the same line, the editor of the Chicago *Defender* criticized the new defenses of slavery in 1914. He found especially distasteful the constant mention of slave loyalty by whites.

It is well enough to praise the slaves for that fine quality of loyalty which they showed, but it is not well to use that loyalty in these days, as a half-way implication that slavery was a just and pleasant institution. The very loyalty of the slaves seems pathetic. Their eyes were not open to see the vision of freedom. Slavery had hemmed them in and kept them down intellectually and spiritually. They did not know enough to strike for themselves. . . .

The journalist welcomed interest in the ex-slaves by the Confederate Veterans, who hoped to honor their former servants by building statues in their memory. This represented, he said, progress on the part of southern whites, who finally realized that they owed the blacks "something besides cuffs and knocks." While the editor judged stone monuments acceptable tributes in their own way, he concluded that "the colored people of the South need justice far more than they do monuments."[51]

Blacks without question approached the study of slavery in ways completely foreign to their white contemporaries. Whereas whites treated the slave as a passive, anonymous figure—an "unperson"—blacks portrayed him as a real person with mature emotions and human sensitivities. Blacks often objected forcefully to the tendency among whites to write the history of slavery totally from the perspective of the master class. In 1917, for example, ex-slave Charles C. Skinner recalled in the pages of the Bridgeport, Connecticut *Farmer* the day-to-day horrors of enslavement. Born a bondsman near Edenton, North Carolina, in 1850, Skinner was separated from his mother at age nine. As a young slave he fanned flies in the big house and performed odd jobs for his masters. Once, Skinner remembered, he received a whipping when he accidentally broke a kitchen utensil. "Slavery was a cruel condition [he explained]. Nobody, unless a victim of the practice can realize the sufferings of mothers as they saw their children snatched from their arms and sent to distant plantations with the knowledge they were never to see them again." Luckily Skinner made his way to Maine in 1864 and worked for the next twenty-five years in a shoe factory. Few whites could describe the coarse texture of slave life the way the ex-slave or the descendant of slaves could. Analyzing the available works on slavery in 1919, Carter G. Woodson grumbled that only a handful gave "insight as to what the Negro was, how the Negro developed from period to period, and the reaction of the race to what was going on around it."[52]

In their criticisms of white historians, blacks underscored the importance of writing from a black perspective. The black clergyman Thomas N. Baker, for example, condemned the treatment of slave women in the writings of James Ford Rhodes and Joseph A. Tillinghast. These white historians, wrote Baker, were "so prone to 'Jim Crow' the Negro, that they feel they must use a 'Jim Crow' logic in discussing him." In 1903 Du Bois lambasted Tillinghast's *The Negro in Africa and America* (1903) because it interpreted slavery as a positive influence

in the elevation of primitive African savages. The black scholar challenged Tillinghast's "picture of the better side of slavery— . . . too
excellent to be wholly true." Woodson, dean of American black historians, was only one of several blacks who lashed out against Edward
B. Reuter's *The Mulatto in the United States* (1918). According to
Woodson, Reuter's book signaled "the return of the antebellum proslavery philosopher disguised as a scientific investigator."[53]

Blacks gave no quarter to Ulrich B. Phillips, the foremost white
student of slavery of his day. In 1913 Du Bois damned Phillips's arrogant
proslavery statements in a sarcastic editorial in the *Crisis*, the organ of
the National Association for the Advancement of Colored People. Specifically, Du Bois attacked Phillips's statement that since the end of
slavery the efficiency of black agricultural laborers had declined while
that of their white counterparts had increased. Phillips, mocked Du
Bois, "is white and Southern, but . . . has a Northern job and . . . knows
all about the Negro." Du Bois chided him for making an unfair comparison. Much of the land cultivated by blacks was inferior to that
worked by whites. Blacks, Du Bois continued, were forced to toil upon
the unfertilized and "slavery-cursed Mississippi bottoms where the soil
has been raped for a century." Du Bois went on to criticize Phillips's
insensitivity to the unequal conditions under which black and white
farmers lived and labored. With typical Du Boisian invective, he asserted that Phillips would be well suited to head the U.S. Department
of Agriculture, "not that it takes brains . . . but it *does* call for adroitness
in bolstering up bad cases." Five years later Du Bois blasted Phillips's
*American Negro Slavery* (1918), berating it as "curiously incomplete
and unfortunately biased." He faulted Phillips not only for his inability
to treat blacks as "ordinary human beings," but also for his unwillingness to recognize growth and change in blacks from the fourteenth
to the twentieth century.[54]


V

Slavery's black critics lashed out again and again at the most vulnerable weapon in the proslavery arsenal: the slavery-as-school analogy.
True, some blacks joined Washington and referred to slavery as a school,
but most found the analogy simply repulsive. That blacks were content
as slaves, they said, was a white man's myth—the propaganda of those
who could not free themselves from treating the Afro-American as a

child. In 1894 Richard T. Greener, the first black graduate of Harvard, condemned the slavery/school analogy, ridiculing the lessons the slaves allegedly received from bondage:

The Negro has no tears to shed over that, "wonderful school of slavery, under Providence," so often quoted. He is no such hypocrite as to go through the pretence of believing that slavery is ever a good, a necessary, or beneficial school. Much less does he grant that any phase of that school, at any stage, affected him morally, socially, or physically except adversely, while he does know from bitter experience, how utterly phar[i]saical, how absurdly hypocritical, and how thoroughly unchristian the entire system was in practice, example and influence.

Put another way, slavery was a school from which pupils never graduated.[55]

A year later, Professor J. W. E. Bowen seconded Greener's critique of the reported school of slavery. Bowen, the son of a slave, received a Ph.D. from Boston University and taught historical theology at Gammon Theological Seminary. In his judgment, slavery was a "pit of seething, reeking, and nauseating corruption"—"a dehumanized and bestialized thing"—where blacks were "worked like dumb, driven cattle . . . crushed with the iron hoof of oppression and repression; [and] whipped, torn, bleeding, in body, mind and soul." Blacks, charged Bowen, must challenge the whites' version of slavery as the halcyon days of purity and moral uplift for the Negro. What sort of school, asked Bowen, taught with the slave driver's whip and bloodhounds? Bowen, Greener, and other blacks agreed that the intellectual and religious qualities blacks possessed emerged in spite of, not because of, slavery.[56]

Black writers found the slavery-as-school analogy vulnerable to two specific criticisms. First, conditions under the peculiar institution placed the bondsmen at near subsistence level. Notwithstanding the apologists' assertions to the contrary, housing, food, and clothing under slavery degraded the Africans, who succumbed to burdensome tasks as well as dehumanizing tortures. Such an environment served to diminish self-respect and growth in the bondsmen.[57] One black writer after another commented that the modicum of care the slaves received resulted from the masters' financial, not humanitarian, interests. William H. Crogman, for example, found the conditions of slave life not a positive

influence on Africans, but rather "a long step backward." Forced to
live in "hovels," dress in "rags," and eat "coarse" food, the slaves
were systematically overtasked. Even Washington, who pointed repeatedly to the educational benefits of slavery, admitted that the bondsmen labored under brutal conditions. Another ex-slave, Dr. William A.
Sinclair, recalled life in thralldom as "gruesome and unholy," "bru-
talizing," and "debasing." After emerging from slavery he earned a
medical degree at Meharry Medical College in Nashville. Sinclair recalled the "bestialities of the slave system" in South Carolina, most
notably the barbaric tortures administered to the slaves. Others, most
notably Woodson, condemned miscegenation as the most heinous product of an ungodly system. They blamed the South's mulatto population
on the lust of the master class. Slave owners, Woodson explained, raped
slave women at random. In doing so they not only disgraced themselves
but diluted the racial purity of the proud Afro-Americans. Along this
line, Woodson reproached white historians, "ashamed of the planters
who abused helpless black women," for "trying to minimize the prev-
alence of this custom." Because of these conditions, charged ex-slaves
Allen Parker and Frederick Douglass, plantation paternalism never could
have existed. In their opinion the celebrated give-and-take between
master and slave belonged in the realm of fiction. Parker, for example,
recalled the dynamics of master/slave relations in North Carolina.

There was always a kind of strife between master and slave, the master on the
one hand trying to get all the work he possibly could out of the slaves at the
least possible expense, and the slaves on their part trying to get out of all the
work they could, and to take every possible advantage of their master, naturally
feeling that all they could get out of him was a poor sustenance for the work
they did.

Douglass stripped bare the alleged mutuality of plantation paternalism.
Under slavery, he quipped, "The master is always the master and the
slave is always the slave."[58]

   The second major criticism leveled at the slavery-as-school argument
concerned the blacks' alleged degradation resulting from emancipation.
Repeatedly since Reconstruction, slavery's defenders had pointed to the
reversion of the blacks to barbarism without the enlightened guidance
of the peculiar institution. Certainly, black authors admitted, enslavement taught the bondsmen all sorts of lessons—lessons in blind obe-

dience, servility, hatred, and humiliation. H. T. Kealing, editor of the *A.M.E. Church Review*, blamed slavery for a long list of what he identified as deficiencies in blacks: shiftlessness, incontinence, intolerance, extravagance, and improvidence. He maintained that slavery imbued blacks with sloppy, erratic work habits and tutored them in the arts of lying, cheating, and double-dealing. Black writers also complained that slavery prepared the freedmen to despise and disrespect one another, and to fear spies in their midst, who, as in the days of slavery, would betray their secrets to the whites. In the opinion of Benjamin G. Brawley, dean of Morehouse College, slavery left in blacks a bitter legacy of contempt for labor. Yes, he lamented, the peculiar institution served as a school all right. It taught lessons that would have to be unlearned.[59]

## VI

While most blacks in these years added little that was new to the old slavery debate, some went on to break fresh ground and sketch out the contours of later scholarship. The most salient contributions along these lines examined the bondsmen's responses to captivity. Black writers celebrated the strength of their enslaved forebears who, unlike the weak American Indians, withstood slavery's cold brutality. Only an unusually hearty and spirited race could weather centuries of oppression yet reproduce at an unparalleled rate and retain a sense of communal vigor and pride. These writers identified a black subculture among the slaves— the slave community—in which members shared a group life, a common world view. This society enabled the slaves to endure the horrors of their situation and, all the while, to contribute a unique Afro-American cultural legacy. The community of slaves included, in addition to field hands and house servants, talented slave artisans, gifted slave poets, and mysterious slave preachers. Blacks could look back to their slave heritage with admiration because the black "genius" persevered amid conditions that would have destroyed the creative instinct in a lesser race. According to Brawley, blacks possessed an "instinct for beauty" that gained force, did not wither, even under brutal enslavement. In his path-breaking volume, *The Education of the Negro Prior to 1861* (1919), Woodson disclosed the persistent strivings of slaves for education. His research dealt a powerful blow to the stereotype of the bondsmen as mindless, satisfied beings.[60]

Like all of Woodson's writings, his monograph on black education underscored the importance of black contributions in the American past. He remained convinced that the slaves worked actively to secure education and training, and he cited the prohibition against teaching slaves to read and write as an extension of slavery of the body to slavery of the mind. Such stifling of the black intellect, he said, bore bitter fruit: the "Negro traits" whites found so objectionable in blacks. Denied an education, he complained, no wonder the bondsmen behaved as "shiftless, undependable beings, seeking relief whenever possible by giving the least and getting the most from their masters." In spite of this closed society, Woodson maintained, approximately 20 percent of the slaves received the "rudiments of education" before 1835, and 10 percent continued to gain some form of training after that date. Too often, though, the masters taught them "to mistreat and malign each other." They tutored their chattels "to be low and depraved," argued Woodson, so "that they might never develop sufficient strength to become a powerful element in society."[61]

Black writers focused far more often and more clearly on the varieties of slave resistance than even the white neoabolitionists did. Some blacks expressed pride that their slave ancestors had laid the foundation for black protest and self-help in America. Bondsmen, they noted with esteem, broke their chains in diverse ways. Most battled slavery symbolically by seeking refuge in their music, leisure activities, and religious folklore. Any and all forms of freedom from the master's dominance, physical or intellectual, constituted a victory in the slaves' fight against the system. Slave songs, according to Kelly Miller, represented "the first expression of the imprisoned soul of an imprisoned race"—"the smothered voice of a race crying in the wilderness." "They breathed the prayer and complaint of souls overflowing with the bitterest anguish," added Frederick Douglass. One early student of slave culture interpreted the slaves' "ring plays" as a "safety valve, a sweet solace, a blessed forgetfulness" when the hardships of bondage became too oppressive. True, some writers construed the slaves' faith as a religion of resignation, but others portrayed it as a form of dissent, a mode of implicit resistance. Dr. Sinclair, for example, maintained that the bondsmen "hoodwinked" their masters by singing religious songs "while the words echoed and re-echoed deep down in their hearts" the thirst for liberty. Through song and prayer the bondsmen vocalized their agony and their innermost appeals for freedom.[62]

Black writers of the pre–World War I period identified yet another medium through which their forebears resisted enslavement—slave folk culture. While Joel Chandler Harris's "Uncle Remus" tales perpetuated the plantation myth for white readers, black writers focused on the slaves' superstitions and presented very different conclusions. Voodoo rites, Obi worship, and tales of conjures appealed as subjects to black writers for two reasons. First, these customs symbolized important remnants of the African past. Second, they powerfully influenced the slaves' world view. Because of the conjure-doctor's alleged ability to cast spells with poisons and charms, he held a measure of control over both the slaves and their captors. In articles in the *Southern Workman,* two students from Hampton Institute assessed conjury's broad social role for the bondsmen. It provided an explanation for the harsh world around them and offered a means of obtaining justice for a people denied access to courts of law. Another black student of slave superstitions, Clement Richardson, argued that the slaves' supernatural myths afforded them some degree of control, change, and excitement in what he perceived as their hopelessly dull and monotonous routine.[63]

In his collection of folktales, *The Conjure Woman* (1899), black lawyer and novelist Charles W. Chesnutt underscored the role of the conjure story as a medium of slave protest. Chesnutt became intrigued with the folk culture of the slaves while teaching in Freedmen's Bureau schools in North Carolina. Strongly impressed with Harris's cycle of animal tales, Chesnutt adopted them as a literary form, but he differed from Harris both in method and argument. Whereas Harris's stories drew exclusively on genuine folktales, Chesnutt's stemmed almost entirely from his imagination. Chesnutt improvised freely with his folk sources, while Harris worked to maintain the integrity of the old tales. But Chesnutt, unlike Harris, excluded any positive images of slavery from his pages. Instead, his tales of slave magic and conjuration exposed slavery's cruelties and injustices, its vile economic underpinnings, and its potentially destructive effect on the black family.[64]

On the surface Chesnutt's book appears to be an entertaining collection of tales set in slavery times. The tales offered parables for blacks and whites without seeming to upset the late nineteenth-century southern racial caste system. Yet on another level,

Chesnutt provided white and black readers alike with an uncompromising denunciation of slavery. He examined the anguish of husbands and wives helplessly torn from one another; the powerlessness of parents to keep their children in the face of the master's whims to the contrary. He destroyed the myth of the good master as well as the happy but bitterly untrue idea that slavery somehow fostered humanity among the slaves. Chesnutt's tales showed clearly that slaves presented human values only through struggle. He condemned the complicity of the nation's legal system in denying the most basic human rights to slaves.

Chesnutt, better than any other black novelist, assailed slavery's denial of black humanity, a denial that removed from the bondsmen the right to shape their own destinies. They were judged not by their work, but by the color of their skin.[65]

In *The Conjure Woman* Chesnutt actually worked a conjure on his audience. He intentionally manipulated the language of his main character, Uncle Julius McAdoo, the venerable ex-slave. When Uncle Julius spoke of the supernatural—men changed into trees or animals, whites transformed into blacks—he was uncovering the essential inhumanity of the slave system, its barbarity, and the strength of the slave family to endure. In "Mars Jeems's Nightmare" the brutal slaveowner, Mars Jeems McLean, is goophered into a black slave and discovers firsthand the harshness of slavery when he is forced to work under his own overseer. Chesnutt credited the blacks with the power to use nature to fight enslavement. He portrayed whites as constantly at odds with nature, exploitative, and greedy.[66]

Not only did Chesnutt's folk stories attack slavery, but they provided folk evidence that blacks responded to slavery in ways other than obsequiousness. Chesnutt's slave characters retaliated against their masters overtly and covertly, maintained group solidarity, and sought to retain their humanity in spite of gross inhumanity on the part of the whites. Drawing upon African influences, Chesnutt argued that slaves used their folk culture to interpret their world and to shape a community totally alien from that of their masters. In this manner the slaves actively resisted their bondage and controlled their own lives, no matter how oppressive slavery became.[67]

Most black writers, however, dealt less with symbolic slave resistance and more with the variety of artful intrigue employed by bondsmen to protest the slave regime. Day-to-day resistance to slavery took various forms—disobeying orders, running away, attacking overseers, organizing secret societies, aiding the Yankees—each revealing the blacks' constant desire for freedom. Just as they detailed with admiration the

Africans' skills as warriors and craftsmen of weapons, these authors identified a militant spirit in the blacks throughout slavery. As early as 1883, historian George Washington Williams asserted that masters remained in constant fear of slave revolts—the only "safety valves" available to the slaves. Williams argued that the small number of slave insurrections resulted not from any fear on the part of the blacks, but because of a lack of leadership among them. Although "under-fed and over-worked; poorly clad and miserably housed," the slave rarely became the "too goodish, too lamb-like, too obsequious" Uncle Tom figure. "The lion slumbers in the Negro," concluded Williams, and this spirit was strengthened, not destroyed, by enslavement. Four years later William T. Alexander added that slave restiveness left southern white society "always on the alert, always with its hand on the sword."[68]

To blacks living in the shadow of slavery—and later, under the specter of Jim Crow—rebellious blacks such as Denmark Vesey and Nat Turner became folk heroes. Historian John Wesley Cromwell, in *The Negro in American History* (1914), referred to slave revolts as "a constant menace to the safety and security of slavery." He maintained that before the American Revolution alone, approximately twenty-five insurrections had occurred. In his *Negro Year Book: An Annual Encyclopedia of the Negro, 1916–1917,* Monroe N. Work upped that figure to thirty-four, including nine revolts in the antebellum period. Lawyer and civil rights activist Archibald H. Grimké regretted that despite Vesey's brilliant planning and "underground agitation," his uprising failed when he was betrayed by a co-conspirator. According to Grimké, Vesey was a "grand master in the art of intrigue" among the slaves and free blacks—one who helped train the blacks "in the habits of deceit, of deep dissimulation . . . that *ars artium* of slaves in their attempts to break their chains." In the same vein, Cromwell glorified Turner's revolt as an example of the assertive, active black who struck "to help himself rather than depend on other human agencies for the protection which could come through his own strong arm." And finally, Kelly Miller applauded Toussaint L'Ouverture's revolutionary deeds. "Where else," asked Miller, "in the course of history has a slave with the aid of slaves, expelled a powerfully entrenched master class, and set up a government patterned after civilized models and which without external assistance or reinforcement from a parent civilization, has endured for a hundred years in face of a frowning world?"[69]

Such emphasis among early black writers can be misleading. Grimké, for example, applauded slave insurgence when writing about Vesey, but in another instance he asserted that the bondsmen remained passive, lacking feelings of resentment and revenge. Similar complexities and subtleties appear throughout the early black scholarship on slavery. Clergyman and missionary Alexander Crummell presents an excellent case in point. Though he was an unflagging critic of slavery, Crummell's contradictory statements are still apt to confuse. In an 1891 sermon, "The American Negro, before the War, and Now," he condemned slavery for denying the bondsmen education. But in "The Discipline of Freedom," he praised enslavement for the discipline it instilled in the blacks—a trait the Episcopal minister found drastically wanting in the mass of his race. On the one hand, such authors celebrated advancements under slavery as proof of the essential strength and equality of their race. Only an exceptional people, they reasoned, could have withstood the outrages of American slavery. The editor of the *Afro-American Ledger*, for example, lauded the bondsmen for hammering out the "internal elements for the construction of real family life" in spite of slavery's wickedness. Yet at the same time, blacks admitted the degradation of the black man wrought by enslavement. They criticized the behavior—subservience, negligence, extravagance—that blacks learned as slaves and retained as freedmen.[70]

## VII

The paucity of professionally trained black historians goes a long way toward explaining the inconsistencies and weaknesses in the bulk of the work of the pioneer black writers. Few blacks studied slavery in a systematic manner, and—understandably sensitive on the subject—they countered white racism with their own filiopietistic interpretation of the black past. Most of the studies analyzed here presented slavery in a defensive, biased, partisan, and moralistic tone. Propagandists for black advancement in the early twentieth century, black writers were prone to exaggerate the achievements of their race under the peculiar institution. Their documentation, for example, for accounts of slave resistance and miscegenation was woefully thin. Only rarely did black writers examine newspapers as sources, and none consulted the plantation records that were becoming increasingly available. Like their white peers, blacks overemphasized the content of slave laws without analyzing their enforcement. They failed, too, to define such terms as *backward* and *primitive* when discussing ethnology and cultural relativism. And black writers virtually ignored the economics of slavery. In the end, their very close identification with slavery denied them the necessary distance—the detachment—to assess objectively such a highly charged emotional question.

Even so, the early black writers on slavery wrote with a mission: to demolish what Robert Bone has termed the "prettification of slavery" by the proponents of the new proslavery argument. Among works written by blacks, only those of the two professional historians, Du Bois and Woodson, can be subjected to fair yet rigorous historical criticism. But to the black writers' credit, even without historical training in the graduate seminars they prefigured much recent scholarship. They examined questions and adopted themes that did not become popular among white historians until the 1960s and 1970s. Blacks probed aspects of slavery, including the slaves' meetings, their garden truck patches, preachers, and teachers, that still cry out for careful study by scholars. Emphasizing race pride and unity, African creativity and nationalism, these blacks anticipated the racial mood of the Negro Revolution of the 1960s. Years before the appearance of Melville J. Herskovits's writings, and a half-century before John W. Blassingame published *The Slave Community* (1972), they observed the survivals of African culture and identified a subculture among American slaves. Their research in black folk life—songs, dances, jokes, and religious practices—foreshadowed the recent work of Sterling Stuckey, Lawrence W. Levine, and Charles W. Joyner. By arguing that the bondsmen resisted enslavement and struggled to acquire the rudiments of formal education, these pioneer writers outlined themes popularized by succeeding generations of scholars. They shared with later historians a sensitivity to the long-range effects of slavery upon American life. In sum, blacks outdistanced the white neoabolitionists in their repudiation of the new defenses of slavery. They transcended the slavery debate of their time and made lasting contributions to the literature on slavery. But most importantly, the vast majority of the early black writers rejected the new proslavery argument point-blank. In doing so, they exposed the virulent racism that lay at its core.[71]

## NOTES

1. Bruce, *The Blot on the Escutcheon*, (Washington, 1890), 11–14.
2. Benjamin T. Tanner, review of James H. W. Howard, *Bond and Free*,

in *A.M.E. Church Review*, 3 (October, 1886): 207; anon., "Ante-Bellum Echoes," Richmond *Planet*, n.d., reprinted in Indianapolis *Freeman*, February 11, 1893; editorial, "Forgotten History," Washington *Bee*, December 23, 1899.

3. Henry M. Turner, *The Barbarous Decision of the United States Supreme Court Declaring the Civil Rights Acts Unconstitutional and Disrobing the Colored Race of All Civil Protection* (Atlanta, 1893), 3, 45, 61; *Address of the Minnesota Civil Rights Committee to the American Public* (St. Paul, 1891), [3]; Kelly Miller, "The National Bird—Eagle or Jim Crow?" unpublished manuscript, n.d., Kelly Miller Papers, Howard University; W. H. Crogman, "Twenty-Sixth Anniversary of the Emancipation Proclamation," *Talks for the Times* (South Atlanta, 1896), 204; Charles B. Purvis to Jonathan P. Dolliver, February 14, 1909, Whitefield McKinlay Papers, Manuscript Division, Library of Congress; Archibald H. Grimké, "Reaction and Danger," unpublished manuscript [1916?], Archibald H. Grimké Papers, Howard University; A Georgia Peon, "The New Slavery in the South," *Independent*, 56 (February 25, 1904): 409–414; Charles W. Chesnutt, "Peonage, or the New Slavery," *Voice of the Negro* 1 (September, 1904): 394–397; editorial, "New Southern Slavery," New York *Age*, December 19, 1907; " 'Negro Is Still Slave,' Declares Prof. Du Bois," Cincinnati *Times-Star*, December 5, 1910; A Negro Nurse, "More Slavery at the South," *Independent*, 72 (January 25, 1912): 196–200; editorial, "Slavery Not Dead," Washington *Bee*, February 28, 1914; Lafayette M. Hershaw, "Peonage," *The American Negro Academy Occasional Papers No. 15* (Washington, 1915), 5, 11.

4. Booker T. Washington to George Washington Cable, October 8, 1889, Booker T. Washington Collection, Howard University; Washington to Emily Howland, December 27, 1894, Miscellaneous American Letters and Papers, Schomburg Center, New York Public Library; R. L. Smith, "The Elevation of Negro Farm Life," *Independent*, 52 (August 30, 1900): 2104; editorials, "Slavery in the South" and "Slave Pen Abolished," Washington *Bee*, March 9, 16, 1901; James Weldon Johnson, "The Hour of Opportunity," New York *Age*, October 18, 1917; D. E. Tobias, "A Negro on the Position of the Negro in America," *Nineteenth Century*, 46 (December, 1899): 959, 961; W. E. B. Du Bois, "The Spawn of Slavery: The Convict-Lease System in the South," *Missionary Review of the World*, n.s., 14 (October, 1901): 737, 740; editorial, "The New Slave System of the South," *Colored American Magazine*, 6 (August, 1903): 618; cartoon, "The New Southern Slavery," New York *Age*, December 13, 1906; editorial, "Portuguese and American Slavery," Cleveland *Gazette*, April 10, 1909.

5. T. Thomas Fortune, *Black and White: Land, Labor and Politics in the South* (New York, 1884), 235–236; idem, "The Negro's Place in American Life at the Present Day," in Booker T. Washington et al., *The Negro Problem: A Series of Articles by Representative Negroes of To-Day* (New York, 1903),

227, 229; George W. Woodbey, *What to Do and How to Do It; or, Socialism vs. Capitalism* (1903), in Philip S. Foner, ed., *Black Socialist Preacher* (San Francisco, 1983), 40, 59; Booker T. Washington to Francis J. Garrison, August 31, 1903, Miscellaneous American Letters and Papers, Schomburg Center; Benjamin T. Tanner, "The Afro-American and the Three R's," *Independent*, 47 (October 17, 1895): 1387; Alexander Crummell, "The Prime Need of the Negro Race," ibid., 49 (August 19, 1897): 1065; Kittredge Wheeler to Du Bois, July 20, 1903, in Herbert Aptheker, ed., *The Correspondence of W. E. B. Du Bois*, 3 vols. (Amherst, 1973–1978), 1:59.

    6. *Open Letter to President McKinley by Colored People of Massachusetts* (Boston, 1899), 11; anon., "Choose Ye . . . Whom Ye Will Serve!" *Howard's American Magazine*, 4 (April, 1900): 388; Frederick L. McGhee, "Another View," ibid., 5 (October, 1900): 95–96; W. E. B. Du Bois, "Of the Culture of White Folk," *Journal of Race Development*, 7 (April, 1917): 445–446.

    7. Charles B. Purvis to Francis J. Grimké, November 16, 1912, in Carter G. Woodson, ed., *The Works of Francis J. Grimké*, 4 vols. (Washington, 1942), 4:128; Robert Graves to the editor, New York *Age*, October 26, 1916; Francis J. Grimké to U.S. Employment Service of the Department of Labor, September 24, 1917, in Woodson, ed., *The Works of Francis J. Grimké*, 4:197; F. H. Miller to William Pickens, March 15, 1918, Pickens to Miller, March 20, 1918, William Pickens Papers, Schomburg Center. The latter two references discuss the virtual reenslavement of blacks in service battalions and stevedore regiments in the U.S. Army during World War I.

    8. Wells, *Southern Horrors: Lynch Law in All Its Phases* (New York, 1892), 24; idem, *A Red Record: Tabulated Statistics and Alleged Causes of Lynchings in the United States* (Chicago, 1895), 8; editorial, "Let My People Go," Indianapolis *Freeman*, September 24, 1892; Holsey, "Race Segregation," in *The Possibilities of the Negro in Symposium* (Atlanta, 1904), 112. Numerous blacks remarked that, in spite of the Thirteenth Amendment, their race remained enslaved by caste and color. See, for example, Archibald H. Grimké, "John Brown and the New Slavery," unpublished manuscript, n.d., Archibald H. Grimké Papers; editorial, "The South Hysterical on the Negro Problem," *Alexander's Magazine*, 3 (March 15, 1907): 223–226; Mary Church Terrell to the editor, Charleston *News and Courier* [1907], Mary Church Terrell Papers, Manuscript Division, Library of Congress.

    9. Scarborough, "The Race Problem," *Arena*, 2 (October, 1890): 564; Hershaw, "Peonage," 5, 11; Brawley, *A Short History of the American Negro* (New York, 1913), 60; Brown, ed., *Economic Co-Operation among the Negroes of Georgia* (Atlanta, 1917), 10.

    10. Williams, *History of the Negro Race in America from 1619–1880*, 2 vols. (London, 1882), 1:109, 24, 119, 323, vii, 307, 385, 299; 2:91, 82 545, 547, 548; John Hope Franklin, "George Washington Williams and the

Beginnings of Afro-American Historiography," *Critical Inquiry*, 4 (Summer, 1978): 657–672; Alexander, *History of the Colored Race in America* (New York, 1887), 119, 121, 143–145, 178, 147, 148, 180, 182; Schomburg, "The Negro Digs Up His Past," in Alain Locke, ed., *The New Negro* (New York, 1925), 231.

11. Alexander Crummell, "The Need of New Ideas and New Aims for a New Era," *Africa and America: Addresses and Discourses* (Springfield, MA, 1891), 14–19; editorial, "Emancipation Celebration," Indianapolis *Freeman*, December 4, 1897; editorial, "Emancipation Celebration," New York *Age*, August 13, 1908.

12. Washington, "The Influence of the Negroes' Citizenship" [speech, July 10, 1896] in Louis R. Harlan, ed., *The Booker T. Washington Papers*, 13 vols. (Urbana, 1972– ), 4:191, 193; Kelly Miller, "The Race Problem in the South— a Negro's View," *Outlook*, 60 (December 31, 1898): 1059; William H. Councill, *Lamp of Wisdom; or, Race History Illuminated* (Nashville, 1898), 16; Willard B. Gatewood, Jr., ed., *Slave and Freeman: The Autobiography of George L. Knox* (Lexington, 1979), 43.

13. Gatewood, ed., *Slave and Freeman*, 35; Washington, "The Economic Development of the Negro in Slavery," in Washington and Du Bois, *The Negro in the South* (Philadelphia, 1907), 16; Miller, "The Negro's Part," *Radicals and Conservatives and Other Essays on the Negro in America* (New York, 1908), 107–108; Councill, "The Future of the Negro," *Forum*, 27 (July, 1899): 575. Other examples of a modified proslavery argument in black thought of these years include C. H. J. Taylor, *Whites and Blacks* (Atlanta, 1889), 5–9; H. M. Turner, "The American Negro and the Fatherland," in J. W. E. Bowen, ed., *Africa and the American Negro* (Atlanta, 1896), 195; Theophilus G. Steward, "The American Freedman," Indianapolis *Freeman*, April 17, 1897; C. H. Turner, "New Year Thoughts about the Negro," *Southwestern Christian Advocate*, 34 (January 26, 1899): 3; Irving E. Lowery, *Life on the Old Plantation in Ante-Bellum Days* (Columbia, 1911); John Wesley Gilbert, "A Voice from the Negro Race," *Methodist Quarterly Review*, 60 (October, 1911): 717–718.

14. Miller, "The Race Problem in the South—a Negro's View," 1059; Robert Bone, *Down Home: A History of Afro American Short Fiction from Its Beginnings to the End of the Harlem Renaissance* (New York, 1975), 52, 54, 72, 73.

15. Griggs, *Imperium in Imperio: A Study of the Negro Race Problem; A Novel* (Cincinnati, 1899), 209, 231, 232.

16. Thomas, *The American Negro: What He Was, What He Is, and What He May Become* (New York, 1901), 20, 21; Bone, *Down Home*, 73.

17. *Southern States Farm Magazine*, 5 (January, 1898): 509; Harlan, *Booker T. Washington: The Making of a Black Leader, 1856–1901* (New York, 1972); idem, *Booker T. Washington: The Wizard of Tuskegee, 1901–1915* (New York, 1983), ix.

18. Samuel R. Spencer, Jr., *Booker T. Washington and the Negro's Place in American Life* (Boston, 1955), 195, 196–197.

19. Washington, *The Story of the Negro*, 2 vols. (New York, 1909), 1:13–14, 23, 27–28, 29, 31–54, 65; 2:265; Washington to Charles G. Harris, May 22, 1897, in Harlan, ed., *The Booker T. Washington Papers*, 4:281–282.

20. Nolen, *The Negro's Image in the South* (Lexington, 1968), 146; Harlan, *Booker T. Washington: The Making of a Black Leader, 1856–1901*,ii; August Meier, "Toward a Reinterpretation of Booker T. Washington," *Journal of Southern History*, 23 (May, 1957): 220–227.

21. Thornbrough, "Washington, Booker T.," in Rayford W. Logan and Michael R. Winston, eds., *Dictionary of American Negro Biography* (New York, 1982), 635. From 1905 to 1912 Park wrote most of Washington's publications, including *Story of the Negro* (1910). See Harlan, *Booker T. Washington: The Wizard of Tuskegee, 1901–1915*, 290–291.

22. Louis R. Harlan, "The Secret Life of Booker T. Washington," *Journal of Southern History*, 37 (August, 1971): 395; Washington, "The Negro's Life in Slavery," *Outlook*, 93 (September 11, 1909): 71; idem, *The Story of Slavery* (Dansville, NY, 1940; orig. pub., 1913), 23–32.

23. Washington, "A New Emancipation," *Our Day*, 16 (February, 1896): 69–70; idem, "Out of Bondage," ibid., 81, 79; Washington to Mrs. George W. Allen, April 16, 1915, Booker T. Washington Papers, Tuskegee Institute.

24. Washington, "The Future of the American Negro," *Missionary Review of the World*, 21 (June, 1898): 430; idem, *Working with the Hands* (New York, 1904), 16, 17; idem, "The Influence of the Negroes' Citizenship," "The Progress of the Negro" [speeches, July 10, 1896, January 16, 1893], in Harlan, ed., *Washington Papers*, 4:191, 193; 3:286; Washington, *Up from Slavery* (New York, 1967; orig. pub., 1901), 24.

25. Washington, "The Race Problem in the United States," *Popular Science Monthly*, 55 (July, 1899): 318; idem, *Up from Slavery*, 15, 19, 21, 44; idem, *The Story of My Life and Work* (New York, 1900), 30, 32, 34, 36; idem, *Up from Slavery*, 19, 56, 25; idem, *The Story of the Negro*, 1:183; idem, "The Progress of the Negro," 286; idem, "Remarks," *Journal of Social Science*, 34 (November, 1896): 87.

26. Washington to J. E. MacBrady, July 3, 1900, in Harlan, ed., *The Booker T. Washington Papers*, 5:570; Harlan, *Booker T. Washington: The Wizard of Tuskegee, 1901–1915*, 403. The section on slavery in Washington, N. B. Wood and F. B. Williams, *A New Negro for a New Century* (New York, 1900), was reprinted from Norman B. Wood, *The White Side of a Black Subject* (Cincinnati, 1896).

27. Washington, "The Economic Development of the Negro Race in Slavery," in Washington and Du Bois, *The Negro in the South*, 16, 19, 24, 25; idem, "Out of Bondage," 84; idem, "The Negro's Life in Slavery," 71, 78;

idem, *The Future of the American Negro* (New York, 1899), 54–55; idem, "Christmas Days in Old Virginia," *Suburban Life*, 5 (December, 1907): 336–337.

28. Washington, "The Economic Development of the Negro Race in Slavery," 20, 21; idem, *The Future of the American Negro*, 53–54, 55; idem, *Up from Slavery*, 20–21.

29. Washington, *My Larger Education* (New York, 1911), 5–7, 27; idem, "The Best Labor in the World," *Southern States Farm Magazine*,5 (January, 1898): 496; idem, *Up from Slavery*, 16, 17, 23, 24.

30. Anon., review of Washington, *Working with the Hands*, in *Publications of the Southern History Association*, 9 (May, 1905): 201; Genovese, "The Legacy of Slavery and the Roots of Black Nationalism," *Studies on the Left*, 6 (November–December, 1966): 14.

31. Washington, "Out of Bondage," 84; Harlan, *Booker T. Washington: The Wizard of Tuskegee, 1901–1915*, 92.

32. According to Genovese, "The crucial point about Washington, as Du Bois drove home, was that the poor man embraced a free-market ideology at the very moment oligopoly was making a mockery out of its premises." Genovese to John David Smith, June 28, 1978, in possession of the author.

33. Harlan, *Booker T. Washington: The Wizard of Tuskegee, 1901–1915*, 205.

34. Du Bois to Albert Bushnell Hart, [April, 1905], W. E. B. Du Bois Papers, University of Massachusetts, Amherst; Du Bois, *The Negro* (New York, 1915), 150; idem, "Serfdom," *Voice of the Negro*, 2 (July, 1905): 481.

35. Du Bois, "The Study of the Negro Problems," *Annals of the American Academy of Political and Social Science*, 11 (January, 1898): 12, 14.

36. Ibid., 14.

37. Du Bois, *The Philadelphia Negro* (Philadelphia, 1899), 67, 71, 147, 161, 178; idem, "The Negro As He Really Is," *World's Work*, 2 (June, 1901): 853–854, 861, 863.

38. Du Bois, "The Spawn of Slavery: The Convict-Lease System in the South," *Missionary Review of the World*, n.s., 14 (October, 1901): 737, 740; " 'Negro Is Still Slave,' Declares Prof. Du Bois."

39. Du Bois, "The Future of the Negro Race in America," *East and the West*, 2 (January, 1904): 8, 7, 19; idem, "The Negro As He Really Is," 858; idem, "Georgia Negroes," *Colored American Magazine*, 16 (May, 1909): 270–271; idem, "The Economic Future of the Negro," *Publications of the American Economic Association*, 3rd ser., 7 (1906): 219–220; idem, "The Training of Negroes for Social Power," *Outlook*, 75 (October 17, 1903): 413; idem, "The Relation of the Negroes to the Whites in the South," *Annals of the American Academy of Political and Social Science*, 18 (July, 1901): 138.

40. Du Bois, "The Southerner's Problem," *Dial*, 38 (May 1, 1905): 316;

idem, "Marrying of Black Folk," *Independent*, 69 (October 13, 1910): 813; idem, "Georgia Negroes," 271; idem, "The Training of Negroes for Social Power," 413; idem, "The Negro and Crime," *Independent*, 51 (May 18, 1899): 1355; idem, "Social Effects of Emancipation," *Survey*, 29 (February 1, 1913): 571; idem, "Discussion," *American Journal of Sociology*, 13 (May, 1908): 834; idem, "Storm and Stress in the Black World," *Dial*, 30 (April 16, 1901): 263.

41. Du Bois, "The Enforcement of the Slave-Trade Laws," *Annual Report of the American Historical Association for the Year 1891* (Washington, 1892), 163, 168, 173, 174.

42. Du Bois, *The Suppression of the African Slave-Trade to the United States of America, 1638–1870* (New York, 1896), xxxv, 1, 6, 71, 109, 115, 169, 197, 198.

43. Sterling A. Brown, "A Century of Negro Portraiture in American Literature," *Massachusetts Review*, 7 (Winter, 1966): 81.

44. Du Bois, "The Religion of the American Negro," *New World*, 9 (December, 1900): 619–620.

45. Ibid., 618, 615; Du Bois, *The Souls of Black Folk* (Greenwich, 1961; orig. pub., 1903), 189, 186–188.

46. Du Bois, *Dusk of Dawn: An Essay toward an Autobiography of a Race* (New York, 1940), 115, 117; August Meier, *Negro Thought in America, 1880–1915* (Ann Arbor, 1971), 203; Elliott M. Rudwick, *W. E. B. Du Bois: Propagandist of the Negro Protest* (Philadelphia, 1960), 50.

47. Du Bois, *The Philadelphia Negro*, 71; Du Bois, ed., *The Negro American Family* (Atlanta, 1908), 21–22; idem, *The Negro*, 188.

48. Du Bois, ed., *Economic Cooperation among Negro Americans* (Atlanta 1907), 12–18, 20–21, 24–25; idem, "The Negro's Fatherland," *Survey*, 39 (November 10, 1917): 141.

49. Du Bois, "The Problem of Housing the Negro—the Home of the Slave," *Southern Workman*, 30 (September, 1901): 486, 488–491.

50. Ibid., 491–493.

51. Douglass, *Why Is the Negro Lynched?* (Bridgwater, England, 1895), 16, 29; Work, "The Songs of the Southland," *Voice of the Negro*, 4 (January–February, 1907): 51; Grant, *Out of the Darkness; or, Diabolism and Destiny* (Nashville, 1909), 33; editorial, "Monuments or Justice—Which?" Chicago *Defender*, May 30, 1914, Slavery File, Tuskegee Institute.

52. "Maine Slave Still Remembers Whipping He Received in 1853," Bridgeport (CT) *Farmer*, March 9, 1917, Slavery File, Tuskegee Institute; Woodson, "Negro Life and History in Our Schools," *Journal of Negro History*, 4 (July, 1919): 275.

53. Baker, "The Negro Woman," *Alexander's Magazine*, 3 (December 15, 1906): 76, 77; Du Bois, review of Tillinghast, *The Negro in Africa and America*,

in *Political Science Quarterly*, 18 (December, 1903): 697; Woodson, review of Reuter, *The Mulatto in the United States*, in *Journal of Negro History*, 4 (January, 1919): 106.

54. Du Bois, "The Experts," *Crisis*, 5 (March, 1913): 239–240; idem, review of Phillips, *American Negro Slavery*, in *American Political Science Review*, 12 (November, 1918): 723. For similar criticism of Alfred Holt Stone, see Du Bois to Stone, March 30, 1908, Du Bois Papers.

55. Greener, "The White Problem," Indianapolis *Freeman*, September 1, 8, 1894.

56. Bowen, "The Comparative Status of the Negro at the Close of the War and of To-day," in Bowen, ed., *Africa and the American Negro*, 166, 167, 168. See also George William Cook, "Is There a Problem?" unpublished manuscript [1905?], George William Cook Papers, Howard University.

57. Francis J. Grimké, "Pride: A High Look and a Proud Heart," n.d., in Woodson, ed., *The Works of Francis J. Grimké*, 2:541; "Missouri Former Slaves," Philadelphia *Sunday Item*, July 24, 1892, and "Stories of Runaway Slaves," Detroit *News-Tribune*, July 22, 1894, reprinted in John W. Blassingame, ed., *Slave Testimony: Two Centuries of Letters, Speeches, Interviews, and Autobiographies* (Baton Rouge, 1977), 501–511, 513–533; Frederick Douglass, *The Reason Why the Colored Man Is Not in the World's Columbian Exposition* (1892), reprinted in Philip S. Foner, ed., *The Life and Writings of Frederick Douglass*, 4 vols. (New York, 1955), 4:471–473; Crogman, "The Negro's Needs," *Talks for the Times*, 144; Wesley J. Gaines, "The Evils of African Slavery," *The Negro and the White Man* (Philadelphia, 1897), 22–31; Nathan B. Young, "A Race without an Ideal," *A.M.E. Church Review*, 15 (October, 1898): 606; Louis F. Post, "The National Afro-American Council," *Howard's American Magazine*, 4 (November, 1899): 39; T. W. Jones, "The Negro as a Business Man," in D. W. Culp, ed., *Twentieth Century Negro Literature* (New York, 1902), 371; Mary White Ovington, comp., "Slaves' Reminiscences of Slavery," *Independent*, 68 (May 26, 1910): 1131–1136; George W. Forbes, "Colored Slave Owners and Traders in the Old Days," *A.M.E. Church Review*, 29 (January, 1913): 300, 301; Joseph C. Price, "The Race Problem Stated," unpublished manuscript, n.d., Carter G. Woodson Collection, Manuscript Division, Library of Congress.

58. John W. Gibson and Crogman, *Progress of a Race; or, the Remarkable Advancement of the American Negro* (Naperville, IL, 1902), 43, 45; Sinclair, *The Aftermath of Slavery: A Study of the Condition and Environment of the American Negro* (Boston, 1905), 3, 6, 9, 11, 14, 15, 17; Woodson, "The Beginnings of the Miscegenation of the Whites and Blacks," *Journal of Negro History*, 3 (October, 1918): 335, 339, 349, 351; Parker, *Recollections of Slavery Times* (Worcester, 1895), 62; Douglass, "Slavery," unpublished manuscript [1895?], p. 13, Frederick Douglass Papers, Manuscript Division, Library of Congress.

59. Kealing, "The Characteristics of the Negro People," in Washington et al., *The Negro Problem*, 174–180; Francis J. Grimké, "A True Pride and Race Development," unpublished manuscript, n.d., Francis J. Grimké Papers, Howard University; Fortune, " 'Good Indians' and 'Good Niggers,' " *Independent*, 51 (June 22, 1899): 1689–1690; Du Bois, "The Social Evolution of the Black South," *American Negro Monographs*, 1 (March, 1911): 1911; Robert R. Moton, "Status of the Negro in America," *Current History*, 16 (May, 1922): 226; Washington, *Working with the Hands* (New York, 1904), 16; Brawley, *A Short History of the American Negro* (New York, 1913), 60.

60. Joseph T. Wilson, *The Black Phalanx* (New York, 1890), 96; Washington, "The American Negro and His Economic Value," *International Monthly*, 2 (December, 1900): 672–674; Kealing, "The Negro's Contribution to His Own Development," in I. Garland Penn and J. W. E. Bowen, eds., *The United Negro: His Problems and His Progress* (Atlanta, 1902), 207; H. H. Proctor, "From the Address of Dr. Proctor," *American Missionary*, 59 (November, 1905): 284; editorial, "Afro-American Womanhood," New York *Age*, February 22, 1906; Archibald H. Grimké, "Modern Industrialism and the Negroes of the United States," *The American Negro Academy Occasional Papers No. 12* (Washington, 1908), 5; W. S. Scarborough, "The Negro and the Trades," *Southern Workman*, 26 (February, 1897): 26–27; John S. Durham, *To Teach the Negro History* (Philadelphia, 1897), 17, 33, 47; Du Bois, ed., *The Negro Artisan* (Atlanta, 1902), 13–21; Thomas J. Calloway, "The American Negro Artisan," *Cassier's Magazine*, 25 (March, 1904): 435, 440, 445; Wilson, "Some Negro Poets," *A.M.E. Church Review*, 4 (January, 1888): 237; Monroe N. Work, "The Spirit of Negro Poetry," *Southern Workman*, 37 (February, 1908): 73–77; Brawley, "Three Negro Poets: Horton, Mrs. Harper and Whitman," *Journal of Negro History*, 2 (October, 1917): 384–392; Leonora Herron, "Conjuring and Conjure-Doctors," *Southern Workman*, 24 (July, 1895): 117–118; Alice M. Bacon, "Conjuring and Conjure-Doctors," ibid. (November, December, 1895): 193–194, 209–210; Robert R. Moton, "Sickness in Slavery Days," ibid., 28 (February, 1899): 74–75; Clement Richardson, "Some Slave Superstitions," ibid., 41 (April, 1912): 246–248; Miller, "The Historic Background of the Negro Physician," *Journal of Negro History*, 1 (April, 1916): 101; R. R. Wright, "The Negro as an Inventor," *A.M.E. Church Review*, 2 (April, 1886): 398, 410; Brawley, "The Negro Genius," *Southern Workman*, 44 (May, 1915): 306, 307; Woodson, *The Education of the Negro Prior to 1861* (Washington, 1919).

61. Woodson, *The Education of the Negro Prior to 1861*, 2, 10, 170, 198–199, 85, 228, 200.

62. Alexander Crummell, "Comments on a Lecture Delivered by Mr. J. W. Cromwell," unpublished manuscript, July 21, 1890, Alexander Crummell Papers, Schomburg Center; Douglass, "Slavery," p. 21; B. F. Lee, Jr., "Negro

Organizations," *Annals of the American Academy of Political and Social Science*, 49 (September, 1913): 129; Miller, "Negro Musical Gift," *Washington Post*, May 10, 1903, clipping in Miller Papers; idem, "The Artistic Gifts of the Negro," *Voice of the Negro*, 3 (April, 1906): 253; Douglass, *The Life and Times of Frederick Douglass from 1817 to 1882* (London, 1882), 28–29; Daniel Webster Davis, "Echoes from a Plantation Party," *Southern Workman*, 28 (February, 1899): 59; anon., "The Plantation Melody," *Colored American Magazine*, 11 (July, 1906): 59–61; H. H. Proctor, "The Theology of the Songs of the Southern Slave," *Southern Workman*, 36 (November, December, 1907): 588, 655, 656; William H. Thomas, "Religious Characteristics of the Negro," *A.M.E. Church Review*, 9 (April, 1893): 392–393; Harris Barrett, "Negro Folk Songs," *Southern Workman*, 41 (April, 1912): 238–245; Sinclair, *The Aftermath of Slavery*, 15.

    63. Herron, "Conjuring and Conjure-Doctors," 117–118; Bacon, "Conjuring and Conjure-Doctors," 193–194, 209–210; Richardson, "Some Slave Superstitions," 248.

    64. Chesnutt, "Superstitions and Folklore of the South," *Modern Culture*, 13 (May, 1901): 231–235; Bone, *Down Home*, 81–89.

    65. Eugene Terry, "The Shadow of Slavery in Charles Chesnutt's *The Conjure Woman*," *Ethnic Groups*, 4 (1982): 124.

    66. David D. Britt, "Chesnutt's Conjure Tales: What You See Is What You Get," *College Language Association Journal*, 15 (March, 1972): 269–279.

    67. Gloria C. Oden, "Chesnutt's Conjure as African Survival," *MELUS*, 5 (Spring, 1978): 38–48.

    68. Moton, "A Negro's Uphill Climb," *World's Work*, 13 (April, 1907): 8740; John W. Cromwell, "The Early Negro Convention Movement," *The American Negro Academy Occasional Papers No. 9* (Washington, 1904); Work, "Secret Societies as Factors in the Economical Life of the Negro," in James E. McCulloch, ed., *Democracy in Earnest* (Washington, 1918), 344–345; Gaines, "The Negro in Slavery Days," *Alexander's Magazine*, 6 (September 15, 1908): 203; P. M. Lewis to the editor, Indianapolis *Freeman*, August 25, 1894; anon., "White Slavery: A Fragment of American History," *A.M.E. Church Review*, 17 (October, 1900): 132–133; Du Bois, ed., *Economic Co-operation among Negro Americans*, 20, 24, 25; idem, *John Brown* (Philadelphia, 1909), 79, 81, 82, 84; idem, *The Negro*, 196; Williams, *History of the Negro Race in America from 1619–1880*, 1:305, 299; 2:82, 545, 547, 548; Alexander, *History of the Colored Race in America*, 147.

    69. Fortune, *The Negro in Politics* (New York, 1886), 6; Cromwell, *The Negro in American History* (Washington, 1914), 12; Work, ed., *Negro Year Book: An Annual Encyclopedia of the Negro, 1916–1917* (Tuskegee, 1916), 108–112; Grimké, "Right on the Scaffold; or, The Martyrs of 1822," *The American Negro Academy Occasional Papers No. 7* (Washington, 1901), 5, 8, 9;

idem, "Prejudice, Preparing, Eruption," New York *Age*, November 30, 1905; Cromwell, "The Aftermath of Nat Turner's Insurrection," *Journal of Negro History*, 5 (April, 1920): 233; Miller, *As to the Leopard's Spots: An Open Letter to Thomas Dixon, Jr.* (Washington, 1905), 13. See also Linda O. McMurry, *Recorder of the Black Experience: A Biography of Monroe Nathan Work* (Baton Rouge, 1985), 79–81, 92–98.

70. Grimké, "The Ultimate Criminal," unpublished manuscript, n.d., Archibald H. Grimké Papers; Crummell, "The American Negro, before the War, and Now" [1891], and "The Discipline of Freedom," n.d., unpublished manuscripts, Crummell Papers; anon., "That Wife of Mine," *Afro-American Ledger*, June 26, 1915, Slavery File, Tuskegee Institute. S. P. Fullinwider notes similar tensions and contradictions in black thought of these years in *The Mind and Mood of Black America* (Homewood, IL, 1969), 1–71.

71. Bone, *Down Home*, 10; Woodson to Archibald H. Grimké, July 29, 1921, and enclosed "Questionnaire on Negro History," Archibald H. Grimké Papers.

# 8

## *American Negro Slavery:* The Triumph of the New Proslavery Argument

Blacks had no more formidable opponent in their fight against the new proslavery argument than the pioneer white historian Ulrich B. Phillips (1877–1934). Phillips dominated slavery scholarship in the years before World War I and rose in stature to become regarded as far and away the leading expert on the subject up to the 1950s. Phillips's writings epitomized the merger of postbellum proslavery ideology and turn-of-the-century "scientific" historical method. A native of Georgia, Phillips defended his section from neoabolitionist attacks long after Appomattox, and urged his fellow white southerners to thwart the exploitation of their region by northern capitalists. He considered the South a section distinct from the rest of the country, the product of "natural organic life," not "forces of perversity." In upholding his region's past and present, Phillips drew upon the best "scientific" historical training then available. Schooled in William A. Dunning's seminar at Columbia University, Phillips worshiped at the shrine of primary sources. His generation believed that "objective," nonpartisan history resulted from allowing the facts to speak for themselves. "The historian's chief concern," he wrote early in his career, "is with facts, their authenticity and accuracy; and interpretation is a secondary consideration." Yet Phillips's blatant proslavery interpretation—his assemblage of the "facts" pertaining to the peculiar institution—earned him the reputation as the most articulate and the chief scholarly spokesman for the new proslavery argument. He, more than any other writer, combined sectional and racial bias under the imprimatur of "objective" historical scholarship. In spite of his defense of slavery, Phillips made lasting contributions to our understanding of slavery. His work demands careful attention both for its proslavery content and its role in the ongoing slavery debate.[1]

# I

Phillips was born in 1877 in the western Georgia town of LaGrange, not far from the Alabama border. His father came from yeoman lower–middle-class stock, but his mother, whom Phillips considered his constant "comrade and source of inspiration," had a plantation background. Before the Civil War her family had owned 1500 acres of land and twenty-four slaves in Troup County, Georgia. Phillips once recalled that "a sympathetic understanding of plantation conditions was my inevitable heritage from my family and from neighbors, white and black, in the town of LaGrange." On another occasion Phillips explained how his knowledge of plantation conditions stemmed largely from his own "observations in post-bellum times." In the early 1890s the Phillips family moved to the site of the first capital of Georgia, Milledgeville. In 1891, their son entered the Tulane Preparatory School in New Orleans. Two years later Phillips, "an ungainly, retiring, country boy," enrolled in the University of Georgia in Athens. He stayed at that institution for seven years, earning a bachelor's degree in 1897 and a master's degree in 1899.[2]

Phillips's mentor at Georgia, John H. T. McPherson, had roots reaching back to Johns Hopkins and its famous seminar on slavery. In 1890 McPherson had completed his dissertation on the history of Liberia under Herbert Baxter Adams. While still working on his master's degree under McPherson, Phillips attended the 1898 summer term at the University of Chicago, where he enrolled in a seminar offered by Frederick Jackson Turner, then a visiting professor from the University of Wisconsin. Phillips found inspiration in Turner's emphasis on regionalism, his vision of the frontier as process, and his insights into American sectionalism. For his part, Turner was favorably impressed with the twenty-one-year-old graduate student from Georgia. He encouraged Phillips in his master's project—mapping the social and economic characteristics of Georgia's different geographical sections. Turner predicted that when Phillips had expanded and extended his research, he would contribute "just that kind of a study of the politics of a southern state that we most need.'' There began a relationship of mutual admiration that matured for more than three decades.[3]

Phillips took his doctoral work at Columbia University, not Johns Hopkins. Had he planned to concentrate on slavery or some narrow aspect of southern history, he most certainly would have studied at Johns Hopkins with Adams and, after Adams's death, with James C. Ballagh. But Phillips favored broader training with more of a political science orientation. William A. Dunning, who later would train a generation of students of Reconstruction, seemed to fit the bill. Phillips also recognized that Johns Hopkins's graduate program in history was on the wane at the very time when Columbia was establishing one of the nation's foremost Ph.D. programs. Phillips compiled an excellent record at Columbia and became the first student to receive the Schiff Fellowship for two consecutive years. His professors praised his ''discriminating mind,'' ''excellent character,'' and ''engaging personality.'' In 1902 Dunning enthusiastically approved Phillips's dissertation, ''Georgia and State Rights,'' an expanded version of his master's thesis. Later that year this study received the Justin Winsor Prize and subsequently was published by the American Historical Association.[4]

From 1902 to 1908 Phillips served on Turner's staff at Wisconsin, thrilled to be associated with the man who had so influenced his early belief in economic and geographic determinism. His years in Madison launched Phillips's career in several important directions. First and foremost, he immersed himself in primary source materials that illumined the previously neglected field of southern economic history. Writing in 1905, Phillips explained with considerable prescience that ''when I shall have obtained a sufficient grasp of economic development I shall turn again to politics and try to work out the bearings of questions of industry, commerce, and society upon political policy with special regard to sectionalism.'' Soon after, in a grant application to the Carnegie Institution, he explained the breadth of his research plans. ''It is not the condition of negro labor that concerns me, but the economic and social forces which are essentially historical forces.'' These, he continued, ''controlled the historical development of the South, politics included.''[5]

Phillips's publications in the first decade of the twentieth century dealt with hitherto unexplored economic themes—plantation slavery and transportation in the Old South. His major articles in the *Political Science Quarterly* and *American Historical Review* quickly marked Phillips as a rising star among students of slavery. In those works he first expressed what later would become central tenets of his books: the unprofitability of black slave labor and slavery's ill effects on the South's economy. He also made salient contributions to the still neglected field of southern transportation history. In *A History of Transportation in the Eastern Cotton Belt* (1908) Phillips argued that, despite inherent difficulties, by 1860 a railroad network had been established in the South that adequately served the region's transportation needs. But in relating this interpretation to his conclusions on slavery, Phillips charged that by extending and intensifying the plantation system, the South's railways encouraged planters to overproduce staple crops. Railroads, then, were partially to blame for the region's historic failure to diversify its agricultural products.[6]

While in Madison, Phillips also caught the fever of Progressivism then sweeping the nation in general and Wisconsin in particular. He campaigned privately and publicly for educational and agricultural reform in his native Georgia modeled closely on the "Wisconsin Idea." In essays in the *South Atlantic Quarterly, Sewanee Review,* and *World's Work,* Phillips implored southerners to provide scientific and agricultural training, to limit their cotton production, and to diversify their crops. From his studies of the one-crop system of the Old South, Phillips discovered clues to the agricultural woes of the New South. He advised reducing cotton acreage and reestablishing plantation-sized agricultural units, but with free black—instead of slave—labor. Phillips judged the small post–Civil War farms cultivated by tenants or sharecroppers as beneficial to neither blacks nor whites. He maintained that a return to the efficient plantation system would provide black workers with the guidance of what he deemed the superior race. Whites in turn would gain a constant and cheap labor supply and retain hegemony over the black working class. The idea of utilizing the plantation as a mode of racial control remained central to Phillips's proslavery thought throughout his subsequent writings. For him it bridged the gap between history as theory and history as relevant to contemporary problems.[7]

Phillips's important scholarly work earned him one attractive professorship after another. He taught at Tulane University (1908–1911), at the University of Michigan (1911–1929), and at Yale University (1930–1934). He welcomed his years in New Orleans as an opportunity to gain access to those primary sources he valued most—plantation records, manuscript census statistics, and newspapers. While at Tulane, Phillips collected plantation records that he later drew upon heavily in the writing of his landmark work, *American Negro Slavery* (1918). Phillips, according to Wood Gray, had the knack for working and reworking these sources "until almost the last possible bit of utility had been squeezed from them." For example, in 1909 Phillips published verbatim approximately four hundred documents in *Plantation and Frontier*, the first two volumes of the highly acclaimed *Documentary History of American Industrial Society* (1909–1911). Much of this archival material—including excerpts from planters' diaries, travelers' journals, and merchants' account books—Phillips employed again and again in books and articles.[8]

During his eighteen years at Michigan, Phillips established himself as the nation's foremost student of southern history and slavery. These were his most productive years. In 1913 he edited a valuable collection of the papers of fellow Georgians Robert Toombs, Alexander H. Stephens, and Howell Cobb, and published a political biography of Toombs. But his reputation as a historian of the South resulted from his two best-known works, *American Negro Slavery* and *Life and Labor in the Old South* (1929). He also contributed path-breaking articles treating comparative slavery, the economics of slavery, and slave crime. In 1927 Phillips and one of his doctoral students, James David Glunt, co-edited *Florida Plantation Records from the Papers of George Noble Jones*. The following year Phillips published his seminal essay "The Central Theme of Southern History." In Phillips's judgment, throughout southern history one desire solidified whites of all classes: the desire to keep their region "a white man's country." Despite the notoriety this essay has received, in it Phillips simply amplified a theme implicit in many of his writings dating back to the early twentieth century. Other southern white conservatives, notably Walter Lynwood Fleming and Walter G. Brown, had been stating the same point for years. In any case, the article added yet another star to Phillips's luster.[9]

While at Michigan, Phillips began what he often referred to as his "big job," a three-volume history of his beloved South. The first volume, *Life and Labor in the Old South*, was so well received that it won a large cash prize from Little, Brown, and Company. The volume's success earned its author the prestigious year-long Albert Kahn traveling fellowship, which Phillips used in 1929–1930 to observe blacks and other working-class peoples in tropical climates throughout the world. All of this spotlighted Phillips even further. In 1929 Yale University enticed him away from Michigan with an offer that he considered "flattering" and especially conducive "for authorship." Upon returning from his world tour he hoped to complete the next two volumes of his trilogy—on the coming of the Civil War and the modern South—but he died of throat cancer in 1934, at age fifty-six.[10] All in all, Phillips left a legacy of outstanding scholarship, a corps of devoted students, and the racist caricatures of his prolific pen.

## II

Phillips published nine books and nearly sixty articles. Historian Wendell Holmes Stephenson estimated that Phillips wrote approximately 4800 printed pages, most of them treating slavery, the aspect of the Old South that he knew best. Phillips's early writings on slavery provide an essential backdrop to his seminal *American Negro Slavery* and to the more broadly based social history, *Life and Labor in the Old South*.[11]

Phillips's first discussion of slavery appeared in *Georgia and State Rights* (1902). In this work Phillips devoted his attention to southern politics, which, according to Louis Filler, always was the historian's "first love." Even so, slavery played an important, albeit small, role in Phillips's pioneer analysis of political factions in the early history of his native state. He maintained, for example, that after the start of the abolitionist crusade, slavery became inseparable from other elements of the state rights ideology. For Georgians, slavery became an essential thread holding together the fabric of their social and economic life. By the 1850s, argued Phillips, the number of bondsmen in Georgia almost equaled the number of whites; and, just as important, "their value as property was considerably greater than that of all the land in the State." Even though politics, not slavery, was the focus of his doctoral thesis, Phillips nicely presented the contours of the institution as it existed in Georgia. With his penchant for hunting down obscure, hard-to-find documents, Phillips devoured all the legal digests, state documents, and newspapers he could locate. In a compass of only eleven pages, his first book gave a clear indication of the tone of his many later writings on slavery.[12]

Ironically, Phillips's brief sketch of slavery in *Georgia and State Rights* became—with the exception of an essay on slave labor in the Charleston District—his only study of the peculiar institution in a single North American state or community. In it he traced Georgia slavery back to its origins in the eighteenth century and found in the antislavery restrictions of the colony's founder, James Oglethorpe, a possible key to later Georgians' defenses of the institution. In a manner comparable to that of his contemporaries at Johns Hopkins, Phillips outlined the various slave regulations in effect in Georgia. While he admitted that some slave laws were indeed severe—one even "positively barbarous"—Phillips asserted that Georgia bondsmen fared "neither better nor worse" than blacks in the other slave states. He argued, too, that harsh slave laws rarely were enforced. Bondsmen generally were protected by the collective power of public opinion. "As the years passed and as masters and slaves came the better to understand each the nature and disposition of the other," slave owners generally "rendered informal justice." These early themes, reminiscent of proslavery defenses, served as the nucleus for Phillips's conception of an organic plantation paternalism.[13]

Phillips presented another of his fundamental arguments when he declared that "slavery [in Georgia] was distinctly a patriarchal institution." Offering visions of both romanticized courtly masters and realistic planter-capitalists, the historian argued that masters generally showed much "consideration" for their slaves. Frequently, owners of only a few bondsmen worked alongside their chattels in the fields. Harsh overseers, Phillips proclaimed, were the exception, never the rule; rarely were slave families in Georgia separated by sale. On the contrary, genial treatment characterized slavery in his native state, said Phillips. "As compared with the free blacks in New England," he added, "the slaves in Georgia were frequently the better clothed, better fed, better taught, and better treated by their superiors." Slave cabins often equaled those of the poor southern whites. Phillips displayed his racial prejudice in explaining, "That they [the cabins] were not always clean was due to the habits of their occupants."[14]

Throughout his monograph, and his later writings as well, Phillips expressed a distaste for the abolitionists. He blamed the Civil War upon William Lloyd Garrison and other Yankees. Prior to the start of the abolition agitation, wrote Phillips, many southerners considered slavery an evil, but northern extremism solidified the South in defense of its peculiar institution. Phillips remained convinced that northerners were misled by erroneous descriptions of slavery published by Frederick Law Olmsted and Frances Kemble. He designed his description of slavery's "softer side," then, not as a justification of black bondage but as a corrective to years of misinformation. The young historian wrote confidently that southerners "intimately acquainted with the negro character and with the mild nature of his servitude" were most qualified to discuss slavery.[15] Contrasted with Phillips's later writings, this concise summary of slavery in Georgia seems impressionistic, general, and weakened by unsubstantiated statements. Except for its legal aspects, Phillips almost totally ignored slavery's institutional features. Yet his treatment of slavery in *Georgia and State Rights* anticipated many of his future views.

Phillips furthered his discussion of slavery, albeit in an indirect way, in his series of essays published in 1903–1905 that promoted agricultural reform for Georgia and the South. He argued that the plantation represented a unit of labor organization comparable to the modern factory, and one peculiarly suited to southern staples and adaptable to efficient hired workers. He insisted that the economic fortunes of the New South would improve if more blacks could be encouraged to work for their former masters, "the most substantial, practical, and valuable friends . . . [the Negroes] have ever had."[16]

In Phillips's opinion, by re-establishing the plantation system, the South would move down the path to what he frequently termed "conservative progress." Phillips reminded his readers that before the Civil War the plantation had served a vital social function, creating an environment under which master and slave lived in peace and harmony. The Georgian predicted that the reinstitution of the plantation system would guarantee a social order in which the whites would remain unquestionably dominant. Phillips warned, however, that the South could not afford again to be weakened by those excesses in the old plantation system resulting from slavery. The South must diversify its crops, establish factories, and allow free speech.[17]

In his major works Phillips developed many of the themes that he first introduced in these early essays. In 1904, in "The Plantation as a Civilizing Factor," he employed his analogy of the slave plantation as an educational institution—what Phillips termed "the Virginia training school" of slavery. By emphasizing the differences between slavery in South Carolina, which had inherited characteristics of the West Indian system, and the unique system that evolved in Virginia, Phillips also introduced his use of the comparative method. He described the former mode of slavery as commercial, impersonal, and severe. In contrast, the peculiar institution in Virginia resembled more closely life on an

English manor. Masters in the Old Dominion were patriarchs who sought to civilize their chattels.

The great majority of planters were kind masters from interest and inclination, looking after the moral and industrial development of their slaves as a matter of business as well as from higher motives. On the other hand, there was doubtless a large number of instances of harsh masters and maltreated slaves. In fact, the dark side of antebellum conditions was somber enough to cast a heavy gloom over the bright; but the evil features were due chiefly to the institution of slavery and not to the system of plantation industry.

In Phillips's judgment, the Virginia system became the prevalent system in North America.[18]

The clear distinction he drew between the plantation system and slavery became one of the most significant conclusions Phillips reached early in his career. In a review essay published in 1904 he maintained that too many writers confused the two systems. Phillips interpreted the plantation as "the training school," whereas slavery "was necessary at the beginning in bringing negroes into the plantation system." Firmly convinced of the merits of large-scale plantation organization, he hinted that major economic weaknesses had existed all along in the peculiar institution. Slavery in fact "had completed its work and was already an anachronism when the Civil War and Reconstruction overthrew it." Had the war not intervened, he said, "slavery would have been disestablished in some peaceable way." In its wake, Phillips asserted, would have been some "modified form of the old plantation system," an institution that he deemed still "the best resource for agricultural progress and racial sympathy in the present and the near future."[19]

Phillips's first major article on slavery, "The Economic Cost of Slaveholding in the Cotton Belt," appeared in 1905 in the *Political Science Quarterly*. Phillips grounded this piece on an extensive compilation of several thousand slave price quotations obtained from the Georgia state archives, records of counties lying in the Georgia cotton belt, bills of sale in private hands, and, to a lesser degree, travelers' summaries and local newspapers. A pioneering account of the economics of slavery, this article also introduced historians to the use of slave price data as evidence. Phillips considered this new source essential to untangling the organic nature of slave society, for it provided "one of the indexes to the [southern] economic situation at any time." This essay analyzed slavery for the first time on a cost basis. It represents the first of many forums from which Phillips pronounced slavery a successful mode of racial control but an economic failure.[20]

Slavery, argued Phillips, evolved from white southerners' desires for "private gain and public safety." They maintained it initially for economic reasons. But when the blacks became too numerous, the master class transformed slavery into a system of police control and protection. Whites enslaved the blacks, he said, "to keep their savage instincts from breaking forth, and to utilize them in civilized industry." To be sure, slavery proved profitable in the colonial period, serving both economic and social functions. Black bondsmen exhibited special strengths, adapted readily to the southern climate, succumbed less rapidly than whites to tropical diseases, and were easily taught to perform "simple" tasks. Further, slaves provided a "mobile" labor source. Despite these advantages, Phillips explained, after 1815 slaves increasingly became inefficient laborers and slavery an economic noose around the neck of southern progress. "It was only in special industries," wrote Phillips, "and only in times of special prosperity, that negro slave labor was of such decided profit as to escape condemnation for its inherent disadvantages."[21]

Phillips identified many specific economic shortcomings in slavery. It required what he termed "capitalizing the prospective value of the labor of each workman for the whole of his life." Masters had dangerously large amounts of capital invested in bondsmen and, lamented Phillips, wealth invested in slaves was drained away from the cotton belt by the slave trade. Incipient southern industries consequently were deprived of much needed capital. Phillips compared slaves to the industrialists' machines, both representing forms of fixed capital. Just as machines could not be shut down without accruing losses, slaves, he maintained, toiled in the cotton fields even when low prices warranted cutbacks in production and crop diversification. This situation resulted both from the "force of inertia" and basic southern conservatism. In Phillips's opinion, the capitalization of labor in slaves resulted in a "fictitious form of wealth." After 1815 slave prices began a steady advance, yet cotton prices underwent a heavy net decline. The former resulted from speculation among slave owners, the latter from an overabundance of the fleecy staple.[22]

Unlike any previous historian of slavery, Phillips itemized the overall

cost of slave labor. In addition to food, clothing, and shelter, he identified four supplemental expenses: interest on the capital invested in
slaves, "economic insurance" against the loss of bondsmen's services,
depreciation of the value of slaves, and taxes assessed upon the value
of the chattels. After listing these costs, Phillips concluded that slaves
generally were more expensive than free white hired laborers would
have been. True, he admitted that the discipline of slavery remedied
much of the blacks' "inherited inaptitude" toward work. Nevertheless,
Phillips perceived the institution of slavery to be an economic liability
for the South, one inimical to the region's economic development.
Overcapitalized and inelastic, slavery became too rigid to be profitable
as a labor system. Phillips recognized that some masters indeed had
garnered large fortunes from slave labor, but far more lived in uncertainty and perpetual debt. Slaveholding proved to be a risky investment.
It encouraged cutthroat competition and engendered extravagance.[23]

Ironically, wrote Phillips, cotton planters themselves became enslaved "by their two inanimate but arbitrary masters, cotton and slavery."
In an economic sense, their community became abnormal, and masters
were dragged unknowingly into a "vicious circle." Virginians, said
Phillips, routinely "bought fresh lands and more slaves to make more
tobacco, and with the profits from tobacco they bought more land and
slaves to make more tobacco with which to buy yet more land and
slaves." Phillips resorted to one of his favorite analogies.

The system may be likened to an engine, with slavery as its great fly-wheel—
a fly-wheel indispensable for safe running at first, perhaps, but later rendered
less useful by improvements in the machinery, and finally becoming a burden
instead of a benefit. Yet it was retained, because it was still considered essential
in securing the adjustment and regular working of the complex mechanism.
This great rigid wheel of slavery was so awkward and burdensome that it
absorbed the momentum and retarded the movement of the whole machine
without rendering any service of great value.

The "capitalization of labor," continued Phillips, "and the export of
earnings in exchange for more workmen, always of a low degree of
efficiency, together with the extreme lack of versatility, deprived the
South of the natural advantage which the cotton monopoly should have
given."[24]

Phillips revealed a growing appreciation of the dynamic qualities of slavery's evolution over time in essays in the *American Historical Review* and *Political Science Quarterly* in 1906 and 1907, respectively. In "The Origin and Growth of the Southern Black Belts" (1906), he linked slavery and the growth of the plantation system to class conflict in the Old South. Planters, Phillips explained, generally had followed small farmers southward and westward into the southern frontier in search of new opportunities for employing their capital. Gradually this settlement pattern became marked by the planters' encroachment upon their less affluent, weaker rivals, the small farmers. In Phillips's judgment, yeoman farmers could not compete successfully against the planters and their squads of black slaves. If organized properly, blacks furnished "a cheaper supply of labor" than whites and provided "a more effective system of routine work." Exhibiting an insensitivity to blacks as people, Phillips went on to describe the plantation system as "probably the most efficient method ever devised for the use of stupid labor in agriculture on a large scale." Gradually, he continued, southern wealth came to be concentrated within the planter class in distinct geographical areas. Here Phillips revealed the influence of his mentor Frederick Jackson Turner and of the Progressive historians' emphasis on conflict as a historical force. For Phillips, the clash between planter and farmer symbolized the "strife of industrial systems." This led to yet another stage of confrontation—competition among planters themselves for the best lands.[25]

Slavery in the low-lying coastal region of South Carolina and Georgia was the subject of "The Slave Labor Problem in the Charleston District" (1907), and Phillips considered this an excellent example of the complexities of the peculiar institution. Conditions there, he said, more closely resembled those in the West Indies than those in Virginia and the piedmont uplands. Slavery in the Charleston District, one of the blackest of the southern black belts, represented for Phillips the constant tension between "the social and economic points of view" within the dominant class. Adherents to the former attitude, especially numerous following Denmark Vesey's 1822 plot, perceived blacks as potential enemies in a race war. They favored the passage of restrictive slave codes. In contrast, many Carolina slave owners maintained the "private policy" of pitting their slaves in economic competition with white mechanics or upland yeomen. Phillips believed that in practice masters preferred to keep their chattels unskilled and docile rather "than to increase their labor value" by educating them. All in all, he characterized slave life in the low country as generally benign. Phillips insisted that whites only casually enforced slave laws and that, in the main, the two races lived together in relative harmony. Adequately housed, fed, and clothed, blacks had few cares. "Except in emergencies," masters found the selling of bondsmen distasteful. In Phillips's opinion, the sense of noblesse oblige convinced slaveholders that their "dominating consideration . . . was not that of great profit, but that of comfortable living in pleasant surroundings, with a consciousness of important duties well performed."[26]

Successful slave owners, noted Phillips in 1909, rose to the top much like the shrewd, "high-grade captains of industry" of late nineteenth-century America. In order to procure the most labor from their slaves, masters relied upon kindness and custom rather than cruelty and the law. "The actual regime was one of government not by laws but by men," he insisted, slaves living under what Phillips described as "a paternalistic despotism." Sometimes, he explained, slaveholders would threaten less tractable bondsmen with sale to the swamps of Louisiana or Mississippi. Such strategy represented more fiction than fact because, explained Phillips, the volume and evils of the domestic slave trade were overdrawn by the abolitionists. Even though slave trading "was looked upon askance by society," the historian remained convinced that "the traders as a class hardly deserved all the ill repute which tradition had given them." Phillips went on to admit that white Virginians and Kentuckians had earned "considerable income from the occasional sale of slaves," but he doubted that forced couplings were typical. More likely, asserted Phillips, "the matter of breeding was . . . left almost or quite universally to the inclinations of the negroes themselves." "In truth," wrote Phillips seemingly without emotion, "the slaves bred spontaneously and the masters sold off the increase."[27]

In his early essays Phillips also assessed another controversial aspect of race control, slave rebelliousness. He admitted that slave runaways and "desperadoes" confirmed the fact that "malajustments" indeed crept into the slave system. And he affirmed that the system was "by no means perfect as a method of racial adjustment, nor was its working constantly smooth." In fact, throughout his early writings Phillips pointed out a basic flaw in slavery: "with all its variety and considerable elasticity the system . . . was too rigid to be tolerable to all the extremely diverse people who were grouped in the so-called negro race." Even so, Phillips never questioned the benefits that slavery allegedly offered the "typical" bondsmen, whom he portrayed as accepting the civilizing influences of enslavement. Phillips acknowledged, however, that slavery failed in the case of certain blacks. It was suited neither to those "too doggedly barbaric to submit to industrial discipline" nor to the class of "exceptional" bondsmen. This latter group, composed of mulattoes, quadroons, and what Phillips called "yellow negroes," grew restless under the restraints of enslavement. "High-grade, intelligent" and "self-reliant," these blacks—like their twentieth-century counterparts—proved to be an enigma to Phillips, whether he was writing about slavery or contemporary race relations. He recognized that for the minority element of "specially progressive" blacks, including such rebels as Denmark Vesey and Nat Turner, "slave status was obviously a misfit." White southerners, concluded Phillips, experienced "much greater anxiety" over slave revolts than previous historians had recognized. Considerations of racial control, then, influenced master/slave relations as well as the shaping of southern political policy.[28]

In the years before the appearance of *American Negro Slavery*, Phillips also continued to sharpen his critique of slave economics. He faulted planters for locking up much of their scarce capital in slaves instead of investing it in diversified industry or internal improvements. "If they acquired any surplus capital at all," complained Phillips, planters "were so eager to buy additional land and slaves that they had little money available for corporation investment." He developed this theme in *A History of Transportation in the Eastern Cotton Belt* (1908). Again and again in this study, Phillips assailed slave labor as "stupid and careless," "as a rule inefficient for any tasks but those of crude routine." Even then the historian rated it "highly expensive." Phillips's main point, though, remained that the "over-capitalization" of slaves resulting from the needless cutthroat competition among masters drained precious capital away from the piedmont of the eastern cotton belt. White southerners consequently experienced great difficulties in raising stock subscriptions for railways and canals. Ironically, he maintained that even the South's limited railroad network became "a source of [economic] weakness and . . . failure." By carrying cotton more rapidly over longer distances the railroads further encouraged the intensification of the plantation system and the increase of limited staple agriculture. Phillips placed the blame on what became one of his favorite rationales for southern backwardness—"the financial burdensomeness of slaveholding."[29]

Phillips's early writings on slave economics reveal a gradual clarification of his economic indictment of the peculiar institution. In his first essays he seemed unsure about the relative efficiency of the plantation system and slavery. This weakness became less pronounced in his later articles. Writing, for example, in 1909, he identified the vital nexus between race and the profitability question. "On the whole, negro slave labor was probably not as productive as free white labor among modern industrial nations; yet in view of its being negro labor, first, last and always, and slave labor incidentally, it was brought in the antebellum regime to have a distinctly high degree of efficiency." Yet in the long run, as Phillips had argued previously, slavery became an economic liability for white southerners. To his growing list of economic weaknesses attributed to slavery—overcapitalizing labor, exporting capital, discouraging industrialization and crop diversification—Phillips added new criticisms.[30] He now blamed the South's susceptibility to damage from financial crises upon the peculiar institution. And he charged slavery with discouraging the immigration of wage-earning whites to the region. Somewhat of a conservationist, Phillips even held slavery accountable for encouraging planters "to skim the field and waste the natural fertility." In short, Phillips judged bonded labor "productive but less profitable to the communities employing it than to the outside world." By the 1850s slave prices had escalated to such inflated levels that "only through the most efficient management" and on the best soils could slave owners realize "a moderately good return on their investment."[31]

In 1913, five years before the appearance of *American Negro Slavery*, Phillips again altered somewhat the focus of his economic analysis. He praised, for instance, bondsmen as the most "efficient laborers . . . the world has ever seen under any form of coercion." Reviving the old proslavery theme, he judged plantation slavery "immensely effective" as a social and industrial school. Comparing antebellum and postbellum per capita cotton production in four Mississippi counties, the historian concluded that without the direction supplied by slavery, the output of blacks had declined by 35 percent. Even though (as W. E. B. Du Bois correctly noted) Phillips ignored the weakened fertility of the soil, he asserted confidently that "emancipation of the rural black-belt negroes . . . diminished their industrial efficiency." Phillips went on, however, to explain that in spite of their decreased efficiency, free black workers lowered the net labor cost per pound of cotton. Antebellum southern whites, Phillips said, recognized that slave labor was less profitable than free labor. But their exaggerated fear of "social disorder" kept them enslaved to the unprofitable peculiar institution.[32]

In his early writings Phillips developed a final theme: the nature of plantation paternalism. Here the historian foreshadowed Eugene D. Genovese's *Roll, Jordan, Roll*, published in 1974. Crucial to Phillips's understanding of black slavery was his belief that there was considerable give-and-take between masters and slaves. The former, out of self-interest and genuine kindness, allowed their bondsmen a degree of latitude in their behavior as well as work habits. "Indeed," Phillips asserted, "the slaves had many leverages, and oftentimes . . . ruled their masters more than the masters ruled them." When discussing slave laws, for example, Phillips credited the benevolent patriarchs with granting their bondsmen a certain leeway in their enforcement. The regulation against hiring slaves "out" often was disregarded "when the interest or inclination of master and slave agreed in favor of its violation." Phillips added that "in quiet times" the slave owner ignored the letter of the law and followed "his own interest in managing his slaves (or letting them manage him)." Writing in 1918, Phillips regretted that critics of the South failed to grasp the "spirit of camaraderie" between the races that flourished under slavery.

Men who view the old Southern regime from afar off and with a theorist's eye are likely to think it was an agency of race alienation. So far as my understanding goes this is fundamentally erroneous. The grouping of persons of the two races in the intimate relationship of possession tended strongly to counteract that antipathy which all races feel toward each other. The possession was not wholly of the slave by the master, but also of the master by the slave.

Phillips considered this paternalism a virtue of the slave regime. "It made for strength of character and readiness to meet emergencies, for patience and tact, for large mindedness, gentility, and self-control." Anticipating the writings of the Nashville Agrarians in the 1930s, Phillips preferred his romanticized perception of the plantation to the "impersonality of modern industrialism."[33]

Before the publication of *American Negro Slavery* in 1918, Ulrich B. Phillips already had established himself as his generation's most significant contributor to the historiography of slavery. His many articles and books charted new directions in the course of American slave studies. He asked new and penetrating questions that redirected much of the old debate. Phillips's early writings marked the forty-one-year-old scholar as the rising star among students of the plantation South and slavery. The appearance of *American Negro Slavery*, however, more than any other work, thrust Phillips into the role of unexcelled authority on the peculiar institution. The volume summarized almost two decades of research and reflection on slavery. It came to represent not only the culmination of Phillips's scholarship, but the triumph of the new pro-slavery argument as well.

## III

*American Negro Slavery* immediately became a landmark in the literature of black slavery. Whereas Phillips's predecessors, notably the graduate students at Johns Hopkins, had examined slavery and the plantation on the state level, this volume analyzed systematically the institution of slavery as it existed in the entire South. The book surpassed in scope and detail all prior works on the subject and foreshadowed all subsequent works on slavery. Phillips indicated its breadth in the cumbersome subtitle, *A Survey of the Supply, Employment and Control of Negro Labor as Determined by the Plantation Regime*. According to an advertisement for the book, Phillips's work told "the entire story of slavery in the United States, giving a vivid description of plantation management and life and an accurate discussion of economic conditions."[34]

More than any previous writer, Phillips recognized the complex nature of the peculiar institution. Alone among the many authors to investigate slavery since 1865, he sensed the importance of portraying enslavement in its broadest institutional features. Consequently, Phillips examined, among other topics, the African origins of the bondsmen, comparative slave systems, and the economics of slavery and the plantation. More than one-half of the volume's twenty-three chapters analyze specific aspects of slavery. *American Negro Slavery* received wide acclaim not only in scholarly but in non-professional circles as well. Writing from Columbia, South Carolina, an editor praised its human interest flavor, the book's "historic and economic quality without departing from the method of the scientific investigator." In 1926 Universal Pictures Corporation of California relied upon Phillips's monograph when filming *Uncle Tom's Cabin*.[35]

*American Negro Slavery* is divided into two major parts of unequal length, quality, and importance. The first consists of ten chapters, approximately 180 total pages. These opening chapters drew on relatively few primary source materials, synthesized existing secondary accounts, and consequently provided the work with a weak foundation. In them Phillips set the scene for his later, in-depth, discussion of the plantation regime. These thirteen chapters, consisting of over three hundred pages, presented the fruits of Phillips's two decades of toil in plantation manuscripts and other obscure records. They established an analytical model for later generations of slave studies. In this second section Phillips sketched the contours of slavery's organic growth, probed its institutional features, and assessed its importance to the southern racial dynamic.

Phillips's early chapters investigated the African origins of American slaves, as well as the Atlantic slave trade. His analysis of West African culture failed to include important revisionist interpretations of African history then available, especially the work of Franz Boas, of W. E. B. Du Bois, and of Sir Harry H. Johnston. Instead, his analysis of West African culture depended on the standard, racist white sources of his day, most notably Joseph A. Tillinghast's *The Negro in Africa and America* (1902) and Jerome Dowd's *The Negro Races* (1907). Sketchy and inadequate in every way, Phillips's treatment of Africa added next to nothing to the subject. For example, he described Africans as primitive and ''savage'' practitioners of polygamy and superstition, and he seemed to have no sense of cultural relativism. The climate of their continent rendered Africans particularly adaptable, he said, to the warm weather of the American South. This armed them with an immunity to tropical diseases but prohibited ''mental effort of severe or sustained character.'' In short, Phillips progressed little beyond images of the ''dark continent'' published again and again by white racists since Reconstruction. But unlike most of his fellow white students of slavery, he at least began his discussion of slavery with a discussion, no matter how biased, of American blacks' African antecedents. Phillips recognized a ''crude comity'' among their tribes, praised the Africans' ancient communication systems, and noted the importance of tribal differences. All the same, Phillips distinguished himself little with his chapter ''The Early Exploitation of Guinea.''[36]

Nor did he earn for himself a lasting place among students of the Atlantic slave trade. In his chapter ''The Maritime Slave Trade,'' Phillips seemed ambivalent about whether the transatlantic trade in humans resulted in more of a blessing or a curse for all parties concerned. Exhibiting his characteristic insensitivity to the entire enslavement process, Phillips wrote that for the Africans "the future [as captives] could hardly be worse than the recent past, that misery had plenty of company, and that things were interesting by the way." On the other hand, Phillips admitted the "wretched," "frightful" conditions aboard the slave ships. And unlike in his previous writings, he now acknowledged the destructive effect enslavement had on the blacks' tribal industries and institutions. In his final assessment, Phillips rated the Atlantic slave trade a mixed blessing. It provided white southerners with laborers but encumbered them with constant debt and complex dilemmas of racial adjustment. Still, he concluded that those blacks transported to America "were quite possibly better off" in their new home than were their brethren in the jungles of Africa.[37]

In his other early chapters—pedestrian accounts of slavery in the northern colonies, the American Revolution's impact on slavery, and the closing of the Atlantic slave trade—Phillips again added little to previous scholarship. Resembling the post–Civil War defenders of slavery, he exhibited hostility toward northerners, whom he held equally accountable with southerners for the slave trade and the growth of antiblack prejudice. Phillips even asserted that "racial repugnance" was greater in the Old North than in the Old South. And he disagreed sharply with Du Bois on the question of the effect of the 1808 prohibition on African importations. Specifically, Phillips criticized the black scholar's large estimate of the number of Africans smuggled into the South from 1808 to 1860. In Phillips's opinion, the great increase in the antebellum South's black population resulted from natural reproduction, not illicit importations of fresh Africans. Had the foreign slave trade not been prohibited, he speculated, the large number of blacks imported during periods of peak demand would possibly have provided an excess of bondsmen during periods of depression. Such a glut in the slave market, said Phillips, might well have forced slave owners to emancipate their blacks so as to free themselves "from the burden of the slaves' support." Underlying all of this was the old proslavery argument that masters provided adequate care for their property.[38]

When Phillips examined slavery in the West Indies, he finally broke fresh ground and, in doing so, applied the comparative method to the study of slavery. Early in *American Negro Slavery* Phillips established the fact that fewer than 10 percent of all Africans brought to the Western

Hemisphere came to North America. He recognized a strong link between slavery in the Sugar Islands of the Caribbean and the institution in the American South. After all, noted Phillips, the systematic plantation work routine itself had its roots in the West Indies. In his detailed analysis of Jamaica's Worthy Park plantation, Phillips identified characteristics that he would later apply to his portrait of mainland slavery. Skilled bondsmen, for example, received incentives to encourage greater productivity. Upon the birth of each child, slave mothers earned rewards—a rug and a silver dollar—for their fecundity. Consistent with Phillips's earlier findings, though, Worthy Park, like many southern plantations, barely showed a profit. In spite of its large size (355 bondsmen), it earned less than 4 percent on the investment.[39]

Phillips also focused on the establishment of slave-based agriculture in North America. Just as he had described the detailed stages of Jamaica sugar growing, the historian now scrutinized the nature of Chesapeake tobacco cultivation and Carolina rice culture. Relying heavily on the works of James C. Ballagh and John H. Russell, Phillips explained how black slaves came to supplant white servants in colonial Virginia upon completion of their terms of indenture. He also examined the size of tobacco plantations in Virginia and Maryland. "On the whole," argued Phillips, they were "organized in smaller units by far than most writers, whether of romance or history, would have us believe." Ever conscious of differences within his beloved South, Phillips contrasted the nature of colonial slave society in the upper South with that of low-country Carolina. Like Edward McCrady and Howell M. Henry before him, Phillips underscored the ways in which slavery in South Carolina resembled the institution in Barbados. The preponderance of absentee landlords in the former caused "the intercourse between the whites and blacks . . . [to be] notably less than in the tobacco region, and the progress of the negroes in civilization correspondingly slighter." Carolina plantations, Phillips remarked, "were less of homesteads and more of business establishments."[40]

*American Negro Slavery* also contains Phillips's fullest discussion of the introduction of the cotton industry into the South and, consequently, its expansion into the western cotton belt. Thoroughly conversant with Matthew B. Hammond's earlier research, Phillips stressed the importance of European demand, the cotton gin, and the emergence of short-staple upland cotton as salient factors in the growth of cotton as the South's leading staple. Much as he had presented his basic argument twelve years previously in the *American Historical Review*, Phillips now emphasized how planter and farmer competed for the best lands along the southern frontier. Paraphrasing an antebellum Alabamian, he sketched how slavery became the key element in the westward expansion of the South's cotton culture, benefiting white southerners "through its tendency to stratify society" and by providing "even the poor whites a stimulating pride of race." Frederick Jackson Turner's imprint, his concept of an evolving, moving frontier, appears all through Phillips's narrative of the westward expansion of cotton and slavery.[41]

Chapter eleven, Phillips's consideration of the domestic slave trade, ushers in the author's analysis of slavery's institutional features. His examination of the slave trade, plantation operations, paternalism, slave economics, and law established *American Negro Slavery* as the most important contribution on slavery between Appomattox and World War I. These sections best illustrate how and why Phillips epitomizes the proslavery synthesis that not only survived emancipation, but became a major bulwark of white racial thought in the Age of Jim Crow.

## IV

Phillips began his consideration of slavery's inner workings by examining the domestic slave trade. He realized full well that few subjects had received such unrestrained condemnation from abolitionists before and since the war as had the intraregional trade in human flesh. After examining thousands of bills of sale, city directories, ship manifests, and other primary records, Phillips concluded that the abolitionists had been less than accurate all along. In contrast to their stereotype of a ruthless industry devoted to human greed and misery, Phillips pictured the trade as "partly systematic, partly casual." Above all he stressed the trade's localized, ad hoc nature. Unlike Frederic Bancroft in his later harsh account, Phillips argued that slave owners more often than not sacrificed profit "in order to keep faithful servants out of the hands of the long-distance traders." Generally, he continued, the only slaves masters eagerly sought to sell were "the indolent, the unruly, and those under suspicion." But when forced by circumstances to relinquish their bondsmen, owners preferred to keep their black family groups intact. On another controversial point, Phillips found little evidence that female slaves were sold expressly for concubinage. His review of slave price data convinced him that skilled male bondsmen, not women, brought in the highest prices. He admitted, though, that "concubinage itself was fairly frequent."[42]

The historian expressed next to no emotion in his description of black people on the auction block. In a patronizing tone Phillips asserted that "it was a matter of pride" for slaves "to fetch high prices." He failed totally to consider that in feigning illnesses or disabilities while on auction, blacks were resisting the system. Instead, Phillips interpreted such behavior simply as a slave's "grudge against his seller," or as a mode of insuring purchase for light service. He went on to equate blacks with animals. Comparing the risks to purchasers in the slave trade with those incurred in horse trading, Phillips conceded that black "human nature is more complex and uncertain than equine and harder to fathom from surface indications." Totally convinced that the domestic slave trade was not the evil the abolitionists had charged, Phillips admitted that slave traders did suffer public contempt and social ostracism. Foreshadowing one of Bancroft's arguments, Phillips explained that when the "better" class of white southerners entered the slave trade, they frequently did so surreptitiously—as "silent partners" of the acknowledged traders. Ironically, noted Phillips, the "social stigma" cast upon slave trading kept competition to a minimum, thereby actually benefiting participants in the traffic.[43]

In *American Negro Slavery* Phillips revealed more of an ambivalent attitude toward the impact of the slave trade on the South's economy than in his previous essays. He praised it, for example, as a constructive force in transporting laborers to newly settled regions of the South. In this manner slave traders made the blacks "much more responsive to new industrial opportunity than if . . . [they] had been free." Phillips also identified benefits to masters as well as slaves in the neighborhood slave trade within each community. For the former the trade served to transfer workers "from impoverished employers to those with better means." Bondsmen profited, in Phillips's opinion, by change in ownership "from persons with whom relations might be strained to others whom the negroes might find more congenial." Only the slave trade's economic inflexibility bothered Phillips; the trade's chief defect involved the principle of "lifetime service." Even though masters could buy and sell bondsmen in response to their labor needs, the historian complained that local fluctuations made planters liable to "slave trading risks on a scale eclipsing that of their industrial earnings." Short-term slave hiring, suggested Phillips, might have saved many a master from the "toils of speculation."[44]

Phillips grew up in cotton country, and his renowned monograph dealt largely with the operation of the cotton plantation. His book pioneered the broad analysis of plantation life, offering various examples and case studies gleaned from innumerable plantation records, farm books, agricultural journals, and contemporary newspapers. Phillips also presented the earliest investigation of the technical aspects of plantation agriculture, one not supplanted until the publication of Lewis C. Gray's two-volume *History of Agriculture in the Southern United States to 1860* (1933). Unlike previous students, Phillips stood back and viewed slavery and the plantation system as an economic whole. He applauded the slave plantation because it enabled full utilization of labor at a variety of tasks throughout the year. Another of slavery's economic strengths, in his view, was the adaptation of work assignments to the varied skill levels of "the slow, the youthful and the aged." Speaking from firsthand authority, Phillips declared that cotton picking, of all the jobs on the plantation, required more perseverance than strength.[45]

Yet Phillips harkened back to his earlier criticisms of slavery's ill effects on the Southland. Slavery led toward the one-crop system, with its short-term profits but long-term deterioration of the region's soils. An advocate of agricultural experimentation and reform since his days at Wisconsin, Phillips bemoaned that few antebellum southerners paid attention to Edmund Ruffin's antebellum findings concerning crop diversification and the use of manures. But Phillips was careful not to leave the impression that large plantations dominated the Old South's agricultural life. On the contrary, he argued that "there were . . . many more small farms than large plantations devoted to cotton; and among the plantations . . . it appears that very few were upon a scale entitling them to be called great, for the nature of the industry did not encourage the engrossment of more than sixty laborers under a single manager." Phillips also emphasized that approximately one-half of the South's annual cotton crop was produced "by farmers whose slaves were on the average hardly more numerous than the white members of their own families." Such small slave owners labored in the fields right alongside their bondsmen.[46]

Notwithstanding this caveat, in *American Negro Slavery* and his other writings Phillips never lost sight of the large plantation. For him, the ubiquitous, grandiose southern estate unquestionably symbolized the Old South. So wedded was Phillips to this idea that in his monograph he devoted an entire long chapter to the types of large plantations. Focusing so narrowly on large units allowed the historian to probe deeply into everyday plantation life. And *American Negro Slavery*, alone among the hundreds of scholarly works on slavery published since emancipation, made the plantation come alive.

Phillips illustrated his book copiously with pen portraits taken from plantation diaries and farm letter books. He employed primary sources to illumine such important but seemingly colorless facets of slavery as the task and gang systems, or to provide a sense of the limitations of plantation medicine. Throughout he allowed the planters to speak for themselves. Without question, Phillips shared their perception of slavery. The historian, in the spirit of the postbellum defenders of slavery, envisioned the plantation as a patriarchal community in which enlightened slave owners supplied helpless slaves not only with comfortable surroundings but with the guidance and regulation provided only by a superior master class.[47]

Phillips, like countless apologists for slavery before him, wrote confidently of the adequate food, clothing, and medical care available to the bondsmen. For the majority of the blacks, he observed, "crude comfort was the rule." In his opinion, slave owners dedicated themselves to the material and spiritual well-being of "their" blacks. But ever a careful student of political economy, Phillips knew that their concern for the slaves' welfare resulted largely from the planters' economic self-interest. Stable marriages, for instance, virtually guaranteed the planters regular increases in the number of their slaves. Christianity, too, served the planter by schooling the blacks in morality, discipline, and respect for their "superiors." Phillips identified inducements—plots of land or cash payments—that masters used to gain maximum performance from their workers. An Alabama planter even instituted "profit sharing" among his slaves. Each bondsman received a half-acre plot with the assurance "that if he worked with diligence in the master's crop the whole gang would in turn be set to work his crop."[48]

Such strategies convinced Phillips that slavery functioned successfully because it was at its core a human institution. Slaves and masters, inferiors and superiors, lived and worked together to fashion meaning in the only world they knew. Assuming as he did that virtually all blacks were mere children, Phillips sympathized openly with those charged with ordering plantation society. When writing of the overseers, for example, he refused, unlike James Ford Rhodes and Albert Bushnell Hart, to make facile generalizations. Phillips viewed overseers as a class of yeomen who themselves aspired to planter status. Success or failure of a crop rested squarely on their shoulders. The management of blacks, "a bed of roses only if the thorns were turned aside," required extraordinary talents. Although he uncovered some exceptions, Phillips concluded that most plantation managers were humane and approached the blacks in the spirit of "harmony and good will." They ruled by moderate control and "as little as possible by fear, and as much as might be by loyalty, pride and the prospect of reward." The overseers, in Phillips's view, "had about as much human nature, with its merits and failings, as the planters or the slaves or anybody else."[49]

The human equation also served as the linchpin for Phillips's most important theme: the paternalism he identified as cementing the master/slave relation. In his early essays the historian had mentioned, albeit briefly, the sense of fellowship that for him explained the modus operandi of slave society. He expanded and refined his consideration of the nature of this bond in *American Negro Slavery*. Phillips described the nexus binding master and slave as one characterized by "propriety, proportion and cooperation." Through years of living together, he said, the two races established a rapport not between equals but between dependent unequals. "The problem of accommodation," Phillips explained, "the central problem of [southern] . . . life, was on the whole happily solved" by slavery. The lives of the two different races became enmeshed, intertwined in a legal and social system. Writing in the heyday of segregation, Phillips looked backward to a civilization in which *separate and unequal* had translated into a rare form of integration. Slavery provided the vehicle for blacks to enter the lives of the whites. The two racial groups thereby became interdependent—the blacks "always within the social mind and conscience of the whites, as the whites in turn were within the mind and conscience of the blacks." To be sure, Phillips noted, the masters controlled the privileges that the slaves enjoyed. But, he insisted, the blacks were "by no means devoid of influence." Slave foremen or drivers, for example, were selected by masters only "with the necessary sanction of" their bondsmen. Whites recognized that blacks shared a vital stake not only in their crop but in their lives as well. A half-century before Eugene D. Genovese would resurrect, broaden, and radically alter it, Phillips presented his theory of plantation paternalism. According to Phillips, the contours of slave society were "shaped by mutual requirements, concessions and understandings, producing reciprocal codes of conventional morality" and responsibility. According to Genovese, central to slavery was a system of "mutual obligations—duties, responsibilities, and ultimately even rights"—"an elaborate web of paternalistic relationships." It included a "dialectic of accommodation and resistance."[50]

But years earlier Phillips had diagnosed the mutual obligations that grew between master and slave, and he was keenly sensitive to how bondsmen often controlled the behavior of their masters. But Phillips stopped far short of Genovese, who credited blacks with transforming "paternalism itself into a doctrine different from that understood by their masters and to forge it into a weapon of resistance to assertions that slavery was a natural condition for blacks, that blacks were racially inferior, and that black slaves had no rights or legitimate claims of their own." Phillips viewed paternalism far differently but as a weapon nevertheless. He considered the "occasional" protests by the slaves analogous to strikes by the labor movement of his day. Whereas the bondsmen sought better treatment, industrial workers clamored for improved wages and working conditions. Just as latter-day employees bargained with management, Phillips reasoned, slaves used their special relationship to win concessions from their masters. "Humble as their demeanor might be," the blacks' "power of renewing the pressure" by forms of misbehavior never could be ignored by the master class. Phillips interpreted the entire plantation status quo as a series of "mutual concessions and pledges." The give-and-take between slave and master gave the Old South its stability. "Concession when accompanied with geniality and not indulged so far as to cause demoralization," he said, made "plantation life not only tolerable but charming."[51]

Phillips conveniently omitted from his paternalism construct any quest by blacks for freedom. Blinded by his racism, Phillips remained as confident in 1918 as he had been in 1902 that the savage Africans benefited from American-style slavery. Since his earliest essays he had emphasized slavery's benign qualities, especially its educational function. The slavery-as-school idea dated to the old proslavery argument and, not surprisingly, found its way into *American Negro Slavery*. Phillips helped popularize the image of the plantation as "a school constantly training and controlling pupils who were in a backward state of civilization." He equated the plantation with the social settlement homes of the Progressive Era. It taught the blacks by precept and demonstration, offering lifelong courses in civilization and vocational training. Even Phillips, however, had to confront an essential flaw in this argument. Plantation schools never graduated their "pupils upon the completion of their training." He considered this an unfortunate part of the system, but wrote with confidence that slavery "did at least as much as any system possible in the period could have done" to uplift what Phillips deemed an "inert and backward people."[52]

If, as Phillips insisted, slavery served principally to control and educate the blacks, what then was its role in southern economic development? Phillips's argument on this point became clearer over the years but his message remained unchanged. In *American Negro Slavery* he again pronounced slavery an economic burden retained essentially as a system of police control: "it was less a business than a life; it made fewer fortunes than it made men." Although Phillips admitted "the routine efficiency of slave labor," he reemphasized the many ways that the peculiar institution restricted the South's economic growth in general and the profits of individual planters in particular. Slave purchases absorbed capital and doomed the region to a non-diversified staple economy. The cost of slaves exceeded that of free laborers. Only exceptional planters—expert managers situated on the most fertile lands—made profits. At its economic best, complained Phillips, slavery served only to make black workers "mobile, regular and secure." He pitied the planters whose "heavy capitalization of the control of labor" placed them in a self-defeating economic cycle. "Thus while the slaves had a guarantee of their sustenance, their proprietors, themselves the guarantors, had a guarantee of nothing."[53]

In 1918 Phillips also added several new arguments to his earlier economic indictment of slavery. He now noted, for example, that the crude nature of bondsmen encouraged planters to become trapped in an established routine and to ignore the development of labor-saving machines. Another drawback of slave labor, he insisted, was that "the performance of every hand tended . . . to be standardized at the customary accomplishment of the weakest and slowest members of the group." Masters had little choice in the selection of their plantation workmen, the character of their work force depending too much on chance. Phillips preferred the dictates of free market capitalism, by which employers selected their workers based on merit and performance, not on chance. Finally, the historian calculated the many expenses incurred in raising slaves to maturity. He concluded that the average bondsman cost too much, frequently not yielding a net return to his master until about age twenty.[54]

Phillips completed his portrait of slave life by assessing three other aspects of the plantation regime: urban slavery, slave crime, and slave law. Relying heavily on the inadequate 1848 Charleston manuscript census, Phillips nonetheless gained a sense of the diverse trades that urban slaves plied. There were domestics, carpenters, stevedores, bookbinders, and cigar makers. Many slaves toiled in southern factories. Phillips identified in urban slavery the same paternalism he found on the slave plantation. Yet he realized that the urban setting lessened the interdependency he judged so much a fixture of master/slave relations. Town slaves, for example, intermingled more frequently with free blacks and other bondsmen than their brethren on isolated plantations did. They also experienced moments of freedom when hired ''out'' as laborers or when working alongside white mechanics in factories. Phillips pointed also to the practice of hiring urban ''slaves to the slaves themselves.'' This, he explained, exhibited an institution ''flexibly responsive'' to changing needs. All in all, in Phillips's opinion the urban scene provided laborers of both races a degree of integration that was absent on the plantation.[55]

A high crime rate existed among the slaves, said Phillips, both in rural and urban settings. This interpretation clashed with W. E. B. Du Bois's 1901 statement that ''under a strict slave regime there can scarcely be such a thing as crime.'' It also raised serious doubts about Phillips's own romanticized image of kind masters and happy slaves. Why would satisfied bondsmen commit felonies, not to mention revolt, against their beloved protectors? Phillips reconciled his findings with the suggestion that slave crime soared in areas where free blacks were most numerous. But he offered another explanation that harkened back to the postwar proslavery ideologues: blacks were inherently prone to crime. In this regard Phillips revised the frequent harangue of proslavery writers that the rape of white women by blacks was exclusively a postemancipation crime. In his opinion, neither rapes by blacks nor their ''natural'' corollaries, prompt lynchings, were exclusively postwar phenomena.[56]

Racial phobias haunted white southerners, Phillips charged. This explained their exaggerated fears of slave revolt. Phillips credited the master class with even-tempered handling of crimes by individual blacks and with a generally sober reaction to the Denmark Vesey plot. Even so, Phillips noted the hysterical response—the execution of innocent blacks and the passage of repressive slave laws—to Nat Turner's revolt. As with almost every other facet of slavery, Phillips ignored how blacks envisioned crime and resistance. He comprehended none of the implications of slave restiveness that were evaluated so minutely by later scholars. Instead, Phillips perceived only the impact of this restiveness on the whites. Their fear of slave revolt, he said, made the South an illiberal society constrained by "a fairly constant undertone of uneasiness."[57]

His analysis of slave law reveals just how Phillips's approach to slavery differed from that of virtually all other scholars dating back to Reconstruction. Most generally began their examinations of slavery with some assessment of slave regulations. But Phillips failed to treat the subject until his concluding chapter. He de-emphasized slavery's legal side, probably in part because the subject had received such widespread attention from others, especially the students at Johns Hopkins. But equally important was Phillips's organic view of slave society. To him slavery evolved more from social habit and custom than from statutes. In line with the writings of James C. Ballagh and John H. Russell, Phillips argued that antebellum slave laws merely codified preexisting racial and industrial conditions that took shape during the colonial period. He conceded that, on paper at least, slave laws appeared harsh and clashed with his benign view of the peculiar institution. But, Phillips insisted, most repressive slave laws were enacted at times of crisis and rarely were enforced. For instance, strictures prohibiting slaves from entering trades if they would be competing with white mechanics usually remained "left in the obscurity of the lawyer's bookshelves . . . to be brought forth only in case of an emergency." Of the slave ordinances passed in the wake of the Turner revolt, Phillips asserted that they, too, "were promptly relegated, as the older ones had been, to the limbo of things laid away, like pistols, for emergency use, out of sight and out of mind in the daily routine of peaceful industry." Only the most fundamental laws, he concluded, those that perpetuated white supremacy, became enmeshed in the social fabric of slave society.[58]

## V

*American Negro Slavery*, more than any previous work, established Phillips as the unrivaled student of black slavery of his day. The book brought national attention to the University of Michigan professor and launched Phillips's career into a new orbit, one that ultimately placed him in what he termed his "very flossy job at Yale." Most importantly, the book's warm reception in the years following World War I signaled the complete triumph of the new proslavery argument. From the twenties through the depression and up to the post–World War II years, white scholars turned to Phillips and *American Negro Slavery* for the definitive account of the peculiar institution. In these years a number of historians, dubbed "the Phillips school," applied Phillips's organization, sources, and interpretive model to studies of slavery on the local level. Phillips reigned as the master of slave historiography from 1918 until the publication of Kenneth M. Stampp's highly revisionist *The Peculiar Institution* in 1956. Even later, Phillips's interpretations continued to find their way into textbooks and lectures. Ultimately the Civil Rights Revolution dethroned Phillips. His blatant racism and disregard for blacks as people joined Jim Crow waiting rooms and segregated schools as discarded vestiges of an unfortunate earlier day.[59]

But not so in 1918. In general, *American Negro Slavery* won Phillips friends among the reviewers. Most praised the book's broad scope and freedom from partisanship. The *Booklist*, for example, complimented Phillips on the wealth of facts he had unearthed, while the *American Review of Reviews* found the book virtually free of any "controversial tinge." Northern critics almost uniformly heaped praise upon a work whose southern bias appeared on virtually every page. The Springfield *Daily Republican*, for example, and other Massachusetts newspapers welcomed Phillips's work and compared it favorably with James Ford Rhodes's neoabolitionist treatment of the same subject. They especially praised Phillips's accounts of slavery in colonial New England and Rhode Island's prominent role in the Atlantic slave trade. The newspapers seemed to welcome Phillips's benign view of slavery because it offered readers an alternative to many northerners' stereotypes of slavery and plantation life. Similarly, the New York *Sun* identified a refreshing fairness in the historian's work—one it judged at variance with much of the other slavery scholarship. Unlike northern writers, said the *Sun*'s reviewer, Phillips viewed blacks "with a sympathy and appreciation rarely found among those who can see nothing but unmitigated evil in the life led by the colored race in America before the Civil War."[60]

Reviewers below the Mason-Dixon line welcomed *American Negro Slavery* even more enthusiastically. For example, the Baltimore *Sun* praised it as "a fair and impartial account"—"as interesting as a romance." Paradoxically, the rural Tifton, Georgia *Gazette* titled its review of Phillips's book "From a Northern Viewpoint," but nevertheless appreciated fully the author's grasp of southern paternalism. It lauded the historian's book for discarding tradition and prejudice in favor of "clear-cut facts." Phillips no doubt valued the glowing comments of Philip Alexander Bruce, a pioneer himself in the study of the economics of Virginia slavery. Bruce barely could restrain himself in extolling the virtues of Phillips's book.

Not only is it a work of extraordinary historical value, but also one that I have found to be most interesting. . . . Most works relating to this subject are disfigured and warped by biased opinion. . . . They are either too northern or too southern—but . . . you have struck the exactly right key. You are calm, impartial, judicial. . . . You have presented the facts as they were, in the spirit of a perfectly disinterested historian. The work is a monument of research, and equally so of fair and discriminating presentation.

Unable to foresee later generations of scholarly debate over slavery, Bruce added, "I venture to say that you have said the final word."[61]

Phillips received kudos from still other members of his guild, who almost uniformly commented upon the breadth and painstaking nature of his research. Writing in the *Political Science Quarterly*, Caleb P. Patterson, a specialist on Texas slavery, wrote glowingly of Phillips's concern with the African background of blacks. Charleston attorney and amateur historian Theodore D. Jervey found convincing the scholar's evidence that the slaves were not overtasked. Even "if much that is submitted were lacking," added Jervey, "the astounding prolificacy of the slave mother would in itself be an argument of the care bestowed upon the race." Economic historian Tipton R. Snavely esteemed the plantation sources Phillips employed in *American Negro Slavery*. They enabled Phillips, he said, to unveil a whole new economic dimension to the peculiar institution.[62]

Some reviewers, however, adjudged Phillips's perspective all too familiar. They condemned Phillips for approving—seemingly endorsing—slavery as the best mode of race relations. The Boston *Congregationalist* said that Phillips "gave so favorable an impression of slavery that no Southern reader can be offended." It further criticized his book as "over-colored by the sources quoted." A Detroit newspaper predicted that few twentieth-century Americans would accept Phillips's belief in a moral justification for the enslavement of blacks. "Prof. Ulrich seems rather to ignore the fact," quipped the reviewer, that "freedom, in itself, counts for something." Phillips's myopic view of plantation life contradicted itself. How, the critic asked, could the same masters and mistresses whom the Georgian so revered also commit "callous," "inhuman brutality?" The professor from Ann Arbor failed to recognize that it was the slaves' "fear and ignorance"—not their loyalty—that restrained them from rising against their masters during the Civil War.[63]

Critics laced Phillips where he was most vulnerable. Historian Frederic Bancroft repeatedly attacked Phillips's analysis of the domestic slave trade. Shortly after *American Negro Slavery*'s publication, Bancroft explained how he was "a good deal disappointed in what Phillips says about the slave-trade and slave-hiring." Second only to Phillips in his knowledge of the primary sources on slavery, the Illinois native espoused a neoabolitionist view with an intensity equal to that with which Phillips held his own proslavery view. Bancroft bitterly denounced the new proslavery argument and the southern "traditions" upon which he blamed the Civil War. And after Phillips failed to support Bancroft's 1915 campaign to reform the American Historical Association, Bancroft began a one-man crusade to discredit his southern rival. Intensely jealous of Phillips's productivity as a scholar, Bancroft delighted in mocking the historian he termed the self-appointed "Sir Oracle of Southern History." Writing to James Ford Rhodes in 1918, Bancroft vented his outrage at Phillips's proslavery views.

Have you read U. B. Phillips's *American Negro Slavery*? In it he attempts some surprisingly contemp[t]uous comment on anti-slavery opinions. I have been looking for someone to give him his deserts. What he says in an alleged refutation about slave-breeding would interest you. In my volume . . . I shall cover that question in a manner that will leave no room for doubt. I have a most deadly array of facts.

Criticizing Phillips soon became an obsession for Bancroft.[64]

Through the years Bancroft continued to assault Phillips whenever the opportunity arose. "Phillips is fond of literary stilts," railed Bancroft in 1924, "and seems to be very proud of some of his performances on them." Seven years later, in his revisionist *Slave Trading in the Old*

*South*, Bancroft repeatedly maligned Phillips for failing to recognize in his own evidence proof of the large-scale slave breeding from which the planters garnered immense profits. He pounced, for example, upon Phillips's statement in *American Negro Slavery* that slave children rarely were sold separately from their parents. "Hardly ever sold separately!" exclaimed Bancroft. Young slaves constituted "hardly less than a staple in the trade." Bancroft later denounced Phillips's sentimental attachment to the planter class and charged that he either withheld or misinterpreted evidence that otherwise would have portrayed the planters in a less favorable light.[65]

Others presented less personal but equally serious criticisms of *American Negro Slavery*. At Hampton Institute, George P. Phenix complained that Phillips had "toned down" slavery's harshest features, that he had left the inaccurate impression that slavery in its most lenient form typified the institution throughout the South. Two other writers, Mariano Joaquin Lorente and Mary White Ovington, denounced Phillips for failing to treat blacks as human beings. The first reviewer lamented that Phillips's book presented little of the black's mind—what he called "his psychology." Ovington, a distinguished author, social worker, and civil rights activist, censured Phillips for his tolerance of slavery and racism. She remained unconvinced that the organic plantation life he so idealized in any way counterbalanced the inhumanities of slavery. Sharply contrary to Bruce's earlier remark, Miss Ovington feared that "unless the descendant of the slave writes an exhaustive book from his standpoint this *might* be the last word on the subject."[66]

Blacks in fact delivered the most severe blows to Phillips's famous book. W. E. B. Du Bois and Carter G. Woodson impugned Phillips with such skill that their critiques remain examples of historical criticism at its rigorous best. Du Bois slashed Phillips for writing an overtly biased economic history of slavery without even focusing on the slaves or consulting slave sources. Like Ovington, the black professor faulted Phillips for his insensitivity to blacks as people with human emotions. Phillips's racism, charged Du Bois, blinded him to the significant accomplishments of blacks since emancipation. The characters of *American Negro Slavery*—"subhuman slaves" and "superman" slaveholders—were drawn not from fact but from "special pleading," "innuendo and assumption." Neither his benign view of slavery's institutional features nor Phillips's explanation of its economic unprofitability proved acceptable to Du Bois. In short, he judged *American Negro Slavery* a shameless "defense of an institution which was at best a mistake and at worst a crime."[67]

Woodson appreciated Phillips's consideration of slave economics but deemed the rest of the book of little value. He, too, blasted Phillips for neglecting the slaves, for not comprehending "what the Negroes have thought and felt and done." The editor of the *Journal of Negro History* differed with Phillips over the blacks' alleged happiness. How, asked Woodson, could a scholar reconcile such an erroneous notion with the large number of slave uprisings? Unlike other critics, Woodson raised serious questions about Phillips's evolutionary view of slavery. He failed to emphasize to Woodson's satisfaction how slavery changed from a patriarchal institution in the eighteenth century to a commercial enterprise a century later. Consequently, Woodson said, many of Phillips's observations on slavery in the nineteenth century were anachronistic. Finally, Woodson attacked Phillips's much-vaunted plantation sources as too one-dimensional—coming as they did from among only "the most enlightened and benevolent slaveholders."[68]


## VI

Phillips left no record of his reactions to these harsh strictures except for a sense of irritation at Bancroft's tart comments. His subsequent research and writing incorporated virtually nothing of the substance of these criticisms. Phillips instead took them in stride as he vigorously continued his research and writing after World War I. He rose to even greater heights in the twenties—the Little, Brown prize for *Life and Labor in the Old South* (1929), the Albert Kahn Fellowship, and finally his appointment in New Haven. Phillips died before he could complete his projected multivolume history of the South. Did Phillips alter his perception of slavery in his last years? Where does he rate in the pantheon of historians of slavery? And what was his role in keeping alive proslavery ideas?[69]

By evaluating *Life and Labor in the Old South* in light of the criticisms of *American Negro Slavery*, a measure of Phillips's growth as a historian emerges. Writing in 1929, Phillips maintained that over the previous decade he had unearthed a wealth of new sources on slavery that enabled him to make "sundry changes of emphasis and revisions of judgment." The result, *Life and Labor in the Old South*, was a masterfully written and richly textured analysis of antebellum southern society. Recalling his earlier emphasis on geography as a determinant in historical development, Phillips now sketched the interrelationship of man, climate, and physiography in the Southland. With chapters devoted even to the South's neglected people—Indians, Latins, yeomen, mountain folk—*Life and Labor* immediately became what J. G. de Roulhac Hamilton described as "a real event in American historiography." Because of its broad portrait of southern culture, Allen Tate judged the book exemplary of James Harvey Robinson's "New History." Some scholars then and now have argued that *Life and Labor*'s analysis of slavery supplemented if not surpassed Phillips's treatment of the subject in *American Negro Slavery*. Henry Steele Commager spoke for many of his peers when he rated Phillips's latter volume "perhaps the most significant contribution to the history of the Old South in this generation."[70]

Regardless of these plaudits, in *Life and Labor* Phillips failed to revise his interpretations of slavery to any significant degree. He incorporated into this volume none of the criticisms leveled at his previous work. In fact, Phillips's basic earlier theme—the duality of slavery as an economic cancer and a vital mode of racial control—remains. Phillips continued, for example, to admit that there were some cruel aspects to the peculiar institution, but he emphasized slavery's overall benign and paternalistic qualities. He repeated almost all of his statements concerning the legal side of slavery and slavery's function as a school offering curricula in civilization to contented pupils. He still adhered to his argument that slave owners provided their chattels with adequate food, shelter, and medical care. He modified neither his view that blacks were inherently inferior nor his belief that they retained almost none of their African cultural traits upon enslavement. And he exhibited neither a sensitivity to environmentalism nor an appreciation of cultural relativism. "The bulk of the black personnel," explained Phillips with characteristic candor, "was notoriously primitive, uncouth, improvident and inconstant, merely because they were Negroes of the time." The bondsmen lacked ambition, Phillips contended. Masters consequently waged an uphill, futile battle to make them into "full-fledged men." Pitted against *American Negro Slavery*, *Life and Labor* appears less racist in tone because of the latter book's broad scope. Fewer racial slurs appeared in 1929 than in 1918, but Phillips's overt prejudice remained.[71]

His treatment of slavery in *Life and Labor*, then, essentially summarized almost three decades of Phillips's thinking on the subject. In fairness to Phillips, one must note that the book did include a few changes in emphasis. Phillips even admitted that some coercive breeding of laborers occurred under slavery. But through it all, Phillips stressed the "personal equation" as the mainspring of life under slavery. Diversity, not uniformity, characterized slave life. For Phillips, slavery "was a curious blend of force and concession, of arbitrary disposal by the master and self-direction by the slave, of tyranny and benevolence, of antipathy and affection." But most of all, it guaranteed racial control of what he deemed an inferior class by its natural superiors.[72]

Since his death in 1934, few historians have experienced such a meteoric rise and fall in reputation as Ulrich B. Phillips. The criticisms made by early black scholars and some whites suggested just how vulnerable Phillips would be to the forces of revisionism. During the thirties and forties historians continued to chip away at Phillips's major themes. Lewis C. Gray disagreed with the economic indictment of slavery Phillips had espoused since early in the century. Gray found slavery a highly profitable business enterprise but conceded that the institution had pernicious effects on the South's economy. In Gray's opinion, Phillips misread the fluctuations in slave prices. Over-capitalization was "at most only a temporary phenomenon," and for the entire antebellum period "there was a considerable reduction in cost of producing cotton." Other economic historians added to Gray's critique. Robert R. Russel absolved slavery from several charges made by Phillips. He blamed the attractiveness of staple agriculture for the backwardness of the antebellum economy of the region. Thomas P. Govan and Robert W. Smith questioned Phillips's bookkeeping methods. The pioneer historian calculated as plantation expenses items that in reality represented profits. And he erroneously used appreciated values of bondsmen as capital investment in figuring profit. Through the years Phillips's work on plantation economics has fared poorly. Today few subscribe to his belief in the unprofitability of slavery.[73]

Nor have historians withheld criticisms of Phillips's method. As early as 1944 Richard Hofstadter, like Woodson before him, impugned Phillips's use of inadequate and misleading data, the records of large plantations. Influenced strongly by Frank L. Owsley's research on the plain folk of the Old South, Hofstadter faulted Phillips for slighting small slave units, which were roughly four times greater numerically than large units. Hofstadter also accused Phillips of holding "certain preconceptions which disposed him to throw out materials that showed the institution in a less favorable light.'' Another critic identified examples of ''unbalanced selection, misquoting and inaccurate paraphrasing,'' which he said ''raise a strong doubt in regard to the objectivity of Phillips' works.'' Recently students have uncovered inaccuracies in Phillips's slave price data for New Orleans and in occupational records from the 1848 Charleston Census. For years unsuspecting historians have relied upon these sources.[74]

Phillips's racism always has been his greatest weakness, and innumerable historians have objected to his racial slurs. In 1943, for example, Herbert Aptheker pointed out that Phillips's racism prevented him from identifying large-scale resistance on the part of the bondsmen. In later years Aptheker described Phillips as ''a devout white supremacist who was as incapable of writing truthfully of what it meant to be a Negro slave . . . as it would have been for Joseph Goebbels to have written truthfully of what it meant to be a Jew.'' Even so, among white, mainstream, ''establishment'' historians, Phillips's reputation remained intact until the 1950s. White Americans in general, and white historians in particular, simply were unaware of how much antiblack prejudice had clouded their writing about the past. It was not until the post–World War II years, in the midst of third-world revolutions abroad and a black revolution at home, that white American intellectuals became ripe for a complete repudiation of Phillips. Racism, still very much a part of American life, then came under fire.[75]

Kenneth M. Stampp led the assault on Phillips. While mindful of his predecessor's significant accomplishments, Stampp reproved Phillips for ignoring slave life on small plantations and farms, for ''loose and glib generalizing'' about slavery, and for failing to view the institution ''through the eyes of the Negro.'' In treating slavery, explained Stampp, Phillips overemphasized the ''mild and humorous side and minimized its grosser aspects.'' Because Phillips was incapable of taking blacks seriously, Stampp concluded that he had lost his relevance for Americans of the 1950s. Summarizing the anthropological thought of his day, Stampp wrote, ''No historian . . . can be taken seriously any longer unless he begins with the knowledge that there is no valid evidence that the Negro race is innately inferior to the white, and that there is growing evidence that both races have approximately the same potentialities.'' To underscore his commitment to racial equality, Stampp assured his readers that ''I have assumed that the slaves were merely ordinary human beings, that innately Negroes *are*, after all, only white men with black skins, nothing more, nothing less.'' He went on to challenge Phillips's benign view of slavery point by point.[76]

In the 1960s, Eugene D. Genovese launched a resurgence of interest in Phillips and his work. More than any other historian, Genovese focused attention on Phillips's contributions rather than on his antiblack prejudice. Thoroughly deploring Phillips's racism and class bias, Genovese nonetheless applauded many of the historian's ideas. ''Phillips,'' wrote Genovese, ''came close to greatness as a historian, perhaps as close as any historian this country has yet produced.'' True, his racism blinded Phillips, ''prevented him from knowing many things which he in fact knew very well.'' And Genovese was annoyed at Phillips because he ''failed to draw the necessary conclusions from his extraordinary lifetime efforts.'' But Genovese praised Phillips because he ''asked more and better questions than many of us still are willing to admit, and he carried on his investigations with consistent freshness and critical intelligence.''[77]

Genovese's influence permeates what might best be described as a Phillips revival. Since 1969 Phillips has been the subject of two biographies and more than twenty articles.[78] Far from uncritical, each acknowledges the historian's racism but places it into the context of racial thought of the Progressive Era. The authors generally are sympathetic to Phillips, despite having been students during the 1960s, when Phillips and his works were anathema. Even today's most ardent critics of Phillips appreciate his importance as a historian of slavery. According to Herbert G. Gutman, historians continue to employ Phillips's ''model of slave socialization.'' They tend to approach ''slave belief and behavior as little more than one or another response to planter-sponsored stimuli.'' Repeating Phillips's essential premise, they ask, ''What did enslavement do to Africans and their Afro-American descendants?'' Observing in 1976 the trend among historians to characterize slavery in the United States as the mildest system in the Western Hemisphere, Carl Degler noted, ''In that respect, at least, U. B. Phillips's interpretation has returned.'' Twenty years after his repudiation of Phillips, no less a critic than Kenneth M. Stampp argued that ''in their day the writings of Ulrich B. Phillips on slavery were both highly original and decidedly revisionist.'' ''He was about as objective as the rest of us,'' explained Stampp at a meeting of the Southern Historical Association in 1982, ''and that's not very much.'' Recently John W. Blas-

singame noted how "the ghost of U. B. Phillips haunts all of us." And
surveying the new slave studies of the 1970s, Willie Lee Rose discerned
three trends: a renaissance of exhaustive archival research, a better grasp
"of human nature even at work in a slave society," and the development
of "a little more courage" on the part of historians. "U. B. Phillips
has not arisen from the grave," she insisted, but "we have survived
the realization that even he may have done some things right."[79]

## NOTES

1. Phillips to Yates Snowden, January 13, 1905, Yates Snowden Papers,
South Caroliniana Library, University of South Carolina; Phillips, "The Con-
dition of Free Labor in the Slaveholding South," unpublished manuscript, n.d.,
Ulrich B. Phillips Collection, Yale University.

2. Phillips to J. Franklin Jameson, August 24, 1906, *American Historical
Review* Editorial Correspondence, Manuscript Division, Library of Congress;
Phillips, ed., *Plantation and Frontier Documents: 1649–1863*, 2 vols. (Cleve-
land, 1909), 1:103; idem, *American Negro Slavery* (New York, 1918), 313n, 384;
E. M. Coulter to John David Smith, November 22, 1976, in possession of the
author. For additional glimpses into Phillips's life, see Bell I. Wiley, "Ulrich
Bonnell Phillips—the Man and the Historian," unpublished notes, November
4, 1963, copy in possession of the author; Writers' Program, *Georgia, Georgia:
A Guide to Its Towns and Countryside* (Atlanta, 1954; orig. pub., 1940),
225, 388; James C. Bonner, *Milledgeville: Georgia's Antebellum Capital* (Athens, 1978), 244, 247; Wendell Holmes Stephenson, "Ulrich B. Phillips—
Historian of Aristocracy," in *The South Lives in History* (Baton Rouge, 1955),
58–94; John Herbert Roper, *U. B. Phillips: A Southern Mind* (Macon, 1984).

3. Phillips to Turner, April 21, 1902, Frederick Jackson Turner Corre-
spondence, University of Wisconsin; Phillips to Robert Preston Brooks, March
25, 1907, Ulrich B. Phillips Letters, University of Georgia; Turner to Phillips,
April 15, 1899, Phillips Collection; Phillips to Carl Becker, October 13, 1925,
Carl Becker Papers, Cornell University; Phillips to Turner, November 22, 1909,
December 16, 1920, Frederick Jackson Turner Collection, Henry E. Huntington
Library.

4. Phillips, draft of unpublished speech, n.d., Phillips Collection; James
H. Canfield to Frederick Jackson Turner, May 6, 1902, Dunning to Turner,
April 20, 1902, Turner Correspondence.

5. Phillips to "My Dear Henry," February 27, 1903, Frank L. Owsley
Papers, Joint University Libraries, Nashville; Phillips to J. Franklin Jameson,
May 16, 1904, Phillips to Andrew C. McLaughlin, July 28, November 5, 1904,
J. Franklin Jameson Papers, Manuscript Division, Library of Congress; Phillips

to Yates Snowden, January 13, 1905, Snowden Papers; Phillips to McLaughlin, March 1, 1905, Jameson Papers.

6. Phillips, "The Economic Cost of Slaveholding in the Cotton Belt," *Political Science Quarterly*, 20 (June, 1905): 257–275; idem, "The Slave Labor Problem in the Charleston District," ibid., 22 (September, 1907): 416–439; idem, "The Origin and Growth of the Southern Black Belts," *American Historical Review*, 11 (July, 1906): 798–816; idem, "Transportation in the Ante-Bellum South: An Economic Analysis," *Quarterly Journal of Economics*, 19 (May, 1905): 434–451; idem, "An American State-Owned Railroad," *Yale Review*, 15 (November, 1906): 259–282; idem, *A History of Transportation in the Eastern Cotton Belt* (New York, 1908), passim.

7. Phillips to Frederick Jackson Turner, June 19, 1902, Turner Correspondence; anon., "Georgians Reach Badger Capital," Madison (WI) *Democrat*, November 22, 1904, in Phillips Scrapbook, Phillips Collection; Phillips, "Wisconsin University Object Lesson for Georgia," Atlanta *Constitution*, December 4, 1904; Wendell Holmes Stephenson, "Ulrich B. Phillips: Newspaper Correspondent," unpublished manuscript, n.d., Wendell Holmes Stephenson Papers, Duke University; Phillips to George J. Baldwin, April 17, 1903, Phillips to Lucien H. Boggs, February 23, 1903, Ulrich B. Phillips Papers, Southern Historical Collection, University of North Carolina at Chapel Hill; Phillips, "Conservatism and Progress in the Cotton Belt," *South Atlantic Quarterly*, 3 (January, 1904): 1–10; idem, "The Economics of the Plantation," ibid., 2 (July, 1903): 231–236; idem, "The Plantation as a Civilizing Factor," *Sewanee Review*, 12 (July, 1904): 257–267; idem, "Making Cotton Pay," *World's Work*, 8 (May, 1904): 4782–4792; idem, "The Overproduction of Cotton and a Possible Remedy," *South Atlantic Quarterly*, 4 (April, 1905): 148–158; John Herbert Roper, "A Case of Forgotten Identity: Ulrich B. Phillips As a Young Progressive," *Georgia Historical Quarterly*, 60 (Summer, 1975): 165–175.

8. Gray, "Ulrich Bonnell Phillips," in William T. Hutchinson, ed., *The Marcus W. Jernegan Essays in American Historiography* (Chicago, 1937), 369.

9. Phillips, ed., *The Correspondence of Robert Toombs, Alexander H. Stephens, and Howell Cobb* (Washington, 1913); idem, *The Life of Robert Toombs* (New York, 1913); idem, *Life and Labor in the Old South* (Boston, 1929); idem, "A Jamaica Slave Plantation," *American Historical Review*, 19 (April, 1914): 543–558; idem, "An Antigua Plantation, 1769–1818," *North Carolina Historical Review*, 3 (July, 1926): 439–445; idem, "Plantations with Slave Labor and Free," *American Historical Review*, 30 (July, 1925): 738–753; idem, "Slave Crime in Virginia," ibid., 20 (January, 1915): 336–340; Phillips and Glunt, eds., *Florida Plantation Records from the Papers of George Noble Jones* (St. Louis, 1927); Phillips, "The Central Theme of Southern History," *American Historical Review*, 34 (October, 1928): 43.

10. Phillips to Yates Snowden, May 26, 1929, Snowden Papers; Wallace

Notestein to Phillips, June 5, 1929, Phillips Papers; Phillips to Notestein, June 14, 1929, Wallace Notestein Papers, Yale University; Phillips to Snowden, June 23, 1929, Snowden Papers.

11. Stephenson, "Ulrich B. Phillips—Historian of Aristocracy," 59.

12. Filler, "Ulrich B. Phillips: A Question of History and Reality," "Introduction" to Phillips, *Georgia and State Rights* (Yellow Springs, OH, 1968; orig. pub., 1902), viii, 184.

13. Phillips, *Georgia and State Rights*, 151–152, 157, 153, 152, 154.

14. Ibid., 154, 156, 154.

15. Ibid., 156–157, 159, 155.

16. Phillips, "The Economics of the Plantation," 233, 235, 236; idem, "The Plantation as a Civilizing Factor," 264.

17. Phillips, "Conservatism and Progress in the Cotton Belt," 7, 8, 3.

18. Phillips, "The Plantation as a Civilizing Factor," 259–260, 261, 262.

19. Phillips, "The Black Belt," *Sewanee Review*, 12 (January, 1904): 76; idem, "The Plantation as a Civilizing Factor," 263; idem, "Conservatism and Progress in the Cotton Belt," 8.

20. Phillips, "The Economic Cost of Slaveholding in the Cotton Belt," 264, 261.

21. Ibid., 259, 275, 260.

22. Ibid., 261, 260, 259, 260, 268–269, 260, 266.

23. Ibid., 268–269, 270, 273–274.

24. Ibid., 274, 260, 275.

25. Phillips, "The Origin and Growth of the Southern Black Belts," 799, 816, 800, 803, 805, 800; idem, "Introduction," *Plantation and Frontier Documents*, 1:70–71.

26. Phillips, "The Slave Labor Problem in the Charleston District," 416, 422, 419, 438, 439, 437–438, 419, 423, 427, 425, 437.

27. Phillips, "Racial Problems, Adjustments and Disturbances," in Julian A. C. Chandler et al., eds., *The South in the Building of the Nation*, 12 vols. (Richmond, 1909), 4:201, 200, 202, 207, 206, 224, 226.

28. Ibid., 226, 240, 234–235, 236.

29. Phillips, "An American State-Owned Railroad," 260; idem, *A History of Transportation in the Eastern Cotton Belt*, 25, 39, 388, 390; idem, "Transportation in the Ante-Bellum South: An Economic Analysis," 451.

30. Phillips, "The Economics of Slave Labor in the South," in Chandler et al., *The South in the Building of the Nation*, 5:122, 123.

31. Phillips, "The Economics of the Slave Trade, Foreign and Domestic," in Chandler et al., eds., *The South in the Building of the Nation*, 5:127; idem, "The Decadence of the Plantation System," *Annals of the American Academy of Political and Social Science*, 35 (January, 1910): 39; idem, "The Economics of Slave Labor in the South," 124; idem, "On the Economics of Slavery,

1815–1860," *Annual Report of the American Historical Association for the Year 1912* (Washington, 1914), 150.

32. Phillips, "Black-Belt Labor, Slave and Free," University of Virginia, Phelps-Stokes Fellowship Papers, *Lectures and Addresses on the Negro in the South* (Charlottesville, 1915), 29, 30–31, 35; Du Bois, "The Experts," *Crisis*, 5 (March, 1913): 239–240.

33. Phillips, "Black-Belt Labor, Slave and Free," 30; idem, "The Slave Labor Problem in the Charleston District," 423; idem, "The Plantation Product of Men," *Proceedings of the Second Annual Session of the Georgia Historical Association* (Atlanta, 1918), 14, 15, 13.

34. Advertisement for Phillips, *American Negro Slavery*, in *Dial*, 65 (September 19, 1918): 193.

35. W. W. Ball to Phillips, June 18, 1918, Phillips Collection; B. E. Brown to Phillips, August 10, 1926, Phillips Papers.

36. Phillips, *American Negro Slavery*, 4, 8, 6, 5, 7, 26.

37. Ibid., 8, 31, 38, 45.

38. Ibid., 102, 104, 131, 133, 147, 148.

39. Ibid., 39, 46, 62–63, 65.

40. Ibid., 74, 84, 88, 85, 87, 91.

41. Ibid., 151, 154, 162, 170, 184, 186, 337.

42. Ibid., 189, 190, 191, 192, 198–199, 194.

43. Ibid., 199, 201.

44. Ibid., 203, 204.

45. Ibid., 209, 210.

46. Ibid., 213, 215–219, 226.

47. Ibid., 226, 228–260, 235.

48. Ibid., 312, 297–298, 263, 277, 296, 316, 269, 279.

49. Ibid., 279, 280, 287, 288, 294, 283.

50. Ibid., 296, 327, 322, 327; Genovese, *Roll, Jordan, Roll* (New York, 1974), 5, 658.

51. Genovese, *Roll, Jordan, Roll*, 7; Phillips, *American Negro Slavery*, 303, 304, 306.

52. Phillips, *American Negro Slavery*, 342, 343.

53. Ibid., 398, 328, 338, 339, 301, 380–382, 395, 396, 397.

54. Ibid., 54, 247, 293, 360.

55. Ibid., 403, 407, 404, 405, 406, 411, 414.

56. Du Bois, "The Relation of the Negroes to the Whites in the South," *Annals of the American Academy of Political and Social Science*, 18 (July, 1901): 132; Phillips, *American Negro Slavery*, 456, 458, 459, 460.

57. Phillips, *American Negro Slavery*, 463, 464, 476, 477, 481, 483, 488.

58. Ibid., 489, 490, 495, 413, 484, 497, 501.

59. Phillips to Herbert A. Kellar, July 4, 1929, Herbert A. Kellar Papers,

State Historical Society of Wisconsin; John David Smith, "The Historiographic Rise, Fall, and Resurrection of Ulrich Bonnell Phillips," *Georgia Historical Quarterly*, 65 (Summer, 1981): 142–145.

60. Anonymous reviews in *Booklist*, 15 (November, 1918): 51; *American Review of Reviews*, 58 (October, 1918): 439; Springfield (MA) *Daily Republican*, August 15, 1918; E. J. C. in Boston *Evening Transcript*, June 22, 1918; anonymous reviews in Boston *Herald Journal*, May 15, 1918; New York *Sun*, September 1, 1918.

61. Anonymous reviews in Baltimore *Sun*, August 3, 1918; Tifton (GA) *Gazette*, n.d.; Bruce to Phillips, March 11, 1919, Phillips Collection.

62. Patterson in *Political Science Quarterly*, 33 (September, 1918): 454–455; Jervey in *American Historical Review*, 25 (October, 1919): 117–118; Snavely in *American Economic Review*, 10 (June, 1920): 336, 337.

63. J. W. B. in New York *Call*, September 8, 1918; anonymous reviews in *Literary Digest*, 58 (August, 1918): 34; Boston *Congregationalist*, January 23, 1919; Detroit *Saturday Night*, April 19, 1919.

64. Bancroft to Theodore D. Jervey, July 15, 1918, Bancroft to Harrison A. Trexler, October 17, 1931, Bancroft to Rhodes, December 14, 1918, Frederic Bancroft Papers, Columbia University. See also John David Smith, "Historical or Personal Criticism? Frederic Bancroft vs. Ulrich B. Phillips," *Washington State University Research Studies*, 49 (June, 1981): 73–86.

65. Bancroft to Theodore D. Jervey, January 8, 1924, Bancroft Papers; Bancroft, *Slave Trading in the Old South* (Baltimore, 1931), 24, 283, 80, 208, 234n, 235n.

66. Phenix in *Southern Workman*, 47 (October, 1918): 504; Lorente in *Public*, 22 (February 8, 1919): 138–139; Ovington in *Survey*, 40 (September 28, 1918): 718 (emphasis added).

67. Du Bois in *American Political Science Review*, 12 (November, 1918): 722, 723, 724, 725, 726. Bancroft praised Du Bois's review but added, "Naturally I had hoped that you would damage him [Phillips] much more, for he is very vulnerable; but all things considered, probably it was best for you to hold the mirror up to him" (Bancroft to Du Bois, December 11, 1918, Bancroft Papers).

68. Woodson in *Journal of Negro History*, 4 (January, 1919): 102, 103; in *Mississippi Valley Historical Review*, 5 (March, 1919): 480, 481, 482.

69. Phillips to J. Franklin Jameson, November 26, 1925, *American Historical Review* Editorial Correspondence.

70. Phillips, *Life and Labor in the Old South*, vii; Hamilton, "Interpreting the Old South," *Virginia Quarterly Review*, 5 (October, 1929): 631; Tate in *New Republic*, 59 (July 10, 1929): 211; C. Vann Woodward, "Introduction," in Phillips, *Life and Labor in the Old South* (Boston, 1963; orig. pub., 1929), v; Commager in New York *Herald Tribune*, May 19, 1929.

71. Phillips, *Life and Labor in the Old South*, 175, 179, 184, 185, 186, 196, 208, 211, 214, 167, 197, 207–208, 211, 161, 163, 164, 198, 199, 210, 187, 196, 194, 197, 160, 163, 195, 199–200, 196, 200.

72. Ibid., 310, 204, 167, 216, 304, 217.

73. Gray, *History of Agriculture in the Southern United States to 1860*, 2 vols. (Washington, 1932), 1:476 and passim; Russel, "The Economic History of Negro Slavery in the United States," *Agricultural History*, 11 (October, 1937): 308–321; Govan, "Was Plantation Slavery Profitable?" *Journal of Southern History*, 8 (November, 1942): 513–535; Smith, "Was Slavery Unprofitable in the Ante-Bellum South?" *Agricultural History*, 20 (January, 1946): 62–64. Eugene D. Genovese is a notable exception to my last statement.

74. Hofstadter, "U. B. Phillips and the Plantation Legend," *Journal of Negro History*, 29 (April, 1944): 109–124; Hofstadter to Frank L. Owsley, May 18, 1944, Owsley Papers; Ruben F. Kugler, "U. B. Phillips' Use of Sources," *Journal of Negro History*, 47 (July, 1962): 167; Robert W. Fogel and Stanley L. Engerman, draft of manuscript on U. B. Phillips's slave price data [1973–1974], unpublished paper in possession of the author; Anne W. Chapman, "Inadequacies of the 1848 Charleston Census," *South Carolina Historical Magazine*, 81 (January, 1980): 25.

75. Aptheker, *American Negro Slave Revolts* (New York, 1970; orig. pub., 1943), 13, preface to 1969 edition reprinted in 1970 edition, 2; Smith, "The Historiographic Rise, Fall, and Resurrection of Ulrich Bonnell Phillips," 152n.

76. Stampp, "The Historian and Southern Negro Slavery," *American Historical Review*, 57 (April, 1952): 615–620; idem, *The Peculiar Institution* (New York, 1956), vii.

77. Genovese, "Ulrich Bonnell Phillips and His Critics," in Phillips, *American Negro Slavery* (Baton Rouge, 1966; orig. pub., 1918), vii–ix; idem, "Race and Class in Southern History: An Appraisal of the Work of Ulrich Bonnell Phillips," *Agricultural History*, 41 (October, 1967): 354.

78. John Herbert Roper, "A Case of Forgotten Identity: Ulrich B. Phillips as a Young Progressive," 165–175; idem, "Progress and History: A Southern Dialectic on Race," *Southern Humanities Review*, 17 (Spring, 1983): 101–120; idem, "Phillips, Ulrich Bonnell," in Kenneth Coleman and Charles S. Gurr, eds., *Dictionary of Georgia Biography*, 2 vols. (Athens, 1983), 2:793–794; idem, *U. B. Phillips: A Southern Mind*; idem, "Introduction," in Phillips, *Georgia and State Rights* (Macon, 1984; orig. pub. 1902), vii–xxxv; Merton Dillon, *Ulrich Bonnell Phillips, Historian of the Old South* (Baton Rouge, forthcoming); G. Ray Mathis, ed., "Ulrich Bonnell Phillips and the Universities of Georgia and Wisconsin," *Georgia Historical Quarterly*, 53 (June, 1969): 241–243; William L. Van Deburg, "Ulrich B. Phillips: Progress and the Conservative Historian," ibid., 55 (Fall, 1971): 406–416; James D. Wilson, "The

Role of Slavery in the Agrarian Myth," *Recherches Anglaises et Americaines*, 4 (1971): 12–22; Allan M. Winkler, "Ulrich Bonnell Phillips: A Reappraisal," *South Atlantic Quarterly*, 71 (Spring, 1972): 234–245; Peter H. Wood, "Phillips Upside Down: Dialectic or Equivocation?" *Journal of Interdisciplinary History*, 6 (Autumn, 1975): 289–297; Ruth H. Crocker, "Ulrich Phillips: A Southern Historian Reconsidered," *Louisiana Studies*, 15 (Summer, 1976): 113–130; Daniel J. Singal, "Ulrich B. Phillips: The Old South as the New," *Journal of American History*, 63 (March, 1977): 871–891; John David Smith, "Ulrich B. Phillips and Academic Freedom at the University of Michigan," *Michigan History*, 62 (Spring, 1978): 11–15; idem, "An Old Creed for the New South— Southern Historians and the Revival of the Proslavery Argument, 1890–1920," *Southern Studies: An Interdisciplinary Journal of the South*, 18 (Spring, 1979): 75–87; idem, " 'Keep' em in a fire-proof vault'—Pioneer Southern Historians Discover Plantation Records," *South Atlantic Quarterly*, 78 (Summer, 1979): 376–391; idem, "Du Bois and Phillips—Symbolic Antagonists of the Progressive Era," *Centennial Review*, 24 (Winter, 1980): 88–102; idem, "Historical or Personal Criticism? Frederic Bancroft vs. Ulrich B. Phillips," 73–86; idem, "The Historiographic Rise, Fall, and Resurrection of Ulrich Bonnell Phillips," 138–153; idem, "Ulrich Bonnell Phillips: The Southern Progressive as Racist," *Yale University Library Gazette*, 56 (April, 1982): 70–75; W. K. Wood, "U. B. Phillips, Unscientific Historian: A Further Note on His Methodology and Use of Sources," *Southern Studies: An Interdisciplinary Journal of the South*, 21 (Summer, 1982): 146–162; idem, "Ulrich B. Phillips," in Clyde N. Wilson, ed., *Dictionary of Literary Biography, Twentieth-Century American Historians* (Detroit, 1983), 350–363; idem, "Rewriting Southern History: U. B. Phillips, the New South, and the Antebellum Past," *Southern Studies: An Interdisciplinary Journal of the South*, 22 (Fall, 1983): 217–243; idem, " 'My Dear Mr. Snowden': U. B. Phillips' Letters to Yates Snowden of South Carolina College, 1904–1932," *South Carolina Historical Magazine*, 85 (October, 1984): 292–304.

79. Gutman, "The World Two Cliometricians Made," *Journal of Negro History*, 60 (January, 1975): 58–59, 219, 220; idem, *The Black Family in Slavery and Freedom, 1750–1925* (New York, 1976), 31–32, 259, 554; Degler, "Why Historians Change Their Minds," *Pacific Historical Review*, 45 (May, 1976): 179; Stampp, "Slavery—the Historian's Burden," in Harry P. Owens, ed., *Perspectives and Irony in American Slavery* (Jackson, MS, 1976), 160; Stampp, comment at Southern Historical Association annual meeting, November 5, 1982, Memphis, Tennessee; Blassingame, "Redefining The Slave Community: A Response to the Critics," in Al-Tony Gilmore, ed., *Revisiting Blassingame's The Slave Community* (Westport, 1978), 158; Rose, "The New Slave Studies: An Old Reaction or a New Maturity?" in William W. Freehling, ed., *Slavery and Freedom* (New York, 1982), 200.

# Conclusion: Proslavery Ideology in the Age of Jim Crow

Phillips's ethos of plantation paternalism capped several decades of post–Civil War proslavery thought. His historical writings combined the best "scientific" methodology then available with an obsession with racial control. Slavery as metaphor, symbol, and subject of historical inquiry remained very much alive in American racial thought from the earliest days of Reconstruction through World War I. As this book has argued, antislavery and proslavery polemicists—planters, U.S. Army officers, missionaries, pioneer historians and social scientists—continued the old slavery debate all the way from Appomattox to Versailles. While neoabolitionists Caroline H. Pemberton and W. E. B. Du Bois employed antislavery themes to fight racial injustice in the New South, proslavery writers like Phillips espoused justifications for slavery that harkened back to antebellum days.[1]

By the end of the nineteenth century, several patterns already had become identifiable in the ways in which white Americans perceived the peculiar institution. First, in terms of the sheer volume and intensity of their appeal, slavery's defenders clearly carried the day. Significantly, the new proslavery argument triumphed at a time when white legislators in the South were riveting the Jim Crow laws into the region's legal structure. With "home rule" finally a reality, whites maneuvered quickly to return blacks to an economic and social status as close to slavery as possible. White hegemony, by way of legalized segregation and disfranchisement, extralegal terrorism and lynching, surfaced as the South's solution to years of racial discord. Black southerners soon were ensnared in conditions of neoslavery—modified serfdom, economic peonage, enticement laws, emigrant agent restrictions, contract laws, vagrancy statutes, the criminal-surety and convict labor systems.[2] With the implementation of legalized segregation and disfranchisement, the inferior status of black southerners became codified much as it had been before emancipation. Concomitantly, northern blacks also experienced racial discrimination and extralegal restraints. The spirit of slavery, of white domination, remained very much alive in the New South. Slavery, if only in an indirect way, helped fuel the racist reaction that enveloped the nation in the 1890s.

The new proslavery argument served as both cause and effect of the many proscriptions aimed at black southerners. It bolstered the entire Jim Crow system of race relations in the South. Biblical,[3] ethnological,[4] educational,[5] and racial[6] defenses of slavery appeared regularly during the 1890s and well into the new century. Again and again white racists spoke of the overall retrogression—moral,[7] social,[8] economic[9]—of blacks since emancipation. They exposed New England's alleged complicity and culpability in the Atlantic slave trade[10] and defended what they deemed the kindly slaveholders and overall paternalism of the old regime.[11] Such diverse Negrophobes as novelist Thomas Nelson Page, politician Benjamin R. Tillman, physician Paul B. Barringer, statistician Frederick L. Hoffman, and planter Alfred Holt Stone incorporated defenses of slavery into their antiblack diatribes.[12] Whites charged that no element in America's past was more misunderstood than slavery, and proslavery theorists rallied to the call. Writing in 1897, for example, the president of Tulane University praised Page's writings for having captured perfectly "the justification of slavery as it existed with us." Another correspondent complimented Page on his perception of slavery, judging it far and away preferable to that of Harriet Beecher Stowe, "that nigger-loving, South-hating hag of New England."[13] Proslavery writers drew repeatedly on slavery as a comparative model. They praised the "old-time" black servants as symbols of virtue and damned their descendants as rapists and malcontents. In the opinion of most white southerners, the loss of discipline among the freedmen had bred social chaos and impeded southern progress. Some argued that the disastrous results of emancipation were grounds enough for the mass deportation of blacks back to Africa.[14] For the vast majority of white southerners as late as 1918, slavery represented the golden age of race relations in America.

But another major trend also emerged in these years, one that placed the slavery theme in a markedly different context. Gradually the peculiar institution became deeply enmeshed in the warp and woof of American historiography. As northerners and southerners slowly distanced themselves from the sectional tensions of the Civil War and Reconstruction, slavery took on an entirely new role as a major subject of historical inquiry. By 1918 black slavery ranked among the most popular topics of study among American historians. The forces of nationalism and scientism of these years inspired hundreds of scholarly monographs and articles on the peculiar institution. The pioneer historians of slavery anticipated many of the topics and themes examined by modern scholars. This first generation of writers introduced the basic sources and methodology employed by their successors, and the questions they raised are strikingly similar to those addressed by present-day scholars. In short, the foundation for much of the subsequent literature on black slavery was laid during a period that historian Rayford W. Logan has described as "the nadir" of black life in America. Yet in spite of all their painstaking research and important conclusions, the early historians of slavery—like the polemicists before them—remained circumscribed by the contours of the antebellum slavery debate. And the vast majority of white historians championed some variant of the old proslavery argument.

No one understood the importance of proslavery ideology to American racial thought in these years better than Frederick Douglass. In one of his last articles, published first in the *A.M.E. Church Review* and reprinted in England after his death, Douglass focused on slavery's broad legacy. "The sentiment left by slavery is still with us," he wrote, "and the moral vision of the American people is still darkened by its presence." Throughout American history whites had sought to control blacks by some artificial means. Under slavery whites rationalized their repressive actions as arising from the fear of insurrection. Under Reconstruction they cried out in fear of black domination, and after redemption of their region in 1877, white southerners invented the image of the black man as rapist. Through all three periods, Douglass explained, ran the single thread of white hegemony. Whites, continued Douglass, had always employed whatever means was necessary or available to control blacks. Under slavery they resorted to violence in all its ugly forms, including corporal punishment, murder, and rape. Douglass noted with much irony how under slavery "no white man was ever shot, burned or hanged for availing himself of all the power that slavery gave him" to violate black women at random. Today's lynchers, he wrote in 1895, "have had among them for centuries a peculiar institution, and that peculiar institution had stamped them as a peculiar people."[15]

It was slavery, said Douglass, not emancipation or the blacks' ethnology, that explained the post–Civil War race problem. Denied slavery first by defeat in war and then by force of law, whites still sought to maintain its measure of absolute control. White racism in the years since 1865, Douglass said, was nothing more than "the work of the spirit of bondage. It comes of the determination of slavery to perpetuate itself, if not under one form, then under another. It is due to the folly of endeavouring to put the new wine of liberty in the old bottles of slavery." Put another way, whites in post–Civil War America still sought complete control over black labor but, as Douglass wryly noted, they were unwilling to pay for it. Years of holding blacks as slaves not in a precapitalist economy, but in a precapitalist labor system, left whites unprepared to view blacks as free men. Their solution was simple: retain their former slaves in virtual bondage. Debt slavery, in the form of the crop lien, kept the black renter always in arrears. Generally paid only with a share of the crop, rarely in cash, blacks always were hard-pressed to accumulate money with which to purchase their own farms. Instead they slipped into the status of quasi-slaves on the soil of other men. The black farmer, lamented Douglass, became "riveted to one place, and is, in some sense a slave." Whites continued to decide what crops would be planted and how the black laborers were to be compensated. The black field laborer, wrote Douglass, "is in fact a slave, though he may be called a free man."[16]

The quest of whites for maximum racial control held the key to American thought on slavery between Appomattox and the end of World War I. Douglass understood this all along. It was easy, he said, for white southerners to proclaim to the world that they would not reinstitute slavery even if they could. Slavery never again could rule in America as a legal institution. But it never had died in the minds of whites or in the dynamics of race relations in the South. White southerners, lamented Douglass, continued to see the black man as slave. They clutched and held dear every remnant of the peculiar institution, refusing to relinquish this measure of control even when forced or when straddled with long-term economic backwardness. The sparks of proslavery thought that still flickered in 1865 smoldered through the Gilded Age and finally ignited in the Age of Jim Crow. Proslavery ideology provided white southerners with a rationale for establishing a biracial society. By never accepting blacks as equals, by viewing them instead as slavelike inferiors, whites retained a sense of control and constancy in a changing world. Whether in post–Civil War polemics or Progressive Era "scientific" historical scholarship, whites concluded that some modified slave status best suited black Americans. The new proslavery argument justified limitations on the freedom of blacks. It furnished an old creed for the New South.

## NOTES

1. For especially complete restatements of the old antislavery and proslavery themes, respectively, see William Mathews, "The Negro Intellect," *North American Review*, 149 (July, 1889). 91–102, and Thomas Smith, "Brilliant Eulogy on Gen. W. H. Payne from Good Old Rebels Who Don't Care," *Southern Historical Society Papers*, 36 (January–December, 1908): 310–340.

2. See Pete Daniel, *The Shadow of Slavery: Peonage in the South, 1901–1969* (New York, 1972), 29, 127; William Cohen, "Negro Involuntary Servitude in the South, 1865–1940: A Preliminary Analysis," *Journal of Southern History*, 42 (February, 1976): 30–60; Daniel A. Novak, *The Wheel of Servitude: Black Forced Labor after Slavery* (Lexington, 1978), 34–37, 76–77; Daniel, "The Metamorphosis of Slavery, 1865–1900," *Journal of American History*, 66 (June, 1979): 88–99. On a related theme, see Donald Spivey, *Schooling for the New Slavery: Black Industrial Education, 1868–1915* (Westport, 1978).

3. See, for example, John S. Fairly, *The Negro in His Relation to the Church: Historical View* (Charleston, 1889), 17; Charles Carroll, "*The Negro, A Beast,*" or, "*In the Image of God . . .*" (St. Louis, 1900), 289, and *The Tempter of Eve; or, The Criminality of Man's Social, Political, and Religious Equality With the Negro* (St. Louis, 1902), 287, 396; B. F. VanMeter, *A Dead Issue and the Live One* (Louisville, 1913), 5, 7–8, 9, 17, 56.

4. See, for example, Frank G. Ruffin, *The Negro as a Political and Social Factor* (Richmond, 1888), 13–15, 20, 25, 27; Robert Bingham, *An Ex-Slaveholder's View of the Negro Question in the South* (n.p. [1900]), 10; Carroll, *The Tempter of Eve*, 280–285, 454–460, 498–499; William B. Smith, *The Color Line: A Brief in Behalf of the Unborn* (New York, 1905), xiii–xiv, 7. See also the entire first number of *American League: Promoted for the Purification,*

*Elevation and Protection of American Civilization*, 1 (June, 1904): 1–16, in Paul B. Barringer Papers, University of Virginia.

5. See, for example, A. D. Mayo, "The Negro American Citizen in the New American Life," in *First Mohonk Conference on the Negro Question Held at Lake Mohonk, Ulster County, New York* (Boston, 1890), 42; H. B. Frissell, "A Survey of the Field," *Proceedings of the First Capon Springs Conference for Christian Education in the South* (Capon Springs, WV, 1898), 4; Mayo, *The Opportunity and Obligation of the Educated Class of the Colored Race in the Southern States: An Address Delivered before the Agricultural and Mechanical College for Negroes, at Normal, Alabama, May 29, 1899* (n.p., n.d.), 4, 25, and *The Duty of the White American towards His Colored Fellow-Citizen* (Washington, n.d.), 4–5; Edgar Gardner Murphy, *The White Man and the Negro in the South* (n.p., [1900]), 46–49, in Edgar Gardner Murphy Scrapbook, Southern Historical Collection, University of North Carolina at Chapel Hill, and *The Task of the South: An Address on the Subject of Public Education in the Southern States* (Montgomery, 1903), 28; John C. Kilgo, *Our Duty to the Negro* (n.p., [1903]), 13; G. Stanley Hall, *The Negro in Africa and America* (n.p., [1905]), 14–16; anon., *The Race Crisis: Uncle Sam, the Innocent Old Negro; I'se Guine Home, I'se Bound fur Old Norf Caliny* (n.p., [1904]), 7; Willis B. Parks, "A Solution to the Negro Problem Psychologically Considered," in *The Possibilities of the Negro in Symposium* (Atlanta, 1904), 141; A. H. Shannon, *Racial Integrity and Other Features of the Negro Problem* (Nashville, 1907), 15, 195, 204; Mrs. Andrew M. Sea, *A Brief Synoptical Review of Slavery in the United States* (Louisville, 1916), 15–17; Mildred Lewis Rutherford, "Wrongs of History Righted," *Four Addresses* (Birmingham, 1916), 15–17; "From Slavery to Riches, Pioneer Negro Points Way to Racial Understanding," Atlanta *Constitution*, October 17, 1920, Slavery File, Tuskegee Institute.

6. See, for example, W. Cabell Bruce, *The Negro Problem* (Baltimore, 1891), 3, 8, 9, 13–15; John Temple Graves, "The Problem of the Races," in *The Possibilities of the Negro in Symposium*, 10, 19–20, 23; Shannon, "The Racial Integrity of the Negro," *Methodist Quarterly Review*, 55 (July, 1906): 531–532; Carlyle McKinley, *An Appeal to Pharaoh: The Negro Problem and Its Radical Solution* (Columbia, 1907), 37, 48, 177, 185; Thomas M. Norwood, *Address on the Negro* (Savannah, 1907), 6, 11.

7. See, for example, "Mortality among Negroes," Raleigh *News and Observer*, October 18, 1895, clipping in John Spencer Bassett Papers, Duke University Archives; editorial, "The Negro Now and Then," Manchester (VA) *Evening Leader*, December 14, 1898; H. M. Hamill, *The Old South: A Monograph* (Nashville, [1904]), 33–35; Norwood, *Address on the Negro*, 23; "Code of Laws for Slaves Governed Each Southern Plantation in Early Days," Montgomery *Advertiser*, August 28, 1918, Slavery File, Tuskegee Institute.

8. See, for example, Charles H. Smith, "Have American Negroes Too Much Liberty?" *Forum*, 16 (October, 1893): 180–182; Atticus G. Haygood, "The Black Shadow in the South," ibid., 172; Walter F. Willcox, *Negro Criminality: An Address Delivered before the American Social Science Association at Saratoga* (Boston, 1899), 8, 14–15; Hall, *The Negro in Africa and America*, 14; Myrta Lockett Avary, *Dixie after the War: An Exposition of Social Conditions Existing in the South, during the Twelve Years Succeeding the Fall of Richmond* (New York, 1906), 182, 194, 196–197, 206, 392, 395; "The Old Black Mammy," Montgomery (AL) *Advertiser*, December 30, 1917, and "Aged Negroes of Slave Days Well Liked at State Capitol," Atlanta *Constitution*, November 31, 1920, Slavery File, Tuskegee Institute; Winfield H. Collins, *The Truth about Lynching and the Negro in the South in Which the Author Pleads That the South Be Made Safe for the White Race* (New York, 1918), 32, 41, 58, 70, 140.

9. See, for example, Wade Hampton, *Negro Emigration* (Washington, 1890), 12; Charles H. Otken, *The Ills of the South; or, Related Causes Hostile to the General Prosperity of the Southern People* (New York, 1894), 236, 238; Robert F. Campbell, *Some Aspects of the Race Problem in the South* (Asheville, NC, 1899), 13; Murphy, *The Task of the South; An Address on the Subject of Public Education in the Southern States* (Montgomery, 1903), 28, 43; D. C. Heyward, "Tells of Low Country Negroes," Columbia (SC) *State*, January 25, 1920, Slavery File, Tuskegee Institute.

10. See, for example, William W. Stringfield, "American or African Slavery," in *War Sketches and Stories* [manuscript ledger], 1899, North Carolina Division of Archives and History, 150–151; W. J. Northern, *The Negro at the South* (Atlanta, 1899), 3; Norwood, *Address on the Negro*, 25; R. A. Brock, "Last of the Slavers," *Southern Historical Society Papers*, 30 (January–December, 1902): 355; Sea, *A Brief Synoptical Review of Slavery in the United States*, 3–10, 13–15.

11. See, for example, R. Q. Mallard, *Plantation Life before Emancipation* (Richmond, 1892), vi, 28, 36, 39, 210, 228, 236, and passim; Omikron Kappa, "Something of Slavery as It Existed," *Confederate Veteran* 1 (June, 1893): 171; Joseph M. Rogers, "The Negro as a Slave and a Freeman," *Self-Culture*, (June, 1897): 224, 229, 230; James Battle Avirett, *The Old Plantation: How We Lived in Great House and Cabin before the War* (New York, 1901), dedicatory page; Hilary A. Herbert, "Grandfather's Talks about His Life under Two Flags," December 31, 1903, typescript, pp. 22, 23, 35, 41, 42, 59, 71–72, Hilary A. Herbert Papers, Southern Historical Collection, University of North Carolina at Chapel Hill; Mrs. E. M. Loughery, *War and Reconstruction Times in Texas, 1861–1865* (Austin, 1914), 19–20; "How Slaves Earned Owners' Confidence" and "Faithfulness of Slaves," Columbia (SC) *State*, April 4, 1915, August 6, 1916, Slavery File, Tuskegee Institute; William Clark

Breckenridge to E. M. Violette, March 8, 1917, quoted in James Malcolm Breckenridge, *William Clark Breckenridge: Historical Research Writer and Bibliographer of Missouriana* (St. Louis, 1932), 202; undated responses of Hampton J. Cheney and Charles S. O. Rice to Civil War Veterans Questionnaire, Tennessee State Library and Archives, Nashville; John W. Fries, "Reminiscences of Confederate Days," 1924, typescript, pp. 3–5, North Carolina Division of Archives and History.

12. See, for example, Page, *In Ole Virginia* (New York, 1887), 10; "Race Wars in South: Views of Thomas Nelson Page on Negro Problem," Washington *Post*, November 28, 1898; Page, "The Lynching of Negroes—Its Cause and Its Prevention," *North American Review*, 178 (January, 1904): 33–48; idem, *The Negro: The Southerner's Problem* (New York, 1904), 54, 289–292, and passim; Page to Emmett J. Scott, February 25, 1904, Thomas Nelson Page Papers, Duke University; Tillman, March 23, 1900, in *Congressional Record*, 56th Congress, 1st session (Washington, 1900), 3219, 3223; February 24, 1903 in ibid., 57th Congress, 2nd session (Washington, 1903), 2564–2565; January 21, 1907 in ibid., 59th Congress, 2nd session (Washington, 1907), 1441–1443; Barringer, *The Sacrifice of a Race* (Raleigh, 1900), 3, 15, 16, 22, 28; idem, *The American Negro, His Past and Future* (Raleigh, 1900), 5, 10, 11, 15, 20, 23; idem, "Negro Education in the South," *Educational Review*, 21 (March, 1901): 241; Hoffman, "Race Traits and Tendencies of the American Negro," *Publications of the American Economic Association*, 11 (August, 1896): v, 6, 55, 148, 176, 329; Stone to W. E. B. Du Bois, July 1, 18, 1903, W. E. B. Du Bois Papers, University of Massachusetts, Amherst; Stone, "Some Problems of Southern Economic History," *American Historical Review*, 13 (July, 1908): 790–791, 794; idem, "The Responsibility of the Southern White Man to the Negro," in University of Virginia, Phelps-Stokes Fellowship Papers, *Lectures and Addresses on the Negro in the South* (Charlottesville, 1915), 12, 16.

13. William Preston Johnston to Page, December 23, 1897, Lemuel M. Park to Page, January 7, 1898, Page Papers.

14. See, for example, Edward P. Humphrey, *An Address before the American Colonization Society* (Washington, 1873); E. T. Winkler, "The Negroes in the Gulf States," *International Review*, 1 (September 1874): 571–588, 594; Humphrey, *The Color Question in the United States* (Washington, 1877); Charles K. Marshall, *The Exodus: Its Effect upon the South; Colored Labor Not Indispensable* (Washington, 1880), 2–3, 10; Francis G. Ruffin, *White or Mongrel? A Pamphlet on the Deportation of Negroes from Virginia to Africa* (Richmond, 1890); R. A. Brock, "The Colonial Virginian," *Southern Historical Society Papers*, 19 (January, 1891): 135–136; Robert Stein to Thomas Nelson Page, January 29, 1904, Page Papers; Arney R. Childs, ed., *Rice Planter and Sportsman: The Recollections of J. Motte Alston, 1821–1909* (Columbia, 1953), 131–132. On the interrelation of postwar proslavery ideology and colonizationist

thought, see John David Smith, "Out of Sight, Out of Mind: Robert Stein's 1904 'Deafricanization' Scheme to 'Hopeland,' " *Phylon*, 46 (March, 1985): 1-15.

15. Douglass, *Why Is The Negro Lynched?* (Bridgwater, England, 1895), 7, 18.

16. Ibid., 29, 30.

# Select Bibliography

In writing *An Old Creed for the New South* the author examined hundreds of sources—manuscripts, government documents, newspapers, books, pamphlets, articles, book reviews, and theses and dissertations. The notes that accompany each chapter serve as a comprehensive guide to those works. Many, but not all, of the published references are cited in John David Smith, "The Formative Period of American Slave Historiography, 1890–1920" (Ph.D. diss., University of Kentucky, 1977), 389–474, and Smith, *Black Slavery in the Americas: An Interdisciplinary Bibliography, 1865–1980* (2 vols., Westport, 1982). This select bibliography identifies only the manuscript collections cited in the notes.

## MANUSCRIPT COLLECTIONS CITED IN THE NOTES

Herbert Baxter Adams Papers. Johns Hopkins University.
Samuel A. Agnew Diary. Southern Historical Collection, University of North Carolina at Chapel Hill.
American Historical Association Papers. Manuscript Division, Library of Congress.
*American Historical Review* Editorial Correspondence. Manuscript Division, Library of Congress.
Edward A. Atkinson Papers. Massachusetts Historical Society.

Everard Green Baker Diary and Plantation Notes. Southern Historical Collection, University of North Carolina at Chapel Hill.
James C. Ballagh Biographical File. University of Pennsylvania.
Frederic Bancroft Papers. Columbia University.
Paul B. Barringer Papers. University of Virginia.
John Spencer Bassett Papers. Duke University.
John Spencer Bassett Papers. Massachusetts Historical Society.
Carl Becker Papers. Cornell University.
John Houston Bills Diary. Southern Historical Collection, University of North Carolina at Chapel Hill.
William K. Boyd Papers. Duke University.
Jeffrey R. Brackett Papers. Simmons College.
William Garrott Brown Papers. Duke University.
Sarah W. Bunting Papers. Duke University.
Armistead Burt Papers. Duke University.
Edward G. W. Butler Papers. Duke University.
Civil War Veterans Questionnaires. Tennessee State Library and Archives.
George William Cook Papers. Howard University.
Alexander Crummell Papers. Schomburg Center for Research in Black Culture, New York Public Library.
John H. Dent Plantation Journal. Troy State University, Troy, Alabama.
William E. Dodd Papers. Manuscript Division, Library of Congress.
Frederick Douglass Papers. Manuscript Division, Library of Congress.
W. E. B. Du Bois Papers. University of Massachusetts, Amherst.
Walter Lynwood Fleming Papers. Manuscripts and Archives Division, New York Public Library.
John W. Fries Papers. North Carolina Division of Archives and History.
James M. Gage Papers. Southern Historical Collection, University of North Carolina at Chapel Hill.
Leon Gardiner Collection. Historical Society of Pennsylvania.
Joshua R. Giddings and George W. Julian Papers. Manuscript Division, Library of Congress.
Gilman Family Papers. Yale University.
Governors' Papers, William W. Holden. North Carolina Division of Archives and History.
Robert Grant Papers. Houghton Library, Harvard University.
Samuel A. Green Papers. Massachusetts Historical Society.
Archibald H. Grimké Papers. Howard University.
Francis J. Grimké Papers. Howard University.
Albert Bushnell Hart Papers. Manuscripts and Archives Division, New York Public Library.
Paul Hamilton Hayne Papers. Duke University.
Benjamin S. Hedrick Papers. Duke University.

Hemphill Family Papers. Duke University.
Hilary A. Herbert Papers. Southern Historical Collection, University of North Carolina at Chapel Hill.
Thomas Wentworth Higginson Papers. Houghton Library, Harvard University.
Nickels Holmes Papers. Duke University.
Mark Anthony De Wolfe Howe Papers. Houghton Library, Harvard University.
J. Franklin Jameson Papers. Manuscript Division, Library of Congress.
Johns Hopkins University Historical Seminary Records. Johns Hopkins University.
Herbert A. Kellar Papers. State Historical Society of Wisconsin.
Joseph B. Killebrew Autobiography. Southern Historical Collection, University of North Carolina at Chapel Hill.
William Thomas Laprade Papers. Duke University.
Legislative Papers, 1866–1867. North Carolina Division of Archives and History.
Thomas R. Lounsbury Papers. Yale University.
Whitefield McKinlay Papers. Manuscript Division, Library of Congress.
Hugh MacRae Papers. Duke University.
James Mallory Diary. Southern Historical Collection, University of North Carolina at Chapel Hill.
Manigault Family Papers. Southern Historical Collection, University of North Carolina at Chapel Hill.
William N. Mercer Diary. Louisiana State University.
William Porcher Miles Papers Southern Historical Collection, University of North Carolina at Chapel Hill.
Kelly Miller Papers. Howard University.
Edwin Mims Papers. Joint University Libraries, Nashville.
Miscellaneous American Letters and Papers. Schomburg Center for Research in Black Culture, New York Public Library.
Edgar Gardner Murphy Scrapbook. Southern Historical Collection, University of North Carolina at Chapel Hill.
Allan Nevins Papers. Columbia University.
Norton Family Papers. Houghton Library, Harvard University.
Wallace Notestein Papers. Yale University.
Frank L. Owsley Papers. Joint University Libraries, Nashville.
Thomas Nelson Page Papers. Duke University.
John Paris Papers. Southern Historical Collection, University of North Carolina at Chapel Hill.
Lindsay Patterson Papers. Southern Historical Collection, University of North Carolina at Chapel Hill.
R. L. Patterson Papers. North Carolina Division of Archives and History.
Lalla Pelot Papers. Duke University.
Penn School Papers. Southern Historical Collection, University of North Carolina at Chapel Hill.

Ulrich B. Phillips Collection. Yale University.
Ulrich B. Phillips Letters. University of Georgia.
Ulrich B. Phillips Papers. Southern Historical Collection, University of North
     Carolina at Chapel Hill.
William Pickens Papers. Schomburg Center for Research in Black Culture, New
     York Public Library.
Thomas Merritt Pitman Papers. Southern Historical Collection, University of
     North Carolina at Chapel Hill.
Nimrod Porter Diary and Notes. Southern Historical Collection, University of
     North Carolina at Chapel Hill.
Race Problem File. Tuskegee Institute.
Records of the Assistant Commissioner for the State of North Carolina, Bureau
     of Refugees, Freedmen, and Abandoned Lands. Record Group 105.
     National Archives and Records Service.
James Ford Rhodes Papers. Duke University.
James Ford Rhodes Papers. Massachusetts Historical Society.
Gallatin Riddle Papers. Western Reserve Historical Society.
Franklin L. Riley Papers. Southern Historical Collection, University of North
     Carolina at Chapel Hill.
Theodore Roosevelt Papers. Manuscript Division, Library of Congress.
David Schenck Diary. Southern Historical Collection, University of North Car-
     olina at Chapel Hill.
James Schouler Papers. Massachusetts Historical Society.
Carl Schurz Papers. Manuscript Division, Library of Congress.
Slavery File. Tuskegee Institute.
Yates Snowden Papers. South Caroliniana Library, University of South Carolina.
Cornelia P. Spencer Diary. Southern Historical Collection, University of North
     Carolina at Chapel Hill.
Cornelia Spencer Papers. North Carolina Division of Archives and History.
Wendell Holmes Stephenson Papers. Duke University.
William W. Stringfield Ledger. North Carolina Division of Archives and History.
Charles S. Sydnor Papers. Duke University.
Mary Church Terrell Papers. Manuscript Division, Library of Congress.
Ella Gertrude Clanton Thomas Diary. Duke University.
Tillinghast Family Papers. Duke University.
William P. Trent Papers. Columbia University.
Frederick Jackson Turner Collection. Henry E. Huntington Library.
Frederick Jackson Turner Correspondence. University of Wisconsin.
Oswald Garrison Villard Papers. Houghton Library, Harvard University.
John Martin Vincent Papers. Johns Hopkins University.
Booker T. Washington Collection. Howard University.
Booker T. Washington Papers. Tuskegee Institute.
Henry Watson, Jr., Papers. Duke University.

Andrew Dickson White Papers. Cornell University.
Carter G. Woodson Collection. Manuscript Division, Library of Congress.
Jonathan Worth Papers. North Carolina Division of Archives and History.
*Yale Review* Correspondence. Yale University.

# Index

## ABOUT THE AUTHOR

John David Smith, Assistant Professor of History at North Carolina State University, received his Ph.D. in Southern history from the University of Kentucky in 1977. He is the author of many articles, as well as *Window on the War: Frances Dallam Peter's Lexington Civil War Diary* (with William Cooper, Jr., 1976), and *Black Slavery in the Americas: An Interdisciplinary Bibliography, 1865–1980* (2 vols., 1982).

# DATE DUE

| | | | |
|---|---|---|---|
| | | | |
| | | | |
| | | | |
| | | | |
| | | | |
| | | | |
| | | | |
| | | | |
| | | | |
| | | | |
| | | | |
| | | | |
| | | | |
| | | | |
| | | | |
| | | | |
| | | | |
| | | | |
| | | | |
| | | | |
| | | | |